A CELEBRATION
OF POETS

WISCONSIN/MINNESOTA
GRADES 4-12
FALL 2009

creativeCOMMUNICATION
A CELEBRATION OF TODAY'S WRITERS

A CELEBRATION OF POETS
WISCONSIN/MINNESOTA
GRADES 4-12
FALL 2009

AN ANTHOLOGY COMPILED BY CREATIVE COMMUNICATION, INC.

Published by:

creativeCOMMUNICATION
A CELEBRATION OF TODAY'S WRITERS

1488 NORTH 200 WEST • LOGAN, UTAH 84341
TEL. 435-713-4411 • WWW.POETICPOWER.COM

Authors are responsible for the originality of the writing submitted.

ISBN: 978-1-60050-327-6

FOREWORD

In today's world there are many things that compete for our attention. From the far reaching influence of the media, to the voices we hear from those around us, it is often difficult to decide where to commit our energies and focus. The poets in this book listened to an inner voice; a voice that can be the loudest of the many voices in our world, but to pay attention to this voice takes self-control. The effect of these words may not be far reaching, but to even make a small difference in the world is a positive thing.

Each year I receive hundreds of letters, calls, and emails from parents, teachers, and students who share stories of success; stories, where being a published writer provided the catalyst to a different attitude toward school, education and life. We are pleased to provide you with this book and hope that what these writers have shared makes a small but meaningful difference in your world.

Thomas Worthen, Ph.D.
Editor
Creative Communication

WRITING CONTESTS!

Enter our next POETRY contest!
Enter our next ESSAY contest!

Why should I enter?

Win prizes and get published! Each year thousands of dollars in prizes are awarded throughout North America. The top writers in each division receive a monetary award and a free book that includes their published poem or essay. Entries of merit are also selected to be published in our anthology.

Who may enter?

There are four divisions in the poetry contest. The poetry divisions are grades K-3, 4-6, 7-9, and 10-12. There are three divisions in the essay contest. The essay divisions are grades 3-6, 7-9, and 10-12.

What is needed to enter the contest?

To enter the poetry contest send in one original poem, 21 lines or less. To enter the essay contest send in one original non-fiction essay, 250 words or less, on any topic. Please submit each poem and essay with a title, and the following information clearly printed: the writer's name, current grade, home address (optional), school name, school address, teacher's name and teacher's email address (optional). Contact information will only be used to provide information about the contest. For complete contest information go to www.poeticpower.com.

How do I enter?

Enter a poem online at:
www.poeticpower.com
or
Mail your poem to:
Poetry Contest
1488 North 200 West
Logan, UT 84341

Enter an essay online at:
www.studentessaycontest.com
or
Mail your essay to:
Essay Contest
1488 North 200 West
Logan, UT 84341

When is the deadline?

Poetry contest deadlines are August 18th, December 2nd and April 5th. Essay contest deadlines are July 15th, October 19th, and February 17th. Students can enter one poem and one essay for each spring, summer, and fall contest deadline.

Are there benefits for my school?

Yes. We award $15,000 each year in grants to help with Language Arts programs. Schools qualify to apply for a grant by having 15 or more accepted entries.

Are there benefits for my teacher?

Yes. Teachers with five or more students published receive a free anthology that includes their students' writing.

For more information please go to our website at **www.poeticpower.com**, email us at editor@poeticpower.com or call 435-713-4411.

TABLE OF CONTENTS

Fall 2009
Poetic Achievement
Honor Schools

* Teachers who had fifteen or more poets accepted to be published

The following schools are recognized as receiving a "Poetic Achievement Award." This award is given to schools who have a large number of entries of which over fifty percent are accepted for publication. With hundreds of schools entering our contest, only a small percent of these schools are honored with this award. The purpose of this award is to recognize schools with excellent Language Arts programs. This award qualifies these schools to receive a complimentary copy of this anthology. In addition, these schools are eligible to apply for a Creative Communication Language Arts Grant. Grants of two hundred and fifty dollars each are awarded to further develop writing in our schools.

Adams Spanish Immersion School
Saint Paul, MN
Lourdes Flores-Hanson
Guillermo Maldonado

All Saints Catholic School
Lakeville, MN
Terri Peterson*

Blue Heron Elementary School
Lino Lakes, MN
Curt Gutbrod*

Breck School
Minneapolis, MN
Kathy Quick*

Campbellsport Elementary School
Campbellsport, WI
Michele Dahlinger
Shelly Gassner
Becky Palmer

Chaska Elementary School
Chaska, MN
Joan Wright*

Classical School
Appleton, WI
Sondra Chen*
Theresa Coenen

Deer River High School
Deer River, MN
Polly Sheppard*

Discovery Middle School
Alexandria, MN
Dawn Prchal*

Dr Dyer Intermediate School
Burlington, WI
Angela Mangold*

Fall River High School
Fall River, WI
Kim Biehl*

Gillett High School
Gillett, WI
Rebecca Rousseau*

Gilmore Middle School
Racine, WI
    Linda Broesch*
    Sherry Coburn*
    Nicole Paul

Harriet Bishop Elementary School
Savage, MN
    Amy Engen
    Sara Gant
    Emily LeClair*
    Tim Noonan
    Patti Schroeder

Hewitt Texas Elementary School
Wausau, WI
    Linda Davis*

Holy Family Parish School
Whitefish Bay, WI
    Kathryn Conole*

Howards Grove Middle School
Howards Grove, WI
    Jean Hawkinson
    Lisa Perronne*
    Deborah Perry

Jerstad Agerholm Middle School
Racine, WI
    Amanda Rogers
    Mrs. Staniger*

Jordan Sr High School
Jordan, MN
    Norma Timmons*

Kennedy Elementary School
Hastings, MN
    Jodi Glazier*

Lincoln Jr/Sr High School
Alma Center, WI
    Diane Kujak*

MacArthur Elementary School
Green Bay, WI
    Kathy Anderson
    Kay Knapp
    Mary Tomasiak*

Marinette Middle School
Marinette, WI
    Sharon Brey*

Martin County West Trimont Elementary
School
Trimont, MN
    Jackie Royer*

Messmer Preparatory Catholic School
Milwaukee, WI
    Erin Dreger
    Adam Gerber
    Megan Mauk
    Phensy Vongphakdy

Montgomery-Lonsdale High School
Montgomery, MN
    Jen Davidson*
    Brett Frayseth

Oak Creek High School
Oak Creek, WI
    Penny A. Kapitz*

Orfordville Elementary School
Orfordville, WI
    Cindy Roth*
    Tamara Wallisch

Osceola High School
Osceola, WI
    Amanda Meyer*
    Brittany Olivieri

Ramsey International Fine Arts Center
Minneapolis, MN
    Alyssa Paddock*

Rib Lake High School
Rib Lake, WI
Gail Curran*

River Heights Elementary School
Menomonie, WI
Lynn Ruhland*

Riverdale Elementary School
Muscoda, WI
Dianne Nachtigal*

Rosholt Middle-High School
Rosholt, WI
Ann Parker*

Round Lake High School
Round Lake, MN
Shari Nelson*

School of Technology & Arts I
La Crosse, WI
Bebe Fehlig*

Shakopee Area Catholic School
Shakopee, MN
Kyle Metzger*

Sibley Elementary School
Northfield, MN
Rebecca Gainey*

St Francis Middle School
Saint Francis, MN
Trina Schultz*

St Joan Antida High School
Milwaukee, WI
Mrs. Knowlton
Susan Lutterbach*

St Katharine Drexel School
Beaver Dam, WI
Debora Rampanelli*

St Lawrence Seminary High School
Mt Calvary, WI
Katie Daane*

St Odilia School
Shoreview, MN
Ben Stangler*

St Paul Evangelical Lutheran School
Lake Mills, WI
Susan Thorman*

Stocker Elementary School
Kenosha, WI
Amy Ashburn
Mrs. Dorey
Meg Fisher
Jill Francis
Nancy Granger*
Mrs. Kok
Marilyn Siedjak*
Monica Sioco*
Margaret Unger
Ruth Walls

T J Walker Middle School
Sturgeon Bay, WI
Kasee Jandrin*

Wagner Elementary School
Litchfield, MN
Nikki Knochenmus*

Waseca High School
Waseca, MN
John L. Moon*

Woodbury Sr High School
Woodbury, MN
Marsha Swails*

Language Arts Grant Recipients 2009-2010

After receiving a "Poetic Achievement Award" schools are encouraged to apply for a Creative Communication Language Arts Grant. The following is a list of schools who received a two hundred and fifty dollar grant for the 2009-2010 school year.

Arrowhead Union High School, Hartland, WI
Blessed Sacrament School, Seminole, FL
Booneville Jr High School, Booneville, AR
Buckhannon-Upshur Middle School, Buckhannon, WV
Campbell High School, Ewa Beach, HI
Chickahominy Middle School, Mechanicsville, VA
Clarkston Jr High School, Clarkston, MI
Covenant Life School, Gaithersburg, MD
CW Rice Middle School, Northumberland, PA
Eason Elementary School, Waukee, IA
East Elementary School, Kodiak, AK
Florence M Gaudineer Middle School, Springfield, NJ
Foxborough Regional Charter School, Foxborough, MA
Gideon High School, Gideon, MO
Holy Child Academy, Drexel Hill, PA
Home Choice Academy, Vancouver, WA
Jeff Davis Elementary School, Biloxi, MS
Lower Alloways Creek Elementary School, Salem, NJ
Maple Wood Elementary School, Somersworth, NH
Mary Walter Elementary School, Bealeton, VA
Mater Dei High School, Evansville, IN
Mercy High School, Farmington Hills, MI
Monroeville Elementary School, Monroeville, OH
Nautilus Middle School, Miami Beach, FL
Our Lady Star of the Sea School, Grosse Pointe Woods, MI
Overton High School, Memphis, TN
Pond Road Middle School, Robbinsville, NJ
Providence Hall Charter School, Herriman, UT
Reuben Johnson Elementary School, McKinney, TX
Rivelon Elementary School, Orangeburg, SC
Rose Hill Elementary School, Omaha, NE

Language Arts Grant Winners cont.

Runnels School, Baton Rouge, LA
Santa Fe Springs Christian School, Santa Fe Springs, CA
Serra Catholic High School, Mckeesport, PA
Shadowlawn Elementary School, Green Cove Springs, FL
Spectrum Elementary School, Gilbert, AZ
St Edmund Parish School, Oak Park, IL
St Joseph Institute for the Deaf, Chesterfield, MO
St Joseph Regional Jr High School, Manchester, NH
St Mary of Czestochowa School, Middletown, CT
St Monica Elementary School, Garfield Heights, OH
St Vincent De Paul Elementary School, Cape Girardeau, MO
Stevensville Middle School, Stevensville, MD
Tashua School, Trumbull, CT
The New York Institute for Special Education, Bronx, NY
The Selwyn School, Denton, TX
Tonganoxie Middle School, Tonganoxie, KS
Westside Academy, Prince George, BC
Willa Cather Elementary School, Omaha, NE
Willow Hill Elementary School, Traverse City, MI

Grades 10-11-12 Top Ten Winners

List of Top Ten Winners for Grades 10-12; listed alphabetically

Aaron Combs, Grade 12
Carroll High School, Corpus Christi, TX

Kellie Lenamond, Grade 12
Home School, Wills Point, TX

Jordyn Rhorer, Grade 12
Lafayette High School, Lexington, KY

Miranda Rogovein, Grade 12
Greenwood College School, Toronto, ON

Sydney Rubin, Grade 11
Cab Calloway School of the Arts, Wilmington, DE

Kyle Rutherford, Grade 12
Rosebud School, Rosebud, MT

Sara RuthAnn Weaver, Grade 12
Grace Baptist High School, Delaware, OH

Jessica Webster, Grade 11
Boyne City High School, Boyne City, MI

Abigail Yeskatalas, Grade 10
Avonworth High School, Pittsburgh, PA

Mariam Younan, Grade 12
Bayonne High School, Bayonne, NJ

All Top Ten Poems can be read at www.poeticpower.com

Note: The Top Ten poems were finalized through an online voting system. Creative Communication's judges first picked out the top poems. These poems were then posted online. The final step involved thousands of students and teachers who registered as the online judges and voted for the Top Ten poems. We hope you enjoy these selections.

Forever and Ever

The twins were my sisters, my best friends, the hope I had when I was in need.
We helped each other through all the tough times.
Sitting under the clear night skies, us sisters of a different family,
Felt the peculiarly pleasant warm breeze of the crisp November night.
We were amazed by the sparkling stars hovering above the haze of the city lights.
As we contemplated what we thought our true cause in life was,
I just absorbed the world around me.
Behind the calm careful words that were spoken,
I could hear the crackling fire spit sparks of orange in the oblivion of night.
My sweet strawberry gum's flavor was altered from the smoke traveling through the air to my nose.
These senses overwhelmed me to the point I thought I would go insane.
But wait, as the new morning dew now formed around,
I began to realize these girls, my two best friends, were making me their long lost twin.

Julia Zimmer, Grade 10
Oak Creek High School, WI

My Mind

My mind is the greatest weapon within me
And…the most dangerous weapon within me…

There is a battle, a struggle for power
Good, evil, does it matter
My actions tell you who is winning
Now I tell my story from…
The beginning

Look down that's where I am
This is me it's who I am
I was always on the run
Back then when Evil won

Stealing, fighting it's what I did
Not to mention the lie I was living in
When my mind was
The most dangerous weapon
When Evil was winning

I've lost the battle but won the war
Now I'm out here to say
That was then, this is now
When the good in me
Came out.

Jarrod Coyle, Grade 10
Visions Jr/Sr High School, WI

Mon Coeur est Noir

From my pain, I have recovered
The light has returned to my soul
Only by you could my flame be smothered
Your lies and deceit could not take their toll

The light has returned to my soul
My happiness has been returned
Your lies and deceit could not take their toll
My lesson has finally been learned

My happiness has been returned
My life has resumed
My lesson has finally been learned
From its grave, our friendship cannot be exhumed

My life has resumed
Je ne veux pas te voir
From its grave, our friendship cannot be exhumed
Á cause de toi, mon coeur est noir

Je ne veux pas te voir
Only by you could my flame be smothered
A cause de toi, mon coeur est noir
From my pain, I have recovered

Cory Smith, Grade 11
Grand Rapids Sr High School, MN

No Pain No Game

Waiting for the immensely loud sounding of the gun,
And the race begins,
Heavy breathing, intensity,
Blood rushing through your body,
Butterflies in your stomach.
Cross country, exhilarating, painful,
Emotions running through your mind,
Cross country is determination.

Gina Quednow, Grade 10
Rib Lake High School, WI

Shrooms

Some say mushrooms are built for fairies,
Some say they are for toads.
I say they're extraordinary, my dad says they grow on cloves.
Mushrooms come in all different ways, short and fat,
Tall and skinny, and some die down during the day.
I've heard mushrooms can be something called trippy,
Which most people say come from the hippies.
Mushrooms are cool and some are sweet,
Be careful of the ones you choose to eat.

Felicia Osborne, Grade 12
Osceola High School, WI

That's When I Knew

I remember the first time I saw you, the way you smiled, that smile took my breath away. Then you looked at me, I could feel the love coming over me, and I wouldn't stop it if I could. I wondered if you could feel it too, then you walked up to me. Suddenly breathing seemed too hard to do and as I started to fall, you caught me. I never wanted you to let me go.
That's when I knew I needed you by my side.

I remember those walks down the hall. When I saw you standing there waiting for me, my face would glow as bright as the sun. We talked about our hopes and dreams as the walls whispered rumors about us, but I didn't notice because I was concentrated on all you said and I knew you were listening to me too.
That's when I knew I could depend on you.

I remember we walked outside; my walk is a ballerina's dance around you. We watched as the cars with their music as loud as thunder, drove past. You grabbed my hands, pulling me gently toward you, embracing me in your arms. You smiled at me as I turned my head laughing, but never daring to pull away. Then you sang that silly love song and we started to dance. The road danced along with us for miles and miles. Nothing had ever been so perfect as that moment with you.
That's when I knew you would never let me go.

I remember you told me that we belonged together as I gazed into your eyes, which looked like my own personal sunsets. I knew that you could hear me catch my breath as you whispered, "I love you sweetheart."
That's when I knew you needed me as much as I needed you.

Cora Schlei, Grade 10
Oak Creek High School, WI

My Big Brother

My big brother
The one who has been there for me since the day I was born
My protector who got in a fist fight with someone who was making fun of me
The one who puts my safety before his own
My coach who taught me the basics of all sports
The one who knows everything about me, telling me things I didn't even know about myself
My doctor who takes care of me without being asked
The one who I know I can go to during confusing family problems, knowing he fully understands
My very own comedian to make me laugh at the stupidest things
The one who everyone can't help but know and love
My partner in crime who is always at my side to start some trouble
The one who never pretends to be something he's not, comfortable being just who he is
My friend who listens and gives perfect advice
The one who I am proud to call
My big brother

Amanda Blenski, Grade 10
Oak Creek High School, WI

The Path*

As I walk down the path all call life. I've found myself tripping and falling down a lot more then normal. But one day I found myself tripping and falling but this time I gave up. So I sat there not knowing what to do anymore, I found myself regretting everything…but why? I have great friends I thought, but was never a great friend in return, I let my friends down, so maybe this is where I belong, lost, dead, never to be seen again, so I sat there for days, then days moved into months and months turned into years. I sat in that spot for seven years. But now I want to move…but I forgot how. I'm all alone, all by myself. I need help but nobody is on the same path as I am, I feel as if I'm all alone and I'll be in this spot forever, "Why me?" I ask to myself "Why this?"…but still no one answered. No one was around, I sat there and thought to myself, if I let the past go maybe I could move, then just as I was going to give up I see a person walking down the path, and with this person four others followed. I watched these people walk towards me, I was scared but yet I wasn't. They grabbed my hand and pulled me up and showed me I wasn't alone. Now I walk down the path with other people like me. I now call them my family.

Cheyenne Hamilton, Grade 10
Prentice High School, WI
Dedicated to my wonderful friends

Darkness

Darkness surrounds you…
  Stumble,
    Trip,
      F
        a
          l
            l…
From your path.
Shunning the light, you run away…
  Blinded,
    Hurt,
    Scared…
You run faster.
HELP
  Help,
    help,
    help,
Yet no one hears you for you are all alone.

Rachel Solberg, Grade 10
Kennedy High School, MN

I Don't Understand

I don't understand…

Why my dad doesn't want to be in my life
Why he can't just call
Why he can't visit me

But most of all…
Why he left in the first place
Why it's so hard to be a dad
Why he can't just come back

What I understand most is…
Why I love my mom
Why I have a happy life
Why I'm happy with the family I have

Alicia Swenson, Grade 11
Osceola High School, WI

My Little Everything

My little everything is my little sister.
She is cute as a teddy bear.
Her cheeks are red as a cherry.
Every time she is something different.
For Halloween she was a wolf.
At her birthday she was a pretty princess.
At night she becomes Sleeping Beauty.
When my little everything sees a camera,
she becomes a model.
I love my little everything.
My little everything has love to give,
happiness to spread,
and more characters to be.

Jaquelline Ruiz-Velasco, Grade 10
St Joan Antida High School, WI

Changes

How we became friends, I don't remember I just know we said best friends forever
Before I came along you said the same to the girl who you now called names
I played along, blinded by your faux personality
We hung out every minute possible to find us fighting was impossible
For a whole year our names were tied together for a whole year you were mighty clever
To hide your true self away from me
Then when school started up again our friendship started to bend
When plans were made for a dance the name called girl took a chance
Asked a boy to go with her
My friends asked me to go too but that's when your anger meter blew
I saw you for who you really are
You blamed me for your horrible time thinking I had done a crime
That's when the back talking started and that's when our friendship parted
We fought more and more each growing day I didn't want to stay
Because I saw the ugly side of you now you have to choose
To stick to your fake act or to pick up a new hat
And start being who you really are
That girl who you called names became my new friend for we both saw in the end
That you were nothing but trouble and we thought as a double
We made a good team

Jordan Cespedes, Grade 11
Champlin Park High School, MN

Fear to Fall in Love

Fear of falling in love or being in love.
What could it be?
Both
You meet him
You like him
You fall in love with him
But you never get to know them well enough
It hurts when they lie
It hurts when he's not with you
It hurts being played by the one you love
It hurts
Lies and more lies
It's scary how good they seem at first they're nice, sweet, so careful but then they leave
you like if you were nothing to them
Saying I love you at first
You don't hurt who you love
Love is something great, amazing, incredible.
But leaving hurts and it hurts a lot
So if you fall in love make sure he loves you too!

Lizbeth Infante Rodriguez, Grade 11
Lincoln Jr/Sr High School, WI

My Guardian Angel

It's hard to lose a best friend,
and that's what you were until the end.
You could make me smile any day.
You were my angel in every way.
Your energy and life made people smile,
Even though you were in pain for awhile.
You lived your life as fully as you could,
and everyone knew you would.
So many people loved you,
but it was your time to go so we knew.
It brought us so much pain and tears
as you lived with your biggest fear.
You tried to stay strong for all of us,
but that night ended with a silent hush.
That night a piece of us died.
That night a stream of tears were cried.
Nothing seemed the same anymore.
The pain hit everyone to the core.
Sadly, the cancer won, and suddenly life just wasn't as fun.
You may have gone but your memories stayed,
and I promise you they will never fade.

Dustin Moore, Grade 11
Lincoln Jr/Sr High School, WI

Pictures Of...

Turning each page, I remembered
Pictures of me; I was so small
Smiles so wide; a heart filled with joy
All the memories, happy and sad
I feel a smile grow across my face
Nothing can be heard but the sound of my laughter
I close my eyes and see it
I am young again, I feel it
The smell of warm air
The wind brushes against my cheeks
Running around, being free
Zoom! I ran so fast with nothing to fear
I was so brave impervious to pain
Time flashes and things change
I open my eyes; the memory fades
I miss the bliss of reminiscing
Such better days they were
Inside, I still look back
And I wish I wasn't dreaming
I would love to go back
If only I could

Lauren Coleman, Grade 10
Woodbury Sr High School, MN

Water

Water trickles through
Tiny little pebbles like
Sand in an hour glass

Andrew Lane, Grade 10
Groves Academy, MN

Dad, I Wish

I wish that I could understand,
Just why you do the things you do,
What you think gives you every right,
To make me miserable, just like you,
I wish that I could change your ways,
That you'd become someone worth crying for,
But that seems like a distant time,
A time not likely while I'm around,
I used to fall for your every lie,
Your guilt tripping and your fights,
But I have grown immune to it, now I hardly even cry,
I wish that you would quit your games,
I'm tired of keeping up with them,
Now I'm saying goodbye to end it all,
Because when I needed my dad, you weren't him,
I wish that I could change the past,
To make you see the way you made me feel,
To show you what you've done to me,
To teach you how, sadly, my pain is real,
I wish that I could tell you more, to tell you exactly how and why,
But the only thing I know right now, is one word, goodbye.

Monica Cook, Grade 11
Boyceville High School, WI

Life Beneath Your Feet

Sleeping under a shyly lit sky,
Awakening to the brightness of the burning sun.
Gently hugging the earth, floating two inches high.
Soft freshly trimmed blades gently intertwine
Glistening dew drops slip off the tips
Quenching the thirst of the earth below
Green as pine needles weeping from tree limbs
Hints of lemon sprinkled grass
Peep through the meadow of green
An ocean engulfing all its surroundings
Flowing waves distracting everything drawing it in.
A mother soothing her tear filled baby
With gentle hushing.
Twinkling eyes of dew watch over blade tops
Holding a breath of vigorous air
The birth of a newborn baby
Grass. Blooming blades of baked grass
Warming the earth with a hush it's back to sleep
A rustle of creatures
Moving unseen under towering blades
Wilting off to sleep

Melissa Schroepfer, Grade 10
IQ Academies, WI

A Day on the Mountain

life is like a day on the mountain
start at the beginning
a bowl of cool moist air relaxes me
tear droplets splash soundlessly
the earthly surface, filled with life
higher up the ladder
hear rumbling rushes
large rocks sit, like ancient ruins
lay on the stony surface
dip my toes into the freezing water
listen to flowing stream
i stare up at the sky
birds chirp happily
singing a song
snap! twigs break. each step taken
air grows colder
climb till i reach the top
snow cap tips, like white frosting
endless blue sky
a day on the mountain

Stella Vang, Grade 10
Woodbury Sr High School, MN

An Aunt's Love

She smiles her beautiful smile
   as she jumps up into my arms
     wrapping them around me
I don't want to let go, she's so warm
   so cozy
    I love watching her laugh and play
my favorite is when she giggles
   I've never seen someone so beautiful
She is my bundle of sweetness
   the one I adore

She fills my heart with warmth
   and makes my world go 'round

   She's wild and crazy
   but I wouldn't want it any other way

Tasha Jenkins, Grade 12
Deer River High School, MN

The Quest

The training of the sword
Working with the bow
The master is impressed
   I beat him
He gave me a quest
   To save a village
   Goblins were stealing from them
It was hard but I beat them
They called me a hero
   Now they will call on me when needed

Cody Jones, Grade 12
Blackduck High School, MN

Life

Life is how you choose to live it.
Life is all about you and the way you can manipulate certain events.
Life has its own battles.
Life has its ups and its downs.
Life is peaceful.
Life is full of astounding pain.
Life is worth living.
Life will bring you satisfaction and acceptance.
Life will bring you tears.
Life is elegant.
Life causes you troubles.
Life brings love.
Life is like a sweet melody.
Life brings you laughter.
Life is what you characterize it to be.
Life is God making the right decisions in producing you, His masterpiece.
Life is full of possibilities.
Life is made up of your choices and how you build on a certain choice you have made.
Life is what you make it, so make it describe you in every way.
Life is worth living so live it up to the best of your abilities.

Cody L. Shakal, Grade 12
Waseca High School, MN

Tribute

This is a poem to my older sister.
Who was my comrade in times of conflict
and always ensured a fun time when we were together.
You are one of the few who will withstand a *Lord of the Rings* marathon
with me and stay comfortable with the silence of this broken house.
You dried my tears, knowing just when to come and when to go.
But when your friends came first, it hurt.
Though I wasn't the complainer with you so I always kept quiet
For you will always understand.
You get that I don't like to share my secrets so you
treat them with the utmost care.
We share our crazy dreams of traveling the world and
anticipate them all to come true.
So I write this poem to my sister for being more than a sibling,
for being my best friend.

Margaret Splinter, Grade 10
Oak Creek High School, WI

Friendship

Friendship is a flower that never stops blooming.
The years are like the water that helps the flower grown.
You have to be able to share and you have to learn
how to care about someone other than yourself.
You have to be honest with them about everything and never try to keep secrets.
You grow protective of it and always try to look after it.
You don't ever want the flower to di so you care for it and treat it gently.
It is the fact knowing you will have someone there for you at all times.
Friendship is the laughter that fills up the room.
It is the sound of happiness all around.

Shaleta Lathon, Grade 12
St Joan Antida High School, WI

I Am…

I am afraid and lost
I wonder where my life will take me
I hear the footsteps of my future ending
I see the time line of my life creep to a halt
I want my fear to leave me so I may enjoy life
I am afraid and lost

I pretend my life is something it's not
I feel love when it's not there
I touch hearts with an acid grip
I worry for who falls in my trap
I cry for the times I know I should have
I am afraid and lost

I understand everyone deserves a second chance
I say I'm not worthy of your thought
I dream that love will still find me
I try, but fail to see the good in life
I hope one day to see the sun again
I am afraid and lost

Samantha Dull, Grade 10
Oak Creek High School, WI

Memorable Hunt

As I sit there in my little stand in the middle of the woods
quiet as can be not a sound anywhere
  no squirrels making a ruckus
no wind howling away at the trees
  …quiet
then faint steps crumple the dead fallen leaves on the ground
  patches of brown move through the trees
it comes into view a
  nice 8 point steps out
so I pull up my gun
  aim…and fire
…the woods are still again…
  nothing moving…
my heart is pounding…
  then I see the rack sitting above ground
job well done…

Cody Willis, Grade 11
Deer River High School, MN

I Love My Friends

From the first time we spoke,
To the times we made each other cry with laughter,
We were there for each other
Through the tough times and
Through the good times,
I will love you no matter how you act or what you say
We will be there through the darkness of the day
And people can talk about us,
But we know that true friends
Love you unconditionally.

Joelle Holzl, Grade 10
Rib Lake High School, WI

My Life Is Like the Sky

My life is like the sky.
Ever-changing clouds and seasons
line my moods.
Thunderstorms bring peace of mind as they
are my favorite lullaby.
Sunlight brings happiness, smiles and
laughter I can barely control.
And overcast days are my downfall.
They cloud my vision
until I am virtually blind.
V's of geese head south for the
winter as they know the horrors
December brings. Bright clouds
to match the bright ground.
Snowstorms terrorize my homeland, blanketing
the grass, streets and trees in powdered white.
Around March, the snow clears
from warm gusts of wind, we
see cerulean skies once again and
I am finally home.

Tasha Holden, Grade 10
Woodbury Sr High School, MN

Life

Hey Mom tell me how you've been,
  Time has passed and we haven't talked,
I don't want you to think that I forgot about you,
  From my point of view I can't complain,
  Working like always you've been,
There are so many things I want to tell you,
Because we never know if tomorrow we'll be here,
  Sometimes we have stepped back,
  I have always wanted to be right,
But I'm tired and don't want to argue anymore,
  Deep inside us we are almost alike,
  Maybe life will separate us more every day,
  Maybe life will move us away from reality,
Maybe you look for a desert and I look for a sea,
Maybe thanks to life I love you and you love me.

Rosa L. Sanchez, Grade 10
St Joan Antida High School, WI

Breaking Down

Feeling down, sad and alone
Closing your eyes wishing it will all go away
Just hoping for one second of happiness
Remembering the thoughts and memories that we shared
Memories that I will never let go and never fade my mind
Feeling scared and helpless
I drop to the ground and cry
Grasping every moment we had together
Sharing feelings and emotions I never knew I had
Tear drop after tear drop, memory after memory
Remembering is the only thing I can do to make the days go by

Tommy Poncek, Grade 10
Rib Lake High School, WI

Soccer Game

Needing a game plan trampling between lines
Suffering along the way whistle screaming
Just fight it
Celebrating victory searching for openings
The goal is a target rushing wind against my soul
Just embrace it
Expecting the unexpected acquiring injuries
Aware of surroundings craving adrenaline
Just enhance it
Drip drip down my neck the game is a war
An eager enemy protecting the curved version of heaven
Just endure it
Sense of accomplishment sacrificing myself
Lurking beneath the goal striving to stay alive
Just conquer it
Leaving with memories
Soaring across the field
JUST DO IT.

Jasmine Mazzotti, Grade 12
Woodbury Sr High School, MN

Friendship

Friends will see you crying,
And ask if you are okay.
Friends will hurt you
And then just walk away.

True friends are different.

True friends will be crying next to you,
For they know the pain too.
True friends will never walk out,
They always walk in.
True friends are like the wind blowing in your hair,
You may not see them,
But they are always there.

Jalea Priebe, Grade 11
Waseca High School, MN

Children

Put on your costume
Get ready for fun
Walking door to door
Be ready to run

You may get a lot of candy
Make sure you brush your teeth
Don't ever get greedy
Watch out for graveyards and what lies beneath

As you walk door to door, look around
When the door opens be polite
Say trick or treat
And have a good night

Kyle Strout, Grade 12
Osceola High School, WI

The Intimidator

Even though you are gone today,
Your memories will last forever.
The man who inspired everyone
Who himself was inspired by his father
To become the best at what he died doing.
The thought of him will always be remembered
When racecar drivers are driving at 200 miles per hour,
At the 4th turn of that one race track
Which took the life of the legend
The legend who had the iron head
And an iron heart.
When you left this world
Everyone cried
Because their hero died.
The hero who drove his racecar not just to win
But to be the best.
He was driven by determination
And waited with anticipation.
Everyone remembers you.
You won't be forgotten, my friend and hero,
Dale Earnhardt

Darrel Kersting, Grade 11
Lincoln Jr/Sr High School, WI

Ki Huka Makoce — The Ancestor Land

Alone, surrounded by nature and rain,
My attention is caught by a voice.
It whispers to me about the past pain,
Of its ancestors, that hadn't a choice.

Speaking of fallen Native Americans of every tribe,
Destroyed and slain by the whites of my kind;
My sorrow for them, one could not describe.
For visions of extinction occupied my mind.

The voice departed, and I began to shed tears.
As I glanced back, not a person was present.
For it was a spirit, passed on for many years,
That derived from the Native American descent.

Alone, surrounded by nature and rain, I now understand.
Everything we stole belongs to the ancestors of this land.

Jacob Loeffelholz, Grade 11
Belmont High School, WI

Midnight

The midnight air smells like an early morning's mist.
When the wind blows it feels like a wet kiss.
Frogs croak and crickets sing.
The tall grasses seem to swing.
As I walk along this beaten path
I listen close and begin to laugh.
But all good things must come to an end.
So we will wait for a new night to start again.

Matthew Conway, Grade 12
Waseca High School, MN

When Justice Finds You

You confuse me.
All you do is mentally abuse me.
At first you said yes,
Now it's just a big mess.
The answer is black or white
Not a shade of gray,
Because in love there is no such thing as halfway.
I don't think it could bring any consequence,
Because right now, you're the only thing making any sense.
There is no way I can convey,
This emptiness I feel inside
And for what I long to hear you say.
Those words I fear, I will never hear.
I've been waiting for so long, and I think you chose so wrong.
But I can't waste another minute
After all that I've put in it.
Someday justice will find you,
And I'll be right there in your memory to remind you,
That it was you who drew the line.
And it was your mistake, not mine.

Jenny Schroeder, Grade 11
Gillett High School, WI

Unforgotten Good-byes

Anguish suffocates the body.
The shadow of death leaves with no remorse,
his trace is but the scent of despair
and eyes that bleed clear.

Faith walks on broken glass,
eternally shattered in fragile minds.
Irreparable.

Blame bleeds through the veins,
with a first class ticket to a heavy heart.
Unforgivable.

Numb bodies, whose prayers
were neither read nor considered,
Weep.

Amanda Nusbaum, Grade 12
Wayzata High School, MN

Football

It all starts on a Friday night
The air is cold as a winter night
The sky as black as dirt
Flick goes on the lights
The field lit up so bright waiting for the battle
Fans come pouring in from everywhere, waiting, waiting
They can hear the battle cries from the teams
The leaders meet in the middle for a coin flip
Then the fans here a boom!
The battle has started

Danny Holicky, Grade 12
Montgomery-Lonsdale High School, MN

I Am Part II

I am outgoing and playful
I wonder when I'll be able to decide for myself
I hear the music, playing all around
I see a door of opportunities
I want to be able to travel the world
I am outgoing and playful

I pretend my family had no problems
I feel that I never have a say
I touch the sand, running through my hand
I worry that he won't see the end
I cry because I have no future
I am outgoing and playful

I understand we're in a recession
I say that I know I will make it through school
I dream to be a dentist
I try to be the best I can
I hope I'll make it through
I'm outgoing and playful

Kaily Hafoka, Grade 12
Osceola High School, WI

Just Because

Just because I am a mother
Don't think I can't achieve
Don't consider me weak
Don't think I make bad choices

Just because I am a mother
It doesn't stop me from anything
It doesn't make me a bad person
It doesn't give you the right to judge me

Just because I am a mother
It doesn't make me any different
It just makes me a stronger person
Still treat me the same

Just because I am a mother please try to understand

Katie Bantz, Grade 12
Osceola High School, WI

Love Is…

Love is…
Like a soft, silky blanket
touching your skin.
Smelling the fresh blossoming roses
on a warm sunny day.
The shouting of a new couple
arguing about the first bite of a warm fudge brownie
as it came out of the oven.
Beautiful as the trees with a fresh coat of snow
along the branches.

Shawna Egge, Grade 12
Gillett High School, WI

Illness

He had everything he ever wanted,
A family, a house, and a job,
But it wasn't good enough.

We couldn't make him happy,
Nothing could.
He became a victim,
A victim of an Illness.

The illness would make everything better.
He couldn't remember who he was,
the Illness destroyed everyone.

Today he is recovering
and forever will be.
We can make him happy,
but not for long.
He tries to stay away,
but it's too strong.
He will forever have this Illness,
Alcoholism.

Ashlea Pan, Grade 12
Montgomery Lonsdale High School, MN

Why?

Why did everything happen so fast
I want to go back and make it last
Everything was so perfect and right
Now we all have to put up a fight
Mom was healthy and Dad was strong
Why did everything have to go wrong
Now Mom has cancer
We didn't want that answer
And Dad needs surgery done
He still will never be able to run
I try so hard not to cry
And tell myself this won't mean goodbye
My whole family is affected
But I know we will all stay connected
It's times like this
That ignorance really is bliss.

Molly Miller, Grade 12
Montgomery Lonsdale High School, MN

Frozen

You warmed my heart,
Brought me back to life,
And now that I may be losing you
The ice creeps back in,
Settling into cracks
that you don't even know I have.
But if my heart isn't warmed,
By you and the life that comes with you,
I won't survive another hit.

Lindsay Hodkiewicz, Grade 11
Rhinelander High School, WI

My Best Friend Hanz

This is a poem to my dog Hanz,
Whom I love so very dearly.
With your red fur and your deep brown eyes
That are filled with compassion, love, and understanding,
Who would spend his days home alone because we had school and work.
But you never held that against any one of us.
You were always looking out the window when the bright yellow bus passed
And were waiting at the door to welcome me after a long day.

When everyone was home, you couldn't get enough attention.
We would sit on the floor, and you would come and sit on our laps,
Trying secretly to eat our ears or lick our faces.
You made those days fun; you brought laughter back into our house.
Every day you looked forward to your walk with Dad in the park.
With him tossing your toy into the field, training you for pheasant hunting,
Your anticipation for his command to "fetch" was fun to watch.
You'd run full out and return with a prance in your step as you enjoyed life.
You, the crazy dog, who ate socks as a hobby,
Which, we didn't realize, soon lead to your rapid decline in health.
So I write this poem to my dog Hanz whose life was cut short by a sock.
You made an unimaginable impact on our lives.

Amanda Thomas, Grade 10
Oak Creek High School, WI

My Story

She said sit down I have some news.
She said don't get mad this is something I think I should do.
We sat on the tire swing talking for hours.
Until it got more serious her tone was getting low.
At first I didn't believe her.
I didn't want to know.
How could they have lied to me this is something I must know.
Trying not to yell at her for she thought this was right.
All this time I couldn't believe that my very own parents lied.
The tears I cried for days and days kept getting worse it wouldn't go away.
I finally confronted them and the news they could not bear.
For they were going to tell me but they didn't know when.
I cried, I screamed, I laughed as well there were so many questions but they were not there.
Every day I stop and think.
What I'd do if I knew his name.
What would he look like is he someone I already know.
How many other kids like me have gone through this war?

Kayla Steffen, Grade 12
Osceola High School, WI

Desires

Desires can drive us to succeed in life;
Or they can make us falter into strife.

They may lead us to discover new talents;
Or they may throw our lives out of balance.

But there is one thing they all have in common;
Whether we want them to or not they control the way we live our life.

Sydney Burns, Grade 12
Waseca High School, MN

Other or the Same

Reflection — Reflection —
There's another world in there,
Looking out,
Looking in —
Do they see themselves,
Or an ironic mockery —
Perhaps they don't see at all,
But hear or taste,
Or even feel —
From their world,
A hidden paradise
Inside a laughing cage
Inside out,
Maybe upside down —
Really right side up,
To them — perhaps us,
The liquid, blurred gaze
Which one is mirror mimicking —
One elder, the other younger
Both the same age —
Trapped in their personal time.
Michelle Schmid, Grade 11
Mayo High School, MN

I Am

I'm an angel, I'm a devil, I am sometimes
in-between, I'm as bad as it can get and
as good as it can be. I'm a million colors
sometimes I'm black and white. You
can never figure me out there's too
many things I am.

I am special, I am beautiful, I am
wonderful and powerful, unstoppable,
sometimes I'm miserable, sometimes
I'm pitiful but that's so typical of
all the things I am.

I'm an angel, I'm a devil, I am
sometimes in-between, you never can
figure me out there're too many things
I am!!!
Kristie Leighton, Grade 10
Blackduck High School, MN

Dragons

Dragons
Spiny, large
Roaring, flaming, growling
My scaly friend.
Lizard.
Samantha Martin, Grade 10
Groves Academy, MN

Between the Lines

I am a girl who loves the color rustic yellow and wishes for rainy days
I wonder if others are thinking what I am thinking
I hear troubled children laughing
I see breathtaking monuments with remarkable character behind them
I want my sister to love herself and see how her unique ways touch people
I am a girl who loves the color rustic yellow and wishes for rainy days

I pretend I will have an exciting life but know I will not
I feel a newborn's heart beat in my arms
I touch the tears running down unbelievable significant faces
I worry for others' happiness
I cry when I see someone else cry
I am a girl who loves the color rustic yellow and wishes for rainy days

I understand one person's action can change another's
I believe everyone is unique and important
I dream of traveling the world and learning every detail of what I see
I try to look through others' eyes and see what they're trying to find
I hope I am different
I am a girl who loves the color rustic yellow and wishes for rainy days
Alyssa Santi, Grade 10
Oak Creek High School, WI

Monday Morning

Fresh, cold dew on the grass,
Waking up early at break of day.
Getting ready for another long week of school
First bell rings,
Students scrambling through their lockers.
Teachers are roaming the halls.
Last bell rings,
Few scurried students rushing into classes.
Monday mornings drag on and feel like you have been there long enough.
Eighth hour comes around.
Finally, the last minute of school.
Tick, tock, students jammed by the door,
Beep! Yes! School's out!
Parking lot filled with traffic as students race out.
Racing home just to wait for Tuesday morning.
Amber Monty, Grade 10
Rib Lake High School, WI

Far-Off Destinations

She walks slowly as the wind wraps tightly around her like a blanket.
Autumn smells swirl in front of her dainty nose.
An array of warm colors in the trees make the biting freeze seem a little less.
Though she shuffles on the path, her spirit has been swept up into the sky
where her thoughts play and dance amongst the clouds.
They flounce and flitter between stars.
Comets and shooting stars whiz past.
They travel past this galaxy unto others.
Peace, contentment, happiness is all she can or wants to feel.
Just to be able to escape and be.
Just BE!
Meghan Krause, Grade 12
St Joan Antida High School, WI

That Ol' Ford

She first saw him, gettin' outta that ol' black Ford,
That warm November night, at their good friend Tim's house.
They both looked, and what thought might be crazy,
But look — hey man, now he's callin' her Baby.

It all started with a simple little smile,
And now that girl — she drives him wild.
She wants to keep him, as he's her fearless — Romeo;
And he says he's gonna save her — his Juliet, forever.

Now Romeo has to leave, for higher speculation,
And asks his darling Juliet, to strive for when he comes home.
Thinkin' they're gonna make it, but you can't always fake it.
For they were both young, becoming troubles, ya gotta face it.

While her Romeo was gone, boy — that girl felt so alone;
To her, that boy means everything — and she's tryin' to make it.
It's hard, she's holdin' her wait, and prays this life — it is her fate.
And next time that boy was home, he got on one knee and said:

Marry me my Juliet, forever we must always be — you are my everything, for you my love will be.
I am your one, and, you, are my only; I'm in love, so, won't you run away with me?
Now take this ring, and always remember me. Then when the time is right, I will surely come for Thee.
We'll drive away, in that ol' beat up Ford, There ain't no turnin' back — Just the pedal to the floorboards.

Amanda Lynn, Grade 11
Tracy Area Jr/Sr High School, MN

The Case of Diamonds

Love is like a diamond trapped in a case
It is extravagant and rare
Extravagant because of the comfort and happiness that it shares
Rare because of the different forms it comes in
But the only way the diamond will shine and sparkle, is if it's outside of its case

A diamond trapped, unable to shine is like living inside a dark hole
Unable to be free to see the beauty and joy it can bring on to others
Therefore, a diamond should be a risk taker and allow its case to be opened
Many keys will come along the way, very willing to open the case
Allowing the diamond to glow like the golden gates of heaven

The diamond allowing itself to be taken away from the norm is an optical illusion, tricky and disappointing
The wrong key to the case is the poison apple eaten by Snow White
Yet the correct key will be the petals of a growing flower, fragile and maturing
But the diamond will never be perfect, it will always have its flaws
Therefore, a diamond is a soldier, battling through thick and thin

Diamonds are not worthless and can never be replaced
But not having it in life can bring sadness and unworthiness in one's state of mind
Many have said that diamonds were once the most valuable things in the world, a girl's best friend
The diamond will eventually die but its presence will never be forgotten
It will always shine, like you seeing the moon at night and the other side of the world seeing the sun gleam

Janellie C. Ortiz, Grade 10
Oak Creek High School, WI

My Father

Father says to his son,
"I will never do to you what my father did to me"
— Son becomes a father —
Father says to his son,
"I will never do to you what my father did to me"
— Son becomes a father —
Father says to his son,
"I will never do to you what my father did to me"
— Son becomes a father —
My father says to me
"I will never do to you what my father did to me"
I become a father…
WAIT…Do I continue or not?

I choose not,
It all stops here!
Now it's my turn, to start a new trend,
A positive one.

Travis Siegl, Grade 12
Visions Jr/Sr High School, WI

You're the One

Sometimes it's embarrassing to talk to you,
You are such the type everyone can always talk to.
I'm always in the way, never seeing what was true,
I can't imagine what I can't do, otherwise known as being you.
The way I am is a fake identity.
The way I scam and act like things are all okay.
And truthfully I'm a wreck, walking in my own pain,
Waiting for your key to unlock the chains.
You're the only one who can save me,
The only one who forgave me.
You can give me that love I never knew,
That love that saves me from the truth.
You're the strength that awakens in my soul,
You're the hope that blossoms and makes me whole.
You're the one that gave me a life to live,
And I thank you with every miracle you give.

Elizabeth Droll, Grade 10
Fridley High School, MN

Guilt

First you see the smiling clown face
That turns into a gloomy one
As you feel the grasp of your loved one
Slowly fading
Feels as painful as when you finally
Broke that jaw breaker you've been sucking on
That disappointed voice you hate so much
Asks why
No answer just looking at the ground
Then you look up because you can't smell
Her perfume anymore
She's gone

Andrea Beaumier, Grade 11
Gillett High School, WI

What Am I?

I wreck houses and uproot trees.
A nightmare I am to the butterflies and bees
Although I cannot be seen.
You can tell where I've been.
What am I?
Yet with all the havoc I cause.
Sometimes I stop and take a pause.
I am loved for the music I can sing.
But hated for the mess I bring.
What am I?
There will be the days that I am gone.
Fear not, for I shan't be long.
When you hear the chimes play.
You know that I have come back to stay.
What am I?
Once you find the answer to me.
Then you'll finally see.
That it was me the whole time.
The wind.

Kyle Blumenstein, Grade 10
Rib Lake High School, WI

A Lost Chance

The yearning for someone but being too shy
To tell her those words, you try with all your might
But instead you go home lonely at night
Her picture keeps interrupting your thoughts as you let out a sigh
She steps in the hallway and says "hi"
You feel warmth inside from a small glowing light
You try to speak but your mind and lips get into a fight
So all you do is wave as a good bye

Your whole body now is filled with regret
The feeling takes over of becoming insane
All you want to do is to just forget
Your world is constantly filled with rain
Lying down, your body in a cold sweat
Finally your eyes close, and away goes the pain.

Ethan Peck, Grade 12
Nicolet High School, WI

Half a Heart

I wave at her but she doesn't wave back.
   I try to catch up.
The wheels on this chair going too slow.
   A wheel breaks.
I spill on the floor.
   People gather around helping me up.
I look on and my heart sinks.
   She's with another boy.
Water leaks from the corner of my eyes.
   People help me back to my un-normal state.
On my way I feel empty inside, my heart is cold, my soul is dark.
   My whole world has fallen apart.

Ben Aguas, Grade 11
Deer River High School, MN

Why This? Why Now?

Things happen that are unexplainable
But why did it have to ensue you?
It all happened so fast
It wasn't your fault

You were suppose to be my bodyguard,
My friend, my sole mate
I know you're in a better place
But I just wish I could see your smiling face

There are no tears anymore
Because the time we shared was unforgettable
Nothing is quite the same
There is one to blame

You're one of life's blessings and joys
A true heart of gold
No one will ever replace you
Because no one is quite like you

Why this?
Why now?

Jillian Turek, Grade 12
Montgomery-Lonsdale High School, MN

A Single Red Leaf

A single leaf dipped in rouge
Hangs amongst a sea of chartreuse
All alone without a like soul
Without a companion to keep it whole

Deepening in shade as the depression sets in
The vibrant blood red stain turns to the deepest plum
Not wanting to be alive
Slowly decaying from the inside

Thinking it's all alone
Without a like soul
It drops from the sky
A fallen angel void of life

To the hard packed earth below
Now it's truly all alone

Michelle Ann Hagen, Grade 11
Osseo Sr High School, MN

November

November enters with a bunch of white snow
Fluttering around like a little butterfly.
It brings brightness to this world.
It does it by making the ground all white.
It does it wherever the snow falls.
The warm air melts away the beautiful snow.

Josh Schmidt, Grade 12
Osceola High School, WI

It's Okay to Cry

Mom it's okay to cry, for how I feel inside, after all, I did a lot to
you though words cannot express how I feel
The opportunities I've had with you, and all I've done was stare
right through you, Mom I know you are aching and it hurts me so
And all I want you to know is that it's okay to cry
Even though I don't want to see you cry but when it happens I'll be
right by your side, I'm not going to leave you ever again, even
though I'm going to be eighteen and I know I can
You are the most beautiful woman on earth, and I'm glad that you
gave birth to me, I promise to not make you cry even though we
still got a lot of building to do inside and out, but once that
building is through I'll still be with you, never alone or too far gone
Just remember it's okay to cry with me by your side and know that
this will never ever leave…

I LOVE YOU
MOM

Eden Mathews, Grade 12
Visions Jr/Sr High School, WI

The Things You'll Never Know

You'll never know how much I cared,
Because I'll never be able to tell you.
You won't find out the way I felt,
Or the way I wanted you too.
You'll never know the way you made my heart melt,
Just by one single look,
Or the way you would stare at me,
It's like you could read my mind like a book.
How much I needed your love.
Held in my heart far above.
These are some of the things you'll never know,
But I truly wish I could tell you.
The truth is, one of the things you'll never know,
Is the fact that I still love you.

Julia Sullivan, Grade 12
Visions Jr/Sr High School, WI

The Beautiful Soul

With every sway of the wind,
she waits
as each bird sings it's morning song,
she waits
and as the ocean glides along the sandy coast,
she waits a bit more
getting impatient she holds her breath,
not knowing that the wind called her name
that the birds sang her tale,
and the ocean wept her tears
she exhales,
and with a glee
she smiles,
never having to wait again.

Stevee Hutchins, Grade 12
St Joan Antida High School, WI

The Game

The nervous tension fills the air,
Pre game practice over the players
Are preparing themselves for the game

One by one they are called out onto the
Ice lining up shoulder to shoulder,
In honor of our nation's flag
Some are totally focused
Others are shifting back and forth
Getting ready for the tough game ahead

The ice is rough,
Torn up from the many sets of skates
That glided over it moments earlier
The arena is dark except for a single
Spotlight shining on the players
That were announced

The atmosphere is tense
Everyone knows this is it,
Win or go home

Jordan Badeau, Grade 11
Gillett High School, WI

The Fear of a Mirror

All shapes and sizes
Everywhere you turn
You can't possibly avoid them
This I'm starting to learn.
They haunt me and judge me
I'm starting to see,
I wish they would leave
And just let me be.
Everyone has one
And thinks they're just great,
If we'd learn to ignore them
We'd rarely be late.
They define our self-image
And all that we are,
With the fear of a mirror
You'll never get far.

Katlyn Schnitzler, Grade 11
Lincoln Jr/Sr High School, WI

Love Is a Four Letter Word

These days the word falls
So easily from our lips.
It's easy to say without meaning.
It's easy to say without feeling.
A word that can make us.
A word that can break us.
We swear by it.
Love,
A four letter word.

Sylva Judson, Grade 12
TAGOS Leadership Academy, WI

Reminders

Sparkling its white coat in the breezy winter morning, snow reminds me of our love
Happy, chirping coming from tall, live trees, birds remind me of you
A cool shower in the middle of a heated summer day
Reminds me of our love
The adorable and unexpected way you did things, lion cubs remind me of you
Whistling memories keep floating through my mind
Helping me once again feel that love
You were a rainbow
Your youthful smile that looked like flowers beamed over me after a depressing rain
Like the brightest stars, your smiling eyes radiated through the thickest of any fog
And our moments were like dreams I lived
That I still maintain
You were a sunset
Your warm heart was always in the right place
Helping me realize what meant nothing
And what I needed to get up and chase
Your heart told you why, your mind showed you how
You never quit believing and I doubted things, but now
I know you were a blessing
You were a beautiful love and a friend, and as always
You knew things would be okay in the end

Huda Karim, Grade 10
Oak Creek High School, WI

Awhile

You are the first to send warm chills through me.
The buzz of something exciting and new.
What we have, took some time but slowly grew,
something as good as this can take time I see.

Now your kisses are on my cheeks, like those from rays of the sun,
sprinkling spots of freckles across my face.
The lifelong impressions may fade, but I know will not erase,
each memory or lesson learned, good or bad, they cannot be undone.

When I'm feeling mad or upset,
you are the best at getting me to smile,
even when I may not want to.

No matter what, you are someone I can never forget,
so I hope what we have can last awhile.
Always know that I love you.

Sarah Amenda, Grade 11
Belmont High School, WI

Where Are You

The wind is impatient
It looks for you and it does not perceive you.
It expands by the arcane forest, but you are not there.
The desperate wind searching for you, but it only finds your smooth perfume.
It does not comprehend the facility that you can escape him.
What the wind does not understand is that you are rooted within me.
There his strength is not able to grasp you like the yellow leaves of autumn.
Although his force could drag me, you will be safe in my heart.

Esperanza Perez, Grade 12
St Joan Antida High School, WI

More Than Just an Ordinary Girl

A girl
A girl everyone sees as perfect
But really
She's screaming on the inside
She wants to be herself
Too afraid
To show her wild side
Purple eye shadow, crazy colors
A nose ring, an added touch
Standing in the street
Wondering who she really is
Mirror in hand
She wants people to see, her wild side
More than her plain exterior
She wants
Dark red lipstick and piercing eyes
Something more than ordinary
Something more
Her

Jessica Fullerton, Grade 12
Gillett High School, WI

Flying to My Death

Have you ever been afraid
That you would die in the air?
My heart's racing as we enter the jet
Ready to take our seats.
I make one last plea to my mom,
"Please don't let me die in the air."
I hear the motor start
My heart jumps with fear
When the jet moves,
I can feel the tears
Holding on tight to my mom,
"Don't cry," she says
All I can think about is dying
In this tiny little space.
Please keep me safe.

Etazhanae Baker, Grade 11
Lincoln Jr/Sr High School, WI

Trapped

In opera houses confidence sings
But inside closets we hear no ring
Of love thyself and all before
So we just fall back to the floor.
They say it's better out in the light
But in the light there is a sight
Of hate and torture knocking on the door
To scare us all back to the floor.
With coats and shoes, with rats and snakes
We all just search for one safe place
To be ourselves and nothing more
So we don't fall back to the floor.

Emma Plante, Grade 12
Osceola High School, WI

I Am…

I am a girl who has strong faith and sticks up for the underdog.
I wonder what is beyond the stars. Is there an end?
I hear "Party in the USA" blasting on the radio.
I see beauty when people smile.
I want others to know Jesus.
I am a girl who has strong faith and sticks up for the underdog.

I pretend to use my phone in awkward situations.
I feel the warmth of the sun.
I touch a hurting heart.
I worry about being accepted for who I am.
I cry when a loved one dies.
I am a girl who has strong faith and sticks up for the underdog.

I understand that there's a bright side to any situation.
I say that everyone should treat others the way they want to be treated.
I dream of going on a mission trip to Africa.
I try to be patient with others.
I hope to make a positive difference in someone's life.
I am a girl who has strong faith and sticks up for the underdog.

Jennie Kranjac, Grade 10
Oak Creek High School, WI

Molly

I long to meet her, if only for a moment.
To see her face, filled with life and shining bright,
Her hair, gently waving and dark like chocolate,
Her eyes, light blue pools of emotion.
But I know that it could only happen in my dreams.
I wish to hear her voice.
Maybe it's wispy like a thinly stretched cloud dancing in the sky.
Or is it strong and rich, filling the room with beautiful music?
I wouldn't mind if her voice sounded strange
Because I know I will never get to hear it.
This woman, as distant as a star, who is only a dream…
Never got to live,
Never had the chance to make friends and make mistakes.
This woman died at birth, a victim of life's cruelty
This woman was my older sister.
I could never confide in her, seek guidance from her, or fight with her
But I know something that I can do.
I can love her.
She is a flower that makes me cry, that brings me comfort.
She is in my heart, a flower that will never wilt.

Sydney Paquin, Grade 10
Oak Creek High School, WI

Is That a Friend?

Someone who can lead the path,
or just to help you with a simple errand.
Someone who can tell an oath
and keep with it till the end.
Is that a true friend?

Someone you can chit chat with
about anything.
Or have a shoulder to cry on
when things get bad.
Is that a friend?

Someone to lean on and
ask for support.
Or someone to laugh with,
while enjoying life,
is that a friend?

A friend is anyone who can
help you through life.
Anyone you enjoy having around
who sees you for you.

Ashley Werth, Grade 12
Gillett High School, WI

The Nonfat Latte

To the girl in the coffee shop,
I don't know your name,
Or anything about you.
I do know, however,
That you like nonfat lattes.
Every morning in the
Coffee shop I see
You in line, as it has
Been for many months.
Every day without fail,
You order a nonfat latte.
Every day I want to talk to you,
But can never find the courage.
Maybe someday I could,
And then I would be
Able to buy you
A nonfat latte.

Joe Reuter, Grade 12
St Lawrence Seminary High School, WI

Sky

Sometimes light, sometimes dark,
it's always there, doesn't move,
full of stars, full of clouds,
the sun shines through the clouds,
sky.

Jessica Kusch, Grade 11
Lourdes High School, WI

The Other Side of Love

Love is hard to find,
Love is hard to keep.
One couple's happiest day is another's saddest.
Two people start dating,
And two break it off.
Someone receives an engagement ring,
And another gets their spouse's wedding band thrown at them.
Two people get married,
And two get divorced.
Two people rejoice over the birth of a child,
And two fight over their custody arrangements.
Some love needs patience,
Other love waits for no one.
Love is a roller coaster,
It has many twists and turns.
It is fun while it lasts,
But when it ends you are sad and feel like someone has punched your gut.
Love is like the weather, it is so unpredictable.
Love fills you with sunlight, and it downpours on you.
Love is pain, love is joy.
You don't really know what you have until it's gone.

Taylor Marsolek, Grade 10
Oak Creek High School, WI

Till the End

You were brave, yet I never saw it,
I only saw your softness, your sadness,
And your small quiet personality.
You were strong, yet I thought you were weak.
I only saw your soft white skin,
And the fact that there wasn't a single fight you had won.
You were truthful, and now I understand.
You told me how your dad beat the happiness out of your mom,
And how your mom forgot you till you weren't there.
You told me you were small sad and weak, but you lied.
For you are bigger than me,
And you are stronger than anyone,
And inside you are one of the happiest and most beautiful people in the world.
You tried your hardest, and so did I.
We tried to keep you above the surface,
To keep us together, forever, as best friends.
But no matter how hard we tried,
We could beat time.
You left, but we are still together,
Till the end.

Samantha Fischbach, Grade 10
Oak Creek High School, WI

Love Is…

Walking down the road holding hands while the fall leaves drift off the branches,
Perfume and cologne linger in the air as the time flies by,
Turn to each other and barely let our lips touch as we continue down the windy road,
Strawberry chapstick lines his lips as I pull away,
Pause from our laughter to say *I love you* in a faint whisper.

Kayla Rohde, Grade 12
Gillett High School, WI

Cry a Little

I was little when you left
Crying and wanting you back
Years later I can't even imagine
Why I would ever think that.
Tears have always fallen for you
But my will is getting stronger
No more nights stricken with shock
Because my tears will fall no longer.
I'm not the only one you hurt
You hurt the both of us equally
He used to forgive you every day
But now sees who I see.
You blame everyone but yourself
For the hurt in your life
It's not our fault ever at all
That yours is full of strife.
Depression hits everyone
But yours is making everyone sad
We don't blame anyone but you
The world's greatest dad.
Emily A. Troff, Grade 12
Montgomery Lonsdale High School, MN

Trooper

She is a trooper
My trooper
Able to do things
I cannot
To see such strength
When so weak
I gladly will admit
She's stronger than I
She is a trooper
Our trooper
Always loving and caring
I admire her
Even in grim times
Her beauty shines
We appreciate the things you do
We love you
Zakri Reed, Grade 12
Deer River High School, MN

Time

The leaves change color too soon
They crackle beneath my feet
As I stride down the street
There is red, yellow, orange to brown
Now the snow is on the ground
The flakes cover the town
What is left is the mud
And the trees start to bud
The sun's rays hit my face
It's summer again, where did the time go
Alyssa Blee, Grade 12
Waseca High School, MN

Taking a Chance

Is it a fear of falling in love or being in love?
It is both.
You never know who it would be,
How they would act around you.
You will never know them at first.
It could be awhile before you really know who it will be.
It could be very scary falling in love with a person you've never met.
You might never know if they really love you the way they say they do.
When you fall in love sometimes you think to yourself,
Does this person really love me the way he/she says they do?
Maybe you will never know it for sure.
You could get hurt by falling in love with someone.
They could make you cry.
They could hurt your feelings.
This you may never know unless you experienced it first.
Love may never be true to you.
Take the chance of falling in love before you die.
Charlene Kinser, Grade 11
Lincoln Jr/Sr High School, WI

Daddy

Daddy, will you ever love me?
Daddy, will you ever realize the hurt you've caused me?
Daddy, remember when I was your Daddy's Girl?
And, Daddy, remember those days when I was your entire world?
Daddy, will you ever choose me instead of her?
Daddy, will you ever see my pain and wonder, "Why did I let this occur?"
Daddy, you've pushed me so far away,
And, Daddy, it means nothing when you say it'll be okay.
You've made someone else your world,
And now I'm just some lost used-to-be daddy's girl.
Aren't daddies supposed to be there to love and always care?
And, if so, Daddy, why haven't you done your share?
Sometimes I wonder why, Daddy, why I love you,
And then I remember: It's my hope of someday you loving me too.
Taylor Dibble, Grade 10
Cameron High School, WI

Addicted to Life

Life is all about addictions, some small but some severe.
If you did not have your vice, would you still want to be here?
Anything can be addicting, so long as it always appeals.
Everyone will realize they're an addict, when they notice how it makes them feel.

Life revolves around addictions. Most minor, but some you crave.
Should you ever lose your passion, what's between you and your grave?
Any addiction holds good, never hold yours in vain.
This is hard to keep in mind when your longings drive you insane.

Life is nothing without addictions, whether it's a want or a need.
If we did not follow our hearts, what kind of life would we lead?
Addictions, vices, cravings, or a hobby you have always kept;
It's inevitable, no matter how we describe it, it's the same concept.
Felix Norman, Grade 11
Osseo Sr High School, MN

I Am Me

I am competitive but intriguing
I hear the sound of opportunity knocking on my door, waiting to see if I'm brave enough to answer,
I see the good in people, when others may not
I want wishing to be as easy as finding a genie,
so the only reason people's wishes didn't come true is because their genie's broke
I am competitive but intriguing

I pretend people's words don't hurt me, even when sometimes they cut into me like blades of ice,
I feel like I have to put a footprint in history to help others find their way
I touch my pen, the trapdoor to my escape, where I can be whoever I want to be
I worry I won't make a difference
I cry when I see my dreams disappear in a blink of an eye
I am competitive but intriguing

I understand I must do the work to get it back
I say to have my desires come true I must first really think what my true desires are
I dream that one day I will change the world with what I write;
that someone…just one person will be changed by my words
I try to guide my little brother to the right path but many times I find him guiding me,
reminding me there's more than one *right* way
I hope that when it's my time to go I won't bother making a fuss about what I didn't do, but what I did to *try*
I am competitive but intriguing
I am me.

Heather Briley-Schmidt, Grade 10
Oak Creek High School, WI

cobble

unlike most
we build down
we strip away the blocks
and separate the interior from the exterior
leaving a skeleton to stand alone on the pavement
wondering when a crooked heartbeat will care to take a breath inside its shell
when a forgotten beast will dwell inside it once again in its limited forensic rooms with pale robes covering the walls
old english photos reminding eyes of the lost buried underground
rhinoceros roots shoot about to arrange a new family tree
and forever down around they go
diving to new roots and ends
building down
unlike most

Ginger Coleman, Grade 11
Northfield School of Arts and Technology, MN

Silence

The silence roars on in my head. How quiet it is and yet it deafens me. They say I need to talk; that they can't help me if I won't trust them. But how can you trust those who judge? How can you confide in a friend who is only there if you pay them? I can trust no one; can be helped by none. And so the silence roars on.

Samantha Hanson, Grade 12
Chisago Lakes High School, MN

Saturday

Love me tender, love me sweet. It's time to see what you mean to me. One foot forward, one foot back. We become one person with every step. I melt with your smile and tremble with your touch. All I feel around you my one and only love is truth. Truth in this world and truth in myself. Truth that was never there before. You keep me safe and give me hope.

Kaitlin Mewhorter, Grade 10
North High School, WI

My First Time

Agony gushing,
Through my veins.
Everyone saying,
It's just growing pains.

Betrayal abounds,
It hurts to breathe.
What tangled,
Mangled webs we weave.

Hidden love
Struggles, withers, and dies.
Trusting loyalty,
Crumbles under lies.

Excuses offered,
For what I give and you take.
Empty promises,
You're my first heartbreak.

Jewel Ball-Rochester, Grade 11
Lincoln Jr/Sr High School, WI

I Am a Southpaw

I am a southpaw,
I am a relentless opponent
in every competition I enter
I am a southpaw,
my stance is graceful,
my hits are deadly,
I am accurate in every
movement I make,
I am an adrenaline junkie
I do anything for the rush
I am a southpaw
I am difficult to predict
my opponent never knowing
which move I'll make,
I am a southpaw.

Manny Aljamrah, Grade 10
Oak Creek High School, WI

Journey Through Life

What is our purpose in life?
To be someone of importance,
Like a husband or wife?
Living life by chance?

Everyone has a different calling.
Specifics are of great importance.
So, how do they sift their calling?

Just follow your heart
And everything
Will fall into place.

Jimmy Nguyen, Grade 12
St Lawrence Seminary High School, WI

Here I Go

Here I go; I'm taking the first step outside of this hole —
The hole is so deep I had to jump high.

Here I go; I'm walking towards you; I'm trying to ignore you
Your love was impossible you just had to say no.

Here I go towards the door; I'm going to walk out
I'm going to leave, you will no longer control me.

Here I go; I closed the door you just watched me leave
You didn't stop I didn't bother to ask why.

Here I go; to a new life a new road
A new journey, new hopes and dreams.

Here I go; there I went. I watched the past repeat itself
I knew I had to change something. It was her or me.

Here I go; finally leaving, finally going to be wanted
Finally going to a place I call home. I'm finally going to tell my story.

So let it be heard
Here I go

Claire Winkel, Grade 12
North High School, WI

All These Things

The way your eyes light up whenever I come close to you.
The way mine light up just the same.
The way my heart smiles at just the sound of your voice.
The way you laugh and speak my name.
All these things.

The way I still feel the butterflies.
The way I know you do too.
The way you make me see the beauty in my flaws.
The importance in all the things you say to me, and all the things you do.
All these things.

All these things are still just things.
Maybe to some people, insignificant and queer.
But they all mean a lot to me.
And you as well, my dear.
All these things.

All theses things made and make me love you.
Just as much your fault as mine.
You're such an amazing person to me.
The feelings I have come natural, without even trying.
All these things.

Allie Rogers, Grade 11
Waseca High School, MN

Welcoming

Hands join and the world disappears.
Feeling content for the first time in years.
The night commences its endless bliss.
Body language signifies a simple kiss.

Our souls touch our hearts meet.
Her hair glows in the light as we stir our feet.

So soft,
So warm,
So beautiful,
So calm.

So lay your head upon my chest.
And put your worries all to rest.
You continue dancing as the song ends.
Swaying with me my beautiful friend.

For it's moments like these,
That can help our lives mend.
It's moments like these,
That I wish would never end.

Eric Hagen, Grade 12
Mukwonago High School, WI

A Hike into the Wilderness They Call Life

My life is a camping trip filled with joy and laughter
or ruined by pestering mosquitoes or lightning and storms
yet I trudge on through rugged paths knowing that eventually,
something good will overlook all the bad
perhaps a radiant autumn day to get my mind off things
but for now I continue on
I venture into the captivated wilderness
never quite sure what the next bend brings
courage encourages me to find out
pellets of hail shower on me but I'm not discouraged
heading back to the campsite
greeted by the smiles of loved ones
THEY scurry into the tent
hoping to escape the storm but I embrace it
we barrel into our sleeping bags
each relishing this weekend and I think to myself,
this is what life is all about and I close my eyes.

Thomas Schneider, Grade 11
Woodbury Sr High School, MN

The Calm

Peace slips over me like a shroud.
It's coolness calming me.
With eyes shut yet open wide to the world around me.
I am one with myself and the universe.
I am calm.
The sweet peace of a tranquil place enveloping me like a blanket.
I am calm, at last.

Taylor Murphy, Grade 10
Neillsville High School, WI

Black Door*

Behind a black door awaits it all
Never ending opportunities
Future possibilities

Behind a black door sits the past that once was forgotten
Here she lies in the mess of a miserable life
The autumn breeze scatters fallen leaves across an empty grave

Behind a black door stands the shuttering lid of a blind eye
A car slides through the impairing snow of a harsh winter night
Family buries a daughter, a sister gone to soon
Not from her own recklessness, but from a harsh mother
Who should have let them pass through the gates

They, at the black door
Awaiting access to the gates of heaven, or the depths of hell

Emily was her name, Eddie was his
Two souls destined to live their live's together
Now they wait for us beyond the Black Door

Bradley Wright, Grade 11
Winona Sr High School, MN
*R.I.P. Emily and Eddie

Violet

Violet!
Neither purple nor blue.
Unique in its own way.
Violet!
If ultra, it would not be visible.
Violet!
Longing for the sun to shine so that it may bloom.
Opening its petals and enjoying every second of this beautiful day.
Violet!
Do you ever feel enraged for being last in the rainbow?
No
Violet is a cool, calm, and relaxing color.
Never angered by a bump in the road of life's path.
Why?
Because…
It's violet!!!

Lisa Schanning, Grade 10
Oak Creek High School, WI

Foggy Mountainside

It creeps and waits till it's least expected,
as a lion silences his steps to pounce.
It blankets dirt roads in a silhouette of gray.
It descends in the dark of night,
and keeps the light a shadow during early day.
Farms, houses, schools, and forests, all covered in white mist.
But it floats away,
the sheets of gray,
and comes again another day.

Brittni Gullickson, Grade 11
Osceola High School, WI

Shadow

A shade of black,
Just slightly lighter.
Always seems to envy
Its close relative.
Never mentioned as much as
Its near-identical twin.
Never referred to as
A color used
To create great paintings.
Never taught to children
In art classes.
Never considered to be
A real color at all.
The color "Shadow"
Regrets these things,
And regrets always
Being forced to live
In black's shadow.

Jake Adelman, Grade 10
Oak Creek High School, WI

Starting Over

Tomorrow comes, and then again, it goes
While my ambition to become something more, grows and grows.
All I've ever wanted was something to live for,
I don't want to be this little person anymore.
I've been basing my life upon what others think,
I wish I could just drain all this hurt right down the sink.
I've fought to become who I am and what I want to be,
I have to remind myself that one day, I *will* be free.
Free from the rules I followed as a child,
When everything was a game and life was so mild.
Now, it's like no one pays attention to what I feel is best for me,
And what I think about the way some things should be.
I understand though, that I'm pretty much on my own,
And I know a lot of what I can do will never be known.
My thoughts build up, yet I keep them well-hidden,
They tell me I'm never right, that they don't need my opinion.
Who am I to speak up if I'm always wrong?
All they do is drag me down, I don't need them. But where, then, do I belong?
I want to know where I am going, I don't need to be reminded of where I've come from.

Tatum Swenson, Grade 10
Rib Lake High School, WI

Anger

As anger starts to build
My face starts to burn.
My eyes start to water,
The room starts to spin.

Why now?
Why me?

But then again…
Could I have stopped it?
Could I change the outcome?
Could I get what I lost back?

NO!!!

So why worry?
What's done is done!
It's time to move on.

Nada Ismail, Grade 12
St Joan Antida High School, WI

Stargazing

I sit down against the breeze, and relax myself against the Earth's curves
That lonesome hillside, which so calms my tangled nerves
A smile spreads across my face, as I look to the stars
My imagination is freed, from behind those wretched bars
I turn my daydreams loose, and they run wild
And I start to feel the joy of a child
My thoughts stray to you, and my smile begins to fade
I used to turn to you for such a welcomed aid
You used to stand by my side, but you've long since strayed
Sometimes it seems as though our friendship had never been made
What I used to think, a yearning heartache
Now seems to have been foolish, for our love could only have been fake
When you gamble like that, you leave your feelings at stake
As you walked over my heart, my broken emotions lay in your wake
With my hands to my face, the teardrops rolled down my nose
I regained my senses, and to my feet I rose
Leaving behind my world of repose
And I put back on the mask that everyone knows

Luke Weldon, Grade 11
St Lawrence Seminary High School, WI

Follow Me

People think everything is free, everything has its price,
'Tis the mantra I follow as a shade of fate, follow me, follow, through the timeless age,
I walk, I walk in the path of the misfit's blood, are you ready? No high hopes, dreams to see?
One by one, people fall to my feet, submissive, reclusive, they dream of me!
Essence, essence my friend, take it in, believe in it, it is their time, their calling,
Do not free them, you cannot free them,
It is too late, they are gone! Dead! Defeated! Downtrodden!
Dare you go against fate? Against the one who directs the sands of time?
Fine! Consign thee to oblivion, cur!
Dance with them, the demons of despair, dance the dance of fate!
May evil be your herald into darkness, betrayer of the future!
Do I stop you? Do you wish for an end to your suffering?
No. Betrayal cannot stop me, nor you,
We stand before the final altar, the altar of infinity, and still I defend you,
Please, I beg of you, beg in the name of my life, forgive thine transgressions, I have forgiven yours.
Is this it? The finale? Does fate's chain snap here?
I forever wish to reconcile, those who you freed, those who I wronged, those who I destroyed,
In the name of my life, where deception's free, follow me, follow, into freedom, into peace.
Still you stand opposed? Still you combat me? Believe me! Believe! I meant no harm, no deceit!
Fate's shade stands without you, as fate's courier fades into awareness,
Follow me, follow, to your shade, the shade which I love.

Ian McDonald, Grade 12
East High School, WI

A Struggling Mother

She wakes every morning
with no hope in the world.
She has to move forward.
She has no time to backtrack.
For her, life is like an abandoned train.
People jump on and off
they always seem to leave something behind.
It makes her life even harder, she feels lost and there's no one there to find her…
She abandoned the things that were left behind.
Now those things are left to find their way
without anyone there to help, protect or guide them in life.
Life will become a big struggle.
The mother who was once there, is now a person that struggles along the lonely road of life just trying to stay alive.

Clowie Stewart, Grade 12
Wisconsin Career Academy, WI

Random Scribblings of an Insomniac

In the midst of what can only be defined as a lyrical drought,
I search to find my voice,
The world is my muse,
I am surrounded by inspiration,
Yet, I find myself unable to properly convey with eloquence and grace that which has inspired me,
That which has given birth,
No,
The very breath of life to my now flickering poetic flame,
A flame that once shone with utter brilliance,
Is now,
A mere,
Soft glow…

Dereya Henderson, Grade 12
St Joan Antida High School, WI

The War Has Just Begun
Our country's had its beatings,
And taken deadly falls.
When the sky is burning red,
Our nation seems so small,
But the war has just begun…

You may not support the troops,
But the troops will always support you.
You can say the war is needless,
But I'll disagree with you,
Because the war has just begun…

They say, "freedom isn't free"
And if what they say is right,
How much does freedom cost?
How many lives to pay the price?
And yet, the war has just begun…

Out status means nothing.
Who cares about the battles that we've won?
Even though the flag flies high,
The war has just begun.
Laura Wright, Grade 10
Lincoln Jr/Sr High School, WI

My First Mare
She is my pride,
Lots of spirit and a little wild.
Oh yes, she's my problem child.
Every time I ride,
I feel something new inside.

Whenever I try to teach her to be mild,
She always becomes a little riled.
Since the first day she arrived,
She's given me quite the fight,
When trying to get her saddled.

Though her trust in me is unsure,
She is my joy and delight.
Even though she gets me rattled,
I love her.
Matt Magby, Grade 11
Belmont High School, WI

Going Fishing
The leaves of fall red, yellow and green,
Are no longer here to be seen.
The ground is covered in a frosty white,
To every ice fisherman's delight.
The wind chill factor is twenty below.
I hope my old truck still wants to go.
Out to the lake in the morning light.
I hope the fish are going to bite.
Justin Judnic, Grade 10
Rib Lake High School, WI

An Unforgotten Death
A grieving death
Clouds in the sky
Where she must lay
Watching over me here on Earth
I can't but wonder what it must be like
Still I grieve with pain for not having her by my side
How hard it is to lose someone so dear
Death is something I never fear
Yet when death takes away someone close
My heart aches with sorrow
She lived her life dancing to music
She died listening to its beat
How I wish I could have seen her move with her hands to the rhythm
I miss her so much with each passing day
My skies went from blue to grey
My grandmother, a lovely woman
I'll always remember her cheerful smile
Death took her away from me
But I am thankful for having spent the time I did with her
For you do not know what you have until it's gone
Luis Miguel Alanis, Grade 12
St Lawrence Seminary High School, WI

Moment Eternal
It's showering
You're outside running
It is warm and the rain is cool
The air filled with the smell of grass
You run through the grass
Kicking up water as you go
Your foot slips on the grass
You turn falling on your back with a
Splash!
You lay there with your eyes closed
Breathing heavy from your play
You relax and feel the cool rain falling like a soft shower upon your face
And you think this is true bliss
Wishing for that single moment to last a
Lifetime
Cameron Drake, Grade 11
Gillett High School, WI

The Prayer
You love my imperfect flesh;
Always extending your undeserved kindness.
I was given a choice; a chance to exercise my free will,
To worship, fear, and love you,
Or to reject, rebel, and hate you.
All you demand of me is exclusive devotion
All you want is love and submission, and then your blessings will flow
without restraint
I choose you, Jehovah, with my whole soul
There will be times I will need to repent, and you will lovingly forgive;
I will be a bright light in this vast sea of darkness.
Celene Bodien, Grade 10
Blackduck High School, MN

Miracle

I've been waiting night and day. I didn't see the time, I waited half my life away.
There were lots of invitations and I know life sent me some,
but I was waiting for the miracle, for the miracle to come.
But, I see my hands were tied. I know I must have hurt people;
to have to stand beneath my window with my bugle and drum,
and I'm up there waiting for the miracle to come.
You wouldn't like it here. There isn't any entertainment and the judgments are severe
when you're waiting, there's nothing left to do.
I haven't been this happy since I came to heights, nothing left to do when you know you've been taken.
Nothing left to do when you're begging for a crumb, nothing left to do
when you've got to go on waiting; waiting for the miracle to come.
I dreamed about my life it was just the other night.
The sands of time were falling from my fingers and my thumbs,
and I was waiting for the miracle to come.
We're never alone were always together.
We know that we're strong.
Never do something absolutely wrong,
while we're waiting for the miracle.
Nothing left to do, when you've fallen on the highway and you're lying in the rain,
and they ask you how you're doing, if you're squeezed for information,
that's when you've got to play it dumb.

Malcolm Lewis, Grade 11
Wisconsin Heights High School, WI

From a Distance

Two peas in a pod is one way to describe them,
but they'd tell you they wouldn't want to conform.
Almost as if they alone are the ones blind of their similarity,
witnesses have to act as their Braille.
Such strange souls are they.
Originally they were merely zoo animals forced to be in the same cage;
now, like inseparable twins.
It can be seen from afar:
their eyes speak in secretive code, their own lovely, longing language.
A painfully slow relationship was formed to the observer's eye;
like watching puppies interact for the first time: each one tentatively eyeing the other
while the owner must watch irritably, their knowledge holding the truth of the future kinship.
Their love soared beyond all others,
knocking away that of those whose suitors knew nothing of the other.
Perfect puzzle pieces can portray this natural connection,
resulting in as cold as ice stares from envious onlookers.
But do they take notice?
No. Blind to their own unique love,
while the world around them are like hawks restricted from landing:
only able to gaze upon what they wish they had,
from a distance.

Emma Palasz, Grade 10
Oak Creek High School, WI

Why Are You So Merry?

Every day someone comes to me
And says, "What's the matter?"
I should say "How are you so merry?"
My worn down mind is severely tattered,
I go about my day consumed by my own apathy.

I'm not attacking you with my rather
Explicit vernacular, I wish not to
Conform because of my internal storm.
Like the biblical apocalypse, the storm,
There's no stopping this.

What is happiness?
Why am I lacking this? I don't want
Attention, I want you to ignore me.
I woke up this morning, hoping there
Was more to life than what I see before me.

There's got to be more than people who
Discriminate; you say you're my friend; ha!
You're so fake. It's not your fault it's my own.
That's why I feel so alone.

Joe Hanson, Grade 10
Random Lake High School, WI

Statistic

I used to live in my own world —
Thinking it could never happen to me.
But that fateful day, he told me all.
The things I tried to ignore:
The late nights, the drinking, the overtime, the trips, the fights.
I never let myself say the answer to this equation out loud,
But I knew all along.
That day I watched the strongest man I know
Break down into tears.
"I don't know what to do anymore," he tells me.
He has tried everything;
I am his last hope.
But I am only seventeen!
How am I suppose to solve this?
The two people I love and respect the most
Are rapidly turning into another statistic.
How do you stop it?

Bobbie Jo Tiede, Grade 12
Montgomery-Lonsdale High School, MN

Freedom

Wind blowing, animals calling
An unlimited buffet
Weightless on my feet
I smell the trees, and flowers under my nose
I see red, white, and blue and only knowing it's the American flag.

Spencer Kurz, Grade 11
Gillett High School, WI

Grandpa

I see you, but this time I walk slow,
Lying still as stone, alone, lifeless,
As I place the flower down, a tear escapes as I go.

I think this can't be happening no, no, no,
But the disease overtook you and left you weak and helpless.
I see you but I still walk slow.

The chemo helped, but the cancer never let go,
You were healthy then sick, it ended in a mess.
As I say a little prayer, a tear escapes as I go.

I watched you get carried into the ground below,
Dressed in black, being overtaken in sorrow.
I see you but this time I walk slow.

Those last few minutes were the hardest, you'll never know.
I wish I could turn back time, I feel so powerless,
As I see our weeping family, a tear escapes as I go.

I whispered 'I love you' as though you didn't already know.
As the casket closes, I suddenly become breathless.
I see you, but now I will always walk slow.
As I say goodbye, tears escape as I go.

Ally Knaust, Grade 11
New Berlin West High School, WI

Untitled

Through a sea of people
And an ocean of thoughts
I managed to find my life
Everything is meant to be for a reason
Whether we know it or not
The Earth is still spinning
Still giving everyone a chance

In the daylight, this is still our life
When it seems as if it's far away
Things just don't feel right
Little things that you do, make the sun shine bright
I want to see the moon shine

When things just don't go the right way
I think of how everyone came all this way
Suddenly, we've got all this time
That we wished for from the start
We all know that this life is mine
Forever, I'll remember this part

Sound waves whipping through many ears
Everyone is now facing their fears
No one can deny any of their true feelings

Danielle Stern, Grade 10
West Bend West High School, WI

Unpleasant Surf

It is the sailor shrieking above the innocent, violent toss of waves
It is the sadness behind circumstance
It is the anger behind discomfort
It is the jealousy behind preference
It is the hatred behind mistakes
It is the love behind desire
All these things so toss me about.
The burn of silver sea salt on all life's wounds,
I have buried them…
Lost far beneath the earth,
Of my quiet glance.
Unable to cross that great ocean.
Unable to be shipwrecked.
Abandoned on an island alone
Lie pressed against the still sands
Staring at the stars
Connecting the constellations
That have always looked down.

Victoria Philllips, Grade 11
Mayo High School, MN

Autumn Nights

What is it like to mend a broken heart?
With your apathetic look, my body shakes.
City streets pull our souls further apart.
I ponder the direction the wind takes.
Do the maple trees of our love still sway?
Thinking of yesterday makes me queasy.
Did my dimwitted heart go so astray?
October nights alone leave me uneasy.
Autumn leaves will drift towards the dirt floor,
But tomorrow the sun will burn brighter.
Moods ease as new faces walk through the door.
Every inch of my physique feels lighter.
Dear alleged prince charming, can you not see?
You sincerely were not the one for me.

Kayla Kuehl, Grade 10
Oak Creek High School, WI

I Remember

that day is one i will *never* forget
It was
chaos
People yelling and fighting
things being thrown left and right
    confusion and crying all around
my mom told him to take whatever he wanted and get out
    he sped down the driveway
we didn't know what the future would hold after that
but we knew it would
    eventually   be OK
but some things still hurt and haven't mended

    but in time they will

Danielle Larson, Grade 11
Deer River High School, MN

A Daddy's Love

Protects you like a warm winter's glove
It tries to protect you from pain
And keeps guys from getting any gain
It helps mend your broken hearts
And it treats you with respect
It cares about you
Even when you don't care about yourself
It is there for you even when you think you don't need it
You won't give yourself away if you have this love
You will respect yourself more if your Daddy is there
My Daddy is here and I know I am safe
I know that I will have someone to help me
Daddy, thank you for all you do
Thanks for being here for me always
I thank God for you every day
You are a blessing,
and I wouldn't want anyone else to take your place
I love you!
Love your baby girl.

Stephanie Bauer, Grade 12
Appleton East High School, WI

Sonnet 1

I will love you forever. Will you?
You stand by me when I do not need you.
But when you are not there I need you still.
You were one of the people that made me feel new.
Yet made me want to destroy and to kill.
When I am with you I feel askew.
I felt light and free. Happy to be me.
You were a leach ready to suck my soul.
But now you are everything. The key.
Now you make me feel like I'm on a roll.
Like an ocean rising and swelling high.
You are my happy place in the storm.
I am now a bird ready to fly.
I am a new person up in the sky.

Sara Hofmann, Grade 10
Oak Creek High School, WI

Perfection

The perfect artist composed the perfect beat
The team across the line perfect for defeat
The perfect day
Making money in the perfect way
The perfect house and family
The perfect life in every way
The perfection we want always out of reach
The lines of perfection never been breached
As you learn perfection does not exist
Your drive for perfection just memories bliss
And yet you're happy just like this
Nobody is perfect no matter what they say
Only perfect in their own way

Tevin Pittman, Grade 12
Osceola High School, WI

Up North

Amazingly clear waters
Wild fields of lily pads
Thick black stone shores
Glaring granite cliffs
Deer drink along the shoreline
Whispering pines calling me
Serene landscape
Wild, and free the eagles soar
Precious wildflowers
Breathtaking sunsets
Smokey blue night skies
Glimmering stars
Peace and serenity
True family time
Never touched, undiscovered
Undefined, no planning
No sense of direction
Life is simple, no past, only present
Live in the here and the now
Whole and now like a dream
Heaven on Earth up North

Shawn Wonsmos, Grade 10
Woodbury Sr High School, MN

Life in the Everyday

Do you ever stop?
Ever think?
Ever hear around you?

Pause,
Ponder,
Listen…

Discover unknowns,
Step back,
Experience.

Let it surround and caress,
Envelope the senses,
Broaden the mind.

Absorb its joy,
Pursue its happiness,
Live it out.

Enjoy it, for it is life!

Kristen Heller, Grade 11
Random Lake High School, WI

The Sound of Madness

Playing in my room I was so closed off,
Until there was a bass filling the entire downstairs.
Loud booming, screaming voices, voices I could not understand.
The stairs became illuminated as I started towards them.
Daddy? Why were his arms open like wings while he was sitting on the stairs?
Mommy? Why was water running down her face?
"She stays here! She stays HERE!" kept echoing in the hall.
The entire time I sat there watching this madness.
What was going on?
Melissa? Where is she? Is she in her room?
In the split second I turned around to look, Mommy stormed away.
Night, night was all around me.
Blackness came in from every door and window.
There was a bit of light though.
The only light was at the back door which I ran to.
I put my hand against the frosted glass.
The blur of the red brake light was bright at first then it quickly disappeared.
Coldness from the night filled my lungs. Why did they just leave me?
Daddy came and got me from the door. It would just be me and him tonight.
Finally, it was silent in the house;
The sound of madness had stopped.

Michelle Amidzich, Grade 10
Oak Creek High School, WI

No Turning Back

When the doctor told me the news, I started to cry
Why me? Why now? Why do I have to die?
I looked up at the doctor whose face was filled with sympathy
He says you have cancer and only a few months to live
There's no way to treat it, I'm sorry to tell you this
He left me with my mother and dad whose heads were in their hands
Weeping they asked how could it be?
Not wanting to believe their little girl will soon be dead
They held me close, as I silently prayed to God
"Let the rest of my life be good, let me enjoy it until the end."
Months passed by as I lie sleeping in my bed
When a man appears in my dreams and tells me it's time
I look at him and ask "Does it hurt to die?"
He shakes his head no and takes my hand
I know I have to leave I can't turn back
Good bye now world, family and friends

Jasemine David, Grade 11
Montgomery Lonsdale High School, MN

Friday Night Lights

Trotting onto our rugged home terrain Friday nights
We hear the distant roar of the home crowd
The familiar smells of freshly cut grass and line paint linger in the air
The stadium lights glisten on our sweat dripping faces
Clouds of steam roll off our bodies
It's time to lay it all on the line and play our hearts out
Because this is game time
The is the sport we've come to know and love
This is football

Derek Thieme, Grade 10
Rib Lake High School, WI

Chartreuse

My color chartreuse, always happy as is
The color that limes represent
And the queen of green
Chartreuse as is, always crazy
Even prettier than a daisy

The color that no other can imagine
No one can understand the graciousness
That this color hides
My color chartreuse,
Never goes out of trend.

Queen of greens, queen of neons
That is my color chartreuse, happy as is
Just look at the happy smile that
My color chartreuse has
Look at its charming eyes
Just watch my color chartreuse
Come alive and rule the colors

Dominika Steinova, Grade 10
Oak Creek High School, WI

It's Life, No Matter, That Still We Lead

For you my reader, I pray you read,
A rhetor's thoughts, a simple creed,
About this life that both we lead.
It's just the beginning, a simple seed,
A single lovely resilient bead,
Adding more with every deed,
Nimbly living, a lakeshore reed.
Spreading rampant a garden weed,
Echoing at wondrous speed,
A mounted fighter, with glaring steed.
There is an end though this do heed,
This world will pass, it is agreed,
For somnolence we are thus freed,
With love or hate or want and need,
It's life, no matter, that still we lead.

Carl Colosky, Grade 12
St Lawrence Seminary High School, WI

I'm Not Getting Out of Bed Today

School's a drag,
Class is boring
Friends are getting old.
Teachers are dull,
The hallways smell,
And the classrooms are oh, so cold.
I want more sleep,
My body aches,
This is where I'll stay.
The blankets are warm,
The pillow is soft,
I'm staying in bed today.

Elyse Barnard, Grade 12
Lourdes High School, WI

Life and Love

Love is so confusing; throughout my life it's been about broken bones and bruising
To others, though, love is just so easy, they don't even have to try
They're always falling in love, and all I do with love is cry
But, when will it get better? All I've become is a big fretter
I just want to live a life with love; although I don't care when push comes to shove
It's hard for me to care when no one's ever there
I have to do things on my own, to take care of myself alone
If someone could just come and save me, save me from becoming crazy
I feel like my life is worthless, and this world is full of cruelty
If only someone would care to help, to be my wheelchair,
Someone to be by my side and not make me feel denied
If only someone would love me and see the things that I see
The things that happen in this world
This world that seems so twisted
This world that made me wounded
That made my life a miserable place and help me find in life, some grace
Help me understand why everything I do is unplanned
Why my life is hard to fix and help me learn the basics
Of how to live the normal life that I've never had.

Shyla Ward, Grade 11
Gale-Ettrick-Trempealeau High School, WI

Who Knew

Who knew something so simple could bring so much joy.
It was far better than anything money could buy.
Nothing in the world could compare; not even a toy.
Oh and nothing could be better than waking to his cry.

Who knew you could grow up with a friend with no words said.
Something that's always a reliable companion
That ball of fur always rhythmically humming at the end of my bed
After hours of play his droopy eyes looked at me like we were champions.

Who knew how fulfilling one's life could be.
His personality made my childhood anything but lonely.
Whether it's the ball of energy he was then, or the tired out soul he is now
The impact he has on me is clear to see.

Lauren Checker, Grade 10
Oak Creek High School, WI

Eating Disorder

To an eating disorder that has changed my life.
You seemed secure and simple on the TV screen.
I used you every day.
I kept my thin physique because of you.
But I hated you, with a passion.
Becoming overly obsessed with you, I reached your peak.
You drained my brain and thoughts.
You hospitalized me.
You sent me to rehab.
Or maybe there was no regret, perhaps you taught me to be strong and overcome.

Rachel Boehnen, Grade 11
Lincoln Jr/Sr High School, WI

Cliques Suck!

High school is the real deal
Nobody cares how you feel
Friends just come and go
Makes your self-esteem go low
Look around, where do you belong
Just keep following your "friends" along
Mean girls are everywhere
Waiting for the minute they can get hold and rip out your hair
Rumors always get spread around
Don't let them knock you down
Cheerleaders are so perfect, yet so fake
They just want to see you ache
We all put on a mask
To hide our flaunts, please no questions asked
Teachers' pets always get good grades in school
No matter how much they try they'll never be cool
People only get in your group by their looks
You're reeled in on a hook
The dorks, populars, gangsters, preppies, emos, and wannabes
Why not set yourself free
Clique is just another word for separating unity

Lissette Delatorre, Grade 10
St Joan Antida High School, WI

My Life Is Like a Dream

My life is like a dream
The moment where I feel like anything is possible
When I am creating the shining stars.
Where there are no mistakes, no rules
The adventure takes me farther, faster.
However I feel, my mind will set me free.
Deep into the blackest parts of the ocean.
Where no man has heard the splash of waves.
Higher then the glistening galaxy.
Where I can touch the brightest of all the stars.
My dreams make me feel alive.
I am a wise super hero soaring above my fans.
Dancing with the marshmallow clouds.
The smell of sweet salt from the water.
The tickling breeze as I stand on the shoreline.
The rough sand between my toes.
In this dream the warriors greet me.
I am the leader I can protect and conquer.
I trot off into the sunset on my graceful mustang.
My dreams might not define who I am or what my life is
But it helps me create it.

Zuma Clark, Grade 10
Woodbury Sr High School, MN

Autumn Moods

My mood is like autumn,
It's always changing,
It changes so fast that I can't see,
I cry every day,
From the hurt I have suffered in my past,
I get aggravated every second,
From insults I am always receiving,
I am depressed each time my heart breaks,
From the love that's fading away,
I am happy every blue moon,
From the limited sparks surrounding my heart,
My leaves are always falling,
My colors keep changing from bright to dark,
Great to worthless,
Hate to Love,
The confusion clouds my head,
I'm sick then I'm healthy,
I'm found then I am lost,
My autumn moods that can't ever stop,
My autumn moods that are confusing,
My autumn moods.

Sandra Dorazil, Grade 12
Wisconsin Conservatory of Lifelong Learning, WI

I Know Many People

I know many people
They are somewhat insane
They like to play jokes
And randomly claim
That they are so crazy
They love to profess
They'd walk right down main street
Wearing a dress
Sometimes I will catch them
Painting their faces
With different shampoos
And making disgraces
I tell them to grow up
But they smile and say
That they're having fun and I'm in the way
I'm scared that someday
They'll get in trouble
They'll blow something up
Just to dance through the rubble
Nevertheless, these people are fun
And living without them would be very glum.

Joel Blomberg, Grade 10
Rib Lake High School, WI

Please Excuse My Temper

I know I have a temper
but I don't know why.
I'm fine one minute
The next my insides are raging
needing to yell and hit something.
Punching walls hasn't worked for a while,
and I don't know what to do now.
You make me mad
and it takes very little but it
happens quickly but takes forever to go away.
It started with a push then a shove
and escalated from there.
I scare myself with my rage more than you'll ever know.
I try to control it then you make me madder
and it comes back with full strength.
Last time I went too far and apologized
for making you cry and pushing you.
I don't mean it but I'm not sure what
to do to make it stop, so please excuse my temper.

Kaitlyn Kittell, Grade 12
Hartford Union High School, WI

Trail of Tracks

Up atop a hill so bold
I see nothing beyond the bitter cold
I look to the floor in my dismay
And see a trail of tracks already made
A trail of tracks upon the snow
A trail I'm forced to follow, but I'd rather say "No!"
A trail of tracks that looks so hollow
A trail of tracks that I mustn't follow
A trail of tracks that, like all, lead to the same place
A trail of tracks I'd avoid with haste
But if each trail is like a strand of thread
That all lead to the same place when all are dead
Eventually many trails of tracks are shown
But as for me, I think I'll make my own

Julian Leyva, Grade 11
St Lawrence Seminary High School, WI

Trees Through the Seasons

O swaying strands of hair
Dancing in the wind,
Dyed a deep orange in the fall.
Your hair falling out in the winter
Like an elder man who has seen so much,
As *you* have lived such a long life yourself.
Your head so bald in the winter,
So freezing cold
With the watery dandruff hiding where your hair has fallen out,
Until spring comes again
And your hair grows back,
Full and rich once again.

Michael Franceschi, Grade 11
St Lawrence Seminary High School, WI

'Til You Return

The day I saw my first desire
It was across the blazing fire.
Trying to play it cool
But failed, and looked like a cute young fool.

Two years down the road
I found you were in Army mode.
Till finally four months later again we met
To scared to embarrass ourselves,
But finally we got used to each other.

For seven months we were together
Inseparable, unable to sever.
I knew the pain came all too soon for you,
Knowing I had to be there for you too.

The happy smiles fade away
As you leave at the end of the day.
You were here when I needed you most,
But you disappeared like a lost ghost.
Here I'll wait 'til you return.
When you are back, of that you will learn.

Kristina Colby, Grade 12
Round Lake High School, MN

Broken

Why do people find it so compelling?
    Why do people look for it so anxiously?
Is it really worth it…
        Falling so hard…
    When all you end up with is
        Pain
Although the hurt they feel,
The tears they cry,
    The countless people who were there to offer comfort
        They still try again
    It is so
        Wrong!
So what is it that keeps bringing shattered hearts back
    …Only to shatter further With more disappointment
Will anyone ever learn…
    Or will this circle of pain and breaking
        Just keep ignorantly repeating…

Aundria Sobolik, Grade 11
Deer River High School, MN

Jealousy Is…

Jealousy is…
The feel of cold, damp defeat
You hear the wailing of the sirens just like out of Odysseus
You see flashes of green in your eyes
You taste the bitterness of unsweetened cocoa.
You can't help but smell the disgusting smell of rotten cheese.

Rebecca Timm, Grade 11
Gillett High School, WI

Lord, Have Mercy on Me

Lord, please have mercy on me!
I've followed all your requests.
What else could there be?
Lord, have mercy on my soul.
I've lost everything and my heart is turning cold.

Lord, have mercy on my loved ones.
They need help and I can't do it alone.
I NEED someone!
Lord, have mercy on my friends.
Help them stick with me to the end.

Lord, have mercy on my heart.
Help me find that one for me.
Let me know where to start.
Lord, let me know it's okay.
When I'm lost, show me the way.

Lord, hear me out when I pray.
Let me know you're here to stay.
Lord, help me be the best person I can be.
Lord, please have mercy on me!

Donja Davis, Grade 10
St Joan Antida High School, WI

Pilgrim's Path

A pilgrim's life is difficult.
My life is proof of that fact.
I often stumble and lose my way
And I forget how I should act.
There are many trials and tears along the way,
And I suffer from fatigue and fear.
But it seems whenever I need Him most,
He never feels near.
I sometimes feel alone,
Like no one understands me.
I feel like an outsider,
Trying to ignore what the world tells me to be.

But sometimes the path seems easy,
As I stroll in the sunshine
And smile as I speak with Him.
I feel so divine.
A pilgrim's life is full of ups and downs
And we don't know what is around the bend.
But we must remember that He is with us
And He'll give us all the strength He can lend.

Michaela DeVaney, Grade 10
Lakeview Christian Academy, MN

Sonsarae

As the rain falls those who are awake pass on to that dreary sleep
to be born another day when the sun rises
good night my darling we shall meet again when it is sunny

Tyler Kirkham, Grade 11
Buffalo Sr High School, MN

Grandpa

Brown, weathered face,
He was a tall, thin, old man with big strides.
Behind his thick reading glasses,
He had eyes with ocean's depth.
His neat silver hair always shone in the sunlight.
With his weary hand,
He always held my small hand tightly.

Born and raised in a small fishing town,
He knew his trade; he was the greatest fisherman.
When he went fishing, he wore his tattered straw hat.
Before sunset, he never came back with empty hands.
Grandpa's table was plentiful with the fruit of his labor.

One stormy night, Grandpa went out to sea,
To check on the nets, he hopped on his old boat.
That was the last time I saw my grandpa.
The deep blue sea that he always loved,
Took my grandpa away from me.

Deep in my memory, he's there.
His genuine laughter still echoes in my heart.
I remember my grandpa.

Dong Hyuk Choi, Grade 12
St Lawrence Seminary High School, WI

Farewell and a New Beginning

It was on August 12 when I had to say goodbye.
All my friends were there to see me for the very last time.
The atmosphere was almost happy in my eyes.
I enjoyed the evening because it was mine.

The next morning was very hard for me,
Just my mum and the closest friends were left.
Just a last view and I had to leave
With my dad in the car to the airport without a rest.

To get number LH 9150, that was my flight,
Straight to the airport, Chicago O'Hare.
One more farewell and I was out of sight.
It took about eight hours until I was there.

My connecting flight ended near the green Wisconsin border,
Where my new family stood, seeming to be waiting for a mail order.

Rosa Hofmann, Grade 11
Belmont High School, WI

My Mother

My mother is a super hero to me
Who feels that she has to do everything for me,
Who needs love so that she can overcome fears,
Who wants me to listen at her first command,
Who fears that something bad will ever happen to me,
Who would like for me to go to college and have a great future.

Daesy Plascencia, Grade 12
St Joan Antida High School, WI

Dreaming…

I am dreaming…
Dreaming…
Dreaming.
Dreaming of hope,
Hope for tomorrow,
Peace in the world…
I am dreaming…
Dreaming…
Dreaming.
Dreaming of love,
The love I want.
Dreaming of comfort,
Comfort I need.
I had a dream,
A message of peace
A message of love
A message of everlasting peace.
I love to dream…
I am dreaming…
Dreaming…
Dreaming.

Natalie Bosin, Grade 11
Visions Jr/Sr High School, WI

The Never Ending Journey

Starting with forever ending with never
The middle acting as a black hole
Life and love searching for the way out
Starting with forever ending with never
Moons and stars swaying around
Life and love searching for the way out
But darkness blocks the path
Moons and stars swaying around
Waiting for the exit
But darkness blocks the path
Lives struggling with the ways of life
Waiting for the exit
Searching for hope
Lives struggling with the ways of life
Beaten paths guiding the way
Searching for hope
Souls knocking on the doors of the exit
Beaten paths guiding the way
Minds grinding, trying to finish the puzzle
The never ending journey

Courtney Carlton, Grade 12
Luxemburg-Casco High School, WI

Sweet Beckoning Amber

The color amber is like the sun. Her rays beat on our cold world making it peaceful
Seizing all sources of hatred into love
The color amber is not immortal yet she feels that every day is a gift
Living life as it were meant to be…happy
She's as passionate as the gods and natural as love
Taking each memory and never dwelling on the past
The color amber is never selfish
Seeing the world and loved ones before herself
Always hesitant like a deer when she has the beauty of a gazelle
The color amber wants to live her life to the fullest even though she knows the consequences
Feeding herself with lush and positive things
Though she cannot live as she was
The color amber needs to be pure but she knows that her sweet yellows and browns
Come with many choices
Though with life, she gains overcoming strength
The color amber is my soul
To be the best she can be, she will love forever
Her world might die…
But the color amber's soul will live forever

Francesca Gayle, Grade 10
Oak Creek High School, WI

Shy

Shy of meeting new people.
Shy of telling your feelings.
Shy of getting out of the clouds.
Shy of not being able to talk to females
Shy is what I felt when I saw you.
Shyness like a little puppy that doesn't want to come out from under the bed.
Shy sitting in this class.
Shy not introducing yourself with a greeting.
Shy like one cloud in the sky.
Too shy to take your order.
Too shy to express myself.
Afraid of doing the wrong thing.
Shy of doing all this
Yup, of all this.

Adam Ripple, Grade 10
Wisconsin Career Academy, WI

Halloween

By myself walking home, night closes in
Heart picks up, fear drops down
Imagination starting to run wild
Pictures of ghosts, blood getting cold, I can't feel my toes
Slow sweat appearing, legs shaking bad, feels like I'm in Iraq
Can't even run, I am stunned by the noises all around me
Looking down the street, a shadow fades in
It turns the corner its eyes staring at me ready to leap!
Backing up was a wrong move, the figure charges like an angry baboon
Glued where I stand can't do anything
I never saw that car coming
Thinking I'm dead I open my eyes only to see bright headlights.

Eric Mattson, Grade 12
Osceola High School, WI

Who Am I

I am a person that laughs and smiles too much
I wonder what the future will bring
I hear guns shooting in Iraq
I see children starving and begging for food within other countries
I want a cure for cancer
I am a person that laughs and smiles too much

I pretend to be a surgeon
I feel the pain of my aunt with pancreatic cancer
I touch her hair with soft hands
I worry what the future will bring to her
I cry seeing her in so much pain
I am a person that laughs and smiles too much

I understand I'm short
I say life is too short to regret things
I dream to be a pathologist one day
I try in school and sports
I hope to be a successful and good person
I am a person that laughs and smiles too much

Tiffany Phan, Grade 10
Oak Creek High School, WI

I Am

I am young and determined.
I wonder what accomplishments I can make.
I hear the wind whip.
I see the rain fall.
I want a good job.
I am young and determined.

I pretend to be here on time.
I feel I need to be awake earlier.
I touch my pen to the paper.
I worry about my grades.
I cry only when I laugh too much
I am young and determined.

I understand the consequences of tardy.
I say I'll be here when I'm not.
I dream of waking up.
I try to.
I hope I can fix this.
I am young and determined.

Andrew Bruss, Grade 12
Osceola High School, WI

Fear of Falling in Love

If you've been hurt one time
You will no longer go back to that moment
when they said they didn't love you anymore.
You lost the butterflies in your stomach,
the sound of forever and always whispering in your ear,
the feeling of someone by you at all times,
and the three most important words being said to you,
"I love you."
But falling in love just doesn't always happen once
You may not think you're ready to make that leap
and cross the bridge that was already broken
but you will have a hand to hold on the way
someone to tell you those three words
you thought you would never hear.
You just don't want to be hurt again
so you have the fear of falling in love.

Hannah Boettcher, Grade 11
Lincoln Jr/Sr High School, WI

The Terror of Surgery

Waiting for the day to come.
The day you dread
They say everything is all right
But you know different.
The doctors leave
Sponges, scalpels, forceps, and more.
You are afraid.
They give you drugs.
The light is fading from your eyes.
You wake up during the operation.
Nobody knows how it feels,
With the cutting, sawing, and stitching even more.
You see your life through another's eyes.
You can smell the fresh air of fall before you die.
One last thought occurs.
Why me?

Kyle Gerber, Grade 11
Lincoln Jr/Sr High School, WI

How I Feel

Sometimes you think I hate you,
And other times you don't,
No matter what happens babe,
Always know I won't.
Even on our off days my feelings for you grow,
I know that sometimes it doesn't really show.
We have had our good times, and we've had our bad,
When I look into your eyes it kills me when you're sad.
No matter what happens you will always be my friend,
I am glad you are in my life, I love you 'til the end.

Jake Walker, Grade 10
Round Lake High School, MN

Home!

I'm remembering the day I entered my room…
It is the day before I left my beloved country.
I take a look under my bed, and I pull out my footlocker,
I start going through it, until I find old albums.
Old albums of my family and me,
I close the album and put it back.
As I'm leaving the room I say to myself,
What lovely moments…
Every time I remember that moment,
I say to myself, "I can't wait to go back home."

Maher Awies, Grade 11
St Lawrence Seminary High School, WI

Where I'm From

I'm from the mansion, the hotel room, the house.
I'm from almost ten different homes, and three different states.
I'm from the 100 degree summers with no AC and the cold, harsh six-feet-of-snow winters without heat.
I'm from the endless backyard and the bunny chasers to the small plot of grass that's called a lawn.
I'm from the glasses that missed the braces and the heavy acne.
I'm from the home cooked meals that I make almost every night,
I'm from the unpaid chores — the dogs, the dishes, the floors,
I'm from seven different schools since I was only five years old,
As well as the never ending push to be only the best: perfect tests, perfect homework, perfect life.
I'm from a huge family — two sisters, three brothers, two parents, two cats, three dogs, and a bird,
But no family support — no grandparents or aunts and uncles, no lifelong family friends.
So no matter how big we seem, we're really so small.
I'm from the 60-hour-a-week working mother, and the stroke-ridden father with no feelings.
I'm from my many lost friends: Gina, Andrena, Tyler, Erika, Lisa, Kim…
And the constant need to be popular, satisfied, and happy.
I am from pain, anger, crocodile tears, lies…but more — the warmth, gut-splitting laughter, and love.
I am from independence, do-it-yourself attitudes, and responsibility.
In the end, all the things I have done, all the things I have seen, all the places I've been, and all the things I can do,
Have shaped me into who I am today, Coral Hsiung.

Coral Hsiung, Grade 11
South St Paul Jr/Sr High School, MN

The First Three Years of My Life

My memory, so strong, so robust
That it has been labeled with a capacity amount of unlimited
It can remember what I wore to my eighth grade graduation
My first girlfriend, my first kiss, my first signs of maturation
But this force, this powerful force of nature, cannot remember my first three years of being
This harsh fact of life is so loud in my head as if it is screaming
Three years that I have no recollection of
Oh! What I would give to be able to remember my birth
My first steps, my first word, my first signs of maturation
I sit and wonder what my life was like
Was I loud and overbearing or calm and nice?
Was I a ray of sunshine, slowly streaming through the window to land on someone's cheek and leave them with warmth
Or was I flash of lightning, loudly letting loose if my demands did not definitely get met
The first three years of my life, I will never get them back, no matter how hard I try
They have flown away, taken on the wings of the butterfly

Happy Musonda, Grade 11
Oak Creek High School, WI

Every Time a Jeep Starts an Angel Gets Its Wings

Jeeps are indestructible creatures made only for pleasure.
And when a herd of Jeeps fire up simultaneously, heaven sings a most joyous song
All the angels gather to sing, but after fifteen minutes are suffocated by the pollution.
And after five hours of riding all you can taste is the mud and dust that has been crusted onto your mouth and face.
When you take that sip of "root" beer, in a can cozy that chalky taste goes away, at least for a few minutes.
And when you get up early in the morning to prep your Jeep,
The cool peanut butter vinyl refreshes you.
And you are suddenly awaked and restored from your serious case of dehydration.
During your mid day run you encounter hundreds of unique vehicles as you have to pull a few out of the deep mud.
And you don't regret paying the extra money for your super comfy Bestop seats
There is a unique smell, a smell of solitude in the morning which leads to fuel.

Brandon Nygaard, Grade 12
Gillett High School, WI

Mountains

Climbing mountains always starts uphill
But after the first incline,
There will
Be a descent.
Yet there might
Be more uphills ahead.
They may be even steeper,
Possibly even more slippery.
But as long as you have started it,
You know that you cannot stop
You just need to keep going.
Conclusion: swallow up
And keep your feet
Moving.
Then
You will
See the other side of the world.

Hoon Park, Grade 12
St Lawrence Seminary High School, WI

Roses

I see this rose at my window,
As I lay on my pillow.
It seems to grow every day,
Especially on Sunday.

Roses are mostly red,
Like your skin had bled.
They also can be romantic,
Which is very classic.

People think they are a sign of love,
Just like a little dove.
So give a rose out to a girl
They will find it just as valuable as a pearl.

Stephanie Jacob, Grade 12
Tracy Area Jr/Sr High School, MN

Green Lake

Vegetables are growing
Tomato green and red

Reflect the scorching sun —
Feel of inner warmth —

The water casts glares
On surrounding boats

That dare to tread upon
The glazed emerald surface, for

Heaven knows — what could
Be lurking beneath the jewels

Jade Taylor, Grade 12
St Joan Antida High School, WI

The Masterpiece

Love is the wind that carries kites
    high into the sky.
Love is the stove that heats up
    the emotions of the soul.
Love is the stuff of legend that
    drives men toward victory.

The love of a friend is a mat to catch those out-of-control tumbles
The love of friendship is an elevating ladder to leap you to higher places
Friendship is a mountain, filled with valleys and peaks
Sometimes rocky and sometimes slippery
Friendship is the lifeblood of love.

The love of a family has no rival
Family is like a starfish, although limbs can be severed,
    They always grow right back stronger than before
Through struggle and strife, the basket weave of a family supports
    Every other weave, and together forms a work of art.

Like copper, the exterior may tarnish, but its core stays pristine
Like obsidian, its edges can be sharp but its beauty present in the rough
Love is like music, for although the greatest masterpiece may be written down,
    It means nothing 'til played.

Trevor Iglinski, Grade 10
Oak Creek High School, WI

Stifled

I see kids in the hallway —
Diseased, tortured, blank with boredom
I see these faces, these worlds,
Every day.

They let it slip through, somehow,
Their faces clear windows.
And they slip through, slip past
The concerned teachers, wrinkled brows

They come to school as much as they can bear it,
Knowing it somehow could be worse,
And go through the motions of their day
Without a slip of the tongue

Dragging their sullen bodies from class to class
With persistent bells to guide them,
Wondering what went wrong with the world.

And I sometimes wonder myself,
As I watch these kids compress themselves,
Ever so gracefully, brimming to the surface with thoughts of their own,
But stifled, for the common dream.

Kahlea Williams, Grade 12
Logan High School, WI

The Road to Nowhere

These wheels burning to where nobody knows
Through the mountains that steal my breath
And with every moment I march through the shadows
Lying deep within their depth

The moon light falls down from the sky
Taking away my heartache
These wheels start rolling so high
Away from the sorrows that I've had to take

The wind around me blows so sweetly
A beautiful kiss upon your face
An orange glow on the horizon starts to burn so brightly
All around this saving grace

These wheels stop for only a moment
To bathe in all this glory
But the moment is shortly spent
Because I never got to say I'm sorry

Logan Fiero, Grade 12
Apollo High School, MN

Golden Locket

Here I sit, once again, holding this golden locket,
Here upon the window sill, the very spot where we met.
I'm staring out at the black night, broken by a starlet,
Broken here and there by a shining white starlet.
Since you left, I couldn't bear to open this locket,
Couldn't open it to see your eyes in this golden locket.
For though both our faces are there, you know it's a habit.
Looking immediately to you, seeing nothing else: my habit.
For there's nothing else I'd rather see on this planet.
They haunt me every second, your eyes of chocolate.
Every second, they're all I see, they and this locket.
But I couldn't bear to think I need to open this trinket,
Open it to remember; you'll be back soon, I'm sure of it.
So here I'll sit and wait, but I won't sleep out of habit,
Being that my sleep is short and restless: another habit.
But I'll sit and wait and grip this golden locket,
Because I'm praying that I won't have to open the trinket,
That I won't need it to remember your eyes of chocolate,
Because you'll be back and I can toss away this locket.

Rachel Martens, Grade 10
Hortonville High School, WI

The Last Fight

I live by the sword
and during the battle
I dive into war
down to the soil
underneath all men
and drop my shield
this is where I am staying
this is my death

Brandon Trampf, Grade 12
Lourdes High School, WI

Bible Camp

Campgrounds filled with laughter
Joyous kids running around
Playing games, having fun
To see all of my friends, to hear them
Is a gift from the Lord
A mighty gift that no one can take away
All studying the Bible
To see who could memorize the most verses
Laughing at those who make fools of themselves
Swimming every day to cool off
Eating in our mess hall after we get back
From our three hour swim
Tubing behind a jet ski
No one wants to go tubing behind the speed boat
Only those who are brave
Laughing…singing…having fun…playing games
Wanting…
MORE.

Krista Noll, Grade 11
Deer River High School, MN

The Glow of Life

Life is like a candle,
That burns into the night.
Even though the winds may be settled,
It will still have to come to a dreadful end.
The light that we give effects those who are near,
And when our glow is gone,
We take a small piece of everything that we are close
to with us.
We stand our guard to last all we can,
But sometimes we are caught off guard.
A wind sneaks up and sweeps us away,
Never to shine another day.
But our memories still glow,
And keep others lit.
We teach while we're here,
And teach while we're gone,
And that's the light that guides us on.

Lucas Richardson, Grade 12
Blackduck High School, MN

Move Your Feet

Oh snap, look at you
Cool, great, fun and new
Good keep working at it
Use the rhythm to stay fit
Music, beat, move your feet

Dance class makes me smile
I'll show you my move
Now show me your groove

Hip hop 'til you drop

Alina Freshour, Grade 10
Alliance Education Center, MN

The Happiness in My Heart

My horse Jo is the cutest thing.
She is in my heart and is sure to cling.

To hear her whinny is a wonderful sound,
And it takes my breath away to see her gallop across the ground.

She sure does know when she's being good or bad,
And can push all the right buttons to make me mad.

Even when our friendship goes through a rough patch,
I somehow smooth things over with a treat or a scratch.

When I see that sparkle in her eye,
It calls me to climb up onto her back, so high.

I feel I'm flying when we ride as one,
Together in rhythm, it can be so fun.

I don't really like to be apart,
Because she brings joy and happiness to my heart.

But the most important thing of all:
Is to always get back on when I take a fall.

Victoria Kronenberg, Grade 11
St. Patrick's Academy, WI

Flying

grounded to the earth, wandering around
the inescapable chains of gravity
holding me down
as the birds flit past i wonder if they pity
this poor bound soul, flightless and gritty

the skies above look down with yearning
as i look blindly for a way to take flight
my ambition burning
could an earthbound misfit try as he might
actually earn shining, shimmering, wings of white?

so i rise up from the dirt and think like a sparrow
people surround me, an unenlightened crowd
i start to float up, and a hawk shoots past like an arrow
i wonder if i look that regal, that righteous, that proud
as the sky swallows me up, a limitless blue shroud

finally flying, finally free
and from above a heavenly bell rings
i look around and what do i see?
hundreds of people, with stunning white wings
escaping away from all earthly things.

Matt Olson, Grade 12
Deer River High School, MN

When...

When I see you
the light comes back into my eyes

When I'm not with you
I feel like I'm dead

When I see you with her
I die a little more

When I'm not around you
nothing is right

When you are around me
everything is just fine

When you are hugging me I don't want to let go
because I finally have you in my arms again

When you are in my arms
I finally have my whole world in my arms once again

When I see you the light returns
back into my eyes

Stephanie Barrett, Grade 10
St Francis Sr High School, MN

The Traveler

I have traveled this road for so long;
It has made me weary,
But I must go on.

As long as Polaris shows me the way;
I will follow and never go astray.

The North Star is my guide,
And in it I confide;
My trust and energy;
To go on.

Tonight the light of the north has failed to show;
The reason for this I know,
As the answer is an unacceptable blow;
To my moral, and my determination;
To go on.

A storm is moving in.

My patience is now growing thin,
As my only companion on this lonely path;
Has succumbed to this storm's wrath.

Matthew Johnson, Grade 11
Montgomery-Lonsdale High School, MN

Ego

This guy thinks he's cool,
Some say he's a tool.
Hollister is what he wears,
Puts extra gel in his hair.

He talks to all the girls,
But he'll never buy them pearls.
A player is what he is,
But I'll never be a girl of his.

He walks around like he's hot,
He thinks he'll have a shot.
I'm not falling for his charm,
He'll only hurt and harm.

So when he asked me out,
I said no and watched him pout.

I hope I hurt his ego,
I would hate to make it grow.

Katie Kopacz, Grade 10
Amery High School, WI

Alone

Going to the movies alone.
Waiting to answer my ring-less phone.
Having a dinner not meant for one.
There's no one around to call me hun.

Lots of couples in this crowded city.
But I tell myself that I'm too busy.
I trap myself in my own mind.
And make my heart become blind.

I want not to be single.
But I'm not one to go mingle.
Closed off to the world once more.
I just want to be opened to soar.

To be touched by the one who freed me.
A touch that can only be done by thee.
There is one that can make me feel young.
But her name shall not be sung.

Dwight Michael Sonsalla, Grade 11
Lincoln Jr/Sr High School, WI

Another Day at the Rodeo

My name rings out in a crowd of screaming fans
I tip my cowboy hat to be sure I make a good entrance
Ride my horse into the sandy rodeo arena thinking to myself
"This is where legends are made"
I ride the horse deep in the boxes' corner
Waiting patiently as the yellow barrier is stretched slowly in front of me
As the barrier tightens I put the string between my chattering teeth
My heart takes control
I look at the black colored calf ready in the chute and sit back in the saddle
Calm and composed on the outside
I nod my head in a relaxed fashion
The chute bangs open as my horse lunges toward the calf
The rope in my hand seems to swing itself
One swing… Two swings…Throw…Right around the calf's neck
My horse hits the brakes with a slightest touch to the reins
I make my get-off and sprint down the rope
Flank the calf…String the front leg…Gather the back two legs
One wrap…two wraps…and a half-hitch
Hands in the air!
10.03 seconds
Ladies and gentlemen a new leader!

Ty Vickerman, Grade 12
Deer River High School, MN

Departure

The dreaded day came as if blown in by a swift wind.
I kept my mind busy and thought of other things with a sigh.
I counted the medals on his breast that were pinned,
For I knew the time was near when we'd say goodbye.

I prolonged the moment as long as I could.
As we held each other in a loving embrace,
I tried to blink them back, but try as I would,
I couldn't stop the tears, now flooding down my face.

To God I silently prayed, "Return him safe and sound."
For his family he must be brave; he would show no fears.
In the soldier's eyes, undaunted courage was found.
But if he could be brave, then so could I, and I swallowed back the tears.

And my heart swelled with an overwhelming pride
As my brother walked away with a valiant stride.

Sadee Eastlick, Grade 11
Belmont High School, WI

Little Fear Inside of Me

Little fear inside of me, you make me fear you all day
You make me fear that you will take my life away
If you take me away I hope it's not soon
These scars you've made started to heal, and now my life is starting to seem so real
My life is working hard to stay healthy; my dream is to be a doctor and to be wealthy
My hopes and dreams might come true, but my life depends only on you
The cancer is gone, no need to take me away; please little fear, please let me stay

Ashley Volmer, Grade 10
St Joan Antida High School, WI

The Blind Side

Our world keeps spinning, round and round
Our sun keeps going, up and down
Our days keep passing, by and by
People are ignoring, what's going by.
People are hungry
Children are starving
They don't have food
They don't have fresh water.
We have nice clothes, they have old rags
We have big houses, they have tin shacks
We have our plumbing, they have their nature
We have our stores, they have their hands.
Our cultures are different
But we are the same
We see the sun, we live the same days
We just don't see, how lucky we are.
Their world keeps spinning, round and round
Their sun keeps going, up and down
Their days keep passing, by and by
People still ignoring, what's all around.

Melissa Tracy, Grade 12
Montgomery Lonsdale High School, MN

You Are

You are the light that guides me
And the darkness that blinds me.
You are the reason that I wake,
Though I sleep so I might dream of you.
You are the air that gives me wings to fly
And the gravity that ties me to the ground.
With you, all things are possible,
Without you, is there a point?
You are darkness; you are light.
You are my greatest dream,
And still you are my reality.
You are the one who stole my heart,
Though I would have willingly given you the key.
You are sickness; you are my cure.

You were here,
And suddenly you had disappeared.
Still there next to me,
Not really there,
You are the one who broke my heart.

Hannah Riggle, Grade 12
De Pere High School, WI

Techno

Techno
Tempo, rhythm
Electrifying, enlivening, exhilarating
The music pounded as the people danced.
House

Michael Pederson, Grade 10
Groves Academy, MN

Invincible Spell

To forsake the past
To let the memories fade into thin air
That is the burden that we share
But with you I feel strong enough
Strong enough to take on the coming dark
Your heart gives me that tiny little spark
To fuel my everlasting fire
Where the purest eyes couldn't see
Your light opened my eyes to all the possibilities
And then I could finally see you and me
With your light banishing its cursed mark
And breaking the chains that kept me in the dark
And together our lights drove it all away
So that the memories never fade away
With the coming of each new day
And now I finally see
Your invincible spell
Everyone can't help,
But believe in you.

Nicholas Vyse, Grade 12
Pardeeville High School, WI

Paradise

in my head exists a place
where the sun doesn't shine as bright
the moon isn't as high
the colors aren't as vibrant
in my head is my
solitary
place
this place is my freedom from this world
it's my quiet place where
everything i want will happen
everything i need will be there for me
everything i have ever wished for comes true
in my head
there
is
a
place…
only in my
head…

Tashina Grauman, Grade 11
Deer River High School, MN

Live

We live for tomorrow
With little or no sorrow
The swelling from the pain
Just shows how much we gain
Sometimes we slip away
And we cannot pay
For the mistakes that we have made
For a moment everything starts to fade

Kirsten Leisch, Grade 12
Osceola High School, WI

I Am

I am a dreamer and I'm shy
I wonder for my future
I hear puddles dry
I see a light in the dark
I want to touch the sky
I am a dreamer and I'm shy

I pretend I am brave
I feel God wants me here
I touch silver stars
I worry about my dream
I cry for my mistakes
I am a dreamer and I'm shy

I understand my mind
I say that life is great
I dream every night
I try to stay awake
I hope for summer flight
I am a dreamer and I'm shy

Marketa Pivodova, Grade 11
Lourdes High School, WI

My Journey

My journey is a long one,
To find myself in me,
The road is long and hard,
But this will make me see,
That though I may not think it,
God is always there for me,
Even in my worst of times,
He truly cares for me.

My journey is a long one,
To find myself in me,
The road is long and hard,
But this is just for me,
To find myself as I am,
The way that God made me.

Morgan Wisneski, Grade 10
Lakeview Christian Academy, MN

My Life

— Kyle
Hunting, fishing, farming, and the outdoors
Brother of Carmen and Brian
Lover of hunting
Who fears a head on crash
Who needs more money
Who gives help when needed
Who would like to see a great future
Who lives on a lake
Paulson —

Kyle Paulson, Grade 12
Osceola High School, WI

Love

Love
Can shine like the sun, living in the young hearts that love unconditionally
Living on in the hearts that found it so many years ago
Holding on in memories sometimes long forgotten
Love
Can break, leaving the warmth of family behind
Forgetting the bond that once brought them together
Leaving the love once there to linger in the past
Love
Is reliable when it wants to be
Questionable when you least expect it to be
Kind and caring when it needs to be
Fun and thrilling when you want it to be
Love
Is like the ocean's waves, beautiful but dangerous, smooth and rough
Sparkling in the sun
Twinkling in the moonlight
Love
Speaks in many different languages, with many disguises
Love is found in people in unexpected ways
And so special when you know it is right

Rachael Baricevic, Grade 10
Oak Creek High School, WI

The Four Little Angels I Never Knew

It was a typical early January morning,
When all at once flames protruded into the sky.
It seemed like Mother Nature was scorning,
And for all of our selfishness, we had to say goodbye.

I never got to meet these four children who are angels today,
But from the way everyone talks of them, I feel like I know who they were.
My siblings and others tell me of how they used to play.
I don't know why this tragedy happens to good people; it makes me unsure.

When this type of tragedy strikes a rural community, everyone knows.
People came from miles around just to help my uncle and aunt.
They had mountains of support, which helped them to deal with their woes.
People were right there to help them move forward when they said, "I just can't."

When things like this occur it's hard to acknowledge anything, but regret.
Jason, Jeremy, Anne, and Brian; the four little people I never met.

Courtney Dietzel, Grade 11
Belmont High School, WI

Summer

Summer is a fun season to have.
You do many wonderful activities in summer —
Play sports, hang out with friends, be with family, and many other wonderful things.
Summer has so many things to offer to everyone.
I love it when it storms in summer. The sound of the thunder
And the rain falling on the roof makes it even better.
Oh, summer, why do you always leave?

Benjamin Cunningham, Grade 11
Round Lake High School, MN

Wednesday in September

Is it true there's a path back home?
The place that I once knew
So long
So far
So distant
Recalling is fading and so it begins
Hard to believe
It was for the better
Easy to picture a different past
Two tears tonight
For the future I won't have
Hoping
Someday
The heaviness leaves
To let my heart be lighter
Able to find the path back
But take the new

Maria Peterson, Grade 12
Century High School, MN

Life

Life is good
Sometimes bad
We often stumble
Then get sad

But when we see
Our reason here
We all shout out
'Cause it's so clear

We're here to help
And serve with joy
So we can be
In His employ

Zackary Swan, Grade 10
Rib Lake High School, WI

A Firefighter Dad

Its sad to think
about being a
firefighter when you have
a family at home
sacrificing it all to
save the lives of others
looking back at the good times
deep in the burning house
a scream of a child
rescued and alive
the all American
Firefighter Dad is
my dad, a role model
to me and my brothers
the job he does for free

Steph Tesnow, Grade 10
Chequamegon High School, WI

In Pain

I find it unnerving
the way people are, it's almost as if
we are our own
        demise
So many times I've seen the *hypocrisy*
and I see me in the shackles of my actions
        and yet, I just sit back and let it grow and fester
A boil on the face of my conscience

And I see others, too
laughing along with their own little devils
        The evils I've known in my life making me sick

Although, I've seen these dark misdeeds stemmed,
        …there is a drop of hope in our pool of dark thoughts and evil intent
The swells and tides of pain and misery that could simply wash us away can be turned
                        by a *single* kind act
And just as hatred grows from vile acts of cruelty, so too does joy grow from kindness
        People see the devils in their minds and find a way to stop believing them,
to stop thinking only for themselves and ward away the cold night with the light of a
flame.   All we need is to be shown the way.

Dale Dowling, Grade 11
Deer River High School, MN

Wondering Soul

In my dreams, I saw a whole new world.
It's not decided in a moment of time.
Even if my tears overflow, or if fear embraces me.
I will never give up on what I believe in.
My desires made me a wondering soul.
I've been wondering for over a thousand years, with no beginning or end.
The moonlight illuminates my heart.
The dance of the burning flowers guides my path.
I reach my hands into the endless river and let them drift.
If I take the red road, then I'll never return again.
For those who care or have pretend.
I wonder why people live?
That in thoughts kept me in this world.
If life would disappear, why even dream.
In the end, the answer was never found, not ever in infinity.
I who continue searching around, kept my soul wondering for all eternity.

PaNhia Xiong, Grade 10
Logan High School, WI

The Armor

I feel like my armor is stronger with you at my hilt
I feel like the universe revolves around my beating heart
I feel like I can fly amongst the great phoenix when our skin touches
I feel like no human may defeat me in battle
I feel like when I am bloody and bruised I will still fight
I feel like I will be victorious in any endeavor
For you alone are my trophy, my queen, my prize
And only when that time comes, and I am triumphant
I will unsheathe my mighty sword, and bury it in the ground

Dalton Brandt, Grade 11
Montgomery-Lonsdale High School, MN

Alone

All alone in this cold old world that she was brought into,
She lives a pretty normal life.
Pretending not to care, and she's all right,
Letting no one see
What lies beneath her smile?
Putting barb wire around her heart,
Trying to keep her from getting hurt.
But it doesn't protect her from out-turnal hurt,
Or even emotional pain.
Crying alone in her room…
Ringing out her pillow…
And soaking it again in her tears.
Knowing she would never be understood
By the two people who brought her into this world.
So here she sits
Trying to think of a way
To get away from them
Knowing they have the power
To take her out of this world
Just as they had the power
To bring her into this world.

Emily Carns, Grade 10
Cuba City High School, WI

Heaven and Hell

What's the difference between heaven and hell?
Is there one? It all seems the same to me.
Does heaven feel like your arms around me?
I sure hope so.
That was bliss I loved so much.
Does hell feel like seeing you with her?
I would think so.
That sight never leaves my mind.
Maybe that's the difference between heaven and hell.
Love and Loss.
That's what I thought anyway.
When I was in your arms, that was the happiest
time of my life.
But you took it all away.
They say heaven is eternal bliss, eternal happiness.
But is it really?
If it is, you must be there.
They say hell is well, hell. Pain and sorrow.
But is it really?
If it is, you must not care.
So, What's the difference between heaven and hell? You.

Lindsay Liljenberg, Grade 10
Osceola High School, WI

The Wind

Loud and hollow the cold wind flows
Over the broken land below.
It is heard by many, near and far.
In the dragon's cave, the snow stirs
Over his shining black scales and pile of gold.
He draws his gold closer and warms
The fire of his being against the cold.
The wind blows through the crowded streets
Of the small, grimy village, bringing winter
In all its harsh cruelty on the shivering forms.
In the forest the wood-elves dance
As is their custom in welcoming the newfound snow.
On the dark plains, the free grass is trampled
By thousands of warring men and steeds
Their armor tarnished by blood and ice,
The wind carrying their screams through the night.
And on top the mountains, in a solitary cottage,
One person hears all of this.
His face and voice, young and fair,
He grips his staff and says
"Let us go and shine the light where it is needed."

Benjamin Postma, Grade 11
Round Lake High School, MN

Fear

I cry when it's dark,
I can't see what is right in front of me,
You cry when it's light
There is something you do not want to see,
We gear what we can't see
As we fear to see
Or taste something that is too sweet,
Something that could rip your heart out,
If you believe,
You might fall,
When the ice is not thick enough,
You might cry when you fall into the icy lake
And the needles push inside you
When the ice reforms
And you can't get out,
Darkness closing around you,
The mud and salty water filling your lungs
When you fear enough, you can feel it
I don't want to believe what I can see
I don't want to live in darkness

Terhi Kakko, Grade 12
Gillett High School, WI

World

World
Dreadful, forbidding
Lying, fighting, disturbing
But we still like it
Terra

Floyd Cuttino, Grade 10
Groves Academy, MN

My Brother

This is a poem to my brother Josh
Who is my only brother
He can be a pain
He teases and annoys you just the same
But then he makes a joke
And smiles at me with those hazel eyes
He will bother you constantly and get you so mad
Then I realize it's not so bad
We fight and argue all the time
But we have to realize we are all that we have
It's just the two of us, just Josh and I
Some days we get along just fine
When we do get along, it's a blast
It doesn't take much to make me laugh
He will make a weird noise or do a goofy dance
Then he will give me that evil glance
There are good days and bad days of having a brother
But it sure would be boring
If we didn't have each other
So I write this poem
As a tribute to my brother Josh

Hayley Danowski, Grade 10
Oak Creek High School, WI

That One Flower

Something so simple,
Can be yet so beautiful and daunting.
Such beauty can cause men to scatter.
While one single rose,
Can change a lover's soul.

Some may count petals,
Instead of wishing upon a star.
While others grow the love,
They lack deep inside.
Their many colors, shapes, and sizes
Help some to see the error of their ways.

The world is turning round,
Everything spinning up and down.
The ones who choose to stop and think,
And take in the smell
May understand what we have come here for.

Brittany Wedig, Grade 11
Belmont High School, WI

Nature Is…

The taste of cold crisp spring water
The sound of leaves falling from the trees
The scene of autumn colors
The wonderful fragrance of wild flowers
And the feeling of chillness from the coldness entering your skin

Clayton Bscherer, Grade 11
Gillett High School, WI

Little Sister

You and I are not the same,
though we be blood and you my brother.
Little Sister is my name.

They watch us race and play our games —
see me stumble, trip, and tumble — discover
you and I are not the same.

You sprint on while I remain,
choking on the dust that hovers.
They whisper, "Little Sister is her name."

For you they clap and dance — exclaim!
Roaring Father, beaming Mother
think that we are not the same.

This thirsting beast I keep contained
and join the praise of others.
(This Little Sister hates her name.)

For you they croon like drunken swallows, proclaim
the song that smothers,
that sings, "Those two are not the same —
Little Sister is her name."

Claire McLaughlin, Grade 11
Edgewood High School, WI

Life Is Beautiful

I look into the sky all I see is a beautiful sunset
I think about life and all the other beautiful things in life
I think about my friends my family
The grass, the trees, the buzzing bees
I think about life and its beauty

I look at the park
I see all the little kids
Smiling back at me
I think about life
And when I was a little kid
When I had no worries
And when I ran free
I think about life and its beauty

I look out my window
I see the birds flying away
I see the squirrels run up in the trees
I think about life
And all the beautiful animals in this world
I think about life and its beauty

Life is beautiful no doubt about it
Open your eyes and you will see as well as me

Lorene Harshman, Grade 10
Altoona High School, WI

When We Will Meet

Grandpa Dale, how I want to see you,
But you have already gone up to the sky.
I really wish you could be in my view,
Although it has almost been three decades since you said good-bye.

I won't let that get me down,
Because I know someday and sometime
I will smile and no longer frown.
But, I might be speechless like a mime.
I never sat on your lap,
Or asked you what it was like to live back in the day.
But someday, I will get a map,
And I will be on my way.

Then when I step into heaven's gate with both feet,
Grandpa Dale that is when we will meet.

Cameron Carey, Grade 11
Belmont High School, WI

My Cell Phone

Without my cell phone I would die
I would be worse than a baby when he cries
Without my communications I would go wild
People might think I was the devil's child

My cell phone is the best
To me it is needed like a good looking sweater vest
With it I get to call my ladies
And that's when they reject me and say "you're crazy"

As you can see my cell phone runs my life
Like when butter gets spread by a knife
Where ever I go it goes
Am I a little crazy? I suppose

Max Traynor, Grade 12
Osceola High School, WI

Fishing Lessons

His hands were stiff and old,
Hers were pink-polished and small,
Together they held the pole,
And together they had it all.
She would touch the worm,
But she wouldn't touch the catch,
When the line tugged she squirmed,
A face of delight under her hat.
He told stories of his life,
And though young she learned,
Under that mid morning sky,
All of his life lessons and turns.
In time she'd earn great admiration,
And in time she'd touch the fish,
But nothing gave her such determination,
As wanting to live like her Grandpa did.

Emily Penning, Grade 11
Worthington High School, MN

I Will Fight

You took my childhood,
My heart,
And my laugh.

Because of you, I taught myself
To give you up
And fend for myself.

I was unwilling
And you tried to break me.

Five years have passed.
I'm done thinking about it.
You're out of your mind.

What you tried to do
Did not work.

I've moved on, you creep.
Abuse yourself next time.
I'm not that same girl anymore.

I will fight.
The next girls will fight, too.

Ashley Gerber, Grade 11
Lincoln Jr/Sr High School, WI

Alone

By yourself…
    Alone in the woods
Thinking about how to get away
To stop the noise
    and thunder
Alone in your sweater
    to keep warm and
not fear on what's come
All by yourself

Time to cry,
    SCREAM
        YELL
Time alone to
    get things straight
To have a dream
    On what life should be

Alone in the woods to miss
    the ones you lost
To wish things were the way
    it used to be

To be alone is to be yourself

Mariah Curnow, Grade 11
Deer River High School, MN

Arrive When You Can

My phone is ringing, deathly chill,
I jump up from my chair to answer!
No one there, my mind again, dear god
I wish my son would call! Never mind.

With my weak and weary will,
I lift myself, filled with cancer,
I walk toward my windowsill,
I sit down again, never mind.

Head in hands, than hands on leg,
I sat down and began to beg,
Please oh please take me away!
I want to die alone, today!

I weep and cry unable to move,
To kill myself is out of question,
I wait for the deathly soothe,
Of death to come! Never mind.

My mind tells me to call my father,
My wife asks, "Why should you bother?"
Gah, never mind what they say,
I'll just call another day.

Jesse Olson, Grade 11
Osceola High School, WI

And So It Rains

Dark clouds
Overcast
Thunder and lightning
And so it rains

Darkness
Silence
I didn't ask for this
And so it rains

I stand here
In the middle of this
Alone in the shadow
And so it rains

It pours all around me
Drenching me
In all my pain
And so it rains

Soak me to the bone
Chill my entire body
Melt away my fears
And so it rains

Krysten Koenig, Grade 11
Gillett High School, WI

Red Rose Petals

You took my heart away, even though I thought you never would
You've turned my tears into red rose petals
You made my sense of insecurity and doubt leave inch by inch

But now as you walk away

The heart you took with love is torn in half
The red rose petals have stopped falling on my face
My hope of love was blown out like a candle
And now every time I want to trust someone I question it more than I should
But you tore me in half like I knew you would

But I am strong
So when the stitches in my heart heal, and the tears have run out
I'll be ready once more for the next person
    To
       Walk
          Away

Rebeccalyn Richardson, Grade 10
Blackduck High School, MN

If Someday

If someday the Earth meets the sky,
no more tears could I cry.
For once, everything would be perfect.
I wouldn't have to spend the rest of my days
stumbling in a forlorn worried haze,
wondering how I could save you.
I would be able to wake up to a world, in which you couldn't disappear.
You would be always at my side, whether far or near.
You could never be a far off memory, or a scattered dream.
There would be no pieces to pick up, everything would be as it seems.
I would never have to worry about you fading away,
for once in my life, I could live in today.
I'd be able to take every moment in, listen to every word you've ever said.
I do not fear the past, only the future that's ahead.

Jenna Rosquist, Grade 11
Lincoln Jr/Sr High School, WI

Silent Killer

They call you the silent killer.
You have already claimed my grandfather's life.
You have taken away happy memories and replaced them with grief.
You knock down the supports of my heart, pillar by pillar.
Now it's my father you try to take from me.
Can you just leave me alone?
Because of you, I visit my grandfather at his gravestone.
I wish you would just let my family be.
Without warning you take the ones I love.
You have no feelings; do you even care?
Do you care you've taken my grandfather's life from him?
I know he watches over me from above.
But taking him from me was still not fair.
Please don't take my father, without him my life will be so empty and grim.

John Henry, Grade 11
Belmont High School, WI

My Fear

Pushed my love, burnt my heart
My life without you
The pounding heart being crashed
Losing my faith in you
Most of all, losing you!

My dreams being taken away
Shattered expectations from you
My eyes losing sight of you
Most of all, you not being you!

You being taken away from me
The pain in my heart
The memories left behind
Face of the inside of you
Pain next to ecstasy
Me not being me!

Sheeza Afzal, Grade 12
St Joan Antida High School, WI

Fly

I walk along the river,
I see all that is green,
There I see a crow which sends me a shiver.
I notice its wings so black and wide,
It cocks its beak and holds its head up high.
It knows I judge it as it must judge me,
Then I see it fly so high.
It gives me the courage I need to survive.
Oh, I spread my wings so high,
I am then able to fly!
I fly with all my might,
I don't know where I'm going,
I just know where my heart is.
I just keep flying…flying.

Montaha Sarsour, Grade 10
St Joan Antida High School, WI

Good-Bye My Friend

Good-Bye, My Friend
My thanks I send
For this love we cannot comprehend
For the hand you lend
True our time together was small
But I do not regret it at all
I am to blame for how easily I fall
How I dreaded our last call
The world seemed fair
Before this loss we shared
This pain I wear
Makes my heart tear
The birds once sang, now they cry
How hard it is to say Good-Bye

Juan Carlos Alanis, Grade 12
St Lawrence Seminary High School, WI

She Is

She is my one true, never-ending love.
And for way too long, I've loved her so.
She is like a majestic, flying dove,
And to her I can never say no.

Many years ago when we were younger,
I would never disobey her wish.
But over time our love began to plunder
And I treated her like a broken dish.

Now I can only mourn, weep and sob.
For I let the love of my life leave.
I should have never let her twist that knob,
On that fateful, snowy, Christmas Eve.

I should not fret for all hope is not lost.
I will get her back no matter what the cost.

Michael Melegrito, Grade 12
St Lawrence Seminary High School, WI

Snow

Snow
Gentle, elegant, delicate
Falls in a soundless cascade
Special, each one unique

Snow
Harsh, glaring, cold
Endless ruthlessness and frost
Laughing, mocking you

Snow
Light, merry, childish
Prancing in the sky
Joy, happiness, and cheer

Elisabeth Karlik, Grade 10
Rib Lake High School, WI

White

When the tide comes in
On a humid, still day
White lace covers everything
A thin mist, then a spray

When the tide comes in
The white birds fly away
Frail lace threaded wings
Cutting the light of the day

When the tide comes in
The waves lick the hot sand
Bubbling, lace edged sheets
Creep up, littering the land

Lauren Thoma, Grade 12
Annandale High School, MN

One Moment

Just one moment
Could change your life
Or just one moment
Could flip your life

Just one moment
Could get all you have waited for
Or just one moment
Could challenge your patience

Just one moment
Could get a family to bond
Or just one moment
Could make your own a stranger

Just one moment
Could put you in dreams
Or just one moment
Could ruin all you have dreamed

Because it is just a moment
Which could
Pass like the wind

Sumra Mian, Grade 12
St Joan Antida High School, WI

Guardian Angel

She brightens my life
like the stars in the black sky
    shining like a beacon of hope
guiding me
    when I am lost

    When things get bad
        when they get worse
she's by my side
    never leaving
    never wavering

    With her right there
        I know
I'll be fine
    no matter how hopeless
        hope is never lost

    Survival without her
        is impossible
My
    Guardian
        Angel

Tyler Nelson, Grade 11
Deer River High School, MN

I Do Not Want to Get Out of Bed

The sun rises up above
as a new day arises
but the covers hold me in
for I do not want to get out of bed today

I hate for the weekdays to come
and the weekends to go
school is a dreadful place
that sucks you in

There are days I would rather lay still
than get up to take a test
or do my homework

I especially hate for 3:30 to come
when work approaches
I hate the smell and orders I am given
When can I got back to bed?

Jolene Schultz, Grade 12
Lourdes High School, WI

I'm Afraid...

I can't lose her,
she is everything to me.
I love her like none other,
her love is strong.
If I lost her I would be lost,
I can't lose her.
I can see the days,
where we are old and frail.
we will still be together,
I will love her forever.
All I know is I can't lose her.
I love her till we part,
at death there will still be love.
I can't describe how she makes me feel,
I can't lose her.

Jared Burns, Grade 11
Lincoln Jr/Sr High School, WI

Thinking Brings Pain

I think about you night and day
I always wondered which way
To heaven or hell you went
I thought you would at least leave a hint
Wondering about you night and day
Makes me go insane
I wish you'd at least come back to say
The simple words
The simple words I never heard
But I always prayed
That you'd say
"I love you"

Athea Hermann, Grade 11
Osceola High School, WI

A Teenager's Attempt at a Love Poem

Because you hold the unexpected
And allow me to laugh
When I would have cried
I like you.

Because you fulfill what I lack
And push me to do what is right
When others would have steered me wrong
I like you.

Because you seem so simple
Yet keep me wondering every night
While my heart keeps watch
I like you.

Because you listen intently
And care with sincerity
While allowing me my distance
I like you.

Genevieve Bern, Grade 11
Worthington High School, MN

Me Without You

A flower without sunshine,
A bird without its wings,
The world without color,
And a song when no one sings.

A movie with no screen,
A concert with no crowd,
A school without its students,
And silence when it's loud.

Thunder without the lightning,
A storm without the rain,
A pool without the water,
And peace when there is pain.

A person without love,
Perfection with a quirk,
This is me without you,
And it just wouldn't work.

Renee Catledge, Grade 11
Grafton High School, WI

Tears Lost in the Rain

Let the rain fall down on me,
Let it wash away my tears,
May I forget what he did to me?
Rain, wash away my fears.

May I forget my sorrows?
Please heal my broken heart,
Let me make it to tomorrow.
Rain, heal what's torn apart.

Forget I ever loved him,
Forget I ever cared,
Make him nothing more than a whim.
Rain, make me forget he was ever there.

I ask you, please do as I say,
Rain, rain, wash him away.

Miranda Robinson, Grade 11
Belmont High School, WI

Empty

The thing we once had
We have no more.
It made me sad
To see you walk out the door.

But it's the best for you
And happy is what I want you to be.
My heart is yours; this is true,
Forever you will see.

You're all I think of
When I can't sleep at night.
You are what I love.
It was at first sight.

I'll take your heart,
So we are never apart.

Josh Womack, Grade 11
Belmont High School, WI

Christmas Peace

Outdoors, flakes fall lightly on top of a white blanket of snow.
Bare trees stand still as they become topped white.
Inside also stands a tree, but the pine is nowhere near bare.
Plethora's of needles stand seven feet tall.
A multitude of white lights shine just as stars twinkle in the night.
The strips of tinsel are silver icicles hanging down from green overhangs.
By hooks are orbs hung of all colors.
Maroon, navy, evergreen, silver, and gold among others are seen on the tree.
At the tip of the mini-colossus lies a five-pointed star.
The topper stands the brightest over the magnificent scene.
A myriad of boxes wrapped in colorful paper hides the bottom of the tree trunk.
Adults and children alike open presents one by one by one.
A homey aroma from a lit fireplace filters throughout the air.
Children are in glee, and laughter erupts from parents.
Love can be felt and seen from hugs given out to one other.
On this Christmas night,
All is peace.

Jacob Jones, Grade 11
St Anthony Village Sr High School, MN

True Light

Where there is darkness,
There is light;
It brings forgetfulness,
But it promises insight.

True light is found elsewhere,
In the darkness unexpected.
With much to find there,
You become redirected.

Let your light shine,
Clearing the shadows away.
The sun's gleam, so divine,
Makes it live every day.

So let the light come to bloom,
And forget the inner gloom.
Valerie Barthels, Grade 11
Immanuel Lutheran High School, WI

Birthday Gift

I feel us drifting apart
being pulled at the seams
here's my heart you hold the key
telling you how much you should love me
words are hard to express
as I'm ripping open your chest
trying to find your heart that's beating
I search and search
worrying and wondering were it had gone
then you smile at me
and from behind your back
you pull out a white paper sack
dripping with blood
I saw what it was
it was your heart for my gift
I smile and grin
because its all I've ever wanted
Jenna Kraft, Grade 12
Ogilvie Secondary School, MN

Grades 7-8-9
Top Ten Winners

List of Top Ten Winners for Grades 7-9; listed alphabetically

Gemma Bush, Grade 8
Dominion Middle School, Columbus, OH

Heather Kinkade, Grade 7
East Marshall Middle School, Gilman, IA

Sasha Kogan, Grade 7
Public School 334 Anderson, New York, NY

Hayley Lange, Grade 7
Mater Dei School-Nativity Center, Sioux City, IA

Colleen Maher, Grade 8
Our Lady Star of the Sea School, Grosse Pointe Woods, MI

Coralynn Nydokus, Grade 9
ES Laird School, Lloydminster, SK

Addie Pazzynski, Grade 9
Waynesburg Central High School, Waynesburg, PA

Taylor Thornton, Grade 9
Shepherd Jr High School, Mesa, AZ

TJ Wells, Grade 9
Cardinal Spellman High School, Brockton, MA

Joanna Zou, Grade 8
West Jr High School, Columbia, MO

All Top Ten Poems can be read at www.poeticpower.com

*Note: The Top Ten poems were finalized through an online voting system.
Creative Communication's judges first picked out the top poems. These poems
were then posted online. The final step involved thousands of students and
teachers who registered as the online judges and voted for the Top Ten poems.
We hope you enjoy these selections.*

The Changes Over the Year

On a grey night, rolling thunderheads are getting swept across the sky.
The moist mist wipes across my arms as I walked along the road.
Colorful trees towered over me everywhere I look.
As I am walking, I know that Clear Creek is following me wherever I go.
Then I walk past a white, picket fence. I notice that the paint is starting to chip.
As I'm walking with the fence, I see a vacant farmhouse, and notice something in the window.
All of a sudden, the wind picks up. I can hear the howling of the wind in my ears.
Then I hear the sound of petite hummingbirds chirping in the distance.
As I walk, I notice the crisp, crunchy sound of the colorful leaves that I'm stepping on.
Then one minute later, a tall, scrawny girl named Nelly walks up next to me.
Nelly invites me over; she welcomes me to rock on her old, squeaky rocking chair.
Then she takes me to her tree fort in her backyard.
The trail that we walk on is covered with dripping, wet grass.
On our way back to the house, we notice that we're soaking,
So we say goodbye and Nelly disappears into the weeds.

Alexandria Bourdeaux, Grade 9
Jordan Sr High School, MN

Hank Aaron

There I was, in Braves Stadium, about to break a record harder than titanium.
I was next up to bat, where I waved to the audience with my hat.
Then I hit my glorious home run, the crowd went wild, it was very fun.

715 home runs, it took a while, but once it was said and done, it made me smile.
I broke two records, home run and RBI, it felt great, the way I made that ball fly.
The next day I could taste the relaxing morning air, and I thought I could be stronger than a bear.

I worked my whole life to achieve this goal, I worked day and night, in the warm and in the cold.
My family was poor and could not afford a bat and ball, so I used wadded up rags for a ball to throw against a wall.
I used a stick for a bat to whack, and when I was done there would be nothing to eat for a snack.

I held the record for many, many years, for many years it brought me many cheers.
Unfortunately, you can't hold a record forever, even though I thought I would never lose the record. Ever.
Later Bonds came from behind, I lost the home run record, but I still hold it in my mind.

Nicholas Galis, Grade 8
Jerstad Agerholm Middle School, WI

The Visitor

The visitor emerges from the clouds and settles on the grass-covered trail.
Autumn's ruby and ginger leaves float to the ground
but the gusting wind picks them up and carries them to a new destination.

Momentarily, the visitor loses his train of thought for a murder of crows
suddenly fights for a mouse, capturing the man's attention.
The visitor shudders and suddenly sees what he is looking for — Old Grandma's Creek.
It sits untouched, waiting for the visitor.

He picks up his speed when he feels the mist and sees the rolling thunderheads creeping toward him.
He scurries past the trees, over the sitting meadow, and around the animals.
Finally his long voyage ends for he sees the white picket fence looming in front of him
and behind it the abandoned farmhouse
but to him he saw his autumn recollections with Grandma and rolling in the leaves.
He sits down on the old chair, now with chipped paint, and says one last farewell to Grandma.

Heather Sharkey, Grade 9
Jordan Sr High School, MN

Lonely

One lonely man.
One box to live in.
Because one dollar a day really doesn't pay.
One snooty person walks on by.
One nose in the sky, one face held high.
Soon someone will understand.
How one is very hard.
One is deathly lonely.
One is very sad.
One day one'll be free from all.
One day one'll find hope.
One day one'll be free forever,
and ever more.

Carl Sadloske, Grade 7
Lincoln Jr/Sr High School, WI

One Time

The last game of my high school career.
Only 5 seconds are left,
And I get the ball.
I am freaking out.
I don't know what to do
I see the basket, I shoot
The ball goes round and round and round
It was the longest 5 seconds of my life.
The buzzer goes off.
The ball goes in.
I made the winning shot,
One of my life goals.
Now I feel like nothing can stop me.

Hannah Langseth-Berger, Grade 9
Round Lake High School, MN

The Soccer Legend

I wish to be a professional soccer player,
win championships,
become rich and give to the poor!
Have kids and a wonderful wife!
Become the world's best soccer player,
right after I
get the milk
feed the cats
and go to school.

Nathan Bowman, Grade 7
Shakopee Area Catholic School, MN

Winter/Spring

Winter,
Fun, windy
Snowing, freezing, cooling
Snow, snowballs, forts, sledding
Melting, warming, falling
Water, grass
Spring

Steven Venske, Grade 9
Rosholt Middle-High School, WI

Volleyball

Bump, set spike
You've been waiting for this night for a week now.
The score is 2 to zip.
The other team has the ball.
They serve the ball it's coming right to you.
You're getting ready to bump the ball hands locked in place.
You squat down just a little.
The ball meets your hands you straighten your legs and there goes the ball
right over the net.
You're smiling big, the crowd is going wild!
You just scored one point for your team.
It's your turn to serve.
You throw the ball up, pull your hand back, and wait for the perfect timing
to hit the ball.
There it goes full speed just clears the net.
The other team doesn't know what hit them.
You get a good run going and the crowd is going wild!
It's game point for you it all comes down to this.
You serve your hope you can win this.
You did it! Your team is jumping up and down and screaming!
You won the game!

Stephanie Werre, Grade 7
Lincoln Jr/Sr High School, WI

Monster

After packing up my tent, I continued on my hike.
Finally, when the grass-covered trail ended,
I saw heavy mist hanging over an algae-covered lake.
The lake then drained into Lost Creek on its south end.
I watched as the bright autumn leaves floated down the winding creek.
After the rolling thunderheads announced the coming rainstorm,
I spotted an unpainted, abandoned farmhouse.
The gale swept the fearless red-tailed hawks from their nests.
I entered the house, and upon seeing a rocking chair, I collapsed into it.
Then I heard footsteps blundering up the porch to the front door.
I threw my terrified body underneath the chair.
The door squeaked open, and a heavyset man walked toward my chair.
Without a moment's hesitation, I dove from my cover and dashed out the door.
I looked behind me as I leapt over a weather-worn fence
and saw a man pointing and laughing at me.

Ben Althoff, Grade 9
Jordan Sr High School, MN

The Hearts Sadness That's Never Shown

What if you don't know who you live for?
Even for yourself.
Who do you live for then?
I live because I was given birth to, given life,
But what good is this life you have if no one believes in it.
And people constantly put you down and treat you like you're nothing.
How do you cope with your birth mom dead
And you're always being reminded of her but they talk down about your mom?
This life I have does not belong here if no one believes in it.
But they can judge me all they want I'm me and that's not going to change.

Victoria Valvo, Grade 8
Cooper Elementary School, WI

I Am

I am Max Flowers
I wonder why I am not good at Math
I hear a flock of geese landing on a pond
I see big bucks walking into sight
I want my grandpa back
I am Max Flowers

I pretend to be in the NFL
I feel when something is wrong
I touch cold frost on my deer stand
I worry about my family
I cry when I think about my grandpa
I am Max Flowers

I understand how to be respectful
I say something that needs to be said
I dream about big bucks
I try to get good grades
I hope to be as successful as my dad
I am Max Flowers

Max Flowers, Grade 9
Discovery Middle School, MN

Chains

Chains all around me.
I'm where nobody is free.
I want to fly away,
and be all I can be.
I hear the foreman shout.
I hear the crack of his whip.
I hear the cry of a slave,
as he stumbles and trips.
A man called Lincoln,
he comes to town.
He says, "Free the slaves!"
The white people frown.
Soon, Lincoln frees us slaves,
and all the chains drop.
I'm free before I reach the grave!
The painful whipping stops!
Chains aren't around me.
I'm where everybody is free.
I can now fly away,
and be all I can be.

Kadija Larsen, Grade 8
Holy Family School, WI

TV

TV
awesome, exciting
advertising, showing, telling
stations, cable, satellite, direct TV
amazing, exhilarating
movies

Alec Ray Kosloske, Grade 9
Rosholt Middle-High School, WI

Laughter

The sound of laughter is a thing of beauty.
It is like a whole different language.
Laughter spreads the gift of happiness.
People are drawn to happy people.
Everybody wishes to be happy.
If you feel sorry for yourself,
You are the saddest person in the world.
Not even your friends want to be around you.
Laughter blooms and never fails to fill the cup of cheer.
Laugh away your worries,
And the worries will turn to calmness: reassurance.
It has a joyful ring and only the heartless will fail to hear it and join in.

Megan Schmitz, Grade 8
Round Lake High School, MN

The Road of Life

Life is a boulevard traveled by many cars
At some points it can be a broken journey,
And at others smooth sailing
You never know how long that highway will last,
For some cars it ends quickly,
And another, extends for an eternity
Sometimes accidents happen during your voyage,
Sometimes you are able to keep on moving.
And other times it seems your path has concluded even though it hasn't
Relish your trip on this road and live like it's going to end in the neighboring mile
Don't ever pull over and consider that this is too challenging,
Keep on driving and your quest will be commemorated forevermore.

Lydia Legler, Grade 8
Cedar Grove-Belgium Middle School, WI

I Will Dream

Today the sun will rise, and I will dream of tomorrow.
Tomorrow the singers will sing a new song, and the dancers will find rhythm.
Tomorrow the teachers will guide, and the children will learn to dream.
Tomorrow the coaches will motivate, and the team will succeed.
Tomorrow the doctors will heal, and the sick will be relieved.
Tomorrow the blind will see, the deaf will hear, and the mute will speak.
Tomorrow the leaders will steer, and the people will believe.
Tomorrow the young will be old, and will lead our world.
Tomorrow the captives will be free, and the people will rejoice.
Tomorrow a parent will comfort, and a child will feel loved.
Tomorrow world leaders will make peace, and the world will be a better place.
Tomorrow the sun will set, and I will dream again!

Lauren Camacho, Grade 7
Lakewood Elementary School, WI

Halloween Night

On a gusty black night,
Mysterious scarecrows lurk around in a large cornfield
The obnoxious turkeys run around the old crooked fence line
Leaves and acorns fall off the tall oak trees, landing in an enormous fire pit,
and this Halloween night, the abandoned granary down by Gravel Pit Creek
is making strange noises that ride the gusts of air into the black night.

Kayli Shutrop, Grade 9
Jordan Sr High School, MN

Tubing
I see the
Glistening water beneath me
Reflecting the shining sun

The joyful ear-piercing screams of others
Echoes in my ears
Happiness drifts in the air around me.

Adrenaline
Rushes through me
As the waves lift me into the sky

My body rapidly slaps
Against this soaked tube which is flailing
Around the sky

The wet crisp air
Surrounds me
On this warm summer day

Finishing with the roaring engine
Of the boat coming
To
An
End
Alicia Bellefeuille, Grade 8
All Saints Catholic School, MN

Father's Tree
When he was six years old,
George was very bold.
Without his dad's permission,
George went on a mission.

George was running around at night,
Chopping down everything in sight.
He chopped his father's favorite tree,
Which was his English cherry tree.

Sometime later his father discovered,
The dead tree that had been uncovered.
His face flushed with fury and anger,
That was noticed by any stranger.

His father's face lost its red,
As little George slowly said,
"Father I cannot lie,
I chopped the tree down to die."

"Never be afraid to tell the truth,
It's more to me than anything."
Said his father.
After all he didn't even bother!
Marisa Ursu, Grade 8
Jerstad Agerholm Middle School, WI

Everyone Has Everything They Need
Everyone has a life
A life to live
Everyone has a chance
A chance to give
Everyone has a family
A family to love
Everyone has something
Something to be a part of
Everyone has a dream
A dream to win
Everyone has an angel
And angel with a grin
Everyone has one true love
To love forever
Everyone has a heart
That stays together
Heather Sawchuk, Grade 8
St Odilia School, MN

The Real World
The world that goes around.
The world that's going to go down.
The people that worry for freedom.
The kids that wonder for the world.
The words that our president will say.
The gun that might be pointed.
The screams that will be heard.
The world that goes around.
The world that might not exist.
The tears that the eagle makes.
The words that aren't spoken.
The wars that we'll relive.
The fights that can be deadly.
The freedom that might go down.
The world that goes around.
The world that's going down.
Shelby Adkins, Grade 8
Kewaskum Middle School, WI

The Precision of Work
Work is blood, sweat, and tears
Poured into a formula of success
Work is a football game of assignments
Blocking, running, tackling.
Work is an everyday objective
Getting what you give
Work is an enduring mission
Taking time and effort
Work is a satisfying smile
Recognizing what you've finished
Work is a career
Calling forth your responsibility
Work is an ability
Asking for nothing but the best
Adam Chier, Grade 8
Cedar Grove-Belgium Middle School, WI

My Team
My team works hard
every single day
in the mud
in the rain
We won one game all season
but it's just another reason
to go for it next year
and get better
in a way losing
is better then winning
start from the beginning
be better than you were
because you're never too sure
if you're the best
but WE will be
Just practice
Michael Bous, Grade 9
Discovery Middle School, MN

Special Place
There's a special place in my heart,
Where no one has ever gone…
It's a special place where dreams,
And secrets, are kept quiet…
So much love is waiting there,
Waiting for someone to come along,
Who can accept all the love I am.
Capable of giving…
Someone who wants to share the dreams,
To hear the secrets, and live the
Love…
My heart has told me,
That you could be that someone…
There's a place in my heart,
That no one has ever gone…
No one but you.
Kylie O'Neill, Grade 9
Lincoln Jr/Sr High School, WI

My Grandpa
What is it about my grandpa
Is it how he brightens my day
Or is it the thought of a warm summer day
But then again he's always there for me
When I was hurt he was there
When I was sick he was there
Or is it that he's in my dreams
To give me a dream of none other
To let me fly higher than the sky
And dive lower than the sea
Or even just to be there
To talk
Have a good time
And of course to be my role model
Anthony LaTour, Grade 7
Shakopee Area Catholic School, MN

If Everything in Life Was Simple
If everything in life was simple…
STUDENTS wouldn't have to study for tests
STUDENTS wouldn't have to practice band instruments
STUDENTS wouldn't have to practice sports

If everything in life was simple…
ADULTS would all have jobs
ADULTS would all have houses
ADULTS would all have healthcare

If everything in life was simple…
THE WORLD wouldn't have poverty
THE WORLD wouldn't have global warming
THE WORLD would get along

But I figured out that this isn't the life that I want, because

If everything in life was simple…
MY LIFE wouldn't be fun
MY LIFE wouldn't be enjoyable
MY LIFE would be worthless

Ellie Northrop, Grade 8
St Odilia School, MN

Locker 272
I am a locker in the seventh grade hall,
Locker two-seventy-two.
I am full of books,
Folders and pencils.
Kids sometimes write on the inside of my door,
Or put gum under my shelf.
I get locked up for forty-five minutes,
Until the kid comes back to the hall.
Sometimes bullies will throw
Kids into me,
It hurts, but I feel worse for them.
My books are never in the same spot,
After an hour they move or leave.
Kids don't think much of me,
But that's all part of being a locker
In the seventh grade hall.

Jesse Christopherson, Grade 7
Lincoln Jr/Sr High School, WI

The Platypus
A mammal, yet lays eggs
Ducky bill and ducky legs
Venom from snakes, hair from bears
This animal seems to be quite rare
Some say that it's the result
Of a scientist at fault
But no it was placed here just like you and me
So of all the animals large and small; elephant to honey bee
The platypus will always be the most special one to me.

William Arnold, Grade 8
St Odilia School, MN

War
War
…Is not a way to deal with things you don't like
…Is the power of the people to fight
…Changes lives, not situations
…Comprehends the daily notations
…Isn't a joke, nor a silly game

You can't mess around or worry about the fame

War
…Is a matter of life or death
…Ruins people's lives like a dose of meth
…Has power over us all
…Isn't heroic, whether you stand or you fall
…Teaches a lesson, both good and bad
…Tells you to stop bombing Japan or Baghdad

Quintin Smidzik, Grade 8
Ramsey Jr High School, MN

Me and My Sis
My sister's birthday is June 26 and so is mine.
My sister is loud and I am annoying.
We go to movies and anything fun.
We argue about all the dumb things.
I help her pick out prom dresses.
She helps me pick out clothes, but we still argue.
We hate having to wash the dishes or clean our rooms.
Somehow, we end up cleaning or washing together.
Our relationship is like an ocean.
rough but can change and be peaceful.
We can always find something to do.
It doesn't matter how bored we are.
I hate the way she hogs the computer.
She hates the way I play the drum set when she is watching TV.
I think we will move away from each other.
However, we will never lose contact with each other.

Shelby Gaede, Grade 7
Lincoln Jr/Sr High School, WI

Two Cats
Prowling and lurking, in the light and in the shadows.
Up streets and down alleys, in and out of gates and bushes.
Ears alert and nose to the ground I walk.
I walk and I walk and I smell a smell I haven't before.

Slowly, lowly, lowly, and slowly I go.
I go to the smell, I go to the sound.
I see something lurking, lurking in the shadows black.
Lurking and looking, looking at me.

To the shadows I go slowly and lowly.
A figure emerges from the shadows, lowly and slowly.
A figure the color of night, a figure of me.
We stare, we smell, we walk away.

Kelly Zimmerman, Grade 9
Fall River High School, WI

Weather

Sunshine
Bright, yellow
Shining, lighting, warming
Summer, heat, starlight, big
Sprinkling, dripping, pouring
Dark, wet
Rain

Tia Zdroik, Grade 9
Rosholt Middle-High School, WI

Joyous Seasons

Christmas,
Merry, joyous
Wrapping, receiving, giving
Presents, Santa Claus, cookies, snowmen
Rising, falling, new beginning
Candy, eggs
Easter

Maria Lewandowski, Grade 9
Rosholt Middle-High School, WI

Light/Dark

Light
Bright, golden
Clearing, glowing, coloring
Energy, sun, bulb, sight
Fading, dying, leaving
Cold, silent
Dark

Owen Neff, Grade 9
Rosholt Middle-High School, WI

Winter/Spring

Winter
White, refreshing
Snowing, wind blowing, shivering
Cold, fun, snowmen, basketball season
Warming, thrilling, budding
Colorful, alive
Spring

Josh Studinski, Grade 9
Rosholt Middle-High School, WI

Kira

A fun, loving puppy
Who can't keep from wiggling
When you come home.
Her breed is brown and fuzzy
Because she's a mutt.
And when she sleeps
She's too cute for words.

Meghan McGinnis, Grade 7
Hudson Middle School, WI

Everlasting Winter Love

"Good grief!" I exclaimed. "It is dreadfully cold!"
"Well," he reasoned with me. "Let's try to stay warm.
We could make hot chocolate with marshmallows too
and have snowball fights at your farm, so go get your boots."

"So, after we play in the snow," I said, "We should go back inside
and grab the blankets and pillows and lie by the chimney fire."
"What if my feet get cold?" he asked, giving me that friendly smile.
I scooted closer to him and suggested we could cuddle for a while.

I hear three simple words — "I love you" — he replies.
I can feel the butterflies flutter from deep down inside.
He looks outside the window and observes it is still snowing
"Even when the snow melts in the spring, my love for you will keep growing."

We decide to go back out into the cold, and I wrap my arms around him.
The snow is falling heavier…The snowstorm is about to begin.
He looks at me with his rosy cheeks, as the snowflakes fall from above.
I wrap my arms even tighter to express my everlasting winter love.

Jasmine Radke, Grade 9
Round Lake High School, MN

The Old Granary

On a black night, we were standing at the cornfield by Halloween Creek.
Scarecrows lurked everywhere I turned my head; I would see another creepy face
attached to a straw-stuffed man mounted on a wooden pole.
Some looked like vampires; some looked like werewolves;
some I didn't know what they were, but they were all chilling.
A large fire pit was lit and burning dry leaves and small twigs; acorns lay everywhere.
Every time I stepped down, I would almost twist my ankle.
When we finally got near the granary, an aged picket fence followed the trail
toward the abandoned building.
Wild turkeys were running free.
We went around a corner in the trail and heard an earsplitting noise
coming from behind us.
We all turned to see what was happening, but saw…nothing.
Fearful, we continued forward.
As we approached, the building's weathered boards creaked.
Wind whispered easily through the cracks, and animals scurried about inside.
Scared out of our minds, we froze.
Our hears raced. Our skin crawled. Our breath came fast.
We all decided that…next year we would come back.

Tanisha Bembenek, Grade 9
Jordan Sr High School, MN

Autumn

The fall leaves lightly float from the trees in the surrounding woods.
Lightly crumpling and cracking under my feet.
I walk slowly to feel the crisp autumn breath against my face and hands.
I sit beneath a large red, yellow, green, and brown leafed tree.
I close my eyes and reopen them to see an explosion of colors.
As the explosion of colors gently fell, the peace and quiet grows as each leaf falls.
The squirrel's hustling and bustling to find food for the harsh winter makes the silence stop.
Giggle escapes from my lips.

Corissa Rathsack, Grade 8
Freedom Middle School, WI

Grandpa

I remember the
warm greetings you gave me
when I would come to your house.
I miss the good times
we spent together
and all the laughs we had.
The days of happiness
and the days of sorrow.
And then one day you
got emphysema and
you suffered.
I remember Mom
was in Colorado
and Dad had to call her
about Grandpa and
ask how to put tights on me.
Then we went to
Grandpa's house and
Watched him die.
Grandpa I love you
with tender loving care.

Kayla Green, Grade 7
Lincoln Jr/Sr High School, WI

Shopping*

Prancing down the aisle,
Trying not to crash.
Need to get a gift,
Need to make it fast.

Looking through the stuff,
Thinking, "This is tough!"
Now through the door and out the store,
I think I've had enough!

Ohhhh, shopping here, shopping there,
Shopping everywhere.
Oh, I have gifts to buy,
With little time to spare!

OHH!
Shopping here, shopping there
Shopping everywhere.
Oh what fun to be done,
Now I don't have a care!!

Albi Maksuti, Grade 8
Thorp Middle School, WI
*Sung to the tune of Jingle Bells

Smile

Just smile and the world
will smile right along with you.
Smiles makeup the world.

Angela LeDonne, Grade 7
Templeton Middle School, WI

Clock

Time goes on.
It's always ticking,
from 1 to 2…2 to 3 and so on.
It's there when you go to bed,
and when you wake up the next day,
5 minutes till your favorite show,
then 4, 3, 2, and now 20 seconds,
19, 18, 17, 16, 15…

People say, "Time's a wasting" but really,
where's it going?
Around the clock again till the next,
hour, minute, second, what?
The thing is time is a never-ending thing,
It'll never stop or slow down,
It just…ticks.

Darby Schmidt, Grade 7
Lincoln Jr/Sr High School, WI

A Lasting Moment

Waiting in the curtains
about to go on
the dancers before you,
amazing
the audience is clapping,
the signal that you're up.

You feel the rush of adrenaline
running
throughout your body
take a deep breath
as they announce your name

It's your turn.
Step onto the stage.
Make a lasting moment.

Cassie Derfus, Grade 8
St Odilia School, MN

I Wish

I wish for a party,
    So I can make friends.

I wish for a dog,
    So I can have some fun outside.

I wish for a car,
    So I can drive to my dad's house.

I wish for a sister,
    So I can tell her how I feel.

But most of all I wish for 1,000 dollars,
    So I can buy a dog.

Lillyth McMullin, Grade 9
River Heights Elementary School, WI

Run

Bag packed
Shoes on
Window open
Family gone
Road ahead
Dark skies
Cold air
No good-byes
To runaway
It was my choice
To be alone
To find my voice
I wanted to, have a chance
To sing my song
To dance my dance
To live my life, by today
Not tomorrow, or yesterday
To finish the journey
To follow the light
Lay under the stars
And whisper "Goodnight"

Maddy Ober, Grade 8
Valley Middle School, MN

Dogs

Cuddle, warm, fuzzy
so many to choose from
tall ones short ones
fat ones too
old ones new ones
special ones too
They can eat way
more than you can
Just eating and sleeping
all day long
From morning to night
you like them as
pets and as friends
Telling secrets to
have adventures with
or just being yourself
they'll love you
always no matter what
Just as long as you love them
and do what you both
like you will be friends forever.

Matt Holicky, Grade 9
Montgomery-Lonsdale High School, MN

Winter

White and fluffy, soft snow
    It is colder than ice is
    It is a great sight

Josh Scozzaro, Grade 8
McKinley Middle School, WI

School

School is not fun
It is really a bore
Everyone sleeps
And usually snores

They load us with homework
Day in and day out
We sometimes cry
And always pout

I really hate school
I think it is lame
I'd rather be home
Playing video games

No one can wait
'Til the end of the day
When the bell rings
"FREEDOM!" we say

Nick Schieldt, Grade 8
St Paul's Lutheran School, WI

Volleyball

Volleyball is the coolest sport,
It is really quite fun.
I love to spike the ball,
I'm always sad when the game is done.

Bump, set, spike is what we do.
We play as a team,
We work real hard,
And when we win we all scream.

We come up with cool nicknames,
We make up drills.
We may not get it right,
But we always give our fans thrills.

As our season ends,
Win or lose,
We have all given 110%,
We're the team you should choose.

Carly White, Grade 8
St Paul's Lutheran School, WI

Hatred

Hatred is fire,
Lashing out at those who would comfort.
Hatred is an angry, brooding soul,
Nursing a hurt that can never be forgiven.
Hatred is a blade,
Blood soaked and lusting for revenge.
Hatred is a broken heart,
One that will never be mended.

Ben Nelson, Grade 7
Holy Family Parish School, WI

Love Is Blind

Love cannot see the outside.
It does not snicker at the face of another.
It rejoices at the size of the only thing it can see.
A heart.
The heart of what it will die for, what it will cry for, and celebrate over.
The true center of what it desires to be with.
Forever.
Love only pays mind to the other love in the people or person.
It is blind to everything else.
Once you realize that your love for those people or person is true.
Pure.
And centered on the strongest and most impacting gift of all:
The heart of another.

Annie Gonring, Grade 7
Holy Family Parish School, WI

Copy Cat

Everything I do and everything
I see, everything about me you
just have to copy! I see
something I like,
and well I buy it.
Then what do
you know, the
next day you
have the same
exact shirt as me.
You said it was the cutest
tee of all and would be all the rage
next fall. My heart starts to race, it's
like there is a fire burning beneath my
face. I know we're such great friends
and will be till the end, but
lately you're more
like a copying
twin. I have to
be honest we
go along so
well but I can
not take it, seriously,
my brain is starting to
swell! But since you are my friend
I must brush it off, and say oh well!

Madelyn Brunes, Grade 7
Shakopee Area Catholic School, MN

Old Wise Pond

Far from the hummingbirds, milkweed, apples, and bees,
sat an old man in his rocking chair
and his visitor who came from the grass-covered trail.
They sat there in an abandoned farmhouse with spiders lurking in every corner.

The men sat there in peace, looking out the window
past the rolling thunderheads and fence,
and through the mist hovering over old Wise Pond.
Remembering the joy it used to bring them, the aged men shared memories.
Outside, the pond glistened in the sun, unbothered by the chaos of children at play.
As a gentle breeze sent the autumn leaves skyward,
the men sat there at rest, sharing in final thoughts of the oh so important Wise Pond.

Nate Beckman, Grade 9
Jordan Sr High School, MN

The Audition

Butterflies flying
Wings hitting my sides
I step up,
3 steps to go,
2 steps,
1 step,
I'm on stage.

My heart pounding,
They can hear it.
"What's that sound?" they say.

I begin
It's over
I leave,
And feel so good

It's a dream
Really?! Wow!
I have to do it again.
Megan Blaschko, Grade 7
Shakopee Area Catholic School, MN

Just Imagine

What would it be like,
if you had the choice
to awake from a nightmare,
or live out a dream…
To be with the one that you love,
or fly with the birds high above?

What would it be like,
if the world was mixed up?
If the grass was dark blue,
and the sky was lime green…
And what would happen if,
boats floated upstream?

So now I have to ask,
because I always wonder.
What would happen if,
our imaginations became…

reality?
Lexi Turgeon, Grade 9
Montgomery-Lonsdale High School, MN

The Pear Girl

There once was a sweet girl named Claire
Whose favorite fruit was the pear.
She thought they were yummy,
Put ten in her tummy
And learned it was better to share.
Clara Temlitz, Grade 8
Pilgrim Park Middle School, WI

Autumn's Cardinal

On a cool autumn day,
Sand Creek was splashing through the crimson and gold leafed golf course.
A light mist wafted just inches above the fairway.
A cardinal started to get ready for the crisp air of winter.
The rolling thunderheads of summer would visit no more.
Just down the road,
the cardinal flew to the old abandoned farmhouse.
Guarded by a white picket fence,
it was surviving the test of time.
If you looked closely,
You would see the cardinal flying
through the bare sticks of trees,
and over the small, grass-covered trail.
He held a secret.
Through the trail,
A small, hidden cottage was built,
surrounded by woods.
It had an ancient quality about it, but yet it seemed new.
Through the tiny window where the cardinal perched,
a rocking chair sat lonely,
waiting for a visitor, as autumn came to an end.
Michael Rutz, Grade 9
Jordan Sr High School, MN

November 4*

On that dark day God took away, the nicest girl in the world.
On that dark day her voice went silent
Doctors tried and tried.
While all we could do was cry.
I was told later that day and all I could do was cry.
On that dark day God took away, the nicest girl in the world.
In some way, big or small, she left a bit of herself with her family.
My family believes that God took her for a reason.
I think she left because she was needed in heaven.
On that dark day God took away, the nicest girl in the world.
She will be missed. Everyone liked her even if they never even met her.
Meghan was and always will be my favorite cousin ever.
She was the nicest person and no one will ever replace her.
Her friends and family will miss her.
Jacob Austin, Grade 9
Lincoln Jr/Sr High School, WI
*Dedicated to Meghan Elizabeth Powell, 1994-2007

Virginia

The beautiful crystal ocean owns its own glamorous, glimmering, golden sand
Feeling the crisp air around me, the bright sunlight on my shoulders
People laughing heartedly, seagulls honking overhead
Mellow swaying trees and plants giving out aromas and scents of maple,
fresh and free
A cloudless sky, crystal-clear blue, gorgeous buildings with elaborate architecture
Radiant flowers and tall, colorful trees raid the perimeter
Children running wild in the grasses, people having a good time
And so am I
Victoria Paquette, Grade 8
All Saints Catholic School, MN

Fear

You tell me you love me
You hug me tight.
All the while
I shake with fright.
You cover my face
With your dirty hands.
You glare at her
Where she stands.
You hold me close,
So near and dear.
All I can think,
Is fear fear fear.
Taylor Boylen, Grade 8
Silverbrook Middle School, WI

You

Your beautiful voice,
This wasn't my choice,
Your deep colored eyes,
That see through my lies,
Your hand in mine,
My life's so in line,
Your lips so smooth,
My body won't move,
Your kiss so sweet,
That nothing can beat,
Perfection so pure,
You don't need a cure.
Samantha Missall, Grade 8
Silverbrook Middle School, WI

Peace

I am the feeling that calms us all
When earthly nations begin to fall.
I am the bond that keeps us close;
No more need for the lethal dose.

I am the forge that builds us strong
When locking out the doers of wrong.
"Our freedom" is to say the least,
I am the answer, I am peace.
Natalie Brown, Grade 8
Pilgrim Park Middle School, WI

Wake Up!

Don't hit the snooze
Or you will lose

Just get in the shower
Please! Give me an hour?

Getting ready for school
This is so not cool
Amanda Jo Hines, Grade 8
All Saints Catholic School, MN

Yesterday, Today, and Tomorrow

Too many times from rarely-seen relatives I hear
What a beautiful young lady you have become

From acting our scenes with Barbie dolls,
To portraying the supporting role underneath the lights of the stage
Done wearing lose and dirty Disney jumpers
Now instead selecting a dress, much more snugly fitting
Mother and father threaten to lock me in a cage

Mom tells stories of the girl that played with dirt
The one whose best friends were various pet worms
Of the little girl who had a haircut like that of a little boy
Who ate napkins at the restaurant, who knew nothing of germs

Now that little girl is a bright young woman
Shopping for homecoming dresses, and preparing for life after graduation
Equipped with a boyfriend, cellphone, and life other than the one at home
Having to make real-life choices, in grown-up situations

Looking back on pictures of myself all those years ago
The only thing I see is a cute little girl,
Completely oblivious to the amazing young woman she is to become.
Melanie Lynn Daas, Grade 9
Rosholt Middle-High School, WI

A Virtue and a Vice

Deceit
Deceit is a collage of silver and gray, like a camouflage
It sounds like a clever liar, the words slipping off their tongue like silk
It tastes like wild berries, sweet, but poisonous
It smells like a looming sickness, waiting to strike
It looks like a spider, waiting to capture you in its web of lies
Deceit makes you feel guilty; how could you ever succumb to deceit?

Courage
Courage is golden, shining, and flashing in the sun
It sounds like a single trumpet, determined to play on
It tastes tangy, strong, and memorable in your mouth
It smells like spring, flower heads daring to challenge winter's frost
It looks like a sunrise, peeping over the horizon
Courage makes you feel strong, for doing what no one else would.
Sarah Nelson, Grade 8
Holy Family Parish School, WI

A Description of Myself by Myself

Colton
Friendly, musical, awesome
Brother of Marc
Lover of saxophone, guitar, and music
Who feels music and school come first, girls come second, and food comes in a close third
Who fears clowns, unorganized things, and dirty everything
Who would like a 4.0, teaching degree for musical/theatrical arts, and banana cream pie
Resident of Rosholt, Wisconsin
Schlotman
Colton J. Schlotman, Grade 9
Rosholt Middle-High School, WI

Emptiness

I cannot hear
I cannot see
There is a dark nothing
All around me
I can't see even five feet
In front of my face
IT seems like I'm trapped
In a dark void of time and space
When someone or anyone calls
It's like a barrier or even walls
Stop the sound from being heard
It is actually peaceful there
When I am here I can think
I almost never have to blink
Every now and then I see a door
I sometimes think about opening it
On the door there is a sign
That sign says reality
I think to myself I want to stay
I'd rather not leave.

Shawn Forsting, Grade 9
Lincoln Jr/Sr High School, WI

The Soothing Sounds of Thunder

In the darkness
I lie alone
I lie awake
Thinking of today's mistake.
Thinking long
And thinking hard
I still can't remember
What went wrong.
As I began to think
I began to wonder
Then I hear
The sound of thunder.
It was distant but yet in my room
So I lay there listening to the booms
Getting louder and louder.
Then came the light
But steady rain as I listen to it
Hitting my roof I'm stuck in a trance
And put to sleep
Forgetting about today's mistake.

Patrick Copeland, Grade 9
Lincoln Jr/Sr High School, WI

Toast

It's crusty, it's sticky
It kind of looks icky
The jam seeps over the side,
But I guess if I must
Before I miss my bus
I'll eat my crusty, sticky surprise.

Katie Gnerer, Grade 9
Montgomery-Lonsdale High School, MN

Winter Galore

Adrenaline flows through my veins.
I am standing at the top
of a thick, snow covered hill.
My feet at the ready,
inching to start down
my hilly yard.
The snowboard takes off,
slicing through
the crisp, powdery, snow.
Starting off great,
I start to lose my balance,
also losing control of my board.
I see the chimney, like a wall,
protected by sharp rose bushes.
I am doomed.
My face slams into the snow.
The cold biting my face.
My legs painfully caught in the bushes.
I safely crawled away.
I will never risk snowboarding again.

Camille Panas, Grade 8
St John Neumann School, WI

Broken Hearts

Your heart was broken, and so was mine,
So we picked up the pieces and gave it time,
Bound together with a broken vine,
Lays in darkness your heart and mine,
Silence beats with a thunderous roar,
For our hearts bleed no more,
Somehow when we gave it time,
Our hearts found a way to combine,
Becoming one your heart and mine,
That's the way they'll stay for all time,
Never to be torn apart,
Sits our silent beating heart,
How we finally learned to love,
Is a mystery to all except God above,
But in the darkest dead of night,
Our heart will help us fight,
To stay together,
To be one forever,
And even in the hardest time,
Will stay together your heart and mine.

Rachel Borden, Grade 9
Discovery Middle School, MN

Remember…

Remember when we used to sing and play
Remember when we talked every day
Remember when we danced in the night
Remember when we got into a fight
Remember when you cried,
Remember that was the day I said goodbye.

Sara Schmitt, Grade 8
St Odilia School, MN

Winter Memories

Do you remember
the winter season?
I remember
snow softly falling,
the fire burning.
I remember
the bitter cold
of the snow.
I remember
feeling the joy and excitement
of Christmas just around the bend.
I remember
tasting the warm fresh baked cookies.
I remember winter.

Erik Schwartz, Grade 8
St John Neumann School, WI

What Winter Means

Snowflakes softly falling.
From the cloudy sky;
Falling onto rooftops,
As the children are passing by.

Coming into the warm house,
From the frigid air;
Having a warm cup of cocoa,
And family time to share.

Opening Christmas presents
From under the Christmas tree;
Sitting by the warm fire,
Thinking, "Wow, what a sight to see!"

Ashlyn Rife, Grade 9
New Glarus Middle/High School, WI

Of That Which Remains Unknown

A soft light glows on the horizon
Growing brighter, ever brighter
As people watch, the light it grows
Ever growing, ever growing
Late and through the night
What is this light, the people wonder
That permeates the dark of night
Strikes fear in every heart?
And like the wind the light is gone
Along with all on earth
Cold, and barren, desolate is the Earth
What was this light?
They would all wonder
If there were but one left to care.

Caleb Postma, Grade 9
Round Lake High School, MN

Autumn's Life

Strong rolling thunderheads roamed the skies over the autumn oak trees
while the leaves danced with pride,
apricot, ruby and ivory colors fluttered in the branches.

Soon, colored gems fluttered down on the soft, jade, grass-covered trail which led to a run-down old farmhouse.
The farmhouse, as old as World War I
had ivory faded walls that once glistened crystal white.

In front of the house rested a dirty, rotten porch
that used to be a great oak porch from England.
On the porch floor, a broken rocking chair strained to sway back and forth.

Behind the house a pond appeared.
It gave off a shimmering shine as it reflected the warm, bright sun.
The pond called itself Gem Pond.

Surrounding Gem Pond, millions and millions of sunset-colored milkweed rose from the ground.
In the middle of the pond jutted up a small island that gave a home to a great apple tree
filled with apples, painted crimson and gold.
Around the little land, a snow-white fence stood guard.

Bees buzzed on their way to their honey home.
A spider sat on its silk web, waiting silently for its prey.
A blue jay chirped a song of morning to the visitor who sat by the apple tree.
The gusts of autumn breeze blew blasts of memories through the man's mind as he faced the autumn of his life.

Lizbette Breeggemann, Grade 9
Jordan Sr High School, MN

Passing Through

West More Creek flows lazily across the countryside
A flock of loons glide across the water
They spread their wings and fly into the air heading south
Running across the field, a weather-beaten wood fence leans and sags
A grass-covered trail that hasn't been used in years winds along near the fence

A visitor to this land, a man in a dark cloak, is walking along the trail
The visitor passes an abandoned farmhouse that has seen better days
He pulls his cloak tight as a sudden gust of wind sends bright fall leaves of all different colors flying across the path
He looks at a worn down rocking chair lying in the grass beside the fence a few feet from its arm rest
Then the man looks up at the grey autumn sky
He considers the thunderclouds forming on the horizon, threatening to burst open

The visitor stops and leans his walking staff on the fence and
Then reaches into his small empty black bag and pulls out an apple
He takes a bite out of the apple, looking at the emerald stone on the top of his staff,
before throwing the apple back into the bag for later
Then he picks up his staff and walks forward into the mist-shrouded horizon
As he walks, he begins to hum a nameless song
The visitor stops and looks up at the dark sky
then he reaches into his bag and takes a last look around the place he once knew
And with a roar of thunder and a flash of light,
The visitor vanishes into the coming night

Spencer Kubista, Grade 9
Jordan Sr High School, MN

Thinking of You*

So many times I've been alone,
But then I think of you and I am home.
Forever I'll pray for you from my heart,
But sometimes I can't think of where to start.
Just know we are all thinking of you.
Living without you is pretty dang tough,
But then I remember
You went through something pretty rough.
Thinking of you and your personality,
I also think of me and reality.
Everyone misses your always loving smile,
And we will be missing you,
For a long, long while.
Just know we are all thinking of you.
You've seen all of us go through life,
Good times and bad,
And you know who we are,
Inside and out.
Loving you is the easiest thing anyone can do,
And we will always know, that you love us, too.
Just know we are all thinking of you.
                        Sarah Erickson, Grade 8
                        Sartell Middle School, MN
                        *Dedicated to Grandpa Lee

Sports

I take sports seriously
I take sports as if it is life and death
I don't care what sport I play
I play it
Football — my favorite.
Everything about it makes me want to play it.
Basketball — most intense.
When the game is on the line, we come out on top
Soccer — just flat out love it
Baseball — I love the feeling of going up to the plate
and getting that clutch hit
I could go on all day about sports
I don't care what sport I play
I just love to play sports
I take sports seriously
                        Matthew Brown, Grade 7
                        Necedah Middle School, WI

Expression

Expression is a delicate flower
Growing, swaying, dying
A blossom doesn't trouble with what others have to say
She will be beautiful being herself
All the colors
Dancing in the breeze
Doing what is desirable to her
The bud knows she is magnificent
And loves the way she is
                        Hannah Dirkse, Grade 8
                        Cedar Grove-Belgium Middle School, WI

Now You Are Gone

I remember you taking me to the park.
I remember your bad singing!
But the most I remember is you on your bed just
Lying there.
Or even the time you couldn't even remember me.
That was the worst day.

Then came around Thanksgiving.
Everyone said you would die, but
I didn't believe it.
All I cared about at the time was if I was going to
Aunt Sue's house or Flood's house.
I wanted to go to Flood's house, but you didn't want me to.
After an hour I decided to go to Aunt Sue's house.
That night my sister, Aunt Sue, and I played karaoke.
Of course I won.

The following morning I woke up and saw my
Dad and sister crying.
I came over to see what was wrong and found out you were dead.
That moment I felt like the whole world stopped.
After that I was never happy again.
                        Amy Johnson, Grade 7
                        Lincoln Jr/Sr High School, WI

My Life and Yours

Life can be strange
Sometimes you don't know what's next
And others have already passed
From their weird personalities
To your family at home
All different in their own ways
To the way they dress to the music in their ears
Being hurt can only benefit you
Only time can heal the broken
Having a good time, then the next bad
When you've been hurt
And only your worst enemy can save you
your life is like no other
Only live yours, be you
Life can be strange
                        Heather Madsen, Grade 8
                        Lakewood Elementary School, WI

The Strong, Courageous Light

Courage is noble strength
That breaks down redoubtable walls that hold you back
So that you can keep moving on
Acting valiantly, even if you don't feel like you are.
Courage is an illumination,
That leads you through obscurity,
So that you can see the challenges ahead of you
And prepare yourself for them.
Courage is your conductor throughout existence.
                        Cara Jones, Grade 8
                        Cedar Grove-Belgium Middle School, WI

Star

Wish
Wish
Upon a
Star, if you
look you'll see so far. Bright,
Bright just like a light
to see a star
no need to fight.
Wish, Wish   upon a
star, if   you look
you'll   see
so   far.

Mya Klehr, Grade 7
Shakopee Area Catholic School, MN

Stars

Stars
0, so bright
Up in the sky,
Twinkling in the night.
Brightly shining,
As a shooting star goes flying by.
Quick make a wish
Before it disappears into the sky!
They are way up in space.
Someday soon
I hope I have a chance
To go to the moon.

Lizzy Ericson, Grade 7
Shakopee Area Catholic School, MN

She Is…

She is power.
She is known by everyone.
She is friendship.
She is modesty.
She is always there.
She is truth.
She is deception.
She is human.
She is worldly.
She is beauty.
I call her love.

Taylor DeVincentis, Grade 8
McKinley Middle School, WI

Love/Hate

Love
Romantic, attraction
Caring, kissing, interesting
Hearts, emotions, sweetheart, picture
Yelling, hitting, fighting
Horrible, falling
Hate

Kimmy Hintz, Grade 9
Rosholt Middle-High School, WI

Parents vs Christmas Shopping

The Christmas season is here,
No stopping Mother Nature this year.
Our wallets are packed,
Yet the toys are beyond stacked.

Children hover and whine over toys, parents are sick and annoyed by the noise.
Shoppers disagree over sales,
While kids follow brightly lit trails.
The stores are stuffed and parents are yelling, "That's enough!"
The toys are bouncing off the shelves,
Santa's taking pictures with giggling elves.

The tension in the workers is enough to blow a fuse,
They are anxiously awaiting their yearly Christmas cruise.
We finally end our shopping in the store; we have stepped through the final revolving door.

The lists are done,
Oh boy! Wasn't this "fun?"
We go find where we parked in the cold,
The children have not been as good as gold.

Home at last!
This bustling-around day has passed.
Tomorrow will be the official shopping day,
Well, whoop de do. Hip, hip, hooray!

Melissa Barth, Grade 8
Thorp Middle School, WI

Caped Crusader

I wear a yellow belt, and blue boots, alone I wander as the owl hoots.
Stopping bad guys, crime fighting's my game;
The Caped Crusader, or Batman's the name.
When I see the bat signal in the sky, It is then that I know it's time to fly.

Bat mobile is my ride, When he sees me, the joker hides.
Through Gotham city I ride around, The Joker I know shall soon be found!
And look! The Joker is here!
He and I both know his end is near.

Then suddenly I burst from the shade, and hit the Joker with a bat grenade!
The Joker is mad, but does nothing,
For he knows something bad is coming.
We put him behind the stark bars of jail; No one likes him, so there is no bail.

The only light comes from a small window,
That does not bother him, though.
For alone, day and night, the Joker will plan the tragic fall of the great Batman!
But I don't care, it's the city I love.
To protect them all, I'll go beyond and above.

The camera flashes, the lights, the fame, But in the end, I'm still Bruce Wayne.
All in all, it's been a good night. And the stars are out and in full sight.
It's time again to wander at night.
But as for the Joker I'll be ready to fight!

Emily Wood, Grade 8
Jerstad Agerholm Middle School, WI

Secret Love

You hurt me
You left me in the rain
So I waited
For someone to take me in
I stood there for days
And now here he is
Ready to save me
And I let him take me in his arms
He helped me get past you
But in the process I fell for someone else
The one that I fell for was him
The one that helped me
Then one day he asked me
What I would do if he said three little words
I said it would make me happy
And then he said
What I never thought he would say to me
I love you
My secret is out

Cheyenne Comerford, Grade 9
Fall River High School, WI

The Legend of Bart Starr

Listen here don't go too far,
Or you won't hear about Bart Starr.
Everybody knew his name,
He was the best in the game.

Bart Starr was great,
He would not stop,
Until he got to the top,
He got good at a very fast rate.

He was the best,
He was tested.
He passed the test,
And never rested.

He did the best that he could do,
Winning Super Bowls one and two.
After all was said and done,
He retired in seventy-one.

Alex Streckenbach, Grade 8
Jerstad Agerholm Middle School, WI

The Baby Bird

Adventure is a baby bird preparing to hatch
It has to be willing to break the shell
So it can see the outside world
It has to be willing to step out of its shell
So it can feel the outside world
It has to be willing to leave its shell
So it can experience the outside world
Adventure is a baby bird starting its new life

Jericho Duenk, Grade 8
Cedar Grove-Belgium Middle School, WI

The Music of Storm

A light beat starts to form like a drum giving a beat to a song.
Tip taps start to be heard and all the creatures take shelter.
A soft rumble starts the melody as light begins to flash.
The wind comes in with a high harmony adding to the melody.
As the rumbles continue to come faster, the wind picks up the tempo.
The sweet, intense music slows and quiets as it moves on to
The next anticipating city, which awaits in silence.

Julie Golab, Grade 8
Pilgrim Park Middle School, WI

Music

Thoughts swirl in my head,
Slowly making rhythm.
Notes come, melody sings.
I dance to my soul song,
The one I've been waiting for my whole life
And now it's here
I've discovered music,
The meaning of life, the reason to live.
Listen.
The sweet tune quickens, my heart pounds,
The end is coming,
It's over.
My eyes shut,
For never to be awakened
'Til the light comes back to warm my face
Compliment my eyes
And wake my conscience.
To sing, to laugh, to love
Another day

Claire VanValkenburg, Grade 7
Hudson Middle School, WI

Dreams

When I fall asleep at night
I slip into a dream
A place that's very far away
Where nothing's where it seems

Sometimes the dream is magical
The streets are paved with gold
A castle shimmers in the distance
The prettiest ever to behold

Other times the dream is scary
I'm running through the night
Away from treacherous villains
It gives me quite a fright

I like it most when dreams are peaceful
I'm sitting in the sun
With birds singing over a bubbling stream
I'm having lots of fun

Eleanor Arnold, Grade 8
St Odilia School, MN

I Say Yes

Standing in the field of empty joy
We are frozen like plastic toys
He screams, "I say yes!"
Frozen stones fall on Jess
His last words still hang in the air
Everyone screaming it's unfair
But they don't really care
Pain screams deep within my soul
Telling me I'll never be whole
I look through bloody tears
He was killed without mortal fear
Next it comes over to me
It gives me the same questions as he
Pain sweeps through my being
All I want is to stop the horrid feeling
I look across his length
My eyes meet its with courageous strength
I scream, "Yes!"

Katlyn Vyse, Grade 7
Pardeeville Jr High School, WI

My Cabin

quiet wooden cabin
soft sound of loons at sunrise
cool breeze off the lake
moisture in the air
serene wooden dock

sparse forest
laughter of kids playing
a cool summer day
fish every night
sweet scent of buns and rolls
coming out of the oven
grassy open fields

flames dancing on the last embers of a fire
smooth smoke of a vanished flame
crackling coals
until late at night

Tristan Goblirsch, Grade 8
All Saints Catholic School, MN

I Am Heather Barten

I am fun and loving
I wonder if I make a difference
I hear a fun happy family
I see a happy family
I want to get more money
I am fun and loving
I pretend to be in Arizona
I feel loved and cared for
I touch my mom's soft black hair
I worry that I will be forgotten
I cry when I think about my grandparents
I am fun and loving
I understand life is what you make it
I say just be yourself
I dream that no one dies
I try to help out a lot
I hope to make a difference
I am fun and loving

Heather Barten, Grade 9
Discovery Middle School, MN

Winter Hunting

The frigid cold stung
my face and my hands.
My feet were freezing
in the brisk Sunday morning air.
I know there would be deer waiting for me,
somewhere out there.
I could barely see,
but I could hear.
The flurries came down.
I curled my toes to get warm in a hurry.
The wind raged like fury.
As leaves cracked, I was very dreary.
Part of me loved staying out there.
The rest of me screamed
"I want to get out of here!"
In the end, I didn't get one,
but I still had a lot of fun!

Paden Toussaint, Grade 8
St John Neumann School, WI

Don't Bother

Don't talk to me anymore.
You make me mad

Don't say "Hi" to me in the hallway
I won't answer, I'll just turn away.

Why did you say that about me?
It's hard, since you used to be my friend.

Don't bother calling or texting me.
Trust me I won't answer.

Maddy Berens, Grade 7
Shakopee Area Catholic School, MN

Dragons

Fierce and feisty
Big and mighty

Built for riding
Built for gliding

Claws of steel
To attack their meal

Heavier than a train
Could take down a plane

Dragons are majestic
But they can be domestic

Gabrielle Houle, Grade 8
All Saints Catholic School, MN

Fall Is Here

Fall is here
Have no fear
Leaves are falling
Children are calling
Pie is baking
Dad is raking
Weather is changing
Leaves are rearranging
Pumpkins are growing
We are mowing
Pools are closed
Leaf piles are open
Fall is here
Have no fear

Kelsey Wroble, Grade 8
St Odilia School, MN

A Mother's Advice

You can't go forward,
Without this,
It's part of you,
Knowing is bliss.

Hold it dear,
You need your past,
Pass it on,
It's meant to last.

The future's great,
It's coming fast,
You have no future,
Without a past.

Alli Kremers, Grade 9
St John's Preparatory School, MN

Abandoned Windmill

Twirling
Swirling
Creaking
Squeaking
Never stopping.

Once a farmsite
Now a field.

Once filled with the world of a family;
Now friends stay for just a while.

Oh time has had its wrath on you,
Poor windmill;
You are not the same.

Once shiny and brand new,
Now rusty and dull.

Oh what a pity, poor windmill;
There is still some life left in you.

Sam Edge, Grade 8
Stewartville Middle School, MN

Wildfire

It hasn't rained for months
Leaving the land dry
And the rivers empty
. . .
A flickering flame
On dry long grass
Spreading to trees and other plants

Animals run from their homes

Some escape
Some burned to death

The breeze hits the fire
Making it burn fiercer

Until rain comes
Dying out the flames
And all is left
. . .
Is ash

Callie Kinser, Grade 7
Lincoln Jr/Sr High School, WI

Birthdays

Birthdays are so fun
They are very exciting
Can't wait till next year!

Rachel Smisek, Grade 9
Montgomery Lonsdale High School, MN

Disney Channel

Hannah Montana is a sweet show
Miley has the best of both worlds
Sing, song, show, glow
That Miley is bold.

Wizards of Waverly Place rocks
Wizards have magic
Spells can have locks
Or they can be tragic

High School Musical sings
Gabrielle is like Taylor, a lot
there is laughter in the bell ring
Sharpay and Ryan are two peas in a pod

Camp Rock is rocking
music is being played
with all singing and dancing
stars are being made

Sondra Struble, Grade 8
Robert J Elkington Middle School, MN

Diamonds

Faint a light
Suffused in shades of blue
Faceted and true
Glimmering as bright
As diamonds do
Many sides
Many stories
Both modest and snide
Like the eyes of children
Astute but wide
A diamond in my eyes

Suspended on a gold chain
Be it a bracelet or ring
It is symbolic of love
Like an everlasting spring
Ice may it be but have you no doubt
It will never melt
A diamond in my heart can be felt

Annie Zinnen, Grade 8
Karcher Middle School, WI

Outer Space

Meet me in outer space
Where the skies are no longer blue
Where everything will fall into place
On the bright side of the moon
Take me where the stars align
Where the planets will collide
Take me somewhere we'll be safe
Standing side by side

Nikki Morabito, Grade 8
All Saints Catholic School, MN

Stormy Autumn Day

I awoke to the brilliant sunlight pouring into my room and
Stumbled over to my window and stared at the vast orchard.
I stepped outside,
Walked through the rows of trees, and picked all of the ruby-red apples.
Milkweed littered the aisles of trees, making a perfect feast for butterflies.
I heard the singing of visiting blue jays perched in the apple trees.
When halfway done with my apple picking, a light mist filled the air.
The sky darkened as rolling thunderheads moved my way.
Lost in the trees, I began wandering on a grass-covered trail.
I passed Little Rock Pond where I usually spent most of my time and
Approached a worn-out picket fence.
In front of me, an abandoned farmhouse stood, a perfect place to wait out the storm.
I went up to the door and saw a spider hurry across the porch.
Finding the door unlocked, I quickly stepped inside before the rain hit.
Inside, faded and dusty furnishings sat waiting patiently for someone to come.
A gust of wind forcefully blew the rain and leaves against the siding.
I covered up with a ragged blanket lying on the floor while the thunder shook the house.
The storm slowly tapered off, and I gradually fell asleep.

Elle Case, Grade 9
Jordan Sr High School, MN

Autumn Walk

We walk along the grassy trail, hand in hand.
Thunderheads cloud the skies.
Rain's coming.
The wind is picking up, rustling the leaves beneath our feet.
Closing our jackets, we reach our destination.
Mystic Creek rumbles and growls its way along the middle of the meadow.
Water runs along rocks of different colors, polishing them smooth.
Sitting down and looking up at the sky, we watch the clouds roll past.
A sailboat and elephant pass by.
As our bodies lie next to each other, mist falls on our faces,
On our cheeks, on our lips, and on our eyelids.
We run for the cover of the nearest shelter and find an abandoned farmhouse
With a picket fence surrounding the run-down home.
Sitting down in the paint-peeled rocking chairs, we watch the rain pour down in sheets.
A woodpecker, the only visitor we have seen all day,
Suddenly disappears into a cavity in a maple tree.
In time, the rain stops and we head back past the fence, Mystic Creek,
And the grass-covered trail — reminiscing of the adventures we had.

Gena Beuch, Grade 9
Jordan Sr High School, MN

September 11th

Smiles turned to frowns on that day.
Beautiful blue eyes turned to teary eyes on that day.
Hearts were in two.
Glass shattered like the hopes and dreams of many people watching
that could do nothing.
Families and friends lost wonderful people that they loved on that day.
Angels were crying on the day of September 11th.

Cassandra Harris, Grade 7
Riverdale Middle School, WI

What Did I Do?

What did I do?
What could I have done,
To anger you?
Did I say something, do something?
What did I do?
We had good times, bad times
But we always got through
I sit here wondering
What did I do?
We laughed and joked
And had loads of fun too
We were friends, remember?
What did I do?
You helped me with my questions,
And I helped you
Now, my simple question is:
What did I do?

Mara Bauer, Grade 8
St Odilia School, MN

Bright and Blank

Bright colors are wonderful:
The rainbow in the sky,
And forests on the land
Where colorful birds fly,
Seashells on the sea shore
And tropical plants as well,
Sand buckets and shovels
Where the kids play and yell.

Blank colors are wonderful:
Oh, how I love black and white,
The zebras on the safari
Are surely a great sight,
The stars on the night sky
And bats with hearing senses,
A blank page ready to be written on,
Plus lonely white picket fences.

Alexis Wendling, Grade 8
Pilgrim Park Middle School, WI

Blurry Thoughts

When I look to my left and look to my right
I look for the things that are out of sight
As I walk I look around
Sometimes I stop and stare at the ground
As I think I look behind
I see the things that are clouding my mind
I close my eyes and scream out loud
My eyes reopen as I stare at that cloud
Then it starts to break apart
As I look deep in my heart
I then think about the things you said
Then I wake to see my bed

Austin W. Houston, Grade 9
Waukesha West High School, WI

Broken Doll

Can you see the broken doll?
her broken legs
her broken arms
her snapped neck

But what you don't see
is her
broken smile
broken heart
broken soul
shattered will

can you see the broken doll?
inside of me

inside us all…

Halimat Alawode, Grade 9
Brooklyn Jr High School, MN

A Better Meaning

We share clothes
and laugh together.
Paint each other's toes
and talk forever.
Have movie nights
just you and me
have a sleep over
with a groupie.
Belt it out
to our favorite song
dance all night
and play ping pong.
We are friends
but even deeper
we are sisters
and that's a keeper.

Megan Kazynski, Grade 7
Shakopee Area Catholic School, MN

Being There for a Friend

I'd be your shoulder to cry on
And I'd be your best friend.
Me and you together
Until the end.
When something is funny,
I'll laugh with you.
When something is sad,
I will cry too.
We'll rise and we'll fall together
We'll win and we'll lose forever
We are lost in our own world
You are my precious pearl
In every little thing we share
We let each other know that we care.

Amber Dieringer, Grade 7
Home School, WI

Inside

Inside I'm a wreck
A cloudy headed mess
But outside I'm happy
Always hoping for the best
Inside I am still hoping
But expecting nothing more
Than another day to live
Another worthless chore
You might see me as the peppy one
But inside I'm truly shy
When I'm gossiping in a hushed tone
I'd rather be asking why…
Why be someone I'm truly not
And let the whole world see
A girl who is a total fake
The inaccurate part of me?
So while I'm laughing and cracking a joke
Inside I'm coughing, getting ready to choke
Save me from me, don't let me hide
From myself any longer
From myself inside

Emily Dallmann, Grade 8
Valley Middle School, MN

Polars

Day and Night.
Polars.
Dusk.
Which way does it look?
Black and White.
Polars.
Gray.
Which way does it run?
Left and Right.
Polars.
Straight.
Which way does it turn?
Above:
Polars.
Combined by one word.
Girls and Boys.
Polars.
Sports. Art.
Band. Choir.
Academics. Plays.
WE ARE ONE.

Alex Trekas, Grade 9
Oostburg High School, WI

Love

Love rules the court, the camp, the world,
And men blow and saints above
For love is heaven and heaven is love.

Eric Conniff, Grade 7
Shakopee Area Catholic School, MN

1

You get 1 life to live
1 chance to take
1 shot to make the best of it
You get 1 life to live
Every second counts
Every choice matters
You get 1 life to live
It could be good
It could be bad
Don't waste your life
You only get 1

Erica Ness, Grade 8
McKinley Middle School, WI

Growing Up

Only yesterday,
Everyone called me a little kid.
Who couldn't watch scary movies,
Or play violent games.
I would beg and beg,
But my parents would say,
You are way too young.
I didn't like that,
Not one bit, not at all.
I wanted to grow up faster,
So I went in my room and waited.

Kyle Wallace, Grade 9
Rosholt Middle-High School, WI

Stars

Stars
are bright
in the night.
Shining, glowing, twinkling stars.
They shoot around like cars.
All over the night sky.
Looking at them up so high.
Quite a   delight
these   little stars
in the   night.

Olivia Laux, Grade 7
Shakopee Area Catholic School, MN

Crow and Raven

Violet mountains on the horizon rise
A sickle moon strays into the skies
Beneath the black shadows
Breathing the damp air
There are two
Who are free yet their
Twins in the soul
Ride not under their wings
For their feathers are black
On the silver breeze

Madeline Ince, Grade 8
Black Hawk Middle School, MN

Polluting Can Make Our World a Strange Place

Life is strange in so many ways
How, you may ask
Take pollution as an example
It is ruining our beautiful planet
If we don't stop, our once beautiful planet will look like a giant parking lot,
No one wants to live like that,
Plus we will run out of oxygen
Smoke and fog, fog and smog, it is bad for the air
We will have no water
Water from rain, ditches and drains are harmful to our great bodies of water.
We pollute our land even though you might not think so,
Agriculture, mining, sewage sludge, and dredge spoils all our soil.
Pollution can be caused by noise too,
Road traffic, air traffic and even rail traffic noise all pollutes.
We have a fantastic world and should take care of it pollution is strange in so many ways
But we can stop it.
We should love our planet,
Just as much as it loves us.

Constance Carlson, Grade 8
Lakewood Elementary School, WI

A Time

To everything there is a season, and a time to every purpose under the heavens:

A time for sun and a time for rain a time for pleasure and a time for pain
A time for listening and a time for talking a time for standing and a time for walking
A time to follow and a time to lead a time to take control and a time to heed
A time for excitement and a time for regret a time to forgive and a time to forget

A time to stand back and a time to be bold a time to release and a time to hold
A time to be happy and a time to be sad a time to go easy and a time to be mad
A time to be honest and a time to lie a time to laugh and a time to cry
A time to be patient and a time to hurry a time to be calm and a time to worry

A time to spend and a time to save a time to be strong and a time to worry
A time to spend and a time to save a time to be strong and a time to cave
A time for noise and a time for silence a time for peace and a time for violence
A time to lose and a time to win a time to obey and a time to sin
A time to live and a time to die a time to say hello and a time to say good bye

Ariana Badran, Grade 8
Holy Family Parish School, WI

The Autumn Visitor

On that misty autumn morning, Sand Creek shimmered in the golden sunlight.
The crimson and gold leaves swirled gracefully through the light breeze.
At a broken-down farm, a visitor sat down in a creaking and aging rocking chair.
The visitor looked out upon a grass-covered trail, the one he had walked on to get there.
He heard a sound and looked up at white elegant morning doves and sallow finches;
then came a soft rustling.
He looked to the right and saw the forest of bright greens and vibrant golds.
Then came a low rumble and soon after came the soft tapping of rain upon the porch
and a flash of mighty lightning.
At last, the visitor walked by the fading fence of dark blue and into the storm,
never to return again.

Ali Wallis, Grade 9
Jordan Sr High School, MN

The Race

The thunderous roar of the ground below,
The sting of the whip as it hits my side,
Heart pounding, chest aching, muscles tight.
As I come around the last turn,
I see the finish line.
Thoughts rush through my mind. Will I make it?
Will I finish this?
If so how? Running harder,
With a final blow to my side by the whip,
I leap across the finish line. With my mind clear,
I see that I made it.
I finished the race.

Kaylee Harper, Grade 9
Round Lake High School, MN

Dragon's Breath

I blew right out some dragon's breath
Which made me feel the verge of death.
The frosty flakes, the ice still nights,
The days that never will turn bright.
My fingers gray and turning black
The effervescent days now lack.
My head is down, my cheeks are numb
When he's gone, my friend, the Sun.
I feel the chill that always flies
It burns my skin and makes me cry.
But wait, I shouldn't, I'll freeze to death
For when it's I who breathes dragon's breath.

Caileigh Marshall, Grade 7
Wayzata East Middle School, MN

Fall Nights

Fall nights get colder
As the year grows older,
and the sun sets sooner each day.
Here comes December as it passes November
And the year is drifting away.
The smell of the leaves in that mid fall breeze
Brings joy to the children at play.
The wind in the trees that are losing their leaves
Keep whistling all through the day.
Fall nights get colder
As the year grows older
And now comes the end of the day.

Suzanne Zuba, Grade 8
Kewaskum Middle School, WI

Gentle Lullaby

The sunset is like a million hearts,
Bursting with joy as the gentle waves crash upon the shore.
You hear silent birds flap their wings overhead.
The view is more than life itself.
I call it just beauty.

Mercades Loeper, Grade 8
McKinley Middle School, WI

Predator and Prey

A beetle flies to find a new home
The bird snatches it up for a quick snack
A jungle cat leaps and swallows the bird
The predator has become the prey

Dark shadows stalk the night
Working together they stab the large cat
Eating their food a ship appears upon the shore
White men charge with chains and whips
The predator has become the prey

A single virus infects a man, spreading fast
Soon all are ill, and the ship runs aground
The shadow hunters return home
And the white men all slowly die
The predator has become the prey

A beetle grows within the corpse
Soon its home is but a bone leaving it hungry
A beetle flies to find a new home

This circle shall remain to the end
The creatures may change from one to another
But the circle shall prevail

Justin Davidson, Grade 9
Montgomery-Lonsdale High School, MN

If I Could Grant a Wish for You

If I could grant a wish for you
I would like it and I hope you would too
May you never have the need to be blue
And to yourself, may you always be true

May you take risks that turn out well
May you never get bug bites that will swell
May you work out but never get sore
May you play a game and always score

May you have peace and quiet time
May you always get airplane seats that are prime
May you work hard and be rewarded
By your family and friends, may you be supported

May you always laugh and always have fun
May you have happiness, and of it a ton
May you have food and drink, and of it enough
May you have a house and room for your stuff

On your birthday may it always be about you
May all of your hopes and dreams come true
If I could grant a wish for you
I would like it and I hope you would too

Colleen Flannery, Grade 8
Holy Family Parish School, WI

When You're Here/When You're Gone

when you're here
my heart bleeds
when you're gone
my heart breaks
when you're here
you're the only one I see
when you're gone
you're the only one I think about
when you're here
I can't breathe
when you're gone
I hold my breath
when you're here
I worry
when you're gone
I worry more
when you're here
I love you
when you're gone
I keep loving you

Ashley Carls, Grade 8
Black Hawk Middle School, MN

The Rose

A bouquet in the window
Flowers blooming bright
A frameless sight wanders
Into my mind at night.
I debate at the counter
If a card would be great
I decide not to get one
And I pay the clerk his eight.
I deliver the vase to the teacher
Who says she'll deliver it soon
But then a mild cancer
Turns into a great monsoon.
Cancer takes another life
And all through the halls
People are saluting his window
And tears come in waterfalls...
Cancer, cancer, cancer
An image haunts me night and day.
Cancer, cancer, cancer
One word I cannot say.

Marie Bourget, Grade 7
Hudson Middle School, WI

Horses

Horses
Elegant, strong
Cantering, trotting, strutting
They make my heart beat
Horses

Holly Fields, Grade 9
Rosholt Middle-High School, WI

Autumn's Wonders

On a breezy fall evening,
I sat on my porch rocking in my old rocking chair,
Watching the rolling thunderheads approaching.
While I rocked, a bumblebee buzzed around me.
As I sat there, I heard the black and white geese flying south.
Just then, over the tall grassy hill came Casey my friend, ready for a hike.
While we walked, the orange and scarlet maple leaves fell on the grass-covered trial.
An abandoned broken farmhouse silently sat there.
Around the house, an enormous white picket fence creaked in the wind.
A daddy long legged spider made its home on the white fence.
Behind the old farmhouse, Miller's Pond glimmered.
Strolling around the pond, we looked for monarch caterpillars on the milkweed.
As it started to mist, we hurried back.
We had one more stop to make — the elderly apple tree
Which had the crispest, sweetest, and most delicious apples ever grown.
While walking home, we smiled, filled with the wonderful treasures of autumn.

Dani Allen, Grade 9
Jordan Sr High School, MN

Five Senses in Love and Hate

Love...
Love is red, as warm as wearing a knit sweater made by your grandmother.
It sounds like birds twittering, the sign that spring is coming.
It tastes like the sweetest chocolate, as though you were in Belgium eating it.
It smells like fresh cut roses, enveloping you in its sweet scent.
It looks like a beating heart fluttering with happiness and joy.
Love makes you feel as though nothing bad could ever happen in the world and nothing has.

Hate...
Hate is as black as smoke rising from a chimney.
It sounds like a train screeching to a halt, loud and unsettling.
It tastes like sour lemon juice running down your throat.
It smells like a landfill covered with garbage, that makes you plug your nose and breath
  through your mouth.
Hate looks like war, thousands of people dying to protect their country.
It makes you feel like you can't breath, gasping for air, but can't seem to find any.

Brianna Blankenburg, Grade 8
Holy Family Parish School, WI

My Yard

At my house, a grass trail
Leads to a pond I nicknamed Muddy
It floods when rolling thunderheads come in
In the morning, it is covered in mist
The breeze always blows away the mist
In my field, a lot of milkweeds
Have spiders on them
The red wing black birds always wake me up in the morning
On top of the hill I live on, an abandoned farm is surrounded by a fence
Our yard is covered in oak trees with leaves
Small sour apples are covered in bees
On our patio, a white rocking chair is swaying
Visitors come often to my yard and my house

Andrew Smith, Grade 9
Jordan Sr High School, MN

Love

Love is the key to life
It helps you enjoy the little things
You realize what life is all about
You realize why you wake up
You realize why you live
Love has been here forever
It will never go away
Love is Karma
If you never love
You will never be loved
Love is like peace and happiness
It comes and goes
With the change of the day
God loved us so much that He sent His only son
Down to earth
To help us become better people
Jesus loved us so much
That He died for us

Audrey Kratz, Grade 8
St Maria Goretti Catholic School, WI

Plunging Snow

As I walked out the door on a cold, winter day,
I hear the wind blow snowflakes every which way.

I see the snowman dressed up with a hat,
and at his feet lies a little black cat.

As I grab the handle of my black Corvette.
I hear my neighbors singing a horrible duet.

I slide onto my toasty, warm seat,
sipping hot chocolate that warms even my feet.

I take in the scent of the pine smelling air,
while trying to melt all the snow from my hair.

I turn on the radio hoping to hear the voice say,
kids three favorite words, "No School Today!"

Lauren Fischer, Grade 8
St John Neumann School, WI

A Rose

A Rose
A single rose,
sitting on a table,
having a beauty of its own.
Its meaning is just as mysterious as its beauty.
Its color representing a different feeling.
Its odor takes you to your happy place.
So what does your rose mean to you.

Sarah Baumgard, Grade 9
Round Lake High School, MN

That Special Person

At the end of summer,
you look back and see all the fun you had.
All the sun, all the excitement, all the parties,
all the fireworks, all the good times,

And then you realize,
it doesn't matter what you did but,
who you were with.
The person who made it the time of your life.

You could be having the worst day,
And that person would just walk in the door,
And smile at you,
Giving you butterflies, making everything better.

Then you realize,
You like him and he likes you.
Everything is falling into place.

One day you wake up.
He doesn't like you. He's gone.
It was just a dream.
You tell yourself, but you know better.
He was pretending all along.

Janice Finley, Grade 8
Shakopee Area Catholic School, MN

The Place to Be

The wind is whistling through your hair.
The birds are chirping everywhere.
They are the music of the earth;
The ones that give their songs new birth.
This is the place to be.

You ride over the hills like in a dream,
Jumping smoothly over a stream.
The mane and tail as black as coal,
You know deep down inside your soul.
This is the place to be.

Soaring over the open plains,
Breaking through the invisible chains,
That held you back,
Now you are free,
This is the place to be.

Suddenly the sun fades, and night sets course,
As you dismount from your horse.
You peel off your black leather riding gloves.
You'll be back tomorrow because,
This is the place to be.

Anna Wheeler, Grade 8
St Mark's School, MN

Snowflakes

S nowflakes slithering from the sky,
N earing the end, to the ground.
O utside the weather is cold.
W ind is blowing,
F reezing temperatures plummet.
L oosely falling dancing snowflakes.
A ll is so beautiful,
K indly and gently landing on the ground.
E nding a journey from the sky,
S nowflakes.

Alyssa Rycerz, Grade 7
Thorp Middle School, WI

Perfection?

P retty?
E nvious?
R espective?
F earless?
E legant?
C ourageous?
T errific?
I ntelligent?
O utgoing?
N ice?

Megan Eckstein, Grade 9
Discovery Middle School, MN

Computer

I am very smart
Data is stored inside of me
I don't work by myself
People have to operate me
I can be used for homework
Or just plain old research
People can type on me
I have a mouse and a monitor
I can be big or small
And can stay put or be portable

Kyle LeCaptain, Grade 8
St Paul's Lutheran School, WI

A Special Day

There once was a day,
A day like no other;
The fresh, autumn air,
With a crisp, winter breeze,
Is soothing, yet stinging,
Like a ray, from the sea.
Its beauty and awe,
Its mystique, unmistaking,
Makes a fellow like me,
Not waiting, nor hating.

Jesse Cannella, Grade 7
Prairie River Middle School, WI

Life Like the Weather

Life is like the weather.
The element in our lives
That enables us to have a sunny day or a hurricane.
Passing us by with subtle unimportance.
Like dewy webs speckled with teardrops.
We dance through life in a dark world,
Not knowing how we should open our eyes
To see the beautiful garden we dance in.
Let us open our eyes and experience
The sunny days that lift us,
The rainy days that help us mourn for a loss,
The hurricane that blows us over with a current so strong we can't get up,
The tornado we get sucked into and never get out of
To only later get stopped, to see what we missed.
The lightning we get shocked by;
A realization and hurtful shock
We've been ignoring and missing in life.
And to the cloudy, light, breezy days.
The average day we know only too well.
They don't realize that somewhere not too far,
There's a better life and weather for only you.

Sara Backstrom, Grade 8
Pilgrim Park Middle School, WI

The Only Tigger

My name is Tigger, and I am sad. I've lost my family which makes me mad!
I called, and called, and called. When nobody came I bawled.
Because I have no family; it is not fine and dandy.

So I set off on a trip, and in the woods I found a clip.
But that was the only trace; if there were any Tiggers to chase.
My heart would be happy, if only I sat with my pappy.

As I come back to one-hundred acre woods, I walk around the neighborhoods.
I went to my friend Eeyore who has a small tail. Which was only held on by one little nail.
As I came near he saw my pain and with his hoarse voice he said with a strain.

What Eeyore had mumbled; it had made me feel humbled.
I found out I was wrong for I had a family all along.

Hope Benson, Grade 8
Jerstad Agerholm Middle School, WI

John LaGue

John
Happy, thinking, energetic, and weird
Brother of Steph, Liza, Henry, and Ben
Lover of peaceful spring days, playing in the rain, and competition
Who feels guilt after hurting someone, happiness when I'm myself, and
loneliness in a big house
Who needs food, kindness, and computers
Who gives smiles, laughter, and insight
Who fears loneliness, strangers, and evil
Who would like to see everyone quiet for a day, peace, and kindness
LaGue

John LaGue, Grade 8
Holy Family Parish School, WI

Martin Luther King

You were treated unfairly.
But you stood up for what was right.
You gave speeches that were heard and seen.
You never harmed anyone or got in a fight.

You wanted peace and love to spread.
You never wanted anyone dead.
Violence and hatred you always dread,
You spoke words of wisdom instead.

Equality is what you had in mind,
Since no one should be left behind.
Segregation is what you dread,
But some said, "Martin go take a hike."

To bring peace, no matter what they said,
Fighting for justice and equality instead,
Until the day you were dead.

Mohammed Khan, Grade 8
Jerstad Agerholm Middle School, WI

My Best Friend

We met way back in third grade
Maybe one day she'll be my bridesmaid
We would always laugh at the dumbest things that happen
We never really got into fights which is a good thing to say
She's just like a sister to me
I know her so well
I am glad to call her my best friend

I miss seeing her every day at school
But I know she will always be there for me
I have so many memories of her coming over to play
Having fun outside in the cold weather
I know she wouldn't let me down
I know her so well
I am glad to call her my best friend

My one and only friend
Amber Jackson

Annabeth Cerdas, Grade 8
McKinley Middle School, WI

Volcanoes Having Fun

A volcano is a mountain, a mountaintop,
Spitting out magma red and hot,
With its ridges and bumps and all its edges,
Looking calm at first and then erupting in seconds,
Science warns us when it's about to explode,
While causing earthquakes and destruction unfolds,
The people will hide and try to run,
This is how volcanoes have fun.

Austin Biehl, Grade 8
Marinette Middle School, WI

I Am Ashley

I am funny and loving
I wonder what it would be like in a different world
I hear people calling me names
I see people laughing at me
I want them all to stop
I am funny and loving
I pretend not to hear them
I feel like there is nobody around me
I touch the sky
I worry that no one is there
I cry but don't let them see it
I am funny and loving
I understand that it should not hurt me
I say stop or just agree with them
I dream that soon it will stop
I try to just laugh with them
I hope they will see that it hurts me
I am funny and loving

Ashley Holloway, Grade 9
Discovery Middle School, MN

July 16, 1969 an Eagle's Journey

On that day, a leap in human expansion occurred
Saturn V lifted the Eagle and his comrade Columbus
Into the sky
As it soars, the Saturn V begins to separate
First stage, into space
Second stage, into orbit
Third stage, into deep space
The pair drifts through the black abyss
They see the great barren rock
The pair separate
Columbus watched the Eagle in descent
Staring at the gray barren ground
The Eagle looked at the cold rock
The land was clear when the Eagle veered
Touchdown
Dust exploded from the cratered earth
The Eagle cried to the earth,
"Houston, this is Tranquility Base, the Eagle has landed"

Lucas Ince, Grade 8
All Saints Catholic School, MN

5 Ways of Looking at a Spider Web

A small ladder to heaven.
The necklace of an angel,
threading her miniature beads of pearly raindrops.
A carefully woven veil for a spider bride.
A delicate piece of lace,
fluttering gently in the wind.
A thin road with small, watery cars and
a spider for the crossing guard.

Chloe Corcoran, Grade 7
Holy Family Parish School, WI

All About Me

KATIE
Short, adventurous, brunette
Sister of Nicole
Lover of shopping, shoes, and shorts
Who feels happy, hopeful, and loved
Who fears heights, rats, and bats
Who would like an A in English,
A pet fish, and a genie to make a wish
Resident of Wisconsin
CLEARY
Katie Cleary, Grade 9
Rosholt Middle-High School, WI

Past to Future

It seems like just yesterday
I could not ride my bike
Or reach the freezer
Or open the door
But as the years moved on
I noticed
I can reach the freezer
Ride my bike with no hands
and open the door
Everything changed so quickly
Clayton Jankowski, Grade 9
Rosholt Middle-High School, WI

Music

Rock
Loud, fast
Screaming, shouting, yelling
Emotion, leather, guitars, drums
Slowing, soothing, feeling
Rhythmical, slow
Country
Calvin Lorbiecki, Grade 9
Rosholt Middle-High School, WI

Quickly Changing

Caterpillar
Ugly, slow
Watching, eating, marching
Larva, grass, cocoon, leaf
Engulfing, sleeping, waiting
Vibrant, fluttering
Butterfly
Katelyn Mueller, Grade 9
Rosholt Middle-High School, WI

My Hero…!!!

My hero is the one I look up to with pride.
My hero is the one that is not ashamed to cry.
My hero makes me laugh even when I am about to cry.
My hero is the one that will give me wings to fly.
My hero is a person like you and I.
My hero is the one that will stay strong through it all.
My hero is the one that I miss the most.
My hero is the one that will protect us both.
My hero is the one that brings me hope.
My hero is the one I give respect and my support.
My hero is the one that is not afraid to die.
My hero is the one that has wings to fly.
My hero is the one fighting for our country.
My hero is the one that will not look away from mercy.
My hero is the one that will keep a promise.
My hero is the one that will keep me strong.
My hero is the one that won't scream and shout.
My hero is the one that looks out if something is up.
My hero is the one that keeps me out of trouble.
My hero is the one that says I love you very much even when my heart has been crushed.
My hero is my brother a platoon marine in San Diego, California.
Shelby Drentlaw, Grade 9
Montgomery-Lonsdale High School, MN

Love

Love:
No one really knows what it is,
But they know when they are in love.
They get the butterflies, every time they think about that person.
They can't sleep because; they can't wait 'till the next time they're going to see them.

Love:
It puts a smile on your face,
Because you know he may be the one.
It can also bring tears to your eyes too,
When you realize, maybe he's not.

Love:
It may be just a four-letter word,
But the meaning means so much more.
It can be a heartwarming feeling,
Or maybe, it can be heartbreaking too,
But everyone will find that certain someone
Who they're in love with,
But it takes time, and the feeling will last forever.
Jennie Aellig, Grade 9
Fall River High School, WI

Five Ways to Look at a Butterfly

An angel wrapped in silky smooth colors…
A bird that never grew in size but in beauty…
A giant's light so that he may see in the darkness…
Mother Nature's voice, for she speaks beautiful words of wisdom…
A woman's hope, so she may see her life is as important as anyone else's.
MacKenzie Lillund, Grade 7
Holy Family Parish School, WI

Can You Imagine

Earth without gravity
A sweet tooth without a cavity

A prince without a princess
Basketball without a full court press

People without mouths
Birds not migrating south

Clocks without time
Circuses without mimes

Giraffes with glasses
School with no classes

A raven without wings
A canary that never sings

A game that never ends
A movie star with no friends

A backpack without straps
An iphone without apps
Elise Blust, Grade 8
Holy Family Parish School, WI

Crayola Crayons

Crayola crayons
Wonderful and bright
The way they glimmer in the light.
Lovely green and blue
Remind me of grass with dew.
Exotic orange and pink
Remind me of a sponge in the sink.
Ever so yellow
Twinkles and says 'hey there fellow!'
While scary red
Makes me think of the dead.
These colors so bright
The way they gleam in the light.
Livy Wassen, Grade 8
Sartell Middle School, MN

Grandma

5'6" of pure farmer.
Brown eyes and graying brown hair.
Driving tractors and tossing bales.
Made delicious food.
Put in a long hard day's work every day.
Made excellent homemade cookies.
Spent a lot of time with us.
Then she died.
We will always remember.
All the fun times we shared as a family
Zack Boettcher, Grade 9
Rosholt Middle-High School, WI

Set Me Free

I'm here with these wings
Standing on the edge of the cliff…
But I cannot fly;
I'm bound here to find my calling
Here to see the world in shades of gray
Nothing seems as it really is…
My heart is breaking and aching, and it wants to shatter
But I hold onto winter's last breath
And try to breath in what I can
I know that life is hard
My hopeless dreams that seem so far to reach; no matter how hard I try
In my mind believing in such silly thoughts
With a past so hard to forget
I know I can't change the past; but what will the future bring
Still I won't give up
I'm here with these wings
Standing on the edge of the cliff…
I feel as if invisible chains bind my wings to the ground
It seems I have taken so many burdens for my sins that I must pay
I've cried so much, that I don't have any more tears to shed but now I cry tears of blood;
My curse; please help set me free so I can fly with the wind
Mai Nag Moua, Grade 8
Wayzata Central Middle School, MN

Life or Death

Living is exciting.
You can do anything you choose.
There are many adventures that you can encounter,
But you have to watch out for the unexpected.
Bad things in life can lead to death.
If you die, you don't know where it will take you.
This place could be a happy place or it could be terrifying.
This place where death may take you could be cold and dark.
You don't know what it is like.
If you don't know what death is like, then how do you know if you will like it?
Death could be uncanny, so you make the choice;
Life: where there are opportunities
Or
Death: the unknown.
Marnie Destree, Grade 7
Lakewood Elementary School, WI

My Preface

Grace is my name,
What most people know me by.
But there is a person underneath my name.
A whole personality,
Unique, different from anyone else.
A personality that is as diverse as night and day,
One that consists of qualities such as kindness, confidence, and generosity.
One that also includes humor, trust, and humility.
A name is just a title,
A preface into your personality.
My preface just happens to be Grace.
Grace Holzem, Grade 8
Pilgrim Park Middle School, WI

Someone I Admire

She is happy and cheerful, kind and caring
She knows what I want and need
She helps me no matter the situation
She knows what to do when something bad happens
She understands even if I say she won't
She is someone you go to for advice if its needed
When she is hurt I try to comfort her,
But I can't help her how she helps me
I'm not as wise as she
I can't be as patient as she
Even though we may fight,
She is my hero
She is someone I admire
She is someone I love
She is…
    My mom.

Brianna Fischer, Grade 8
Trinity Lutheran School, WI

To Be a Cat

If I was a cat
my eyes would blink when darkness comes
my body stirs with life
I feel like a bird soaring
as I set off on my new adventure
Who knows what will happen tonight
when I look up
all I see is the stars and moon
the grass is a jungle
It grabs and pulls on my feet
like a monster that wants to eat me
I run around playing with my friends,
we all prance in the pretty petunias at the park
having the time of our lives
when it's time to go home
I just think of how much fun it will be tomorrow

Kyra Odegaard, Grade 8
Robert J Elkington Middle School, MN

Christmas

The snow is falling to the ground.
Children laughing and playing all around.
I see the presents under the tree.
Now I wonder which one's for me.
I hear the dogs barking at the window.
I wish they would come and play in the snow.
The snow is cold to the touch.
The Christmas songs are on too much.
I put on the lights to make the tree pretty.
People are enjoying the big city.
I taste the chocolate on my tongue,
baking cookies like we are young.
The Christmas tree smells of fresh pine.
How can I remember which ornament is mine?

Liz Glowcheski, Grade 8
St John Neumann School, WI

The Difficulties of Love

My life like Eden is fruitful in many ways but poisoned by one
My years are but a few, I am still young.
Though my friends of two,
stand together the two,
they break my heart the two
by sharing joy and love.

I once had the chance to be with him, and hear the sound
of his voice in my ear, but I hadn't made the choice;
I wanted to wait and see, I never got a response.
Maybe we weren't meant to be.

I must move on, but I feel an ache where my heart once was,
stolen by him,
and with it he ran to another by whim.

My heart, oh my heart, cries out in need of shelter
or the rain shall surely pelter, it down to dirt.

I shall go through life as a message in a bottle
thrown in the ocean never to be revealed or opened.
For me and him shall never be,
my love and I shall never be.
I will go through life and shall never be,
for he is with another

Meghan Baumhardt, Grade 8
Eastbrook Academy, WI

A Snowflake Knows

A snowflake knows how to form so exquisitely
So that the there are no others like him.
He knows how to sleep
In his fluffy, ivory bed
As though not a care in the world.

He knows when to fall
And land straight on the tongue of a hopeful, little child.
He knows how to make just the right noise
So that when you step on him,
He makes a splendid crunching sound.

He knows how to fall
So that it makes me laugh as he tickles my face.
He knows how to dance around my head
As if he were trying to wish me a Merry Christmas.

He knows how to glaze the trees just right
So he can make the tree flash and glisten
As though it was made out of sparkles.

Then he knows how to wish good-bye
And vanish leaving nothing behind him but a simple memory.
And he knows how to plan for his next stimulating experience
When the Earth is cold enough to welcome him in once more.

Paige Brown, Grade 7
Thorp Middle School, WI

A Walk with Martin Luther King

We look back at Martin Luther King's life,
Which was full of cheers as well as strife;
He changed race relations for all time,
Because he stood up and said it was out of line;
He gave powerful speeches, you may say,
That drew peaceful crowds as long as a day.

He believed in nonviolent disobedience as a way to protest,
He changed the country in ways we could only have guessed;
With the Montgomery bus strike he started out small,
By the end millions would listen to his call.

"Rise up!" he would say in a strong preacher's voice,
And show the world we have a choice;
In Selma, with clubs and dogs, marchers were beaten and battered,
Although hit with water hoses, they knew peace is what mattered.

Because of his leadership, both noble and wise,
The world honored him with the Nobel Peace Prize;
His work to spread peace had just begun,
But his life ended too soon with a gun;
An early end to his life made tears stream,
But his words still echo…"I have a dream."

Madelyn Tabor, Grade 8
Jerstad-Agerholm Middle School, WI

Run Little Child

Run little child, run.
Run away from the terrors of night.
Run away from your fears
And maybe your nightmares won't come true.

Shh little child, shh.
Be quiet now, do not cry; do not be afraid.
It was only a dream.
Come into the light; they can't hurt you now.
If you do not sleep, you will not see the dangers of your dreams.

Pray little child, pray.
Pray that the terrors stay in your dreams of night.
And your joy stays in the light.
Pray that you won't be tired and will not sleep.
Pray that you won't collapse, but will run.
Run away from your fears and
Pray for the light of the sun to shine down upon your face.

Laugh little child, laugh.
Your nightmares are afraid.
Sleep little child, sleep.
Run to joyous hopes and dreams, as your fears fade away.

Mariah Lichty, Grade 9
Discovery Middle School, MN

As the Snow Falls Softly to the Ground

The first snow falls with silence all around,
while the flakes fall softly, softly to the ground.
Children are laughing, the fun's just begun.
Christmas is coming with much to be done.
Car times pack snow with a squeak and a crunch,
Sugary sweet Christmas cookies baking to munch.
Delicious hot chocolate scalds your tongue,
the snowball fights make it great to be young.
Fluffy whipped cream adds a spot to your nose
as fuzzy warm socks cover your toes.
The trees are just skeletons watching over you,
Hear the hum of the fireplace — it's hard to be blue.
A spine-chilling snowdrop tingles down your back.
The street sides are covered in disgusting black.
The big, bright feather flakes float in the air.
They form a thick carpet for all of us to share.

Hannah Schmidt, Grade 8
St John Neumann School, WI

Growing Up

I used to go to elementary school to learn the basics
And now I go to high school to learn the more advanced
Tomorrow I will go to college, and study for a job.

I used to study addition and subtraction
And now I study geometry
Tomorrow I will study calculus.

I used to get shirts from the junior's section
And now I get clothing from the teen section
Tomorrow I will get clothing from the men's section

My parents think I'm growing up too fast.

Alex Cole, Grade 9
Rosholt Middle-High School, WI

Life

Life may be strange,
It may not go as planned,
Life will have its ups and downs,
Some you will like,
Others you won't,
People will come and go in your life,
Some will be nice,
But some won't
You may fight with your friends,
And then laugh at what you were mad about,
Life will never be perfect,
But you can make it perfect to you by
Looking past all the imperfections.

Tiffany O'Dowd, Grade 8
Lakewood Elementary School, WI

A Winter Day

Bright, white snow packed on the ground,
Clouds dropping flakes without a sound.
Like heaven's crying frozen tears.

Kids are laughing, having fun,
In the distant sun.
Individuality: each kid and flake is different.

Stick out your tongue and taste
the frozen water, don't make haste.
Take your time to take in this day.

Now, the sun is getting low,
There's hot chocolate inside, let's go.
Take a sip,
the warmth trickles down your throat.

Dinner's done, smell the chicken and rice.
The scents in this house
make it all the more nice.
That was yummy, any dessert?

This winter day is over, time for bed.
The day may be over,
but there's more winter ahead.
It's so cold outside, but my blanket is warm.

Megan Horejs, Grade 8
St John Neumann School, WI

Christmas

'Tis my favorite time of the year, the Christmas season
Family and friends gather laughter and happiness to spare
Food to eat all day and all night waiting for Santa to stop by
Presents in jeopardy of being shaken too much
Stories I've hear a thousand times before, but still want more
'Tis my favorite time of the year the Christmas season

Recording all the Christmas classics, annoying the parents
The lights all around flickering all different colors
Carols echoing throughout the town
Looking for flying reindeer
Plots to hide in Santa's sleigh and go to the North Pole
'Tis my favorite time of the year the Christmas season

Playing game, gift making little cousins cry
Alliances, making sure you get the fun presents
Staying up until one in the morning just for Santa
The fire keeping my feet toasty with a good book
Smells of aunts and Grandma's cooking
Sneaking cookies that are for later

I'm smiling for so many reasons
So I can only sum it up in one phrase
'Tis my favorite time of the year, Christmas season

Celeste Friederich, Grade 9
Montgomery-Lonsdale High School, MN

Questions

Sissy?
Do you remember?
When we were little girls in the city?
When it was just me and you and mommy and daddy?
Do you remember when two little brothers came along?
Remember how happy we were?
Then how come it ended up like this?
How come mommy and daddy hate each other?
How come I just want to cry?
When will we be a happy family again?
What if daddy'll like some strange lady?
What if mommy changes her last name?
Why do all the other kids get parents that love them?
Did I do something wrong?
Sissy, I'm scared.
Can I sleep in your bed tonight?
Cause when I wake up from my nightmare
I'll have a new question
Don't worry it's not for you this time
But I know I'll cry when I ask,
Mommy, Daddy what happened to us?

Michaela Murphy, Grade 7
Shakopee Area Catholic School, MN

My Life

I used to bike down the back
roads on cool summer evenings
when the last bit of sunlight still
would light my way.
I would swim in the lake on hot
summer days and read books on lazy
rainy afternoons.
Now I walk through fog and trample
through small piles of leaves with
only the whisper of the wind in my ears
while mice scurry by my feet.
Tomorrow I will trudge through snow banks,
glide across ice, and dress like an Eskimo
while snowflakes dance around me and
stars twinkle on cold clear nights.

Neal Kluck, Grade 9
Rosholt Middle-High School, WI

Winter

The time of year
Where it seems impossible to be bored
There is so much to do during this snowy holiday season
You can ski, sled, and snowtube
If it's too cold outside
You can hide under blankets inside
Or after a long day of playing
Hot chocolate tastes great
But soon everything will be melted
And winter will be gone

Christina Nelson, Grade 8
St Odilia School, MN

What Tomorrow Will Bring

We don't know what tomorrow will bring,
But don't let today bring you down.
You may never find that pot of gold,
But I know you'll still find luck.
You didn't wish upon that star,
But your dream will still come true.
You may never be famous,
But you'll still have fans.
You may never travel the world,
But you'll still have adventures.
You may lose once in a while,
But that's what makes you stronger.
You may never be number one,
But I know you'll come close.
You may get lost in the sea,
But eventually you'll be found.
You may dream big,
But you never take a chance.
Take a risk tomorrow,
Otherwise it will be like yesterday again.

Brandi Shramek, Grade 8
Lincoln Jr/Sr High School, WI

Outside My Window

Outside my window
Is a world of hate,
Society is crude
And people always discriminate
Outside my window
Is a world of disaster
We are grown on violence
There is not too much laughter
Outside my window
Is a world of madness
When there is just chaos
No one sees the big mess
Outside my window
Is a world of potential
To do things that are impossible
To be everything they don't recall
Inside my window
Is my world of tranquility
And I hope some day
The world outside shall join me.

Alexis Hogue, Grade 8
St Paul's Lutheran School, WI

Track

Track
Fun, entertaining
Running, jogging, walking
The runners try as hard as they can
Track

Samantha Gosh, Grade 9
Rosholt Middle-High School, WI

A Recipe for a Perfect Brother

Take 3 cups of shining brown hair,
A handful of golf balls,
One flat football,
One flat basketball, and
3 different video games.
Put the golf balls,
The football, and
The basketball in a large bowl,
Blend and stir until the mixture is your skin color.
Then pour it in a little boy shaped pan,
Bake in an oven,
At 380 degrees until golden brown
You can tell it's done when you hear a kid yell, "Go Packers!"
Let stand for 30 minutes to 1 hour,
Sprinkle on a little happiness,
And you end up with the perfect little brother who wants to play catch.

Matthew McCarter, Grade 8
Thorp Middle School, WI

Rebel

When I got home she came to me with big sad dog eyes and a wagging tail.
After supper, she would clean up the floor, my plate, and every dish she could when
we were done.
When I went to bed she was always by my side, watching over me.
On the weekends, we would play with her Frisbees,
All you could see was a black and tan dog having fun.
When you came she was full of energy ready to play.
At Christmas, she would take all the candy canes off the tree she could reach.
When she was mad she took my dad's hat.
When I was little she would let me ride her.
She was always ready for a snack.
When I was sick she was by my side.
When I was upset she was by my side cheering me up.
When I think about how much I miss her I get a tear in my eye.
Every time I think of her I wish she wasn't gone.
Rebel was my friend, my dog, as patient as any dog could be.

Rachael Nerby, Grade 7
Lincoln Jr/Sr High School, WI

Sadie

A dorable little fluffy one **B** undle of laughter, full of fun
C hewing, chasing, till the break of dawn **D** igging holes in the neighbor's lawn
E nergy is her middle name **F** illed with so much, she's hard to tame
G rowing older every day **H** appiness so great, I couldn't say
I ntrigued by everything in sight **J** oyful play from day to night
K nowing by my side she'll always be **L** oyal, loving, and best friend to me
M elts my heart with her longing cries **N** ever tiring of her puppy sighs
O ne million dollars could not replace **P** uppy kisses on my face
Q ueen of the house, you could easily say **R** owdy and mischievous in every way
S tares at me with her big brown eyes **T** iny will always be her size
U ndeniably she belongs with me **V** igorous, playful sight to see
W alking on her two hind feet **X** hausting jogs up and down the street
Y earning to make this time go slow **Z** ooming by the years will go

Emily Lein, Grade 8
St Odilia School, MN

Us

You sit there and look at me,
with those piercing hazel eyes,
you tilt your head in confusion,
one thin eyebrow up.
Your mocking smile turns into a sneering grin,
as you throw your head back and laugh,
you sound like a menacing hyena teasing it's prey.
I know your face, your cold character,
your face goes hard,
you look like me, you are me,
your thin lips quiver.
A glistening tear slips down your pale cheek,
you don't say anything, you don't have to,
you hate me, and the feeling is mutual,
you are an empty bomb shell, a lifeless soul,
you are the replica of what I've become,
the thing I despise most of all.
I bring my arm back and swing it swiftly,
you fall into pieces and crash to the ground,
I stare at you, and see thousands of us,
and I drop to my knees.

Carly Foor, Grade 8
Oregon Middle School, WI

What Would Happen if I Had a Million Dollars

I could buy myself a sports car
I could buy myself a jet
I'd buy myself a mansion
I'd never be upset.

I could buy a gross of toothpaste
My mouth always clean
I could buy a billion Q-tips
I could buy two pinball machines.

I could buy anything I wanted.
Expensive merchandise to odds and ends
I could buy anything I wanted
Because I was born to spend.

Maureen Brandl, Grade 9
Rosholt Middle-High School, WI

Opaque Night

Sitting outside in the opaqueness of night
Listening to the leaves tumble around in a gust of wind
Hearing the shallow trickling of Cherokee Creek
Seeing the crooked wooden fence wrapped around the grassy patch
next to the lonely abandoned granary
Watching turkeys nest in the cornfield,
no longer fearful of the scarecrows surrounding them
Laughing at squirrels in the tree, scurrying about,
collecting acorns for the long cold winter
Hearing the crackle of a blazing fire in the rusted fire pit
Seeing all of this and realizing just how much I love fall

Rachael Langager, Grade 9
Jordan Sr High School, MN

Light

So dark, so mysterious.
Like a soul left for disaster,
Inside, your dear soul calls for me;
Something I cannot resist.
My mind falls deep, deep, down,
Into your hands of compassion.

What you are,
What you do is…something I understand.
But yet I cannot fathom the mere thought of you.
The sense of the light in your eyes,
Is taking my heart,
My soul,
Me.

The grade and loveliness of this life;
This light in my soul which had gone out,
You have brought back.
The truth of which is you have…
It is love…
I am in love.

Kayla Ann Olsen, Grade 7
Trinity Lutheran School, WI

Missing You

Today I sat on my couch thinking of you, missing you.
I wondered when you were coming home again.
Wondering if we were ever going to see each other again.
Today I cried for hours
Because I've been missing you so much.
I can still hear your laugh,
When we are together.
I can still hear your voice,
When you're talking to me.
I can still picture you sitting next to me,
Holding my hand.
I can still feel your lips touch mine,
As we kissed.
Today I'm still sitting on my couch,
Missing you.

Hailey Mayer, Grade 9
Round Lake High School, MN

Camera

I bring to you fun.
I take pictures for you.
I capture bad and good times.
I will always be at your birthday parties.
When you go on trips I will go and take pictures.
That will last a lifetime.
I was there when you were born I got to see it all.
And that one time you fell
I was there like all the other times.
Me and you have bad and good memories.

Miguel Ramos, Grade 7
Lincoln Jr/Sr High School, WI

This Mystery

This mystery is something called everything,
Invaluable, untouchable;
It, in plain, is the root of all being.

No price can pay this simple thing,
No queen's jewels, treasury of kings,
Nor dragon's horde, or golden-goose wing.
Never before has it seen a match;
Perhaps very close. But only perhaps.

It is a mother's smile and a father's praise,
The setting sun on summer days.
Can it be measured? I think not.
How could you, scholar, on standard's dot?
That citrus kiss beneath the skin,
That inner warmth hidden within?

Wait not; it is neither lingering nor fleeting,
But mortal hearts cannot be cheating;
Someday, this world we will be leaving.

But fear not! It is a feeling, easily shared,
Your hand in mine, mine in yours.
So go out into your world and care,
And always know that love is there.

Kristina Kusel, Grade 9
Kohler High School, WI

For a Non-Shoppertunistic

So crowded and busy
It makes me dizzy
I want this and this
When all is done it will be bliss

I must be the first
This is the worst
Who else must I shop for
There are sales galore

People shoving
This is not very loving
Little ones scream, adults yell
I think I will go and wait in my shell

People get mad
It really is quite bad
Sales, and oh look and another sale
Stores send coupons by mail

There is such a thing called shopping online
That way other people and I are not intertwined
Now I am tired
But inspired
I think I will make a poem on how today transpired

Emily Gerkin, Grade 8
All Saints Catholic School, MN

Yesterday, Today, and Tomorrow

I used to be tucked into bed.
And now I crawl in by myself.
Tomorrow I will be in the nursing home.

I used to be dressed day and night.
And now I can do it without any help.
Tomorrow I will once again be getting dressed by someone else.

I used to be driven all around town.
And now I practice driving all on my own.
Tomorrow I will be driving slowly because I'm too old.

I used to cry and whine when I didn't get my way.
And now I can get what I want by myself.
Tomorrow I will need assistance.

I used to crawl around in little diapers.
And now I dress in clothes that keep me covered.
Tomorrow I will wear clothes like my mother.

I used to have good eyesight 'cause of my carrots.
And now I must wear glasses or my contacts.
Tomorrow I will get Lasik surgery.

Emilee Wadzinski, Grade 9
Rosholt Middle-High School, WI

I Am a Deer

I am a deer
Looking up in the trees
For the people dressed in orange,
Dodging the bullets being shot at me.
All I hear is gunshots and yelling,
Trying to spook me so I will move.
During the day I run and hide,
During the night I eat with delight.
Corn and acorns all over for me,
And with all my friends.
All I smell is gunpowder.
I feel like if I don't run and hide, I might die,
But sometimes that is not good enough.
I am a deer, and this is what I do
When you are waiting for me to arrive.

Joshua Syryczuk, Grade 8
Thorp Middle School, WI

Equal

Let's go to a world without any hate.
Leave the people behind who only discriminate.
No judging of each other,
because of our color.
Only to love and be friendly and kind.
A world where we leave no one behind.
Let's get together hand in hand.
Let's all be equal is what I demand.

Victoria Duarte, Grade 8
Pilgrim Park Middle School, WI

Summer Beach

I feel the warmth of the sand
I feel the refreshing water
I feel the sun beating down
I feel the breeze passing by
I see the kids running around
I see the shells beneath me
I see the birds flying around
I see the beautiful water
I hear the kids splashing
I hear the parents talking
I hear the wind singing
I hear the birds chirping
I feel, see and hear all at the beach

Amy Clysdale, Grade 8
St Odilia School, MN

Day and Night

As the morning begins
The pink sky turns to blue
The blindingly bright sun rises
To a place where everyone can see
Giving radiance to the whole world
Giving us the gift of sight
When the sky darkens
And day turns to night
With no guarantee that it will begin again
The moon shimmers in the blackness
The stars twinkles in the darkness
They are burning out light bulbs
They are misplaced with the coming day

Katie Moynagh, Grade 8
St Odilia School, MN

My Family

They are the peanut butter in a
    sandwich to hold me together
A bubble to protect me
    when things get out of hand
My jacket
    to keep me in line from danger
The roof to keep
    me out of the cold and rain
They are my rock
    without them, I am nothing

Elsie Kunz, Grade 7
Holy Family Parish School, WI

Bowling

Bowling
Fun, exciting
Rolling, striking, sparing
Fun as a swim on a warm summer day
Bowling

Dwight Groshek, Grade 9
Rosholt Middle-High School, WI

I Am Ashley Janae

I am meticulous and warmhearted
I wonder why people don't treat others the way they want to be treated
I hear Jesus whispering in my ear
I see the sun reflecting off the ocean on my wedding day
I want children everywhere to know Jesus loves them
I am meticulous and warmhearted

I pretend I'm always with the ones I love
I feel Jesus wrapping his arms around me
I touch the soft, silky sand with my toes
I worry about what tomorrow will bring
I cry when things don't happen the way I think they should
I am meticulous and warmhearted

I understand that the most important things in life aren't things
I say Jesus is always there to hold your hand
I dream about being a stay-at-home mom
I try to put a smile on someone else's face
I hope the perfect guy will be standing on the beach waiting for me someday
I am meticulous and warmhearted

Ashley Janae Bents, Grade 9
Discovery Middle School, MN

I Am

I am insightful, methodical, and sometimes rather absurd
I wonder what challenges await me later in life
I hear 'Stockholm Syndrome' by Muse
I see that everything is good even if it doesn't seem so at first glance
I want Michigan to win the national title
I am insightful, methodical, and sometimes rather absurd

I pretend that I am a pro football player
I feel the laces of the ball as I catch a touchdown pass
I touch the button on my alarm clock to make it stop disturbing my dreams
I worry that I won't succeed in life
I cry when life begins to overwhelm
I am insightful, methodical, and sometimes rather absurd

I understand that sometimes change is imminent
I say that life would be boring without change, though we often dislike it
I dream of warm pancakes and sausage on a snow day
I try to do my best, but often become a perfectionist in the process
I hope we will have hope
I am insightful, methodical, and sometimes rather absurd

Alex Adrian, Grade 7
Holy Family Parish School, WI

5 Ways of Looking at a Smile

A bright light filling a dark room with radiant light.
One flower filled with bright colors in the middle of a grassy field.
A memory that will make the whole day worth while.
The little thing that will take away all the stress and frustration in the day and
    turn it into happiness and joy.
The one thing that can never be replaced.

Caroline Young, Grade 7
Holy Family Parish School, WI

Destiny
Faster
Chasing, running
Adrenaline pumping
so close to the goal
So far from the prize
down the wooded path you run
hunting, seeking
just out of reach
not knowing, just feeling
believing, not seeing
creating life, causing death
honoring heroes, disgracing fools
come my sweet
destiny

Alex Eckert, Grade 8
St Odilia School, MN

Set Free
Though they may be gone
They never really leave
Their love, their caring, their kindness
Can all be set free

The tears you cry will guide them
The love you have will stay
The pain that hurts so much
Will always be repaid

And now you cannot see them
But you'll always feel their touch
The loved one that you lost
Will always mean so much

Gabrielle Koel, Grade 9
Discovery Middle School, MN

The Big Show
The curtain rises
And I feel all those eyes
Staring back at me!
My heart is pounding
The stress is mounting
As I do my right-split-leap
The audience ooo's and ahh's
Then comes the applause!
I know they're proud of me
As I take my bow
WOW! WOW! WOW!
I did it! I did it!
ME!

Meredith Turner, Grade 8
Ashby Public High School, MN

My Grandpa
My Grandpa had a busy life
with 14 kids and a lovely wife.
Seven girls, and seven boys
can you imagine all the toys?!

I never got to meet my Grandpa.
I only got to meet my Grandma.
I've seen pictures and heard stories,
but of all different categories.

Like when he was a child,
acting crazy and wild!
To when he was a guy,
now living up in the sky.

I really miss my Grandpa,
But at least I have a Grandma.

Anna Dvorak, Grade 8
Black Hawk Middle School, MN

Brightly Shining
I am silver or gold
I am beautiful and bright
I sound like a bird
I can sing alone
Or with a friend
I am quiet
I am loud
I am slow
I am fast
I can sound like a chime
Blowing in the wind
Native Americans played me long ago
When I was made from wood or bone
Until I was made from silver and gold
Then I shone brighter
As beautiful as before
I am a flute

Michaela Hertling, Grade 7
Wabasso Public School, MN

Fear
A boy walks down a dark street
His heart a beat
Badump, badump
As shadows
Dance and prance
Birds squawk
And ghosts haunt
BUT WHY?
During the day?
The fear, goes away
Is fear just an illusion
That's my conclusion

Nathaniel Gillen, Grade 8
All Saints Catholic School, MN

Insecure
Do you really love me
Or is it all a joke
Do you really care
Or do you just pretend
Do you really want to hear it
Or do you just tune me out
Do you really want to see me
Or do your eyes burn at the sight of my face
Do you really want to be my friend
Or do you just feel bad
How will I ever know what is truth
And what is false
I guess for now I'll have to go along with it
And maybe someday I won't feel so
INSECURE

Courtney Wosepka, Grade 9
Discovery Middle School, MN

Knowing
I am the feeling you feel
When you know
That somehow
some way
You are tied to someone
Even if you don't know
Who or what
They are.
You just know
They need you.
It may never make sense.
But when it happens you'll know.
'They need help,' you'll feel it.
'Cause I never fail.
I'm the oddity.

Kelly B. Susa, Grade 7
Lincoln Jr/Sr High School, WI

Tragedy
Screaming voices
Loud noises
Blaring sirens
People crying
Broken glass
Huge crash
Great explosion
Sliding erosion
Comforting words
To people hurt
Falling tears
Many fears
Loving sympathy
Terrible enemy
This is what happens in a tragedy.

Molly Barton, Grade 9
Grand Rapids High School, MN

Candy Land

I lay in a land full of
Gumdrops,
Candy canes,
Sweet tarts,
Lollipops,
And rainbow Nerds
Endless fields of candy powdered snow
Across as far as my eyes can see.

Strawberry milkshake creeks and little waterfalls
Flow through the deep made ditches
Gingerbread houses and Gingerbread people
Line the land
Frosted snowmen waving wherever you go.

Cotton candy clouds sail endlessly across
The endless swirling sweet atmosphere.

Candy cane sleds and Lifesaver tubes
Sled down the tall hills of stacks and stacks of candy
Little kids made of frosting
That is why Candy land is the place for me.

Brandon Vetrone, Grade 7
Lincoln Jr/Sr High School, WI

Your Sport

Intensity rises, it's time to play your game
Back to the court, you won't leave here the same

It's the championships, you're down by two
Coach yells for us to want it, because it's nothing new

Your teammates cheer, we wanted this from the start
The pressure is on, just play with your heart

Push away the bruises you will see tomorrow
Don't think too much, stop your sorrow

Become a warrior, look at the score
Don't mind it, just play your sport

Chelsey Skluzacek, Grade 9
Montgomery Lonsdale High School, MN

Volleyball Tryouts

Stiff, clumsy, sore
I didn't get out of bed the day before
Nervous, pale, sick
I hope it's me they pick
Shaken, red faced, un-new
I didn't make the team because I had the flu
Tired, hurt, sad
I can feel myself getting mad
Cold, alone, crying
Nothing left, just keep trying.

Cassie Greening, Grade 7
Shakopee Area Catholic School, MN

Abandoned

My name is Abandoned.
I live in the house of Lost Hope.
My favorite game is the quiet game.
My soul is hidden,
By an unreadable mask.
Silence covers the thoughts inside.
My favorite color of eye shadow is,
The deep concealing shade of indigo.
My eyes are full of sorrow.
My mouth is full of secretive words.
My heart is full of pain and denial.
My hands are like paper.
My eyebrows are your every happiness.
They know you don't appreciate the many things you have.
Your smile, cursing me into a bottomless pit.
My favorite food is oatmeal.
Because the world is,
Bland, plain, and pointless to me anyway.
I drive on dismal roads,
But I love to stroll in the valley of silence and beasts.
Because I am abandoned.

Angelica Lane, Grade 7
Greenfield Middle School, WI

Why Does It Matter?

Why does it matter? Please let me be.
No need to be mad, just let me be me.
Why does it matter? What I do,
What I feel, who I am to you?
Why does it matter? If I'm having fun,
When I'm doing no good, doing no wrong.
Why does it matter? What have I done to you?
You treat me like nothing, but I am something I tell you.
Why does it matter? Who I become in the future,
Who I was in the past, it's present now, forget the rest.
Why does it matter? If new questions arouse,
Sending new ideas up and around.
Why does it matter? If I'm doing nothing wrong,
If there is nothing to do, no things to be done.
Why does it matter? Don't you see?
There's nothing you can do to change me.
So why does it matter? Just let me be.
I'm not a cold empty shell, I am me!
So why does it matter anyway? I am fresh and free,
And it doesn't matter, because I am being me.

Michaela Gombar, Grade 8
McKinley Middle School, WI

I Have Nothing to Lose

I have nothing to lose when I jam to music.
I have nothing to lose when I dance around the kitchen.
I have nothing to lose when I sing along with the radio.
I have nothing to lose when I'm exhausted and the song is over.
I'm not a rock star yet... so I have nothing to lose.

Molly Pass, Grade 7
Shakopee Area Catholic School, MN

The Dream of Martin Luther King

Hear me as I tell you a thing
About a man they call Martin Luther King.
On March fourth nineteen sixty eight
Lay dead a man who was so great.

Martin Luther was a peaceful man
Him and the people would walk hand and hand.
I looked into Martins eyes and could see something true
The legendary love he had for me and you.

King stayed at the Lorraine Motel booked in 306
At 6:01 King was standing on the second floor balcony.
When a shot rang out with the triggers clicks
When the world heard of this every man fell to their knee.

After chest surgery he was lying in the bed
7:05 is when he was announced dead.
When this great man spoke
The goodness of mans heart awoke.
And that is why I believe in the dream
Of this great man, Martin Luther King.

Savannah Ramos, Grade 8
Jerstad Agerholm Middle School, WI

Country Sunset

Long shadows prance across the soil,
like panthers stalking helpless prey.
A gleaming sphere of fire
faintly illuminates the sky.
Waves of heat slither through the dimming light
as if snakes across fine-grained sand.
In the house, a light goes off,
like an idea, suddenly forgotten.
Clouds roll across the stars,
engulfing their shimmering light.
The darkening figures of trees loom in the distance,
dancing like ballerinas across the ground.
As the horizon gulps down the last breath of light,
dreary creatures are swept into the land of good night.

Aidan McCarty, Grade 7
Brookfield Academy, WI

My Sad Story

Why oh Rocco did you have to go.
You were so nice, everyone should know.

Why did you get those tumors, why oh why?
We attempted to save you, we really did try.

If we kept you, you'd be in so much pain.
It would hurt so bad you would go insane.

I miss you so much, Rocco, you were like a true human guy.
But still, oh why oh why, Rocco, did you have to die?

Chase Rizo, Grade 7
Shakopee Area Catholic School, MN

Disappear

I likely shouldn't be here I'm a mess,
Everything is getting to me because all this stress.
I hardly ever know what to say,
When my emotions get in the way.
I can never get the words I need to convey,
Im trying to get us on the same page when I can't.
I always try to get it better afterward,
When all the wrong impressions are said and heard.
I wish I could explain,
But nothing's ever the same.
I know I don't say all the right words,
Maybe I giggle at the wrong time.
Sometimes I may curse and whine,
The last thing I want is to let you down.
All that I wanted was to make you proud,
I can't clarify why I act this way.
I know I don't make all the best moves,
If I can let the trees do the talking,
And I can let the ground do the walking.
I can let my mouth do the listening,
So can I just let the memories disappear.

Aleta Davannavong, Grade 8
Oak Grove Middle School, MN

Don't Blend into the Wallpaper

Black and white is monotonous and exceedingly boring.
change it.
Add a simple pop of color, and then you'll break away.
From the torrents of your soul,
through the chambers of your heart,
across the deep seas of your mind,
and around the fabrications of your body.
You are you, no one else.
Many people's goal in life is to be immaculate and perfect,
but the truth of it is perfection is nothing but a myth.
Inside everyone is a distinct, authentic human being,
they just need to show their true colors.
Uniqueness is respectable,
originality is key.
Break away from the wallpaper,
and then you'll be set free!

Rikki Doers, Grade 9
Lincoln Jr/Sr High School, WI

Dad

Hardworking,
Hazel eyes and light brown curly hair.
Owning several companies,
But all is for his family.
A farmer building fences and growing crops for his cattle.
Grilling ribs or pork tenderloin are his specialties.
A man strong in his faith for the Lord,
Serving Him by going on mission trips to Peru.
A busy man.

April Disher, Grade 9
Rosholt Middle-High School, WI

Halloween

Pumpkins are orange
Skeletons are white,
On their wicked brooms
Witches take a flight.

On Halloween day
The children eat a lot,
They yell *trick-or-treat*
With a big loud knock.

Zombies rise from the dead
Ghosts come from below,
Ghouls let out a huge scream
And out a yell you will blow.

You see monsters comin'
When the night turns black,
You should just run away
And never come back!!
Jordan Phillips, Grade 8
Messmer Preparatory Catholic School, WI

Dance

I look at everybody's feet
They move to the beat.
While I struggle to keep up
My feet mess up

Right step, left step,
Shuffle step

It's just too hard to be
On guard!

My feet going out of control
My tears running down my face,

"I can do it!" I said without a doubt,
While I manage to figure it out!
What a great dance class
To explore did you learn
A lesson or did you ignore?
Sydney Poshusta, Grade 7
Shakopee Area Catholic School, MN

Standing There

There they stand in front of the gate
Their faces down in hope.
No time is left for them to go
The night has come, the sky is dark.
Their hope has gone for now
Until tomorrow has come.
Their families are there to go along.
For their job isn't done until they are home.
Joe Salzman, Grade 9
Fall River High School, WI

Lost Soul

My mind's spinning because I don't know what to do
My heart's beating so hard you could hear it across a room
My vision gets blurry and my soul empties

I notice the first tear drop and try to hold it back
It builds up so fast, I start bawling my eyes out
I begin to hyperventilate as my body tries to control my sorrow

The memories my mind's sorting through
And the moments my heart's craving for
Are making the tears come faster

My legs feel like Jell-O and I collapse to the floor
I curl up in a ball and rock back and forth,
Trying to convince myself that it's just a dream

I close my eyes and see his face
He has no expression to it,
Because he and I know we can't see each other anymore

I start trembling because I can't handle the pain and suffering any longer
The feelings I had for you are lost in a deep, dark hole that I yearn for
We both know that we have to move on…

But if it's meant to be, somehow we'll find each other
Livia Desylvester, Grade 8
All Saints Catholic School, MN

What a Day

One day I was enjoying a new autumn day
By walking along on a grass-covered trail.
The beautiful orioles were chirping above where the dead leaves lay
When all of a sudden, a major gust pushed a gigantic hay bale my way.

I jumped back and hit a decaying wooden fence.
Behind the fence an abandoned farmhouse stood.
Along the abandoned farmhouse, Sandy Creek flew by;
And on the front porch sat a rocking chair.
Then it started to mist, which I knew meant rain, so I ran to the farmhouse.

As the rolling thunderheads rumbled above me,
And the rain plunged into the soil,
I sprinted toward the old farmhouse.
Suddenly, a thought raced through my mind,
"I am a visitor and shouldn't enter."
But as I thought about the menacing storm,
It made me run even faster.

When I finally reached the house,
I turned to look at the storm.
As I turned, the sun peeked through the clouds,
The rain stopped, the storm slowed,
And that day, I didn't have to enter that scary farmhouse.
Nicole Szyszka, Grade 9
Jordan Sr High School, MN

Isn't That Weird

Why is our world turning into nature's nightmare; trees being cut down and animals taken from their homes?

Why is the human race complaining of the earth being destroyed when we are the first to destroy it?

Isn't it weird?

Why do we watch one suffer when we know they need help?

And why aren't we there when our suffering needs healing?

Isn't that weird?

Why are we the first to throw stones when we are one in the same?

And why are we the ones quick to hurt one another when we fight not to be hurt?

Isn't that weird?

Every day we destroy what we built, what we are so lucky to have.

Isn't it weird?

Every day we fight for what's right and yet we do the wrong!

Isn't it weird?

The world is a strange place and so are the people in it.

Kyle Samuelson, Grade 7
Lakewood Elementary School, WI

All the Way Gone

As I sit in these ugly colored gray seats as I stare out the window
looking at houses, trees, and everything else.

Then I received a message on my phone that was from my best friend.
The message said she was moving 2 weeks, 2 weeks!

Two weeks go by fast and then when I see her I didn't realize my best friend was moving in a week or 2.
A week passed and today was her last day.

I want to cry, but I won't because I don't want people to know.
She was my friend, my best friend, and now I'm never going to see her again.

The days are over and still now we say goodbye…
and she is all the way gone.

Lacey Winters, Grade 7
Necedah Middle School, WI

Autumn's Gift

With a blurry reflection, Milford Pond stared back at me.

Rolling thunderheads growled and screamed across the land, making immense vibrations that shook the valley.

Particles of mist sprinkled the grass that sparkled and shined when the sunlight hit the blades.

In the silence, a white, rickety fence guarded its chosen territory.

Whispering winds played a muffled tune through the cracked exterior of an abandoned farmhouse.

As the sun began to slowly rise, a feathered visitor chirped a smooth melody.

Leaves wrestled against the ground and some triumphed as they flew into the striped sky, amber jewels.

As it danced through the trees, the delicate breeze made the sound of a creaking rocking chair.

Grass-covered trails led to a pool of white sand and blue silk.

As the sun rose, a spider's web glistened, and the spider was awakening from a quiet night.

Apples on trees gleamed a crimson glow.

On their way to blossoms, bees buzzed and fluttered around obstacles.

Some milkweed swayed from side to side as the wind tenderly pushed the stalks.

Ivory tufts exploded from the pods and floated on a breeze, only to settle on autumn's sun-drenched gifts that October morning.

Kelly Gindorff, Grade 9
Jordan Sr High School, MN

Dreaming of Tomorrow

Tomorrow, I want to seek out the perfect tree,
Prickly branches and all,
But for today, I guess I'll search high and low for Dad's saw…
If only it could just hear my call!

Tomorrow, I want to string up twinkling, dancing lights,
But for today, I guess I'll untangle them.
Hey, three aren't shining! That's not right!

Tomorrow, I want to string popcorn and cranberries,
But for today, I guess I'll just eat the popcorn,
"May I please?"

Tomorrow, I want to relive the days of the wise men,
Following the star,
But for today, I guess I'll place the star on the top of our tree,
Up so, so far.

Tomorrow, I want to find next year's tree,
Go on the tree hunt all over again,
But for today, I guess I'll wait 'till next year —
Will this time never end!?

Brooke Noah, Grade 8
Thorp Middle School, WI

Baseball

Today's game is going to be amazing
A baseball game is what I'm craving

You can try and swing but it's going to be a strike either way
That's what the kids on the other team have to say

Then I come up to bat, trying to forget what they say
Here comes the pitch, CRACK, I blow the team away

Here I come rounding third base
Then I score and rub it in their face

As I walk into the dugout
My team begins to scream and shout

Isaak Lipetzky, Grade 7
Shakopee Area Catholic School, MN

Volleyball

Thud!
The echo of a volleyball rebounding off skin fills the gym
Should I go for the ball, or do I dare?
The ball hovers over the net,
Bump, set, spike!
Yeah!
We all jump for joy as we complete this difficult task.
The scoreboard reveals the great victory…
We won!
That was a nice dream.

Bianca Peterson, Grade 8
All Saints Catholic School, MN

Time

Time,
It flies by,
It goes slow,
Sometimes I think to myself, "Oh no! Where did the time go?"
And
Sometimes I think to myself, "Why is the clock so slow?"
It's almost as if the world has stopped,
And all you hear is "Tick! Tock!"
Time is a form of hatred
It messes with your head,
Like when you try to sleep,
You lay there counting sheep,
While the clock just sits there mocking you,
Time is a description of your life
And the fight — you fight out of self pity.
Time is life,
Life is time,
Your time is short
But others are shorter,
Just stop and think…
Live for the others.

Ericka Polar, Grade 8
Trinity Lutheran School, WI

Autumn's Bounty

With scarlet and ivory leaves covering the ground,
Fall brings forth a comforting and mysterious time.
A menacing scarecrow towers in the cornfield
As he protects his harvest.
The black nights creep in, bringing gusts of unpredictable
Yet peaceful winds.
Wild turkeys roam outside the fence,
While on the other side, Breezy Creek rushes along its path.
Halloween night sends chills down spines;
Yet, cozy firepits bring close friends together.
The last acorns quiver in the trees,
As squirrels and chipmunks ruthlessly capture food for winter.
The abandoned granary eerily looms in the field,
But reminds us all of the coming harvest.
Fall brings forth a comforting yet mysterious time.

Hallie Anderson, Grade 9
Jordan Sr High School, MN

That Giant Buck

One day I told my friend
this story from start to end
about that buck up on my wall
hanging there so broad, so tall
I hear a noise, I can hear him walk,
right at me, while I try not to talk
my heart starts pounding harder and harder
from the adrenaline of seeing that giant monster
the buck was so big you would say I'm a liar
but now I have proof cause I saw him then fired.

Nick Prahl, Grade 7
Shakopee Area Catholic School, MN

The Christmas Play

Red and green have filled the room.
Many bodies, some with gloom,
Shivers of worries, and whispers of fright,
Goodies and cookies to last the whole night.
You can hear sighs of relief as children start to settle,
The piano player takes her place, foot on the pedal.
We take our seats while the children line up,
They are tense but very ready.
It begins.
The lights go on, and the music starts.
Lines are recited.
Angel wings glistening in the light,
Children are anxious for their part to come.
All is well, and faces are filled with cheer,
For now that is it,
We all can hardly wait until next year.

Shelby Hurst, Grade 7
Thorp Middle School, WI

Not Your Song

Tell me you love me, say it out loud,
Hug me so gently, blocking the crowd,
Whisper my name, so delicately,
Or is that too lame, for your friends to see?
Are you ashamed, did I do you wrong?
Is this my fault, like all the love songs?
The perfect guy, so kind and so loving,
It made me sigh, at the sound of your voice,
But just as it's perfect, something goes bad,
Then me as the girl, I have to be sad,
I'm supposed to beg, say I want you back,
It's part of the song, but those lyrics I lack,
I won't cry or mourn, 'cuz you were wrong,
It's my heart that's torn, so don't lead me on,
The lyrics are changed, so don't come along,
Saying you're different, 'cuz this ain't your song.

Maddie Zumbach, Grade 8
Valley Middle School, MN

Nature Is Restored

Indoors, lamps take the place of sunlight
Outside, lustrous diamonds are set in black velvet
Moonlight streams down on a bat in mid-flight
The curtain has risen, the stage is set.
A wolf howls mournfully at night's white eye
Alone and desolate atop the hill.
The powerful zephyr carries his cry
Ears prick up at the noise, and then are still.
The silence is broken, the night unfolds,
Now going back to an earlier day
Before man wielded fire, when beasts were bold
And little creatures roamed about unafraid.
Such is the darkness so many abhor;
Until Dawn's first light, nature is restored.

Philip Steigerwald, Grade 8
Pilgrim Park Middle School, WI

Halloween

Halloween is here
BEWARE
Witches fly
Across the sky
Pumpkins stare
With their evil glare
Ghosts and goblins come out at night
Waiting to give kids a fright
Monsters and aliens sneak around
Skeletons and vampires emerge from the ground
Halloween is here
BEWARE

Abby Emch, Grade 8
St Odilia School, MN

You and Me

You see me stare
You see me look
But you can't see
How much you mean to me
Why can't you understand?
You're the only person I care about
You're the only person I want to love
You go for those girls but they don't
Know you like I do
We flirt so much people think we like each other
So why can't you understand
I want you to hold me forever

Caitlyn Cantero, Grade 9
Fall River High School, WI

Journey Back in Time to See

To journey back in time
Read the lines
To see shoe shiners
And bookbinders
To see blacksmiths
And monster myths
To hear a great speech
Or walk on an unknown beach
All you need to do
Is read a book that is true
And it will take you on a journey back in time to see
What there is to be.

Katelyn Litke, Grade 8
Cloquet Middle School, MN

War

War is like a messy room because it never gets cleaned
Up until the mom or kid wins in the fight.
And when it gets cleaned up
The room gets messy in a matter of days.
Which all that means is another war starts.
So I think the U.S.A. should clean up its room.

Anthony Seebruck, Grade 7
Necedah Middle School, WI

Red Fruit

These mortals play God
For what they don't know
And yet they think
They know all
Give them a grain of sand
And they think they hold the world
But all they obtained is a sin
One of pride not deserved

They know little if not nothing
And for this
They seek knowledge
And twist around their humanity
Their simple desires take them over
Leaving them to die a little inside

But humanity was lost long ago
For the knowledge they sought was held in a package
A package of red and sweet desire
The one bite left them full
But empty of truth

Rosemarie Konkol, Grade 9
Armstrong High School, MN

A December Day

I walk outside,
trudging around in the heavy snow,
cold air in my lungs.
It is completely quiet except for
the occasional howling of the wind
and the soft breeze on my face.
I feel cold snow on my hands,
and the soft insides of my warm boots.
I smell the scent of evergreen trees,
and hear my family beckoning me inside.
I dash inside and taste hot chocolate,
and smell fresh cookies coming out of the oven.
I feel the heat of the blazing fire in the fireplace,
and fall peacefully asleep in my warm bed.

James McSweyn, Grade 8
St John Neumann School, WI

Gymnastics

I see, the floor.
I see, the beam.
I see, the vault.
I see, the bars.
I see, myself spinning through the air on the floor.
I see, my legs as straight as a pin on beam.
I see, my hangs bounce off on vault.
I see, my hands all chalky on bars.
My heart is beating,
And the next thing I knew I won!

Emily Clysdale, Grade 8
St Odilia School, MN

Good-bye

At first it didn't hit me
That you were really gone
I hid my tears and sadness
And pretended that there was nothing wrong
But now I understand
That you're in a better place
I just wish that I,
Could still see your shining face
I will always love you
I thought you'd want to know
You're up with God in heaven
But it still hurts me to let you go

Sarah Connell, Grade 9
Discovery Middle School, MN

Good Bye

No amount of words;
Can describe how you feel.
The pain inside me;
Is too powerful and real.
He was good and kind;
But now he is at his end.
To gracious heavens;
Our love we send.
When good-byes are said before they are due;
Friendships remain, they are only being renewed.
Even though he is too far away to see;
Just know that he loves you, and he is finally free.

Abby Braun, Grade 8
Silverbrook Middle School, WI

Memories

Sitting in the moonlight by a vast open lake,
under the ice the memories of first light remain.
I think I'm in one place but appear in another, I stand up,
Look around and a Horcrux is underwater.
You look for a red bracelet of a broken family chain
Or try to kill away your enemies' last remains.
All of the sudden you appear in a meadow,
You see a small girl with red hair and freckles.
Then you see a man fall from the tallest tower,
While a special wand changes its powers.
In the end a family is reunited, and a war brings triumph
With deaths memorable, and unforgotten.

Hanna Gregorio, Grade 9
Fall River High School, WI

Her Perfect Imperfections

My best friend
Looks in the dusty full length mirror
Hanging on her wall in the room in which she sleeps
Every morning when she opens her hazel eyes
To pick out every perfect imperfection she wishes to fix.

Carrissa Ann Wright, Grade 9
Rosholt Middle-High School, WI

The Undesired

Many people judge you, make fun of you,
And spread rumors about you.
Make you feel like you are two inches tall, worthless,
Insecure, heartless, unloved the undesired.
But have you ever thought,
That maybe there's something wrong
No they aren't puzzles that you can just piece together
They are human beings with feelings
But do you see that?
They don't care how it affects you
All they care about is looking good
But it hurts inside, it hurts so badly
That you don't want to even wake up anymore.
How do you think we get cutters?
Emos, and Goths in this world?
They express themselves the only way they know how.
You make them the way they are.
By labeling them, you set an imaginary line
In which they are too afraid to cross.

Aly Gerber, Grade 9
Lincoln Jr/Sr High School, WI

The End

Throw open the door
I'm not staying here.
Get in my car, never
looking back in the rearview mirror.

Every bad day, every silver tear
doesn't mean much to you.
With all those lies to people,
you make me look like a damn fool.

I'm leaving, I can't stay here.
You could consider me already gone.
I'm so confused and stupid.
I should've left at dawn.

Now I'm driving full speed
never to look back again.
Phone's shut off, don't try and call
hasta la vista, goodbye, shutting down, the end.

Jordyn Sachtjen, Grade 8
Manawa Middle School, WI

A New Day

The mist rises off the water now.
The new day is haunting me somehow.
The moon is escaping out of sight.
While the dawn approaches, signaling end of night.
You never know what will happen this day.
But you want to remember it in a good way.
Do something that will always make you proud.
Do something good here, help someone out now.

Marianna Esveld, Grade 9
Fall River High School, WI

Dream Away

During the night I count the sheep
I hear nothing, not even a peep

The sky turns black and fades away
The moon glows like a bright ray

As I shut my eyes and begin to dream
I think of wonderful, peaceful scenes

Magical and bright the characters are
They truly belong up with the stars

The night suddenly comes to an end
The memorable characters are now my friends

Hush now
Dream away…

Halle Erickson, Grade 7
Shakopee Area Catholic School, MN

Anger

When I am mad, it all bursts out.
It bottles up inside, until it gets big and stout.
When it explodes, all my feelings are set free,
I get mad again for hurting the ones around me.
It doesn't help when they encourage my anger,
Because it listens and becomes major.
My anger seems to have a mind of its own.
Sometimes I get angry for no reason alone.
Why has this burden been placed upon me?
For all I want is to be happy.
Sometimes I cry, but it's the anger talking.
Once in a while I calm by walking.
I'm not always angry though. I'm happy a lot.
It's just when someone tips it off,
I start to get very, very hot.
It may seem to you that I have an anger issue,
When all I really need is a friend and a tissue.

Catelyn LaCour, Grade 8
Round Lake High School, MN

Elders

Precious as a jewel,
but delicate as glass.
They come from a historical time,
but they're built to last.
Their memory, generally a sponge,
holding dear memories, but leaving others forgotten.
Being sociable and speaking to you,
with a voice as soft as cotton.
Their hands, sleeping on their lap,
until they want to shake yours.
"Please visit again," is their last request,
and, indeed, it's an easy made chore.

Mark Leonard, Grade 7
St Stephen's Catholic School, MN

Charred Remains

The rolling thunderheads complemented the swirling mist in the great storm.
It had started out as a clear autumn day when we saw the storm approach.
We had wandered down by Silver Creek just before we saw the dazzling lightning draw near.
Sprinting toward home, we rushed over the barbed wire fence.
The lightning struck an abandoned farmhouse, and it went up in a roaring blaze.
A large wind came up and spread the fire to some nearby trees.
Startled by the immense heat, the seagulls were screeching in a very peculiar way.
The leaves on the gigantic oaks were shriveling up in the immense heat.
A visitor to our home shuddered, awestruck as the barn was razed by fire.
The only thing left in the barn, a rocking chair that my grandpa made me the year before he died,
sat among the charred remains.
Soon, the fire was traveling down the grass-covered trail toward our house.
We were next on its list to devour.

Jake Andersen, Grade 9
Jordan Sr High School, MN

A Cozy Christmas

As I sit by the window, it snows
I see the thousands of twinkling Christmas lights that line the bushes all the way down my block
The radio hums next to me softly playing carols
Downstairs the stocking are all hung and the Christmas tree is decorated
There is an expectant feeling in the air, as if we will suddenly see St. Nicholas bounding down the chimney
As we walk out the door to make snow angels, snowmen, and have snowball fights, Jack Frost nips at our noses
When we come in all tired and hungry we munch the goodies and sip hot chocolate while
We wait for the pork roast to finish cooking
After dinner we are filled to the brim but there is yet room for dessert
We have snicker doodles and goodies that came in our stocking that morning
We wind down by playing some card games and cribbage
My cousin and I giggle in our beds until early in the morning without a wink of sleep the whole time
A perfect fairy tale Christmas once more

Laurel Adams, Grade 7
Holy Family Parish School, WI

The Howling of Halloween Night

The moon lightened the black night.
I lay back down in the cornfield, counting the starts above me.
When I looked to my right, I found a scarecrow watching the field.
The water of Firefly Creek was moving slowly and calmly.
When I heard the metal gate hit the fence pole, the notes became songs in the moonlight.
When I looked up the hill, I found an abandoned granary.
The calm but howling wind was blowing the mist into circles.
It knocked down leaves and rolled them across the road.
The squirrels were snacking on acorns from the tree above.
In the field, I heard the turkey gobbling.
I see the other side of the hill, and I felt the warm, toasty fire pit smoke around me.
Pumpkins arrived and stared, trick-or-treating screaming of the frightening Halloween night.

Meredith Hyatt, Grade 9
Jordan Sr High School, MN

The Meadow

I know these things:
My life is like a meadow
The sweet song of sparrows and robins
And the hummed tune of the crickets
Is the music that rushes through my soul,
Like a good friend, pulling me up
When I feel down and always
With me when I'm happy.

I know these things:
Sometimes it will storm,
And the things that make this meadow radiant will hide.
The flowers that bloom with myriad hues will close up.
The fauna that give it a life; a pulse, will take shelter.
And the great cyan ceiling will fade to an ashen frown.
And all that will remain is a field of shadows.

I know all of these things.
But I also know
That after every rain, without fail,
There is a rainbow.

Kenzie Webster, Grade 9
Woodbury Sr High School, MN

Baseball Rumble

The pitcher throws the ball.
The umpire makes the call.

The catcher throws it back,
And the pitcher plans his attack.

The pitcher's attack is swift,
The defender feels its drift.

The batter bounces the ball down the line,
The third baseman gets to it in time.

He picks it up looking to make the out.
The batter is running he'll make it no doubt.

Robby Deziel, Grade 8
All Saints Catholic School, MN

Alone

As the November sun begins to set,
The white haired, wrinkled, and bent woman sits alone.
She sits on a rocking chair on her front porch.
She sits there even with rolling thunderheads and mist.
She just gazes as gusts of wind rustle the autumn leaves.
The robins search for worms in front of her weathered farmhouse.
She likes listening to Sherman's Creek run through her yard
As she waits for any visitor to come up the grass-covered trail
And through the old white fence.
As the November sun disappears over the horizon
The old woman still sits… Alone.

Morgan Huss, Grade 9
Jordan Sr High School, MN

Winter

We walk through the door, and it's instantly warm,
My sister's cheeks red as a rose.
The white winter world disappears behind us,
it's snow soaked right through our clothes.
Into the kitchen where it's warm and it's dry,
hot chocolate is just being served.
Who couldn't love this, who can't enjoy?
To me, that would be absurd.
Decorations wait to be put on the tree,
there are tinsel, bulbs, and a star.
Lights are strung on, the tree looks great.
For this, some people travel far.
At last, I'm dry and finally warm,
with a book, I sit by the fire.
This time that I love in the Christmas season,
fulfills my every desire.

Maeve McDonald, Grade 8
St John Neumann School, WI

Life Is Like a Quilt

Life is like a quilt.
Each piece so strongly built.
Sometimes you may have a knot.
And wished that you never had gotten caught.
It represents things you love.
And the things you want to be free of.
Someday this quilt will rip.
Tough times will make you slip.
The pieces may be any size.
Someday your luck may rise.
This quilt was a present,
To show what her life really meant.
It represents the good and bad,
Many pieces are striped and plaid.
This quilt took a lot of endeavor,
So she will live on forever and ever.

Maggie Larson, Grade 9
Lincoln Jr/Sr High School, WI

Life

Life is a thing that sometimes isn't at all fair.
Life includes people who really don't care.

Life is something that can get on my nerves.
Life can also include low-life jerks.

Every single day my life is the same.
People can breeze through it, like it's some kind of game.

Sometimes you don't appreciate others.
But together, we are all sisters and brothers.

In life, there are people who are crude and mean.
But, you just have to deal with it when you're a teenager like me.

Emily Goodhall, Grade 8
McKinley Middle School, WI

Becoming Snow

The morning mist rolled slowly over the cold ground.
It flowed through the spaces in the wobbly fence with the peeling white paint.
It passed the unstable farmhouse where warm fires once burned.
A dusty rocking chair creaked in the same spot it had sat for the longest time.
A "Home Sweet Home" mat was lying in front of the door to greet any visitors,
But the only visitors nowadays were the woodland animals and the fog itself.
The old owners used to sit on the porch and watch the approaching thunderheads.
The slight breeze that made the rocking chair creak annoyingly, now pushed the fog from the decking.
It flowed downward on a grassy path toward a ravine.
The trickling nose of Wishbend Creek came accompanied by the songs of the cardinals.
As the fog oozed slowly onto the water, the flow took mist with it, away from the farm.
When the fog hit the sunlight it slowly evaporated into the atmosphere.
The next day the fog returned, but not as fog.
It had become a white fluffy blanket, the first blanket of snow of the season.

Nick Haeg, Grade 9
Jordan Sr High School, MN

Listen

Listen!
As the wind whips its way through the tree branches, shaking and rattling, snapping and tearing.
Listen!
As the lonely owl "hoos" through the night, echoing distantly, hauntingly,
through the thin black fabric of midnight's quilt which lays around the world now.
Listen!
As the call of a loon, so distant from shore, echoes over the water, residing in your heart and soul,
so calmly, so peacefully, setting you at ease.
Listen!
To the quiet lapping of the waves upon the shore, upon a piece of driftwood, upon a distant dock,
and maybe the one next door too.
Listen!
As the cricket plays his harmonious song, joining in a whole orchestra, singing a lullaby in the pure, rich, blackness of nighttime.
Listen

Micala Burns, Grade 8
Oak Grove Middle School, MN

The Changing Seasons

Large thunderheads charge toward the small town of Jordan.
On this dreary day, a light mist shines on all the fallen leaves from the rain showers the night before.
The normally shallow Jordan Creek rages through town, swollen from all the rainwater.
A soft breeze rolls by, predicting more rain.
It seems very silent without the birds chirping their morning songs.
A damaged abandoned farmhouse, which has seen its fair share of storms,
has taken the beating of the storm very well, and looks like it's bracing for another.
The fence that used to surround the house is long gone, blown away by the wind.
An old man sits on his childhood rocking chair and reminisces about his past.
A lost visitor and his two sons stumble up the jagged staircase to ask directions home.
His small children frolic in the prairie grass-covered trail, exploring the landscape.
On this autumn day, the clouds race by, and the sun comes out.
Everyone feels cheerful after they know they are safe, but that will not be the last of the storms.

Reece Oleson, Grade 9
Jordan Sr High School, MN

If Only

If only you would look into my eyes
See the joy, the fire
See the passion, and laughter
But you will never know me
For your soul is fraud, and tainted by society

If only you would look into my eyes
Instead of my outer self
But you could careless
For you only care about popularity

If only you would look into my eyes
See the need for acceptance and understanding
But your eyes are blinded
For your eyes are hazed, and will always be

If only…

Samantha Carver, Grade 9
Discovery Middle School, MN

Girls

When people hear my philosophy,
"Girls are a waste of time."
They think such a though is a catastrophe.
As if to think this thought is a crime.

Girls are demanding.
Time, money, and hearts are on the line.
Life, school, and work is commanding.
Self-esteem is on the decline.

People share their precious points with them.
Boy's hearts get broken.
They could write a book like "Anthem."
Girls say "Take this as a token."

Girls want to change us and have their way.
All us guys can do is pray.

Justin De Cleene, Grade 9
Bay Port High School, WI

6 Trucks

6 little kids
Play with 6 trucks
With 6 wheels on each truck
That has 6 little firemen in each truck
With 6 imaginary fires going on
The 6 trucks try and put them out
There are 6 people stuck in a building
6 firemen climb a ladder
It only took 6 minutes to put out the fire
The 6 people were rescued
But had to stay in a hospital for 6 days
They imagined 6 hours but it was only 6 minutes.

Nick Shoemaker, Grade 7
Lincoln Jr/Sr High School, WI

Darkside of the Sun

I used to laugh I used to talk I used to sleep
Until I saw the dark side of the sun
Now…I cry I falter but who cares
I cut I bleed I shatter but who cares

I used to sing I now believe
I used to try but now I die
I had a lot of fun not on the dark side of the sun

Nothing is equal not the same
But I'm dangerous maybe insane
I'm strong I have strength I stood up I fell

Yes I falter and shatter and maybe stutter
But they make me stronger
On the dark side of the sun
Yes I'm strange I have rage
I may cut but I fight

This is my home
It's my life it's my way of saying
I've been through a lot
But in the end, my mistakes
My pain, my heart can take it 'cause I'm strong
On the dark side of the sun.

Lola Alugo, Grade 8
Wayzata Central Middle School, MN

Life Is Like…

Life is like a roller coaster.
Sometimes it takes you to the top…
And sometimes it will take you to the bottom.

Sometimes you have to wait in line.
It takes patience and tolerance.
But it's always a wild ride.

Life is like ice cream.
Sometimes it's sweet and refreshing…
And sometimes it's drippy and messy.

Sometimes it's not so satisfying…
It may be warm and melting.
But you always have to get that last lick.

Life is like the ocean.
Sometimes it's calm and still…
And sometimes it's wild and wavy.

Sometimes you stand alone…
It may be tough and difficult.
But you're not the only fish in the sea.

Life is how you make it!

Lindsay Powell, Grade 8
Pilgrim Park Middle School, WI

A Job Well Done
Work
Hard, complex
Carrying, doing, checking
Knowledge, skills, hammer, boxes
Slowing, tiring, irritating
Happy, done
Play
Renae Bembenek, Grade 9
Rosholt Middle-High School, WI

From Life to Death
Life
Exciting, full
going, doing, seeing
Family, friends, pets, everything
Withering, graying, shrinking
Coffin, gone
Death
Erin Wierzba, Grade 9
Rosholt Middle-High School, WI

Time
Midnight,
Cold, night
Chilling, cooling, sleeping
Stars, moon, constellations, darkness
Learning, eating, sitting
Sun, day
Noon.
Jordan Dobbe, Grade 9
Rosholt Middle-High School, WI

Lizard
The leaves move as he begins to hide,
There is a large tree at his side,
The space between them not very wide.

If anything comes near,
He begins to fear,
Some screams you will hear.
Sarah Cook, Grade 8
Pilgrim Park Middle School, WI

My Brother's Bedroom
My brother's room reeks,
His socks really stink.
If I step in, I'm afraid I'll sink.
Piles and piles of junk,
I swear there is a dead skunk
Looks like he had run,
But now I think I'm going to run.
Haley Moore, Grade 8
McKinley Middle School, WI

The Terrible Tuskegee Study
Nobody likes secrets. They aren't any fun.
But not that long ago there was a terrible one.
It was kept from a bunch of men, 399 to be exact.
It never should have happened, and that is a fact.

They thought they had bad blood, or so they were told.
They really had syphilis. They shouldn't have enrolled.
Many people were affected. Twenty-eight men died.
They weren't given the cure. Penicillin was denied.

At least 40 women were infected, 19 kids contracted it at birth.
All those involved were black, but what were their lives worth?

They were poor and offered free healthcare. What would you have done?
Well they had taken it, and then the evil had begun.

They should have asked questions. They didn't think twice.
They thought it was free, but their life was the price.
There eventually came an apology, although it was 65 years late.
I suppose it's better late than never, but why'd those people have such a fate?

So now I ask, Why did it happen? They should have known it wasn't right.
They shouldn't have treated people like nothing, but they did in spite.
Danielle Ekker, Grade 9
Kewaskum High School, WI

A Little Like Me
I have a big brother who is not at all like me.
When he was little he never climbed a tree, this is not at all like me.
I would climb to the top and let out a scream.
I have a big brother who is not at all like me.
When he was little he liked to stay clean, this is not at all like me.
I planted flowers with Grandma I was never clean.
I have a big brother who is not at all like me.
He was always quiet, you never knew he was there, this is not at all like me.
I would run around screaming in my underwear.
I have a big brother who's a little like me.
When he plays cards he likes to win, this is a little like me.
When I win I sit and grin.
I have a big brother whose a little like me.
Even when we argue, he still loves me, this is a little like me.
Cymbria Sasman, Grade 7
Lincoln Jr/Sr High School, WI

The Catch
Crab fishermen risk their lives to bring home the riches
On a trip to Alaska, my grandparents picked up the live squirming crab
fresh out of the ships holding tank.
Before the crab is stuffed into a pot of boiling hot water,
they scream, holler, pinch, and scurry around the Styrofoam box.
I crush the legs in the crusher, pull the pincher, and eat the meat.
The wonderful butter lures me from miles away like doe scent lures a buck.
Large lively crab tastes like heaven on Earth.
I couldn't live without crab!
Austin Olson, Grade 7
Lincoln Jr/Sr High School, WI

Don't Let Me Go

I'm hypnotized,
I'm mesmerized,
My eyes don't lie,
Don't let me go.

I'm falling through a haze,
I'm desperate for yesterday,
I'm trying to hold on,
Don't let me go.

I touch your hand,
The rush again,
It still feels good,
Don't let me go.

I'm meant to be with you,
We'll break down all the barriers,
And overcome this wall,
You can stop all the fighting,
So please don't let me go.
Chelsey Knuth, Grade 8
Lake Shore Middle School, WI

I Am…

I am passionate and deep
I wonder why I'm here
I hear my heart breaking
I see it fall
I want to be loved
I am passionate and deep

I pretend I don't care
I feel everyone blames me
I touch my own soul
I worry everything gets worse
I cry because I can
I am passionate and deep

I understand only some things
I say live your life
I dream to find the truth
I try to do my best
I hope to understand everything
I am passionate and deep
Katelynn Dau, Grade 8
Marinette Middle School, WI

Horizon

Light falls behind the horizon,
the stars emerge,
the creatures of night crawl.
The moon shines bright watching,
and protecting in the darkness.
Ivy Anderson, Grade 8
St Odilia School, MN

Death

Death
Inescapable, unavoidable
Bringing a whole ray of emotions
Disbelief, relief, belief
Confusion, hate, love, understanding, pessimism, optimism

It's scary, but also amazing
It gives meaning to carry on the deeds of the dead and the spirit of life
Caring, loving, easy going, anything, everything

The good in the world works for her
But she loves the bad in it also
Because she fixes the bad so that
It has a chance at this thing called life

Some people believe there are few rules in life
For her, those were:
Be nice to everyone
Treat others how you want to be treated
Tyler Wastl, Grade 8
Black Hawk Middle School, MN

Faces of the Seasons

On a bitter freezing winter day,
    The white-washed fence glistened in the snow.
    The rocking chair sat on the porch of the abandoned farmhouse,
    Swaying back and forth in the cool winter breeze.

On a pleasant spring day, everything was waking up from its winter's nap.
    Soon the rolling thunderheads covered the sky.
    The rain started to drizzle over the thirsty earth.
    Within a matter of time, the grass-covered trail leading up to the house filled with water.

On a perfect summer day, the red robins sat on their perches.
    Their songs filled the warm dry air.
    The summer visitors were leaving as the days got shorter,
        and as the sunlight stopped warming them.

On a brisk autumn day, the morning mist covered the hillside,
    And the maples shed their burnt orange and burgundy leaves.
    Soon the freezing of Creeks Bend River signaled that this season too had come to an end.
Nick Hunstad, Grade 9
Jordan Sr High School, MN

Everyone's Different

We are all different in some way.
You meet different people every single day.
We all have different personalities,
That is part of reality.
Some people are odd and some are just strange.
And you have to deal with it because your personalities you cannot change.
So no matter how you look, or how you act,
Life can be strange and that is that.
Sydney Van Zeeland, Grade 8
Lakewood Elementary School, WI

It's Home, My Home

From the crisp air, to cooling waters,
From the hot sun, to the park's teeter-totter.
It's home, my home.
From the cozy cabins, to the day's end,
Spending time with my CRAZY family and sweet friends.
It's home, my home.
From sitting on the dock, to intense volleyball games,
From the fun fishing tubing that's insane.
From the night time play, to looking at the bright stars' light,
From the swimming around, to pretty sights.
It's home, my home.
From the early, sleep-in mornings, to intense night games,
From Apples to Apples, to a game of Mafia and being framed.
It's home, my home.
From the rustling creek, to skipping rocks,
From the stinky fish house, to dancing on the dock.
From the place I absolutely LOVE, I can't brag enough,
About this land, and the people I love.
This place I tell about,
It's home, MY HOME.

Nicole Lynch, Grade 8
Necedah Middle School, WI

Sunny Slope

Standing at the top looking down,
Like a sparkling white blanket,
It's beautiful through my eyes,
The wind is blowing, the only sound.

I could stare at this hill for years,
As I snowboard down, I have no fears.
Seeing the trees passing quickly by,
Holding my hat on as I fly.

Swiftly moving but fast I go,
I look around at the pure white snow.
Thinking of absolutely nothing at all,
Besides going faster, risking any fall.

Smiling as I look back at the peak,
Accomplishing my goals all over is what I seek.
My passion for snowboarding will never stop,
As I make my way right back to the top.

Kayla Laufenberg, Grade 9
Lincoln Jr/Sr High School, WI

Belfast

A long lasting war in the streets.
A light switching on and off.
A ticking bomb ready to explode.
A field of green and orange separated by a wall
of hate.
A unique picture that can never be copied.
A light that will never go out.

Riley Grossman, Grade 7
Holy Family Parish School, WI

My Mask

A year ago if you'd peered down deep inside my soul,
You'd find something different; you'd find I'd built a wall.
Perfect Claire, didn't care, what you said rolled off my back,
But that was just pretending, that was just my mask.
Every whisper, every sneer, got trapped behind that wall,
They rolled around inside my ears and tore away my soul.
I'd wake up every morning, snap that mask on to my face,
And screw on my smile, my laugh, it was all fake.
I pretended I couldn't hear you, your teasing and your calling,
But as soon as my mask came off, the tears would start falling.
Slowly, slowly, I pulled myself out of that deep hole,
I only did what I loved, not what the world saw as my role.
I can be who I want; I won't listen to your jeers,
That wall I'd built around my soul now became a shield.
I don't need to be perfect; I just try my very best,
I'll do everything I can do, Jesus will finish the rest.
I try not to judge, I know the pain and sorrow it put me through,
Because I know I'm beautiful — I don't need to hear it from you.
So if I feel the darkness coming, I turn the other way,
Because I am who I am, this isn't a masquerade.

Claire Donovan, Grade 9
Discovery Middle School, MN

The Three Pigs

It all started on a warm day,
When the three little pigs went on their way,
To build houses where they will live,
To cook, clean and raise their kids.
They built their houses of bricks, twigs and straw,
And none of the houses seemed to have a flaw.

Then the Big Bad Wolf came into town,
And blew the first pig's house down.
So the first pig ran to his brother's house,
Faster than a cat chasing a mouse.
Both pigs could hear the wolf out there,
And then there was a knock on the door that was quite a scare!

Now the two pigs were on the run,
So they wouldn't get turned into bacon.
When they arrived at the house of bricks,
The two pigs were in panics.
Then the wolf went down the chimney, and into a pot,
And the pigs ate him before he would rot.

Katie Ashley, Grade 8
Jerstad Agerholm Middle School, WI

5 Ways of Looking at Lightning

God's flashlight sending light so he can see.
God's sparkler saying "Happy Fourth of July."
An angel's hair sparkling in the night, telling us we're
    not the most powerful.
God's hand glowing with radiant light.
Our keepsake of God's power.

Cassie Elliott, Grade 7
Holy Family Parish School, WI

The Trail

A lonely old man walked the grass-covered trail
which meandered around Creek Whatsaka.
The scarlet, gold, and amber colors of autumn circled all around the man as he shuffled along.
A farmhouse loomed at the end of the grassy trail.
The man walked up to the fence that surrounded a weathered, but sturdy farmhouse,
and shoved the creaky gate open.
As the visitor walked up the cobblestone path, a slight mist started to come down.
Crows scattered out of the attic.
The old man knocked and went into the house.
Inside sat a man in a creaky rocking chair.
The man in the rocking chair hadn't expected a visitor,
but welcomed the old friend to lunch.
The men talked about old days and shared stories.
"Remember when Billy set fire to the old barn?"
"That other time when Jim ate the tail off the beaver?"
"Yes, yes, good old times."
After lunch the uninvited but welcomed guest left.
When the man was walking down the grassy trail,
he chuckled as he passed the old tree house that held so many good memories.
Finally, the man reached his house — no longer feeling lonely —
just as gusts of winds brought in rolling thunderheads.

Jordan Remme, Grade 9
Jordan Sr High School, MN

Winter

A ll the leaves have fallen from the trees.
B ears and bees asleep until spring.
C old winter snowflakes fall from the gray sky.
D ecember, the time when the countdown of Christmas starts.
E ggnog waits for you when you come in from the cold.
F resh cut tree in the house decorated with silver and gold.
G reat presents wait under the tree until Christmas.
H oliday songs ring in your head.
I wait for the perfect time to throw my snowball.
J ump in the huge snow piles with great joy.
K ind people stop to sing carols at your door.
L ights flash on the bright Christmas tree.
M istletoe hung in the doorway.
N orth Pole is busy with all of its elves.

O h, the Christmas tree shines brightly.
P lowing the driveway so people can come to our house.
Q uilts are spread out all over the floor.
R eindeer impatient to take to the sky.
S anta gets 1,000 letters from every little girl and boy.
T ucked in their beds, the kids wait for Santa.
U nder the mistletoe waits a kiss.
V ehicles are packed with presents and people.
W reaths are hanging from doors.
X 'mas trees are everywhere
Y ou sit with your friends and family
and watch Christmas movies.
Z azzle others with a little Christmas cheer.

Kelsey Roshell, Grade 7
Thorp Middle School, WI

Time

Time is a continuum, eternal and infinite.
Time is a concept of human mortality, and does not pace itself in a matter of months or years.
To achieve immortality, we must first understand time's essence and solidarity.
Nothing that is timely has anything to do with time, for time does not prepare itself for
certain incidents in a human perception.
Instead, time stretches itself immeasurably and will not discontinue if life ceases to exist.
Only God truly understands time,
And we don't have much time before we see God.
Use it well.

Nathaniel Foss, Grade 8
Holy Family Parish School, WI

Natural Beauty of Autumn

I feel like a visitor walking across the grass-covered trail, walking slowly toward Tree Life Pond.
On the path I look to my left and see rolling thunderheads speeding toward the abandoned farmhouse.
I hear the faint sound of an aging rocking chair swaying in the wind.
The colorful leaves of auburn rustle under my shoes.
I look at one of the trees and examine a spider resting on its web, waiting patiently for prey.
Under the tree, many fallen apples have rotted away to the core.
I step over the broken, white fence and approach the pond which lies covered in mist.
The world seems to open up as I come closer and closer to the shore.
Crows and bees dance around the pond while the milkweed gently sways in the breeze.
The natural beauty of autumn explodes before me.

Erica Stever, Grade 9
Jordan Sr High School, MN

My Eyes

When you look into my eyes you might see a girl who is self-confident and fits in great with her friends.
But maybe look a little deeper in her and to her heart you will see a girl who…
…doesn't feel like she fits in
…doesn't have very close friends
…doesn't have someone to talk to sometimes
…isn't very self-confident
She is now figuring out just be yourself and sooner or later you will find your true friends.
She knows that God made you the way he wanted you to be.
She also knows that it's what you think of yourself not what others think of you.
But when you see all this you will see that she loves you and hopes for the best for everyone!

Shaneé Herd, Grade 9
Discovery Middle School, MN

My Backyard

While sitting on my weathered oak rocking chair,
I looked outside and saw the bright emerald hummingbirds float with the wind.
I saw the autumn mist dripping from the leaves of the red oak, and orange ash.
I saw a grass-covered trail leading to the bridge that went over the family creek.
I saw a worn ash wood fence below rolling thunderheads that threatened the land.
Past all that, I saw our forgotten farmhouse that had a newborn kitten waiting inside.
And then I heard a visitor at the door and saw the mother cat who was calling my name.
Quickly, I went and gave her some food and then watched her hurry back to the forgotten farmhouse.
The cat curled up, fed her baby, and went to hide just as the thunderheads opened up.

Alexis Robling, Grade 9
Jordan Sr High School, MN

Hunting

On a cold and breezy morning
You're in your stand well before daylight
You hear footsteps quicken
In the back of your mind
You know it's a buck dogging a doe
And the doe brings the buck right under your stand
You grunt to stop him and he does
Perfectly at 20 yards broadside, just what you wanted
You draw back and put your 20 pin right behind his shoulder
And let an arrow fly
Perfectly placed
He runs 30 yards and drops
That's a perfect once in a lifetime day of hunting

Tyler Brozek, Grade 9
Fall River High School, WI

My Grandma

Had blackish brown hair
five feet three inches
Always doing something
Making her famous chocolate cake, or her yummy apple pie
Living with three men, she kept everybody straightened up
Sport events and hunting shows, that's what she watched
It was hard not to with three men in the house
She wasn't much of a hunter
But Grandpa got her into it
Shot her first bear not too long before grandpa got in his accident
He's a handful, but Grandma always has it under control
She always told us to remember one thing
"Be good, be safe, and I love you"

CJ Hahn, Grade 9
Rosholt Middle-High School, WI

I Am Myself…

I am myself, in which no one can deny, I am a thought, small in space,
yet so very large in meaning,
I wonder about life, when it will end, or if it has even begun,
I hear the crowd cheering as I cross the finish,
I see the vast sun shimmering in the sky,
I want for all things to be right, even if it can never happen,
I am myself, in which no one can deny, I am a thought, small in space, yet
so very large in meaning,
I pretend to carry the flag on my shoulders, around the track,
I feel the sting of hard rain hitting my face,
I touch the cloth of the comforting pillows,
I worry about myself and others, that we may never come up empty in life,
I cry for the people in our world, who never got their own chance,
I am myself, in which no one can deny, I am a thought, small in space, yet
so very large in meaning,
I understand that life does not always turn the way you want it to turn,
I say my beliefs openly, so no one can reject them,
I dream about the Olympics, as I go from the gun,
I try my best, as I should each and every day,
I hope I can fulfill what God has asked me to do,
I am myself, in which no one can deny, I am a thought, small in space, yet so very large in meaning

Joe Pasbrig, Grade 7
Holy Family Parish School, WI

At the Barn

Horses graze lazily
As a cool breeze makes the emerald grass in the pasture wave to and fro
The breeze is clean and fresh, with a hint of dusty horses present
Horses and riders enjoy jumping in the cross country arena by the pasture
Their shouts and laughter are also carried on the breeze to me
As I walk to the very end of the huge pasture
To where Rowdy awaits me
I jump on the giant Appaloosa's huge spotted back
And we trot slowly back to the barn
Feeling the soft breeze and Rowdy's coarse mane
Hearing the riders shouting happily as they bound over jumps and plunge through the water complex
Tasting the dusty horse smell in my mouth
Watching the looming shape of the barn and knowing that this moment will soon end…
And wishing this moment would last forever

Aisling O'Sullivan, Grade 8
St Odilia School, MN

A Realization

As I lie in bad at night I can't help but think of how things used to be.
When things like fairies existed and all I did was play with my best friend in the old oak tree.
Our biggest fear was getting stung by a bee.
And then I remember that love didn't exist and friendship wasn't a big deal.
My thoughts are confused but my hearts asking, is growing up really that bad?
You have to experience heartbreak but you also get to experience true love and unbreakable bonds.
As my eyes began to droop towards sleep I think of all the things that have broke my heart.
Deaths to losses of friends but then I think, would I be writing this right now if I hadn't had those misfortunes?
And the answer is simple, no I wouldn't.
Sleep finally takes over and I dream of my careless child years.

Stephanie Krus-Reitz, Grade 8
Northland Pines Middle School, WI

The Prize

You never know when the day is going to come,
So live your life, this is your only one.
Even when you have a bad day,
The world will keep spinning
And that is a prize that's worth winning.
So when every day is done,
You should feel like you've won.

Rachel Lee, Grade 9
Fall River High School, WI

Life with You

I fell in love with you the first day I met you.
Your beautiful, vibrant colors lit up my day
You kept me warm when I was cold.
You brightened my day when I was dreary.
I'm so please you are here with me every day
Thank you,
Sun

Carrington White, Grade 8
Trinity Lutheran School, WI

5 Ways of Looking at a Sunrise

A golden haired angel rising to greet the day
The sun and sky playing hide and seek
A shaken up orange soda that has just been opened
A homemade blanket warming the world
Glowing embers about to burst into flame

Kathleen Hessel, Grade 7
Holy Family Parish School, WI

5 Ways to Look at a Sun

The biggest glow stick, peeking into our world
God's giant desk lamp shining on us
Mother Nature smiling on the whole world
A fireplace in the home that we call Earth
A reminder that each day is GREAT!

Jillian Ludwig, Grade 7
Holy Family Parish School, WI

Life…

Time…
It seemed like years in a second
Broken…
Shattered across a thousand worlds
Pieces…
Millions of them all around
Frozen…
In a forbidding time
Black…
Time unchallenged
Gone…
Missing in life
Life…
Ending in despair

Hayley Roberts, Grade 9
Montgomery-Lonsdale High School, MN

The Cabin

The big brown cabin calls out to me.
It tells me if I listen, I will hear,
look and I will see,
inhale and I will smell,
believe and I will feel.

And when I try,
I see the beauty of the waves on the lake,
the gold of the sun,
the rich castles on the beach.

I hear the songs of the crickets,
the buzz of the bees,
the wind past my ears,
a delighted cry of pleasure.

I smell the fragrance of the trees,
smoke burning from wood on a bonfire,
worms wriggling through the dirt,
fish uprooted by the fishers.

I feel wet sand on my feet,
the wind blow through my hair,
the sun shining on my face.
And I smile.

Shannon Elstad, Grade 8
All Saints Catholic School, MN

Broken Headlights

In the back forty
Beat up trucks
Tractors of many kinds
Rust all over
Grown over weeds

In the woods
Flat tires
Home of many animals
Need to be restored

Felt sorry for
Drove past every day
Rusts all over
Chips in the windshield

Many memories
Good for target practice
Moonshine runner
Pitted chrome

Faded paint
Hasn't been driven for years
Wished it could be driven again.
Broken headlights.

Dylan Merten, Grade 8
Sartell Middle School, MN

Oh Stars and Stripes of Mighty Courage

Oh stars and stripes of mighty courage
Resound in me a song of motherhood
Of distant lonely peoples swarming
Towards your wondrous welcoming arms

Oh stars and stripes of mighty courage
Resound in me a song of battle
Of thick red drops of blood
The men that birthed your sprawling lands

Oh stars and stripes of mighty courage
Resound in me a song of vibrant skies
Of wheat quivering in a Zephyr
Waxing strong on rolling hills

Oh stars and stripes of mighty courage
Resound in me a song of glorious life
Of your people countless in number
Your stars shining quiet and bright

Elisabeth Kyro, Grade 8
Wayzata Central Middle School, MN

Lines

The pencil sparks,
And my eyes brighten.
I make the first line
As the image lingers in my head
I try to remake it on my paper.
One line turns into thousands.
They go,
Straight,
Backwards,
Curve,
Point,
Dot.
And they all make up the image I so desperately desire,
To come to life on my paper.
Even with my failing attempts,
To make as my mind shows me,
I accept it as my layout of lines
That make up my passion.

Amanda Brinkman, Grade 9
Discovery Middle School, MN

Motocross

You sit there waiting at the gate
Revving your motor, it's intense
The gate drops, you shift into first and off you go
People racing past
You jump and crash
You get back up and start racing again
You finish in 7th
And felt so proud that you finished the race
What a great day for you.

Chris Counard, Grade 9
Fall River High School, WI

You Never Said Goodbye

Mom can you hear me?
You never said goodbye.
Just thinking of the day I left you,
Makes me want to cry.
The feelings I withhold are getting very painful
Because all you had to say was just a simple goodbye.
As the silent stars go by each night and I start to get older,
I realize that I am getting much, much bolder.
Much of what I've learned so far has made me a better person,
But what you did to me was unfair,
I don't even think you care.
Even though my life's what I make it,
I just wish you would have taken a single step to say goodbye.
I hardly remember you though bits and pieces will always remain,
I'll never forget you through all the pain I feel,
But the question is will you feel the same?

Tia Kendl, Grade 8
Visions Jr/Sr High School, WI

Outdoor Traditions

As I walk out into the cool November morning,
A familiar feeling comes on,
One that thousands of people feel,
You can be young or old,
You can know nothing or everything,
But it's a feeling they all share,
Whether you walk one hundred yards or one,
Whether you go from the ground or in a stand,
They all share that same passion,
Whether it's a hobby or a lifestyle,
It's the same,
It's a hobby or lifestyle that can make a difference,
Whether you do it to feed the hungry or to stop animal suffering,
It's the same,
It's a passion, a hobby, a lifestyle,
But mostly, it's a love for the outdoors and nature.

Trevor Schuch, Grade 9
Fall River High School, WI

Soldier with a Hidden Past

My lover's touch was nothing like his gaze,
His glance was more piercing than shards of glass.
If death is beauty, why then tears are lace
If only he had not been so careless.
I have seen my love in a black casket,
But we knew the consequences of war;
And yet we did not accept it
Then death came knocking at our humble door.
I saw the corpse, yet I could not believe;
The men who brought him told of his last breath,
I learned things I never could have conceived.
My tears flowed when they had finally left,
And yet, by heaven, it made sense at last,
As he now becomes part of my lost past.

Sonia Schaefbauer, Grade 9
Delano Sr High School, MN

Bahamas

The smell of the ocean,
the sight of the sea,
waves folding onto the shore,
and the trees blowing in the salty breeze.

The warmth of the sun shining,
the unwinding feeling,
and yet you will still feel excited.

The cool calm sea,
this makes you feel closer as a family,
the crisp crumbly cooked fish,
sea turtles, starfish, sea horses, and more sea creatures in the sea.

Kids playing,
grownups gossiping,
and maybe a sail boat at sea.

Jessica Sheets, Grade 8
All Saints Catholic School, MN

Christmas

The ground is chilly and crisp
Fireplaces roaring with flames
Hot boiling apple cider, bubbling on the stovetop
Mistletoe hung from above
Christmas lights flickering on and off
Icicles dripping from the roof tops
Presents placed under the tree
with different color ribbon and wrapping paper
Skaters slicing silently over the ice
Cookies are being baked in the oven
Tinsel twinkling in the light
Carolers singing their favorite tunes
Red and white candy canes hung up on the tree
Evergreens reflecting off the moonlit ice
White frosting snow lies on the ground
like a warm, fuzzy blanket
The magical season is upon us.

Samantha Barker, Grade 8
St John Neumann School, WI

Six Points

Six clouds were in the sky
As the six coaches called timeout.
Our quarterback number 6 tired,
Beaten up by six guys tackling him.
The coaches made them have a 6 man line.
Six seconds on the clock
11-6 is the score
They have to get six yards
To get six points for the win.
My six year old brother shaking.
This could be our 6th championship,
And they snapped the ball and six points, we won!

Josh Farnsworth, Grade 7
Lincoln Jr/Sr High School, WI

Just Remember*

You can shed tears that she is gone,
Or you can smile that she has lived.

You can close your eyes and pray she'll come back,
Or open your eyes and see all she's left.

Your heart can be empty because you can't see her,
Or your eyes can light up with the friendship you shared.

You can turn your back on tomorrow and live yesterday,
Or you can be happy for tomorrow because of yesterday.

You can remember her and only that she is gone,
Or you can cherish her memory and let it live on.

You can cry and close your mind be empty and turn your back,
Or you can do what she'd want,
Smile, open your eyes, love, and live on.

Lizzie Hagen, Grade 9
Montgomery-Lonsdale High School, MN
*Dedicated to Courtney Audria Smith. R.I.P.

Black and White

If you looked into my eyes, I'm not sure what you'd see,
You'd either see the brighter or the darker side of me,
There really is no pinpoint to just where they mix,
But wherever they do, it sure as heck conflicts,
I guess it doesn't matter; I guess I'm doing fine,
Although that inner struggle, darts in n' out my mind,
One of these days, I will make my choice,
And maybe then, I'll get back my voice,
It's not that I don't have one, it's the other one I lack,
The one of me together, mix both the white and the black,
So for today I'm waiting, for what I'm not quite sure,
It might be a long journey; it's one I must endure,
And so the night turns 'round to day,
Then back again the other way,
That's how I'll be,
Trapped here, yet free.

All that I wanted, all that I need,
That one final thing; is to be freed.

Halie Nettleton, Grade 9
Discovery Middle School, MN

Life

Life is like a roller coaster with all the ups and downs.
Life is like a novel with many chapters.
Life is like a tornado, it just keeps spinning around and around.
Life is like a child, it gets upset, but can be calmed.
Life is like your first job, it may be fun or it may be stressful.
Life works in many different ways,
Some we don't always understand.
But in the end, everything will be okay.

Emily Gessner, Grade 9
Fall River High School, WI

Tall Tale of a Friend

She fights for her life as she walks down the road.
She fights for her life on the train.
She cries in the rain as it falls.
So nobody knows.

She walks the streets of the black coarse road.
Finds the people are pleasantly strange.
Can't take the change as she goes.
She halts with the wind.

They say she hops on the clouds when nobody's home.
Then they say that she finally falls.
The breeze tends to take her along.
A leaf with the air.

She inhales the light of the sun all alone.
She exhales our happiness now.
She cries on her bed all the time.
Not loving the sight.

Still she puts on a face just to get through the day.
She just wants to tear alone.
We let her go home not a pause.
So nobody knows.

Paige Meierhofer, Grade 7
Webster Transitional School, WI

Flight of an Admiration

When you want to hold the world,
In everlasting harmony,
All you have to do is believe.
But when you can't dream,
Why bother?

When you are on your deathbed,
And don't believe in another life,
You may see a recollection of your life.
But when you achieve nothing,
Why bother?

That is why you must live your life to the fullest,
Because it may be your last day to live.
And if you make a promise to someone,
And refuse to hold your word,
Why bother?

So fly into the sky,
Dive into the depths,
Move yourself to do amazing things.
Because if you do not,
You may not have a second chance.
So bother.

Haydn Tvrdik, Grade 9
Discovery Middle School, MN

I Hate Doing the Dishes

I hate doing the dishes,
it makes me so mad,
when my dad finishes the cake,
and I have to wash the pan.

I hate changing the cat box,
it makes me so mad, when my mom tells me,
"Go do the cat box"
and I go very slowly because I am sad.

I hate doing the dishes,
it makes me so mad,
when my sister says "I'm hungry"
and I have to rinse out the can.

I hate it when the laundry needs folding,
and I am the only one home.
So of course, to please my parents,
I go to the dryer and fold some clothes.

I hate doing the dishes,
it makes me so mad,
when my dad finishes the cake,
and I have to wash the pan.

Sadie Dupont, Grade 8
Holy Family School, WI

Life of Harriet Tubman

It was 1820,
I didn't have a lot of money.
I was a slave who did not rave.
I saved many in my days for that I got a lot of praise.

I may not be Paul Revere but I have no fear.
I led slaves from near to far,
Just hoping not to be locked up behind bars.
The water was so clear,
I could see the dogs coming near.

My dad taught me the woods,
So later we could hide from the men with the hoods.
They come after slaves who don't behave,
Slaves were not allowed to own a stave.
We could smell different things along the ways,
As we touch everything like we were in a haze.

They almost caught us once so we jumped a train,
We had to go down south bound lane.
The sound of the train horn blew in my ear,
As the train we were on started to veer.
When we got off the train we were all in a craze,
We were free, we were free, now we get to laze!

Alicin Levy, Grade 8
Jerstad Agerholm Middle School, WI

Chippewa Bay

Waves shine as they hit the sand,
Water splashes on the land.
Mirror-like water reflects the sky,
Ripples move the clouds where they lie.

Leaves float through the air,
Flying around without a care.
Soft wind wafts slowly by,
As I hear a mourning dove's cry.

The sun's light warms the grass,
Swaying as squirrels run past.
Trees sway with the breeze,
Shadows shift with the morning leaves.

Chickadees twitter and sing
As the sun warms their wings.
Swallows dive toward the lake,
We watch the ripples they make.

As we tell the stories of old,
We light a fire of dancing gold.
We'll never forget this wonderful day,
Sitting here on Chippewa Bay.
Anne Weston, Grade 8
Stewartville Middle School, MN

Run

The timer is ready
On your mark, get set, go!
Get ahead of the others
Don't start off too slow.

Run for the gold
And run for the glory,
Run for the medal
And *New York Times* story.

Run with power
And run with speed,
Run with passion
To be the lead.

Run with confidence
Run for the time,
Run to be the first
To cross the finish line.

Once the race is finished
Once it's over and done,
You scream and shout
Because you just won.
Hailey Koch, Grade 9
Fall River High School, WI

Can You Imagine

A school without work
The world without hurt

Politics without corruption
Minds without obstruction

A leader that doesn't lie
Hungry kids that don't die

A world without oppression
People without depression

A terrorist that doesn't kill
Gas that costs a dollar bill

A storm without thunder
A world without hunger
Luke Harkins, Grade 8
Holy Family Parish School, WI

Making a Difference

Give me a place to stand
and I can change the world
let me hold your hand
and you can change it with me
it might get tough
but we'll keep on trying
we'll keep our chins up
we'll do the right thing

Me and you, you and me
we'll move mountains wait and see
we'll do it all
if I fall
you'll pick me up, we'll keep going
when we're on a roll
there's no slowing us down
because we're making a difference now
Erin Earley, Grade 7
New Richmond Middle School, WI

What's a Girl to Do?

What's a girl to do?
When your best friend comes to you?
His problems seem so real,
I try to make a deal.
But it seems so unfair
No one really cares.
I try to cheer him up
But sometimes it's just not enough
I hope he cheers up soon,
Maybe I will give him a balloon.
He means the world to me,
I want him to be all that he can be!
Rissa Garvick, Grade 9
Round Lake High School, MN

Hope for a Day

If you find out you have cancer today
you may react in a very different way
you may cry, you may shout
you may even pout
or you just might have nothing to say

But don't panic nor fret
or lose hope just yet
the doctors still have good news
your loving family may get a blood check
to find a match of blood to use.

Now this, if found will speed your recovery
but when all is done, and the cancer is gone
you are left with a feeling of hope for a cure
for the day that a cure is found
will be a most wonderful discovery
that day we will never forget.

So don't panic nor fret
or lose hope just yet.
A cure is on its way.
Mitchel Vosejpka, Grade 9
Montgomery Lonsdale High School, MN

We Are One

We are one
Black
White
Brown
Yellow
We are all one
We are one
Thick
Thin
Or even
Slim
We are all one
We are one
Brothers
Sisters
Friends
Enemies
We are all one
God creates us in many unique ways
but we are one race:
Human
Brenna Davis, Grade 8
All Saints Catholic School, MN

Sunsets

Flamboyant flames burst
Signaling the death of day
Bringing in the night
Emelyn Zaworski, Grade 7
Hudson Middle School, WI

Playing the Game

Swish!
Up and down the court they run,
Having tons of good old fun.
Lay-ups and three pointers here and there,
Many players everywhere.
Swish!
Half-time is the time to huddle,
For the other team is in some trouble.
Cheers and hollers all around,
As the teams play out the final round.
Swish!
Now as the final score,
Hornets win, thirty to four.

Cassie Wojtalewicz, Grade 9
Rosholt Middle-High School, WI

Waiting

We wait, we wait
We wait for something
We wait for night
We wait for a fright
We wait for you
We wait for them
We look right
We look left
We cross the street
We wait on this side
We wait on the other side
We wait, we wait

Dylan Brozek, Grade 9
Fall River High School, WI

Book

Each day I am opened and closed.
I have my pages turned harshly.
Each day I am shoved into a locker.
I am put into a small claustrophobic
backpack for a long ride home.
When my use is through
I am thrown on the hard dusty floor.
Being a book is hard if you are sensitive.
I am a book and I am sad.

Hilary Kraus, Grade 8
St Paul's Lutheran School, WI

Hunting

I was sitting in my tree stand for a chance
The weather was cool as the trees danced
As I look up at the sky I saw a bird soared
Then I closed my eyes as the wind roared
Dreaming of a buck so big and bold
When I hear hooves rolling and tumbling
I grab my shot gun and bang!
I got it running away.

Matt Bute, Grade 7
Shakopee Area Catholic School, MN

Configurations

Down it comes,
In all shapes and sizes
Rain, snow, hail.
We don't always know,
but it still comes.
Some of us like it,
Others don't.
It always comes down,
because it always goes up,
Precipitation
Rain…snow…hail…

Bernard Zimmermann III, Grade 7
Trinity Lutheran School, WI

Football

Eleven players make a team.
Eleven positions that
eleven unique players will fill.
Eleven pairs of cleats
on eleven stinky feet.
Eleven mouth guards to fit
and eleven helmets to be smashed
and clashed on eleven other helmets.
Eleven seconds left on the clock.
Eleven points to win the game.
Eleven players will get the glory and fame.

Kolton Flick, Grade 7
Lincoln Jr/Sr High School, WI

The Bee

I am a bee, strong and fearless.
I go out and collect pollen.
More bees come and collect pollen.
We take it back to the hive
And make honey with it.
In the winter, we take a long nap.
Then we wait for spring and
Wait for the flowers to bloom,
Go out and collect more pollen.
We start the process again
The next day.

Storm O'Neill, Grade 7
Lincoln Jr/Sr High School, WI

Happiness/Sadness

Happiness
Warm, delightful
Laughing, joking, running
Chocolate, friends, pets, sun
Sighing, walking, crying
Cold, despair
Sadness

Kristen Lee Lindner, Grade 9
Rosholt Middle-High School, WI

The Opponents

Terrorists
Dark, devastating
Slaughtering, slaying, sabotaging
Murder, mayhem, massacre, manslaughter
Shielding, serving, saving
Brave, bold
Soldiers

Austin Murray Johnson, Grade 9
Rosholt Middle-High School, WI

Music Clefs

Treble
Soprano, high
Playing, piercing, singing
Opera, choir, woodwinds, strings
Descending, falling, breaking
Alto, tenor
Bass

Dalton J. Yaeger, Grade 9
Rosholt Middle-High School, WI

Grades 4-5-6
Top Ten Winners

List of Top Ten Winners for Grades 4-6; listed alphabetically

Hailey Benesh, Grade 6
T J Walker Middle School, Sturgeon Bay, WI

Anne Cebula, Grade 6
Intermediate School 239 Mark Twain for the Gifted & Talented, Brooklyn, NY

Zari Gordon, Grade 5
Walker Elementary School, Evanston, IL

Helena Green, Grade 5
Hopewell Elementary School, Hopewell, NJ

Kristin Kachel, Grade 6
Discovery Canyon Campus, Colorado Springs, CO

Carrie Mannino, Grade 5
The Ellis School, Pittsburgh, PA

Mariah Reynolds, Grade 4
School for Creative and Performing Arts, Cincinnati, OH

Jeremy Stepansky, Grade 5
Hillside Elementary School, Montclair, NJ

Anne-Katherine Tallent, Grade 5
Providence Academy, Johnson City, TN

Claudia Zhang, Grade 6
Rolling Ridge Elementary School, Chino Hills, CA

All Top Ten Poems can be read at www.poeticpower.com

Note: The Top Ten poems were finalized through an online voting system. Creative Communication's judges first picked out the top poems. These poems were then posted online. The final step involved thousands of students and teachers who registered as the online judges and voted for the Top Ten poems. We hope you enjoy these selections.

Fall Is When…

Fall is when…
I can taste the hot cocoa.
It tastes like a waterfall of melted chocolate.
It warms me up throughout my body.

Fall is when…
I hear trick-or-treat on Halloween night.
From door to door I see kids everywhere.
Crazy costumes all around.

Fall is when…
I see haunted houses.
Decked out with decorations like ghosts,
goblins, witches, pumpkins, and tombstones.

Fall is when…
I smell burning candles with scents
like pumpkin pie, pine cone, campfire smoke,
cinnamon, vanilla, and clean linen.

Fall is when…
I can touch wrappers in my bag like
Butterfingers, Snickers, Reeses, 3 Musketeers,
and Tootsie Rolls.

Kade Slattum, Grade 4
Kennedy Elementary School, MN

Barn

I am a barn,
Holding animals in my arms, gates are my organs
My doors are my mouths, telling animals to come in,
Tired animals, my children

I am a barn,
The loft as my bedroom,
The sun as my heater,
The wind as my air conditioner,
The straw as my blankets,
The desk as my organizer,
The water trough as my food

Chickens as my alarm clock,
Cowbells tell me it's time for milking,
Sheep are my leaders,
Horses carry me to wonderland,
Dogs tell me stories, and cats entertain me

I am a barn,
With a lantern hung by my mouth,
Strong and sturdy,

I am a barn

Kylee Kohls, Grade 5
Wagner Elementary School, MN

Dreams*

Hold fast to dreams
For if dreams live
Life is a present
Ready to give.

Hold fast to dreams
For if dreams grow
Life is a garden
Ready to show.

Eva Korb, Grade 4
Classical School, WI
*Inspired by Langston Hughes' "Dreams Deferred"

Dreams*

Hold fast to dreams
Because if you do
Life is a back massage
Ready for you.

Hold fast to dreams
Hold really tight
Life is a bald eagle
Ready to take flight.

Cade Coenen, Grade 4
Classical School, WI
*Inspired by Langston Hughes' "Dreams Deferred"

Racing Roaring Red

Red is a blazing bonfire, a screaming fire truck
and the feeling of being angry.
Red is the taste of spicy wings.
Grandma's roses and pepperoni pizza smell red.
Campfire smoke makes me feel red.
Red is the sound of a tiger's roar and a gunshot.
Red is Mexico, Arizona, and America.
A hot summer day is red.
A scary movie is also red.
Red is the flag of the United States of America.

Alexis Powell, Grade 6
Marinette Middle School, WI

Dreams*

Hold fast to dreams,
For if dreams grow,
Life is a garden
Bright with snow.

Hold fast to dreams,
For when dreams fly,
Life is a beach
With a breeze from the sky.

Gwen Stevenson, Grade 4
Classical School, WI
*Inspired by Langston Hughes' "Dreams Deferred"

Halloween

Halloween is a nice time
to dress up as monsters, ghosts,
or you can go as whatever
you want to be.
As you trick-or-treat you get
candy like chocolate, candy corns,
gummy bears, and more.
So have a nice Halloween
and stay scared.

Stephanie Coleman, Grade 6
Messmer Preparatory Catholic School, WI

Christmas

C hristmas is awesome
H o, ho, ho
R ighteous
I ce is slippery
S ongs are sung
T eeth are chattering
M ost presents are under a tree
A sk for cookies
S anta

Marcos Luna, Grade 4
Luna Home School, MN

Halloween

H appiness in the air
A ll are excited
L oads of candy
L ot of kids walk in the night
O wls hoot
W e all have fun
E vil devils lurk
E mpires of candy
N ight is the time of roaming animals

Matthew Kieffer, Grade 5
Campbellsport Elementary School, WI

Monkeys Climbing in the Trees

Monkeys climbing in the tree
Monkeys playing on the branches
Monkeys rip the leaves off
Monkeys dig holes
Monkeys playing with roots
Monkeys building with bark

Morgan Nyara, Grade 6
St Francis Middle School, MN

the beach at the ocean

the big waves
the long pier
a sunny day
with some clouds
the hot sun

Steven Svare, Grade 6
Harriet Bishop Elementary School, MN

Jelly Beans

A rainbow of colors
tiny and quiet
all different brands and
all of my favorites
watermelon
sour apple
yellow lemon
strawberry and grape
a big wall at target
a great giant list
a taste sensation
I can't resist

Kate Doyle, Grade 6
Harriet Bishop Elementary School, MN

Cloud

Cloud
Flying ice cream
In the sky looking
So yummy when
It goes by.
Pillow of feathers
In the sky looking
So soft like fur on a
Animal.
Foam in the sky
Looking so fun
Just like Legos.

Matthew Jensen, Grade 5
Harriet Bishop Elementary School, MN

Butterflies

Monarchs eating milkweed
On a quiet calm day
Flying through the puffy clouds
With their black and orange wings
People watching the monarchs
Feeling happy and excited
A colorful group
Of butterflies flying away
Butterflies
Butterflies
Butterflies
Please come again

Krista Holmstrom, Grade 5
Harriet Bishop Elementary School, MN

Sports

S uper fun
P lenty
O bvious exercise
R unning fast
T aunting not allowed
S ummer games

Jessica Logue, Grade 4
Chaska Elementary School, MN

On a Fall Day

I see snow like little
diamonds falling from
the sky

On a fall day
after I take the
top off the pumpkins
I stick my hand
inside, it is like wet,
wet mud

On a fall day
crunchy leaves crunch
like chips and like
dried out paint

On a fall day
hot cider flows down
your throat like
a speedy fast
water slide then
poof it's gone

Quinn Kruse, Grade 4
Kennedy Elementary School, MN

Blue

Blue is the color of the rain
Blue is in rainbow after it rains
Blue is the color of sad
Blue is the color of Lake Michigan
Blue is the color of ice
Blue is the color of the sky
Blue is the color of a waterfall
Blue is the color of my desktop
Blue is the color for water on earth.

Melissa Rivas, Grade 6
Gilmore Middle School, WI

Northern Lights

Shining lights of life.
In the blistering coldness of the north.
In the blackness of the night.
Beautiful. Simply beautiful.
Blue, green, red, purple, so colorful.
It goes smoothly across the sky.
When you see it, you're glad you did.
It's something to see.
And it's not fake.
It's amazing!
The lights bounce off the mountains,
Casting large shadows.
Waiting to see it again.
And again.
Those are the Northern Lights.

Alexander Morain, Grade 5
Harriet Bishop Elementary School, MN

Using Tape

Tape can be used for many things
Like wrapping
Oops; I wrapped the wrong thing — meow
You can also use it for
Holding a plastic covering for a wall
Oops; I didn't use strong enough tape
It can take paper off of a wall
Oops, I took some hair off the dog
And for putting paper on the wall
Oops, I put the wrong thing on the wall,
Help me!

Jeffrey Anderson, Grade 5
Riverdale Elementary School, WI

Snowboarding

The urge of excitement,
the wait of getting to the top,
to ride freely to the bottom,
it feels like the ski lift is a snail,
you wish it would go faster,
so you could board free,
finally the wait is up,
the top of the mountain is here,
the fun begins,
the freedom feeling is here,
in a flash it starts all over.

Lucas Fuller, Grade 6
St Francis Middle School, MN

I Wish

I wish I was 18.
I wish for a car
And a house
I wish to have another dog.
I wish to have a cell phone
and a job at thirteen.
I wish for great friends.
I wish to be a football or basketball player.
I wish to never go to jail.
I wish to live forever
and to have a great life.

Hunter Lynch, Grade 4
River Heights Elementary School, WI

Lightning

I am a lightning bolt
A lightning bolt is me
When running down the soccer field
I am as fast as can be

Lightning strikes with accuracy
Just like me toward the goalie
With thunder so loud
I light up the crowd

Trinity Olson, Grade 4
Classical School, WI

All About Me

Trustworthy,
Loving,
Caring,
Wishes to have a horse,
Dreams of being a singer,
Wants to do well in her life.
Who wonders what life will bring.
Who fears her worst nightmare.
Who is afraid of the ocean.
Who likes boys with souls.
Who believes in God.

Who loves Twilight.
Who loves to play volleyball.
Who loves horseback riding.
Who loves meat.
Who plans to be an actress.
Who plans to marry.
Who plans to enjoy life.

Whose final destination is heaven

Cheyenne Marx, Grade 6
Gilmore Middle School, WI

My Hunting Trip

Branches rustling
Leaves rustling
Blowing wind

All in my head
Hearing them is all I need
To get me up to hunt

I listen when we go
I listen on the way
There's nothing in my way

I look up in the sky
To see some birds up high
I look down to see
Some buzzing bees

There's a lot of things to see
But one thing stands out
That's a BUCK!

Janice Asmundsen, Grade 5
Hewitt Texas Elementary School, WI

Dogs

Dogs are fun to have around.
Their fur is soft.
They have a lot of energy to wear out.
Some don't like baths.
Dogs are very fun.

Niko Gibson, Grade 6
St Francis Middle School, MN

Maybe They Will

In the twilight by the seashore
There stood a man watching, waiting
Waiting for the ship to come ashore.
While he paced the shore, the ship comes
Those beloved ones are remembered,
Faraway the clock drums,
It drums the time 1:00, 2:00, 3:00,
Those beloved might be on that ship,
It's now 4:00, 5:00, 6:00,
It's coming closer, closer,
He can't wait till it comes
Closer, closer, closer, closer,
It is almost here.
The suspense is building,
The ship is finally here,
Are the loved ones on it? Yes!!

Brianna Bennett, Grade 6
Buck Creek Mennonite School, WI

Shoes, Shoes, Shoes

Long shoes
Short shoes
Fat, ugly, stinky shoes
Pink, purple, green shoes
Those are just a few
Baby shoes
Adult shoes
Orange, blue, yellow shoes
Lavender, white, red shoes
Your shoes too!
My shoes
Super shoes
And don't forget clean shoes
Last of all
Best of all
I like clown shoes!

Lazer Frey, Grade 4
Boscobel Elementary School, WI

Life Colors

Yellow is the morning sun,
Brown is the breakfast bun.

White is the snow on the ground,
Blue is the color of sound.

Red is the blood in my veins,
Black is the horse's reins.

Silver is the riches I dream of,
Gray are the clouds above.

Pink is the heart in me,
Green is the color I see.

Steven Schultz, Grade 6
Gilmore Middle School, WI

The Finish Line

I'm at the starting line,
Ready for the run of my life!
1, 2, 3 — the race starts!
I take little steps at first.
Faster, faster almost there!
Then, I see it!
I'm at the finish line!

Renee Rodgers, Grade 6
Riverdale Elementary School, WI

My Name Is Like

My name is like a dolphin jumping through cold fresh air
My name is like a paint brush running through a spark of warm dark blue paint.
My name is like my coaches shouting at swim meet "GO GO!" at the top of his lungs.
My name is like a flower that just bloomed in the morning sun air.
My name is like a collage spilling bright beautiful colors.
My name is like an ocean full of bright beautiful colored sea creatures
My name is like a ball that crashed and exploded in beautiful warm colors.
My name is like a plane crashing to the ground in tiny little pieces.

Sophie Bernstorf, Grade 5
Sibley Elementary School, MN

Fall

First fall,
Then the leaves falling.
First the leaves falling,
Then the raking.
First the raking,
Then the fun.
First things first.

Jacob Benish, Grade 6
Hillsboro Elementary School, WI

Senses

I was sitting in the car when
I noticed Sammy falling asleep
I felt very sleepy so I leaned my head onto his shoulder.
I hear my sister's annoying voice in the background.
I barely smelled the cologne from his white sweater.
I yawned and tasted the perfume from my own shirt.
Then I silently fell asleep while my mom was driving us to Sam's home.

Andrea Mares, Grade 6
Gilmore Middle School, WI

Volleyball

First comes the serve,
then comes the pass.
First comes the pass,
then comes the set.
First comes the set,
then comes the kill.
First things first.

Mackenzie Sullivan, Grade 6
Hillsboro Elementary School, WI

Winter

Winter is the coldest season of the year.
It snows, it freezes to 0 degrees.
It rains, the wind blows so hard you feel like you're going to die.
The only good thing about winter is the snow falling to the ground.
The flowers go away until spring.
It snows and snows until about every inch is covered with white beautiful
Snow

Brittany Stevens, Grade 6
Riverdale Elementary School, WI

Quiet Doll

Inside this doll are songs,
Laughter, and joy and yet
She's not able to
Let them out

She sits there pretty in her
Blue and white dress
Just sitting there
On that lonely shelf not able to move

Sometimes we're like this doll
We have these feelings we want to
Let out but somehow
We can't
Inside this doll are songs,
Laughter, and joy but she's not
Able to let them out

Cindy Beckstrom, Grade 6
T J Walker Middle School, WI

Football

Football is a hard sport.
Football is fun when you make a tackle or a big play.
When you run the ball you have to protect it.
When you pass you have to make sure your guy is there and you have to throw it good too.
When you score it feels great and everyone is proud, happy and cheering.

Mitch Ramacher, Grade 6
St Francis Middle School, MN

Video Games

I love my video games, yes I do.
I love my video games, what about you?
DS, PS2, any one will do.
I love my video games, yes I do.
I love the action and the challenge.
Is that fun to you?
And that is why I love my DS and PS2.

Isaha Miller, Grade 6
Hillsboro Elementary School, WI

Spring

Spring energizes me
When the snow melts
New plants start to grow
Birds are singing
The smell of fresh plants soothe me
Animals are starting to come out
Ahh spring

Brandi Parker, Grade 6
Hillsboro Elementary School, WI

Movies

Popcorn, slushies, pop and candy are snacks you bring to all movies.
There are lots of kinds of movies:

Scary movies include *Friday the 13th, Halloween, Amityville Horror* and many more.
In these morbid movies characters run from scary slashers
and many or most end up dead or dying.

Comedy movies include *Tommy Boy, Date Movie, Uncle Buck* and lots of other knee slappers.
These merry movies usually include one or two ditsy characters
and hilarious plots.

Romantic comedy movies include *Wedding Crashers, 50 First Dates, Twilight* and more.
In these mushy movies, a boy falls for a girl and in the end the girl falls for him, too
and the battle for the girl is fought.

Action movies include *Transformers, Terminator Salvation, Star Wars, The Bourne Ultimatum*, and more.
These melee movies may present many intense fight
scenes or bloody brawls.

Whether you watch them at home or at the theater, movies come in different
kinds and we all like them.

Powers Miller, Grade 5
Blue Heron Elementary School, MN

I Am

I am from soccer with its checkered ball,
reading with its awesome books with their dectillions of descriptive pages.
I am from swimming with its smooth waves and
climbing with its long ladders and ropes.
I am from typing and writing like I did with this draft.
I am from colorful drawing with markers and pencils and learning at school and walking home.
I am from memories of holidays and of eating pepperoni pizza.
I am from watching movies and feeding our somewhat wild cat.
I am from traveling to different states to staying at home in St. Paul.
I am from watching noisy birds and squirrels.
I am from looking out the window and seeing a rainy day and going outside on a sunny day to play.
I am from sitting on the fluffy couch and reading big books.
I am from winter and spring and summer and fall.
I am from playing board games with friends
and playing tag with them.
I am from making imaginative maps.
I am from eating delicious apples in the orchard.
I am from playing on the playground and running in the field.
I am me.

Lucas Mueller, Grade 5
Adams Spanish Immersion School, MN

The Important Thing

I float on the ocean, I'm very huge, I was also used in World War II. I was invaded three times and went back to harbor, from hundreds of Japanese fighters. If I sunk we would of lost the war, I was important to the Navy and the Air Force. I had a lot of space but it seemed like nothing because we had men all over the place.

What Am I
USS Enterprise (not from *Star Trek*)

Ryan Callery, Grade 5
Harriet Bishop Elementary School, MN

Math

Math is calming.
It is my preferred class at school.
I like it
  because I know a lot about it.
Whenever it is time for math
  I get exhilarated.
We do math most of the day.
I like adding the most.
  Subtracting can be a little tricky.
Multiplication and division
  are really fast.
Whenever I'm not busy,
  I ask my mom and dad
    to write me a few problems.
If they are busy,
  I make up my own problems.
I do math a lot
  and that is how come
    I like it so much.

Lindsey Bettin, Grade 4
Martin County West Sherburn Elementary School, MN

Weddings

It's the day
It's the time
Your parents tell you to hurry up
You finally get there
So you hurry to get in
The wedding finally starts
But you don't like to look at the end
It's finally the reception
You can't wait to eat
Then it's the dance
You can't wait to dance
You want to leave
But your parents say
We have to stay all night
When it's over you are mad to leave
But you're tired
You fall asleep
as soon as
you get to the car.

Alexis Brolsma, Grade 5
Martin County West Trimont Elementary School, MN

A Day in the Northwoods

A calm lake under a deep blue sky,
The call of a loon meets my ears.
An osprey lands above me on a lazily waving branch,
The smell of wood smoke, the sound of splashing.
The sweet taste of blackberries on my lips.
The breeze gently pushes a hammock back and forth.
A beautiful day in the Northwoods
Mine to share with you.

Morgan Bramstedt, Grade 5
Howards Grove Middle School, WI

Inside America

Inside this old American flag
the sounds of gun shots echo through time
soldiers fall, but no one checks to see who
they are all fighting for freedom

if you get close enough
you can feel inside this flag
the sounds of mothers
playing with children while their husbands
are out fighting
you can feel them watching America being born

those times are gone
now the gun shots are coming from Iraq
but the soldiers who freed our country
are not forgotten as long
as the American flag still stands

Tommy Hauser, Grade 6
T J Walker Middle School, WI

Don't Go Away…

Don't go away…
I feel the hard football as big as a boulder,
when I get the ball my hands seem to fall apart.

Don't go away…
The pumpkin pie tastes as if I'm in heaven
when hot cocoa reaches my mouth my body explodes.

Don't go away…
The huge pumpkin smells as fresh as an air freshener
it looks like a perfect sphere of pumpkin pie.

Don't go away…
The leaves are falling as fast as hail
Gobble! Gobble! I see a turkey running.

Don't go away…

Grant Hollar, Grade 4
Kennedy Elementary School, MN

Germs

Germs are very small,
So small you can't see them at all.
They can get you very sick.
They are in some places
  that you would never believe.
They float in the air.
  They're in your hair.
They are on clocks,
  even in your socks.
Here, well, just put it this way, germs are…

EVERYWHERE

Madeline Ebeling, Grade 5
Martin County West Trimont Elementary School, MN

I Am

I am from unicycling;
actually I am from
falling off the unicycle.
I am an orange letter
waiting silently to be opened.
Who knows what will be inside?

I am from smelling sweet lilacs
and catching my gray cat
before he runs out the screen door.
I am from back handsprings
and upside down cartwheels
tremblingly high beams
and rounded bars.

I am from joyfully reading
hanging on to the plot to the very end.
I am from hot potatoes,
fake pies, and wooden stilts.

I am from the four seasons,
winter, spring, summer, and fall.
They keep on changing, just like me.

Grace Kellar-Long, Grade 5
Adams Spanish Immersion School, MN

A New World

A new world,
Shiny, iron and steel,
Brass and copper,
The only real.
Gold and silver,
On and on,
The world is waiting,
For a new day's dawn.

Tin men, foil wraps,
Bronze cyber trains
On the luminous tracks.
Hover cars and
Space traveling planes,
Metallic coats,
And oil it rains.

An electric world,
Completely clean,
No more pollution,
But no more green.
5,000,000 years of mother invention,
Nature gone by good intention.

Henry Baer-Benson, Grade 5
Adams Spanish Immersion School, MN

Late/Early

Late
Run, hurry
Skipping, scurrying, dashing
School, appointment, sunrise, breakfast
Waking, wondering, waiting
Sleepy, calm
Early

Madeline Biel, Grade 4
Jefferson Elementary School, WI

Sister/Brother

Sister
Older and pretty
Danced, played, laughed
Books, friends, football, baseball
Annoying, boring, running, playing
Funny and crazy
Brother

Anjelica Orta, Grade 6
Gilmore Middle School, WI

Winter

I feel the cold breeze on my cheeks.
I hear kids having fun with the snow.
I see the kids having a snowball fight.
I smell gingerbread cookies in the oven.
I taste hot cocoa on my lips.

I love winter!

Hailey Gentes, Grade 5
Stocker Elementary School, WI

Opposites

Boy
Noisy, trouble
Annoying, bugging, teasing
Cars, racing, makeup, sleep-over
Loving, helping, caring
Simply beautiful
Girl

Brianna Phillips, Grade 4
Jefferson Elementary School, WI

July and January

July,
warm, summer,
calm, beaches, swimming,
steamy, humid, arctic, chilly,
skating, snow, bleak,
icy, freezing,
January

George Rosen, Grade 6
Gilmore Middle School, WI

The Lonely Tree

Inside the lonely tree in the yard
There is sadness
There is a sadness that is greater
Greater than anyone has ever felt

Inside the lonely tree in the yard
Lay old memories
Memories that go way back
Way back to when there was a family
Living in the house next door

Inside the tree in the yard
Is a pain
A pain that this tree has had a long time
The pain that a person has
A person that has lost someone

This lonely tree has lost someone
The kids who played on him
The kids who laughed with him
The only kids who loved him
The lonely tree in the yard

Eric Peterson Jr., Grade 6
T J Walker Middle School, WI

My Cat

My cat,
She is fluffy and cute,
She snuggles and cuddles,
She is old and naughty,
My cat,
We spoil her with treats,
She loves the sun,
Just like my mom,
I love my cat.

Autumn Noble, Grade 5
Riverdale Elementary School, WI

Fireworks

Bangs
Whirls
Crackling

Popping lights of gold,
Red, blue, green, white, and orange

Excitement of flickering lights
Steams of colors
Sparks of color
Darkness of night

Popping
Popping
Popping

Ceejay Fitzke, Grade 5
Hewitt Texas Elementary School, WI

I Am a Fireman

I am a fireman.
I wonder if I will fall.
I hear the sirens.
I see the fire.
I am a fireman.

I pretend to be a hero.
I feel the burning skin.
I touch the little baby.
I worry that they won't make it.
I cry about not saving them all.
I am a fireman.

I understand there are more fires.
I say that I will get all the people.
I dream that I will be successful.
I try to save the world.
I hope that they will live.
I am a fireman.

Matthew Swanson, Grade 6
Gilmore Middle School, WI

Madison

Marketers shout "Corn, 5 cents per pound!"
Street musicians play.
Lady's handing out perfume samples,
I could stay here all day!

In this town, Buckey rules,
And representatives meet.
Thousands of toy shops are everywhere,
Up and down the street.

Oh, look, a shop of ice cream!
That way's a shop of hats.
The Iron-Man contest today,
And a shop fixing bicycle flats!

In this big town of wonders,
I simply must admit,
This town they all call Madison,
Is really a huge hit!

Gianna Creanza, Grade 5
Lincoln Elementary School, WI

Rainbow of Colors

Grey is really boring
Yellow is in the morning
Blue is the peaceful sky
Pink is a cheerful HI!
Gold is found in a treasure chest
Blue is the color I like best
Lime green is the color of a lime
Black shows the darkness of night time

Gillian Proctor, Grade 4
Jefferson Elementary School, WI

Halloween

Halloween is black
Halloween is orange

pumpkins are big
pumpkins are small
pumpkins are short
pumpkins are tall

Johnae Henard, Grade 6
Messmer Preparatory Catholic School, WI

Summer and Winter

Summer
Tropical, Humid
Sprinting, Swimming, Frolicking
Extreme Heat, Bitter Cold
Sledding, Skiing, Snowboarding
Freezing, Snowy
Winter

Joshua Cunningham, Grade 6
Gilmore Middle School, WI

Dragon/Puppy

Dragon
scary, fire
flying, diving, hiding
goblin, black, golden retriever, Labrador
barking, playing, sleeping
cute, fluffy
Puppy

Za Xiong, Grade 5
Howards Grove Middle School, WI

Grandma and Papa

Grandma
Smart, loving
Cooking, reading, shopping
Book, stove, tools, suspenders
Eating, singing, fixing
Funny, kind
Papa

Sydney Johnson, Grade 6
Gilmore Middle School, WI

Bone Trees

As autumn comes
Leaves go.
For this, of course,
Is a sign of winter.
But don't be sad or cry.
They'll be back again soon…
Very soon.

David Ahrens, Grade 4
Breck School, MN

Ice Cream

I like ice cream.
You like ice cream.
We all like ice cream.
I like chocolate.
You like strawberry.
That's ok because it's still ice cream.
Mine's in a cone.
Yours is in a bowl.
It does not matter!
It's still ice cream.

Casey Ekleberry, Grade 6
Riverdale Elementary School, WI

Maple

The leaves turn brown in fall.
The maple trees stand so tall.
It is when the kids have fun
And that fun time is fall.

Crispy brown, orange, and red leaves
They all are there in the fall.
Coming off of playful kids' shoes
In the nice clean hall.
And that windy time is fall.

Amara Neitzke, Grade 4
Classical School, WI

Beautiful Horses

HORSES

H ooves are super strong
O h just don't get kicked by them
R ace horses run like the wind
S tallions are one of the best horses
E at oats, hay, carrots, and apples
S ee them run through the pastures

HORSES

Abigail Hackbarth, Grade 5
St Paul Evangelical Lutheran School, WI

What Is My Dog?

She is a playmate
A peaceful dog
She is a piece of my family
An attack dog
She is a hairy dog
A scavenger
She is a wonderer
A fast dog
She is a silly dog
A happy dog

Nick Shepherd, Grade 6
Orfordville Elementary School, WI

Winter

W hen it's time for winter the snow is here, I come into the
house and the warmth is so dear.
I feel so warm sitting by the fireplace, with a giant smile on my face.
N ight is here but don't fear, because winter time will still be here.
T he cocoa is warm, so get toasty warm.
E at the marshmallows from the boiling hot cocoa.
R emember to spread some warmth and cheer.

Lauren Carr, Grade 5
Stocker Elementary School, WI

Earth Music

The Earth is filled with a special music,
that is here to help you all.
Even when you doubt it all,
you think all hope is lost,
and the hatred absorbs your spirit.
Earth music is here to help you
stand up when you fall.

Christain Holtz, Grade 6
Martin County West Trimont Elementary School, MN

I Remember

I remember all my relatives with tears in their eyes.
I remember the day it happened.
I remember being at the funeral home for hours.
I remember people coming in and out.
I remember staying at the hospital with him.
I remember all the great times we had together.
I remember the day my grandpa died.

Brandon Schrauth, Grade 6
Campbellsport Elementary School, WI

The Rim and the Backboard

They are a pair and they do everything together
They're like Stockton and Malone or Jordan and Pippen
The backboard is the hand that feeds to the rim
They might break your heart or make you love them
You kiss the glass but the rim chucks the ball back
In and out, out and in
The two work as a team

Declan Lang-Backe, Grade 6
Holy Family Parish School, WI

I Remember

I remember going to my friend's birthday party.
I remember playing tag and running through the corn field.
I remember having a chair demolition derby.
I remember dunking for apples.
I remember having a food fight.
I remember having a corn cob fight.
I remember getting hit in the head by a corn cob.

Jacob Johnson, Grade 6
Campbellsport Elementary School, WI

Duba Day

I wake up on a gloomy Saturday;
It's not good for play —
But no tears today,
For Saturday is Duba Day.

It starts in the spring in mid-May
And continues every Saturday,
Never during the week or on Sunday;
Only Saturday is Duba Day.

My brother works there every day
Making pasties by the tray.
"Pulled pork sandwiches on the menu today!"
It's Saturday; it's Duba Day!

Jan Duba makes the rolls at the bak-a-ray.
Steve Duba pulls the pork; what can I say?
He adds Granny's secret rec-i-pay
And ta-da! It's Duba Day.

Whether we drive today
Or we pedal all the way,
We do not delay.
It's Boulder Junction's Duba Day!

Daniel Rubach, Grade 6
Dr Dyer Intermediate School, WI

I Am From

I am from swimming in water as cold as ice
to itching my irritating mosquito bites

I am from skiing in snowy Colorado
to playing in the deep dark shadows

I am from really thrilling skateboarding
to hearing the noisy crowds roaring

I am from soothing classical pieces
to eating sugary Reese's pieces

I am from playing on the warm beach hearing the gulls
to playing some entertaining baseball

I am from catching slimy frogs
to being clumsy and tripping over logs

I am from fishing in Canada
to hearing about my cousin's trip to Grenada.

I like to read and play the entertaining Wii
but that's just me.

Sam Edgerton, Grade 5
Adams Spanish Immersion School, MN

Winter

W hen you're sad try to be happy.
I n the winter so many things can happen.
N ever be angry, be joyful.
T ill after winter ends, still be grateful.
E ven when things seem tragic.
R emember there is still Christmas magic.

Alex Kuehnl, Grade 5
Stocker Elementary School, WI

A Scary Halloween Night

Being out on a dark
night like Halloween.
Ghosts, monsters, all kinds of things.
They will give you a fright,
from Malik Jihad have a
happy Halloween night.

Malik Jihad, Grade 5
Messmer Preparatory Catholic School, WI

Apples

Green ones, red ones, yellow ones
Crunchy ones, soft ones
Tasty ones, gross ones
Big ones, small ones
Clean ones, dirty ones,
I LOVE APPLES!

Michael Sullivan, Grade 6
St Francis Middle School, MN

Swans

Gliding gracefully through the water
Lovely scenes in the air
Beautiful hearts they make together
Swans make peace and harmony
Together they make one
Oh, swans what a beautiful bird

Amanda Jackson, Grade 5
Harriet Bishop Elementary School, MN

Space

Space is as big as life
Planets are as circular as boulders
Stars are as bright as lightning
Comets are as fast as sound
Meteor showers are like sprinkles
Coming out of the shaker

Paige Schultz, Grade 5
Harriet Bishop Elementary School, MN

In the Rain

In the rain
I feel no pain.
Just the sensation
Of relaxation.

Amy Houle, Grade 6
St Francis Middle School, MN

My Name Is Like…

My name is like a group of people laughing
My name is like a candle when the power goes out
My name is like a fish jumping off the rod
My name is like a dancer doing a twirl
My name is like a tornado running around the town
My name is like a train crossing the road
My name is like a horse neighing in the grazing pasture
My name is like the rain thumping on the ground
My name is like a laughing baby
My name is like a horse sweating after a long summer's ride in the woods.

Sydney Philpot, Grade 5
Sibley Elementary School, MN

Inside This Recycling Bin

Inside this recycling bin lay crumpled up pieces of paper from your
mistakes and maybe from recent times.
Inside this recycling bin lay broken pencils from giving up too easily,
and a couple more from months later to let everybody know that you haven't given up.
Inside this recycling bin lay projects you weren't proud of because one,
just one person told you that it was the worst project yet to be seen.
Inside this recycling bin lay memories of your past and all of your mistakes that
gave you a devastated feeling. But importantly inside this recycling bin
lay the memories of your mistakes to let everybody know you have tried
and have never given up and will keep trying from this day on forever and always.

Carly LeCloux, Grade 6
T J Walker Middle School, WI

A Midnight Walk in the Winter

Whoosh, whoosh the wind blowing through my hair.
The night looks so cold, so bare.
The trees like skeletons dancing in the air.
I look at the snowy ground, as if mother nature sprinkled it with care.
Crunch, crunch my footsteps in the snow.
I love the wind, just watch it blow.
A flurry of white rushes by me, I watch and listen to it run.
The night sky like black velvet, all polka dot stars and the moon no sun.
I stare up watching the snow fall.
I don't have a favorite part I love it all.

Lina Colangelo, Grade 5
Sibley Elementary School, MN

The Rose in the Upper Room

In an upper room I stare.
At the magnificent rose that lay there.
Yet I see another and another.
Many roses right before me.
But none can compare to the first.
Absolutely no flower I see.
As I was beginning to leave, I looked back and sensed that every little flower became
drawn to me. The aroma in the room felt like a soft kiss on my cheek.
After this experience my heart was pounding.
Then in all my being I knew that I would return one day.

Madeline Schroeder, Grade 5
St Johns Lutheran School, WI

Basketball

The day I went to my basketball game
Michael Jordan and I played the same
I scored 82 baskets in one day
Just like Kobe Bryant would play

I was on a team called blue ball
I made the other team fall
It was so funny watching them trip
So I did a 360 back flip

No need to boast
We ate them like toast
The score was 92-1
We won by a ton
Brandon Merten, Grade 6
Dr Dyer Intermediate School, WI

Planting and Harvesting

Around and down fields
Past the trees
Across the back
Along the markers
Throughout the field
Underneath the ground seeds go
For this year's crop

Beyond the whirr off the machine
Still more to be harvested
To the fields when everything's ready
Down and up the rows
To make some money
From this year's crop
Caleb Johnson, Grade 6
Orfordville Elementary School, WI

I Can

I can be a man,
I can be whatever I want to be,
I can sing,
I can play sports,
I can go racing,
I can be a winner,
I can be a legend,
Race Null, Grade 5
St Paul Evangelical Lutheran School, WI

Frigid/Heat

Frigid
Breezy, chilly
Freezing, shivering, howling
Ice, snow, rain, sun
Sweltering, sweating, sapping
Steamy, summer
Heat
Kortney Guenther, Grade 4
Jefferson Elementary School, WI

Batteries

Batteries, batteries, small but might.
Batteries, batteries, not tall in height.

If you don't work now right here
Maybe you'll work later there.

Maybe it's small, and maybe it's queer
But it will help but not right here.

I'm not done well, not right now
Because if I were I'd take a bow.

Inside these are electric things
Making your night light go Bing.

So never judge something by size
Because what counts is right inside.
Timmy Ward, Grade 6
T J Walker Middle School, WI

Winter

You get up in the morning
Look out and see
White everywhere
It's like a blanket for nature
You run outside
Build a snow fort
Then you go against your friend
Then both of us get sleds
And hook them up to the four-wheeler
Go out on the lake
Take all the jumps we see
Get our face pounded in the snow
Then we go back home and get warm
With hot chocolate galore
We get back on the four-wheeler
To start a new adventure
Never let go always hold on
Justin Sierakowski, Grade 5
Blue Heron Elementary School, MN

Maxamillion

Oh, Maxamillion,
my favorite dog.
I love it when we
go out to jog.
You've been a handful
from the start
You always have a place
within my heart.
You run hard and
you run far.
You're so big
you barely fit in our car.
Maria Holschbach, Grade 5
St Katharine Drexel School, WI

Horicon Marsh

H ear the animals in the forest
O h, it was the best field trip ever
R an away from the snake
I saw two black and yellow snakes
C an see a lot of geese in the sky
O ur first trip in fifth grade
N ot that warm out

M any animals creeping around
A lways see beautiful sights
R ushing wind blowing on my face
S tood on top of a pile of rocks
H aving so much fun at the marsh
Miya Leistekow, Grade 5
St Katharine Drexel School, WI

Basketball

Dribble
Dribble
Shoot
Score
Squeaky feet
Sweaty jerseys
Fly'n shoe laces
Coaches
Crazy parents
Refs
Last buzzer…
Home team wins!!
Hooray!!!
Callie Gudmonson, Grade 5
Harriet Bishop Elementary School, MN

Autumn

Plucking yummy apples
Eating delicious pies
Dressing up in fun costumes
Trick or Treating with friends
Carving big, round, orange pumpkins
Raking elaborate colored leaves
Brown grass crunching when I walk
Starting to wear warmer jackets
Turning the hot heat on
Animals going into hibernation
Birds migrating south
Everyone feeling cold but happy
I love AUTUMN!
Marissa Marsolek, Grade 5
Harriet Bishop Elementary School, MN

what trees do

whispering treetops.
wiggling from side to side.
beautifully swaying.
Savannah Soderholm, Grade 6
Dr Dyer Intermediate School, WI

Winter

I feel all the goodies sitting in our stockings.
I hear Santa saying, "HO HO HO, Merry Christmas!"
I see the train going round and round on Christmas Lane.
I smell my mom's delicious snicker bar cookies.
I taste fresh lasagna from the Christmas Eve table.

JC Ovitt, Grade 5
Stocker Elementary School, WI

Winter

I feel the snow when I reach down to touch it.
I hear kids playing in the snow and having fun.
I see snow falling on the ground.
I smell cookies in the oven that can't wait to be eaten.
I taste cookies and chocolate melting in my mouth.

Rollan Garcia, Grade 5
Stocker Elementary School, WI

Soup

It's tasty and watery like happiness racing down your throat
It's warm like standing close to a campfire
It sometimes has noodles, crackers, meat, and veggies
It's like eating fresh food from the farm right out of your bowl
It warms you when you're cold like you're an iceberg in lava

Johnathan D. Mulvihill, Grade 5
Blue Heron Elementary School, MN

Winter

Through the winter months so bleak
Summer heat and spring we seek
There in the midst of fall we see a flicker of winter
Winter dominates spring, summer, and fall
Oh the winter months so bleak

Alexander Schneider, Grade 6
Riverdale Elementary School, WI

Snowboarding

Snowboarding is basically all about balance.
You need balance to go far.
You also need balance to stay up.
If you want to go fast you're going to want to lean forward.

Johnathan Palluck, Grade 6
St Francis Middle School, MN

Pumpkin Pie

Yummy, pumpkins
Smooth, cozy, luxurious
Pumpkin seeds, pumpkin pie, pumpkin guts, pumpkin shells
Giggles, oven, rising, rumbling, explosion

Madison DeBoer, Grade 4
Stocker Elementary School, WI

Family

My family is really nice because they care for me.
They help me with my homework.
They love me because I'm their daughter and sister.
They are exciting because they can do things that I can't.

Autumn Durm, Grade 6
St Francis Middle School, MN

Beach

Cool water, coral reef, colorful fish, dark blue water, no people,
Waves swirling, no wind, are there jellyfish,
Warm out, bright sunshine, white sand,
Ocean, ocean, ocean.

Madeline Mulcahy, Grade 6
Harriet Bishop Elementary School, MN

Horses

Horses are as graceful as a bird soaring through the sky.
Horses are as lovable as a newborn puppy snuggled up in its bed.
Horses are as hard working as a lumberjack chopping down wood.
Horses are as exciting as going to outer space.

Alaina Sauer, Grade 6
Harriet Bishop Elementary School, MN

Dogs

Dogs are really fun pets.
They like to play with their toys and go on long walks.
They sleep and eat just like everyone else would.
They need lots of care but they are still really fun!

Cassidy Adamson, Grade 6
St Francis Middle School, MN

Pencil

A pencil has a sharp end that looks like a sword.
The eraser looks like a chewing thing.
It's supposed to be used for writing
But people use it as a weapon.

Brody Childs, Grade 5
Harriet Bishop Elementary School, MN

Basketball

Basketball is awesome, it is my favorite sport.
I like running, and trying, to get the ball.
I like, shooting the ball when I get it in the hoop.
I really hope I never stop playing basketball.

Jordan Miley, Grade 6
St Francis Middle School, MN

If I Were a Mother's Hug

If I were a mother's hug —
I'd be gentle.
I'd be comforting.
I'd make people happy.
I'd love people silly.
I'd always have open arms.

McKenna Meyer, Grade 4
Amery Intermediate School, WI

Colors

Green are my eyes,
Changing brown to yellow.

Blue is the sky,
With white clouds that are shy.

Red are my nails,
Fading to pink and orange.

Purple is my pen,
Writing my name on my paper.

Gray is my polo,
Sitting still on my back.

What colors explain you?
Joleena Redmond, Grade 6
Gilmore Middle School, WI

Arya

Arya's a pretty lazy dog,
Who steals my brother's bed,
And loves to walk and play,
She'll run away if the gate's open,
And won't come back for hours.

Arya loves other dogs,
Like she loves people,
She'll jump on them and lick their face,
She's a black and white husky.

She'll steal food if you're not looking,
She growls at her toy,
My dad calls her meatball,
And I call her pup,
She's the best dog ever.
Matt Anbro, Grade 5
Blue Heron Elementary School, MN

Poetry

Poetry
Like a ripple in the water
Magnificent, intricate
Poetry
Like a paint brush on a canvas
Poetry
Singing for the soul
Poetry
Like music without a tune
Poetry
Words woven together
To make something new
Poetry
My way to escape
Shannon Paramesh, Grade 5
School of Technology & Arts I, WI

Football

Under the sun
On the turf
Against the Bulldogs
On the ball
Near the five yard line
Into the red zone
Across the pylons
In the end zone
Through the uprights
To win the game
Seamus Floyd, Grade 6
Holy Family Parish School, WI

The Bowling Ball

Inside this bowling ball
the cracks and the oil lay.
And you can't see a speck.
The thick hardness
of the inside makes a great roll.
With three holes poking on the
hard inside surface.
As I hit the alley I feel the
hard bounce and when I hit a
strike I feel the momentum.
Jacob Hartl, Grade 6
T J Walker Middle School, WI

The Dragon

The dragon flying and free.
Flying at speeds of
hundreds of miles per hour!
Faster then anything
Sparks of golden fire!
Used in battle sometimes.
A mythical animal that the Chinese
believed in a long time ago.
Used in myths or stories
and very different animals!
Joseph Mickelson, Grade 5
Mazomanie Elementary School, WI

Dreams*

Hold fast to dreams,
For when dreams come alive,
Life is a birthday,
That for me is in July.

Hold fast to dreams,
For when dreams play,
Life is a video game,
That brightens the day.
Joel Heuring, Grade 4
Classical School, WI
*Inspired by Langston Hughes' "Dreams"

Basketball

B ouncing balls
A thletes
S hoes squeaking
K ids shooting baskets
R **E** ferees
T all kids dunking
B alls being dribbled
A nnouncers
S **L** am dunk
L unging to the basket
Brittany Schaller, Grade 5
Howards Grove Middle School, WI

Basketball

B ouncing basketballs
A lways running
S weaty kids
K eeping score
Ch **E** ering parents
T eaching plans
B asketballs
A im for the backboard
Whist **L** es blowing
L ots of kids cheering
Emily Kulow, Grade 5
Howards Grove Middle School, WI

Michael Jackson

He is very flexible
He's a great dancer.
Michael Jackson is famous because
He's the king of pop.
Some of his famous songs and moves are
Moonwalk, Spin twirl,
"Man in the Mirror,"
"Beat It," "Thriller,"
"Billy Jean."
Michael Jackson is the best!
Elle Hemauer, Grade 4
River Heights Elementary School, WI

Storm on the Plains

Coming soon
Now it thunders
Whipping into gusto
The wind
Lightning lights the sand
Rain hits my face
Racing the storm to my hole
I watch very scared
Sand fills everywhere
Storm on the plains
Sofia Herling, Grade 5
School of Technology & Arts I, WI

This Is My Dad

This is my dad,
He is brave and bold.
I love him very much,
But he is kind of old.

This is my dad,
He cares very much.
He loves me a lot,
I'm his little honey bunch.

This is my dad,
I'm his hunting buddy.
We hunt in the fall,
Where we get pretty muddy!
Tito Housey, Grade 5
Howards Grove Middle School, WI

The Blue Candle

Inside this blue candle
Lies something mysterious
Maybe it's a scent
Maybe it's a dream

I almost could hear it ask
As its scent filled the air
Why do you make me wait
Just burn me please

I walked away but I came back
I couldn't stay away
It almost made me cry
As I lit the single blue candle
Jacquelyn Hill, Grade 6
T J Walker Middle School, WI

Tyler Dembosky

T y is my nickname
likes to pla **Y** pool
L ikes bowling
E arly riser
R ides his bike

bore **D** a lot
lik **E** s to swim
M akes high scores on pinball
B ounces on his trampoline
goes **O** n Club Penguin
S ledding is fun
coo **K** s
pla **Y** s with his cousin
Tyler Dembosky, Grade 4
Tess Corners Elementary School, WI

The Bullet in the Clip

Inside this bullet
243. Bullet
That's inside the clip
That's inside my gun
It holds lead
But not just lead
A soul

Inside this bullet
That's in the black clip
It holds happiness
My happiness
To kill my
First buck
And others' happiness

Inside this bullet
There is more than
Just lead,
A soul, happiness,
There is hope,
Inside this bullet
Isaac Arneman, Grade 6
T J Walker Middle School, WI

Angel Tears

I hear the sounds of
Angel tears hitting my bedroom window
The pitter patter of the tears soothes
Me and relaxes me.

The angel tears make the
Windows blurry, confusing me about the
Outside world.
I think to myself,

Why are the angels crying?
Is it happy or sad?
All I know is that the angel tears have
Broken free of their well-made

Aqueducts, causing them to
Splatter across the canvas of our
World, tears hitting my skin,
Wetting down my hair,
And filling my soul with
Love.
Madeline Sarkis, Grade 6
T J Walker Middle School, WI

Crystals

Some may think crystals are gems.
But crystals to me are a magical thing
But it only happens in a season.
Alli Gregor, Grade 4
Tess Corners Elementary School, WI

Oh, Eeky Creaky Tree

Oh, eeky creaky tree
You are so high in the sky
You're dead and droopy
And very spooky
It makes me want to cry.
Woodpecker holes all over you
You are the best tree of all
The thing that I'll remember most was…
That you were really tall.
Clark Crombie, Grade 5
St Katharine Drexel School, WI

Sea Animals

There are many different sea animals
Some are very shy
Some are many colors
Some are mean
Some eat other animals
Some eat plants
Some are scared
Some are not
Ashleigh Quance, Grade 6
St Francis Middle School, MN

Our Only Difference

There are people on the streets.
From Kids to Adults,
From Americans to Europeans,
From Farmers to Musicians,
But we all share one thing,
That's the world we live on,
To the air we breathe.
Diversity is our only difference.
Jessie Meng, Grade 6
Wayzata Central Middle School, MN

Halloween

you see the black cats
you see the midnight bats

you hear the squeaky floor
you hear the scary crows

you know the ghosts are there
you know they are everywhere
Kenny Words, Grade 6
Messmer Preparatory Catholic School, WI

Pancakes

Pancakes
fluffy, sweet
sticky, syrup, buttery
warm, steamy, so tasty
Waffles
Ariana Daniels, Grade 4
Jefferson Elementary School, WI

Vampire

Who: Vampire
What: is going to suck blood
When: at 12:00 midnight
Where: inside H. Express
Why: because I woke up thirsty…

Rashaun Jackson, Grade 6
Messmer Preparatory Catholic School, WI

Winter

I feel snow.
I hear wind.
I see Christmas lights blinking nonstop.
I smell the food in people's houses.
I taste the hot cocoa.

Hailey Tilander, Grade 5
Stocker Elementary School, WI

Band

B ooming instruments playing
A ctive music bouncing along
N atural musicians playing loud
D rummers pounding the beat

Fai Haw, Grade 5
St Paul Evangelical Lutheran School, WI

Fearful or Fearless

Fearful or fearless
No matter what you are
Believe in yourself
Let courage show you the way

Izabel Janz, Grade 6
Campbellsport Elementary School, WI

The First Summer Day!

Summer is here! Summer is here!
Finally it is here. No school,
no school I say. It is finally here.
It is time to play I say!

Christopher Griffith, Grade 6
St Francis Middle School, MN

Deer Hunting

When you go deer hunting
You have to be quiet
You have to listen very closely
And try to stay warm

Justus Young, Grade 6
Riverdale Elementary School, WI

Flower

Gently swaying in the light breeze.
Bees softly landing upon the delicate petals.
Children laugh and smell them.
Deer bound and frolic through them.

Emily Bohn, Grade 6
Campbellsport Elementary School, WI

I Am a Police Officer

I am a police officer.
I wonder if I'm going to bring anyone to justice on my shift.
I hear the sirens when I turn them on.
I see the criminals trying to run away.
I am a police officer.

I pretend that nothing is more important than catching that criminal.
I feel frightened when I go out into the dangerous streets.
I worry that I might not come home to my fun-loving family.
I cry when I don't do something right.
I am a police officer.

I understand that I am not perfect.
I say I can achieve anything if I try hard enough.
I dream to make the world a better place for everyone.
I try my very best at everything I do.
I hope to be successful and the best I can be.
I am a police officer!

Lucero Jaimes, Grade 6
Gilmore Middle School, WI

Make-believe

He causes great fright in the night.
Is he a joke or is he just broke.
He is out there trudging along.
There he caught his prey he'll give it a shake, did you hear that bone break?
Is he really alive?
He will crush all in his way.
He will mush all who stray.
His matted hair is very scary.
He isn't scared to use his claw or his jaw.
On a moonlit night you may catch a sight of THE BEAST OF BRAY ROAD.
Is he a man or a wolf?
Have you seen THE BEAST?
Is THE BEAST OF BRAY ROAD even really alive?
IF HE IS HE HAS A VERY STRANGE LIFE!
ROARRRRR!
Or was that the wind?
RUN AWAY!!!!!!!!

Trenton Howell, Grade 6
Dr Dyer Intermediate School, WI

My Colors

My Red is the fiery tail of a fox extinguishing in its own beauty…
My Orange is the crisp autumn leaves falling in my hair…
My Yellow is the golden field of wheat on a farm…
My Green is the trees leaves falling and growing through the seasons…
My Blue is a waterfall guarding a secret cave in the heart of a mountain…
My Violet is a fresh grape being picked off a vine…
My Black is the shadow, guarding my bed when I go to sleep…
My Gray is the dust worn off in a musty chest, hiding its secrets…
My White is the crisp page in a new book…
My Pink is the warm, dreamy sunset…
My Brown the sand shifting in a desert endlessly…

Hibah Hassan, Grade 5
Harriet Bishop Elementary School, MN

Bliss

As I gape longingly at the serene bliss of nature.
It calls me closer.
As I advance upon the shallow river bank.
I see a small school of fish.
Glimmering in the afternoon sun.

The wind blows.
Cool against my face.
Blowing through my hair.
It rustles the leaves.
The forest is alive.

The trees are swaying.
The birds are chirping.
Leaves are falling.
Subtle ripples appear in the water.
I've never felt more at peace.

I could stay here forever and never leave.
So quiet and calm.
Yet lively and exciting.
I take it all in.
As I gape longingly at the serene bliss of nature.

Waylon Alvarado, Grade 6
Lincoln Middle School, WI

I Am From

I am from excitement
I am from running, daring free time
I am from spending time with my family
I am from around the people I trust
I am from around the world.

I am from going to different states on vacation
I am from eating spicy food. I am from my awesome school
I am from learning
I am from my family's history
I am smart in my own family

I am from soccer
I am from learning sports
I am from playing with great friends
I am from running
I am from jumping around most of the time
I am from skateboarding

I am from having birthday parties
I am from talking to my dad in Mexico on the phone
I am from looking at pictures of my dad
I am from talking to my dad on my birthday
I am from Mexico

Jack Salcido, Grade 5
Adams Spanish Immersion School, MN

Wide, Willowing White

White is fresh, crunchy snow, gooey marshmallows,
and the freezing winter.
White is the taste of mint ice cream.
Vanilla candles and coconut milk smell white.
Blizzards make me feel white.
White is the sound of mooing cows and crashing waves.
White is Antarctica, Greenland, and snow-covered Russia.
Fluffy summer clouds are white.
Brand new, squeaky-clean, white boards are also white.
White is fresh, frozen ice.

Dustin Saylor, Grade 6
Marinette Middle School, WI

On Thanksgiving Day, My Birthday

In 1999 I was born
at the Fairmont Medical Center
the 24th of November.
That day my dad
was coaching girls basketball.
My grandma came and got my sister.
She was setting the alarms off
in the hospital.
I am Maia.
On Thanksgiving day I was born.

Maia Taylor, Grade 4
Martin County West Sherburn Elementary School, MN

Blue

Blue is the waves in the ocean.
Blue is sad when you fall and scrape your knee.
Blue is the chirping Blue Jay outside my window.
Blue is my favorite color.
Blue is the tasty blueberry pie my mom makes.
Blue is the shirt I'm wearing.
Blue is the icy cold wind in winter.
Blue is the sky with fluffy clouds.
Blue is the color of my eyes.
Blue is both cold and sad.

Holly Barron, Grade 6
Gilmore Middle School, WI

The Road to Success

The road to success is not straight
there is a loop called failure a
curve called confusion speed bumps
called friends red lights called enemies
caution lights called family you will have
flats called jobs. But if you have a spare
called determination the engine called
perseverance insurance called faith and a
driver called Jesus you will make it to the
end of road success embrace the smell of accomplishment.

Passion Carson, Grade 6
Ramsey International Fine Arts Center, MN

What Fall Is

What fall is
Cleaning out pumpkins
You reach your hand in and take pumpkin guts
Squish!
The gooey pile of pumpkin guts feels like a pile of wet mud

What fall is
Coming in from playing in the leaves
I have some hot apple cider
It feels like a hot tub in my mouth

What fall is
Listening to the colorful leaves flying on the ground
Going from yard to yard
Crisp grass like a cookie.
Snow falls like sprinkles on a cake.

What fall is
Grass fading to yellow like kids turning pages.
Hot candles burning like a roasting pig
The smell of the cool crisp air.

Jacob Walz, Grade 4
Kennedy Elementary School, MN

Secrets

Inside this tattered American flag
Lie tears and blood
Screams of terror and anguish
Things it has seen should never be shared
That is why it is silent
Waving freely in the wind.

On top it's just a flag
Woven carefully at a factory
Packaged up
Then just sent off

Like people
Most of us grew up with a mama and a papa
Then just sent off
On top we all look alike
Two eyes, ears, a nose and a mouth
But on the inside we differ greatly
With our own secrets

Inside this tattered American flag, is you
Hannah M. Bremer, Grade 6
T J Walker Middle School, WI

Pumpkin Pie

Pumpkins, pie
Slushy, soft, crusty
Good, beautiful, awesome, tasty
Steaming, popping, talking, clinking, laughing
Cameron Sloan, Grade 4
Stocker Elementary School, WI

Pugs

Who is my Pug?
A loving member of my family
An animal with a smashed face and curled tail
One to be always friendly
A playful pooch
One to scratch and bite
There to bark at everything
To snore real loud
Tear up the furniture
To purr like a cat
That is my pug!

Joelle Strand, Grade 6
Orfordville Elementary School, WI

The Occasional Oddball Oozy Orange

Orange is an ordinary orangutan, squishy squash,
and a fabulous friendship.
Orange is the taste of an oversized orange.
Plump pumpkins and candles smell orange.
Stressful sunburns make me feel orange.
Orange is the sound of a crunchy carrot and
hollow Halloween music.
Orange is a pumpkin patch, frolicking in Florida,
and the admirable autumn.
Haunted houses are orange. A hopeless Halloween is also
Orange. Orange is jolting Jupiter.
Lexi Bretl, Grade 6
Marinette Middle School, WI

The Transition

After the last burgundy leaf falls
A crunchy blanket covers the cold ground
Not leaving a bare spot uncovered
The last of the leaves fall to the ground
And all the beauty is gone
But wait,
The first of the snowflakes start the next blanket
The blanket that will cover the leaves until spring
Until then,
We will have the white beauty of the winter
For the whole winter

Clare Weber, Grade 6
Hudson Middle School, WI

Fish in the Current

Fish swim with the flow,
They come out of hiding at night,
Fish can go fast like the wind or they can go slow,
When it gets dark they are out of sight.

Fish are the breeze
They follow the wind as it travels west,
You can catch them if you please,
You know wind and fish are simply the best!
Bryn Goldinger, Grade 4
Classical School, WI

Misery and Sorrow

Misery and sorrow is a day with no light
Surrounded by shadows and fog
Running as fast as you can
To the cries for help
But no matter how fast or how far you run
It seems you can never catch them
But it never lasts forever
As it turns into joy and happiness
Like a ray of sunshine giving you hope
It leads you to positive thoughts
A breath taking ocean
Taking all your misery and sorrow away
Now it has gone
But it is like a cold
It makes you choke like being rolled in the waves of a storm
It will come back so be prepared.

Stephanie Larson, Grade 6
Holy Family Parish School, WI

Seasons

Summer summer, such a sunny time.
On earth it makes you think of
Playing outside, lemonade stands and friends.

Fall is a season of change.
Leaves change color and it gets colder
Until you reach winter.

Winter is the coldest of all time.
It is good for snow days, sledding
and hot chocolate.

Spring brings new life.
It starts to warm up and flowers start to bloom.
Trees start to grow new leaves.
Snow melts away.

Jacob Schneider, Grade 5
Blue Heron Elementary School, MN

Safari

Their guns cocked,
their spirits high,
they seem like heroes yet they die.
Their outfits tan,
their heads held high,
their psyche filled with lies.
They hunt for lust, not for food or sport.
They plot their demise against creation.
They come from rich families, powerful too.
They drink and smoke in moderation,
but they kill for no good reason.
They praise themselves,
they celebrate death.
How long will it be until they turn against themselves?

Malik Selle, Grade 6
Ramsey International Fine Arts Center, MN

Colors

Yellow is the first day of summer,
White is snow; it's just a bummer.

Gray is the color of my bus driver's hair,
Brown is the color of my dining room chair.

Blue is the best color of all,
Green is the coat my sister bought at the mall.

Silver is the color of medal I earn,
Red is my horrible sun burn.

Pink is the flower on Mother's Day,
Orange is the heat wave today.

What are colors to you?

Dawson Snyder, Grade 6
Gilmore Middle School, WI

Wonderful Winding White

White is a silvery full moon,
bright shooting stars,
and beautiful, sweet,
comfortable, fluffiness.
White is the taste of vanilla ice cream,
and crystally sugar tastes white.
White smells like sweet lavender candles,
and the smell of winter
outside when it's coming.
Peace makes me feel white.
White is the sound of a wedding veil,
the end of May,
and a valley of beautiful sweet smelling lilies.
A frosty night is white.
Life and dreams are white.
White is calm, happy, and proud!

Savannah Prucha, Grade 6
Marinette Middle School, WI

In the Season Of

In the season of winter
Joy goes through every house,
Candles light up every window, night is every day,
Riddles get past every night.
In the season of summer
Storms pass by like trains, everybody
Swims like there is no tomorrow, eagles soar
Through the sky like jets, rainbows stretch after storms like
Tornadoes in the sky.
In the season of fall leaves fall like
Helicopters passing by, blossoms start to die,
The invisible sun never show until spring comes
People wear fur
Dangerous ice and no more sun.

Damian White, Grade 5
Wagner Elementary School, MN

Inside This Apple Sauce Cup

Inside an apple sauce cup
lays white mold
tiny flies, stinky, smelly apple sauce
nasty.
Tipped over everywhere on papers and books.
Someone who is nasty.
Who is stinky.
Someone smelly.
Then throws it all away.
Like all the other garbage.
With some old milk and some rotten foods from lunch.
That's what's inside the apple sauce cup.

Santos Garcia, Grade 6
T J Walker Middle School, WI

Halloween

Halloween night might be a fright,
A cool breeze blowing in the night.
Rustling in the leaves might be,
A thief ready to steal all the candy.

Everyone's costume might be spooky,
Or they might even be a little kooky.
Some are cats,
Others are bats.

There are witches, demons, devils, zombies too,
Halloween night can be really cool.

Drew Foley, Grade 5
Seneca Middle School, WI

Glorious Green

Green is glistening clovers.
Green is sparkling grass.
Green is beautiful clear glass.
Green is the taste of fresh, crisp lettuce.
Green is the smell of a warm summer's breeze
and bright green leaves.
Green is the feeling of jealousy and envy.
Green is the sound of the ocean and a meadow.
Green is a river, a dragonfly, and a leprechaun's house.
Winning the lottery is green!
Saint Patrick's Day is also green!
Green is HAPPINESS!!!

Taylor Montgomery, Grade 6
Marinette Middle School, WI

Buildings

Standing in the sky, so big and tall.
I wonder what will happen if you ever fall.
What do you do in the blistering hot sun?
Standing still all day like no one else will.
So many in the city, I can't count them all.
Standing in the sky, so very big and tall.

Laura Wyatt, Grade 6
St Francis Middle School, MN

Baseball

The sun is high in the sky
there are few clouds
It's just right to play baseball
Here comes the white, round ball of wonder
Right into my mitt
Sttttrrrike 1! Yes!
It is 6-5 in the bottom of the 9th bases loaded
2 outs
we need to win
this is the path to fame
the championship, the world championship
one of the most popular sports in it
Foomp! a fast ball on the outside corner Strike 2!
The championship is so close
Whap! he hit it!
The outfielder is running, he jumps and catches
the ball of wonder on the top of his mitt
He caught it We win! We win!
I'm jumping on the outfielder before anyone else
even though I'm way in at catcher.

So we won.

Gavin Fletcher, Grade 5
Blue Heron Elementary School, MN

I Remember

I remember a tall, wide, and green tree.
I remember a colorful decorated Christmas tree.
I remember seeing gifts under the tree.
I remember seeing my family every Christmas.
I remember seeing my Uncle's dog.
I remember opening several presents.
I remember getting up to see what was under the tree.
I remember going to different houses.
I remember passing out gifts under the tree.
I remember the fluffy snow.

Kyle Roever, Grade 6
Campbellsport Elementary School, WI

Little Cramped Room

I feel like storage in this
little cramped room. There are
only two tables in this
room and the teacher
said it used to be
an old speech
room. There are
so many cabinets
that are filled
with storage
and many
instruments
in this little
cramped room.

Dawson Burkhardt, Grade 5
Martin County West Trimont Elementary School, MN

Beaming Blasting Blue

Blue are the clouds, the gentle dusk,
and the softness of day.
Blue is the taste of sweet, pure water.
Summer rain and Lake Michigan smell blue.
Gentle ocean breezes make me feel blue.
Blue is the sound of church bells,
and a train whistle.
Blue is the autumn sky and the
North and South Poles.
Discovering science is blue.
Wisconsin Dells is also blue.
Blue is sorrow, reading, and joyfulness.

Eva Miller, Grade 6
Marinette Middle School, WI

Luscious Lime Lovers

Lime green is a sun filled forest, an inchworm,
and full of light.
Lime green is the taste of a nice green apple.
Peppermint and pickles smell lime green.
Shining love makes me feel lime green.
Lime green is the sound of a water trickle and a
blowing breeze.
Lime green is a meadow, a quiet field of trees,
and a yard of fresh grass.
A rush of fun is lime green.
The flutter of spring is also lime green.
Lime green is the light inside of you.

Emily Buettner, Grade 6
Marinette Middle School, WI

My Very Best

I may lose or be victorious
I don't care if I look bad or glorious
I may not be the very best
But I try harder than all the rest
I don't want to know my future in case it's bad
But I won't be the least bit sad
If I don't know right before
I'll try harder just a little bit more
If things don't go the way I planned
I'll wipe my anger away with the back of my hand
Every day is another test
To see if I can be my very best

Danica Fliss, Grade 6
St Gabriel Catholic School, WI

Winter

W arm taste of hot chocolate.
I t's time for the winter games.
N o more time to wait for Christmas, it's finally here.
T he big man is coming to give us presents.
E at some cookies, but don't forget Santa.
R udolph is coming with all his friends.

Deandre Ross, Grade 5
Stocker Elementary School, WI

Yodeling Yummy Yellow

Yellow is a flickering candle flame,
blonde little girls' curls,
and a million dollar smile.
Yellow is the taste of tangy,
delicious lemonade.
A roaring fire and
a field of sunflowers in September
smell yellow.
A warm sunny day makes me feel yellow.
Yellow is a twinkling star,
and the shining full moon.
Yellow is an Aeropostale store,
a wonderful, fun-filled circus, and a country fair.
A Florida vacation is yellow.
Exciting bright ideas are also yellow.
Yellow is a walk on the beach!!!

Megan Padgett, Grade 6
Marinette Middle School, WI

Muffy and Tye

Muffy and Tye are the best dogs ever
Muffy and Tye will sleep forever
Tye is my sister's, Muffy is mine
They are four years old and chase cats all the time
When they aren't sleeping, they have their own ways of fun
Tye will sleep, and Muffy will run
If anything moves, Muffy is scared
But if anything moves, Tye doesn't care
Muffy doesn't like being without Tye
Tye doesn't like long car rides
When a car comes by, they run around
When a person comes by, they bark really loud
Muffy is small and Tye is big
They don't like toys, they like to dig
When I open the door, they run to me
But most of the time, they are just lazy

Sophia Biel, Grade 5
St Katharine Drexel School, WI

I Am From

I am from summer, fun blue shine.
I am from riding my bike and swimming in a great big pool.
I am from long relaxing hikes in the parks of St. Paul.
I am from a cold Minnesota winter when it's cold outside.
I am from dressing very warm wearing very comfy clothes.
I am from funny looking snowman, while blending snowstorm.
I am from the colors of fall when the leaves finally fall.
I am from raking leaves up and jump on my pile,
and here it comes my baby pup.
I am from the colors of fall when the funny leaves fall.
I am from the colors in fall red, yellow, and green
leaves quietly lying on the ground.
All the seasons are fun.
I am from summer, fall, winter, and spring.

Andres Martinez, Grade 5
Adams Spanish Immersion School, MN

Sam Prepares for an Exam

Sam has an exam.
She hoped it would be a grand slam.
She studied all night,
Working hard without a fright.
She finally had to take a break
Because she had gotten a headache.
She had to stay up so late
Because she had a lot on her plate.
She knew she could ace this test
If she could just get a little rest.
It was getting so late that her tummy started to rumble.
It seemed that everything she studied was turning into a jumble.
So she went into the kitchen downstairs
And happened to find some deliciously sweet and juicy pears.
She gobbled them up, one by one,
Saying to herself "yum, yum, yum."
She went back to study at her desk,
When finally decided to get some rest.
She woke the next morning with the sun in her eyes,
And she realized that her brain was finally organized.

Catherine La Rosa, Grade 5
St Eugene School, WI

Musical Town

I live in the town of music
Musical words I talk with a beat
Musical laugh, musical life
I go with the notes
Live musically
I live in the town of music

I live in the town of music
Never is there silence, always is there noise
Beautiful music
Music sounds like rivers, music sounds like silk
Music sounds like glitter, music like joy
I live in the town of music

I live in the town of music
Music like butterflies wings
Music echoes like rain
Music like gold and shiny bells
Music has no emptiness
I live in the town of music

Carli Christensen, Grade 5
Wagner Elementary School, MN

Moose

My dog is black and white.
He's as little as can be.
When he stands up he's as tall as your knee.
My dog is a Shih Tzu.
He's really sneaky you see.
When he has something you can only coax him with a treat.

Abigail Martinson, Grade 4
MacArthur Elementary School, WI

I Am

I am from cooking with strong-smelling spices
To eating delicious rices
I am from cute cats and playful dogs
I am from balancing on big logs
I am from the busy state fair
And I love brilliant fireworks
I am from a vacation every summer
And camping all the time
I am from Minnesota
And I was born in Minneapolis
I love my normal family
And our pets
And even though we fight,
I guess my sister is all right
I am from blaring music
To quiet slow tunes
I love the big woods
And the speeding wild
I love to read
And watch TV
But that's just me.

Sara Melby Funk, Grade 5
Adams Spanish Immersion School, MN

Writer's Block

The blank page taunts me
It's so annoyingly plain;
This block in my mind
Is making me insane.
No thought can enter in;
The gate's firm in place,
And though ideas hint and linger
They're gone before I can chase.
Though I search and I hunger
For a worthwhile scenario
They flit away like butterflies;
I watch as they go.
Then like a gift sent from above,
With a flash and a racket,
An idea's suddenly there —
Then gone, before I can attack it.
They call this horrid affliction
Quite simply, 'writer's block',
I wish before it'd entered
It would've politely knocked.

Caroline Daniels, Grade 6
Frank Lloyd Wright Intermediate School, WI

Deer Hunting

Finally, deer hunting, my favorite time of year.
I pull on my camo jacket and bright orange hat.
My dad and I walk out in the woods and get up in our deer stand.
We get ready for the sun to start going down.
I just can't wait.

Riley Kelly, Grade 6
St Francis Middle School, MN

Soccer Net

White square bars with different colored netting attached waiting to be shot at.
The keeper's water bottle sitting next to the goal with the keeper on the goal line trying to save penalty kicks.
Multicolored soccer balls flying through the air towards the net with anxious players sprinting close behind trying to score.

Courtney Anderson, Grade 6
Harriet Bishop Elementary School, MN

Dancing Bones

One fearful night the bones were stirring up the night with a jiggle and a wiggle around their coffins they went. For they were stirring up some jolly fun on the very fearful Halloween night with a jiggle and a wiggle all together around and around their coffins they went.

Calli Gerber, Grade 6
Riverdale Elementary School, WI

Life

Life is like a piece of thread,
Being cut shorter and shorter the older we grow.
We make it how we want it to be; meaningful, or random,
Never knowing what will happen next.

Life can be your trusted companion,
The best friend that's always by your side.
Or life can be your fiercest rival.
Terrorizing you from the day you were born.

Life is the bursting yellow sun,
Lighting up our lives with happiness.
But sometimes it's the ugly, gray storm cloud,
Blocking the sun, drenching us in tears
When we're tearing through the patches of thorns
That block our dreams, causing us to suffer.

Life is the loyal angel,
Comforting and watching over us,
Always allowing us to keep pushing on
Through the hard times of our lives.

Life is the bittersweet taste of a perfectly red apple
Off the tree of love that teaches us
How to love and respect one another.

Lillian Krohn, Grade 5
Lineville Intermediate School, WI

What I Found in My Locker*

Two week old socks that walk on their own,
A not done slip that should have gone home.
A pack of gum that I should have not stole,
A miniature fleet of termites out of control.
A book from the library called *The Spy*,
And my dad's badge from the FBI.
An old picture of the Loch Ness,
And a copy of the Gettysburg Address.
And one more thing I must confess,
A note from teacher, clean this mess!

Anjelika Anker, Grade 5
PEM 4-6 Grade School, MN
*Patterned after "What I Found in My Desk" by Bruce Lansky

I Am From

I am from the deep woods to the water
to the hot fire to the cold wind
I am from the cold lakes of Minnesota
to the busy city of St. Cloud with the wide wind at my side

I am from the skate park to the book on my shelf
to the messy room I grew up in
I am from a noisy family with a purring cat
and although we fight my brother is all right

I am from the city with rushing cars
to the calm country with the wind
to the woods with that sweet pine smell
I am from the stinky smell of fish to the treats of cookies
to the sound of the rushing water

I am from the sound of playing to wild parties
to the sound of the black crow crowing
I am from the singing crickets to the good treats of BBQ
to the great smell of hot chocolate

I am from flying hedgehogs to drawing squares
to eating pineapples and pears
to a loving mother
But hey! That's just me.

Maggie Cudahy, Grade 5
Adams Spanish Immersion School, MN

Great Gurgling Green

Green is an open field, a tall maple tree, and
feeling clean and fresh.
Green is the taste of delicious, green tea.
New, crisp money and daisies smell green.
Being happy makes me feel green.
Green is the sound of nature in the springtime
and croaking frogs.
Green is Ireland and wavy green grass.
Helping the planet is green.
Recycling is also green.
Green is the way we should be living.

Wyatt Watson, Grade 6
Marinette Middle School, WI

The Rusted Trumpets Song

Inside this rusted trumpet,
There are notes that haven't been played.
It sits there waiting for someone to pass by,
So it can wave to them.

Inside that rusted trumpet,
Songs have been played,
Only once though.
It sits there waiting,
Waiting for someone to blow into it again.
It cries for the love it once had.

Inside the rusted trumpet,
It wishes to be nurtured again,
The trumpet wants to be picked up again.
Now the trumpet is in shows, it's clean, it's warm,
And most of all it's happy.

Maddy Parenteau, Grade 6
T J Walker Middle School, WI

My Best Friend

My best friend is probably not like yours.
My best friend is one whom you wouldn't expect.
My best friend is not a valuable possession or a person.
My best friend is a dog!
She is a chocolate lab.
She is five years old.
Angel is my best friend because…
She listens to me when I need someone to talk to.
She loves me just like I love her.
She protects me when she senses something wrong.
She gives me a friend to play with.
The reason I love her the most is…
She comforts me in sad times
Like when my other dog died.
Angel is more than my best friend,
She is a family member.
  I love her dearly!

Whitney Smith, Grade 6
Martin County West Trimont Elementary School, MN

At the Park

One day I went to a park and stopped at a tree.
This tree had facial features and started to look at me.
Then he stopped smiling and gave me a wink.
It said, "Go over to the fountain and get an ice cold drink."
So, when I got to the fountain and pressed the button on the side
It seems as just slightly it was staring at the slide.
Then I heard a gurgle that came from the spout.
It said, "Go out and play and mostly run about."
So, then I stepped on every white base and it was very hard to tell
But, that base had a fence with a very similar facial tell.
Then I thought real hard on what to say and do
"Always trust your instincts." said Mr. Magoo.

Sydney Jensen, Grade 4
Ashby Elementary School, MN

Just Me

My eyes are as shiny as the stars at night.
My hair is as golden as my golden retriever's smooth coat.
My teeth are as white as a snowshoe rabbit's hair.
My skin is as tan as a Hawaiian beach.
My heart holds excitement.
That is yellow as fully ripe bananas.
I live on a basketball court.
And drink sweat.

Bryan Sturdevant, Grade 6
Dr Dyer Intermediate School, WI

Video Games

Yeah, video games —
I think that video games are really fun
and powerful and that is why I play them
here are a few reasons to show you.
One they are fun and cool to play.
Two they are powerful and thrilling to look at.
Three it gives you good finger muscles to use while playing them.
Yeah, video games.

Max Mazurek, Grade 6
St Francis Middle School, MN

School

I think school is fun.
In a school there is a principal's office.
You get a lot of homework
Teachers can be mean or really nice.
If they are mean, try to be on their nice side.
In middle school you get eight or seven classes.
You don't get a homeroom.
You can consider focus learning as a homeroom.

Ariel Orr, Grade 6
St Francis Middle School, MN

Crayons

This yellow is a beautiful sunset in the sky.
My green is the slime behind a snail.
This red is a brick sizzling in the sun.
My blue is the bright gigantic ocean.
This yellow is a stripe in the rainbow after a rainy day.
My green is a bright lizard crawling all around.
This red is blood gushing out of my knee.
My blue is the sky all around us.

Kara Odom, Grade 5
Harriet Bishop Elementary School, MN

Smack Smack

Smack! Smack! Hear the shoulder pads clack.
Click! Clack! Let's get the plaque.
Tick! Tock! The clock goes out.
Smack! Smack! Hear the shoulder pads clack.

Smack! There goes the sack.

Justin Orcutt, Grade 5
Mazomanie Elementary School, WI

Things I Like in October…

Things I like in October…
Candy in a plastic bowl
and steaming hot cocoa that's sizzling

Things I like in October…
Scratchy bark on the tree
and candy that rots teeth

Things I like in October…
Apple pie that is hot like hot lava
and turkeys going gobble gobble

Things I like in October…
Apple cider that flows down your throat like a river
and slippy slidey icicles that are hanging from tree branches

Things I like in October…
Deer running through the woods
and leaves that make a lot of smoke in the fire

Corey Franzen, Grade 4
Kennedy Elementary School, MN

Monster in My Closet!!

There's a monster in my closet
Oh what should I do?
Should I hide under my bed?
Oh, I know what to do
I will jump out the window!!!
Now I don't want to hurt myself.
Oh, I know what to do
I will call my friend Nadiah
She will know what to do
"What?", I said
"Tell my mom or dad
What will that do?"
Guess what I told them. They said,
The monster in my closet was just
A pair of worn out jeans
And an old dirty sweatshirt that is two sizes too big.
It's almost like the worn out jeans
and the dirty sweatshirt said,
"Got ya."

Lily Sederberg, Grade 5
Blue Heron Elementary School, MN

All About Me!

My hair is long and blond like the golden garland
My eyes are hazel like the Christmas tree in the snow
My hands are as cold as an icicle on a winter day
My teeth are as white as freshly falling snow.
My heart holds joy
That is bright orange like a fire going.
I live in electronics
And eat keys

Cheyenne Guthman, Grade 6
Dr Dyer Intermediate School, WI

The Beat of the Drum

The beat of the drum is so rythmatic
Some people think it's automatic.
The beat of the drum goes BOOM, BOOM.
The beat of the drum makes people want to move.
Indians play the drum in their songs.
That is when they get up
        and dance to the beat of the drum.
The beat of the drum goes BOOM, BOOM.
The beat of the drum makes people want to move.
    The drum is a supreme instrument.
The sound it makes is so fantastic.
The beat of the drum
    can do or mean anything.
What does it do for you?
What does the beat of the drum
    mean to you?
The beat of the drum
    can be expressed
        in so many different ways.

Jordan Gregory, Grade 6
Martin County West Trimont Elementary School, MN

The Lost Christmas Tree

Inside this Christmas tree
Lie feelings of the past, present, and future
Sad times, happy times,
Emotions

Inside this Christmas tree,
Hides moments in the past
That we love and cherish
Every year

So whenever you're putting
Up your Christmas tree
Instead of thinking about
All of the presents you will be receiving,

Stop, think about
The true meaning of Christmas,
Family, friends, everyone coming together,
That is truly the most wonderful thing in the world.

Mikayla Franda, Grade 6
T J Walker Middle School, WI

Listen

I lay, I lay while my mind floats and listens.
Listens to birds sing their songs,
listens to the rustle of leaves.
Listens to clouds start to brew, clouds, rain.
Creatures run, duck, and cover from the
wetness of the rain,
but I stay, stay to listen to the wondrous
sounds of nature.

Elena Kahn, Grade 6
Ramsey International Fine Arts Center, MN

This Lonely Tissue Box

Inside my tissue box
Lay tears from my memories
Of my best friend
She passed and now I still hear her paws pat
When I pass my tissue box.

It's there when I laugh
And when I cry
But waits with excitement
When I pass by
Hoping I will pick one up and share my feelings.

When I share my feelings
The tissue feels them
But the tissues hiding in the tissue box are breathing
Almost waiting to see the world
Even if only for seconds

They are all grateful for what they do
And how they help me to stop crying
And get over what I have had to face
How they love when all I do is just let all my feelings go.

Allyson Jean McLean, Grade 6
T J Walker Middle School, WI

My Friend Moved Away

My friend moved away,
On a midsummer day,
I cried and cried till our next play,
Then she past away,
Now there's night no day.
My
   friend
      now
         peacefully
           lay.

Chame A. Noble, Grade 6
Ramsey International Fine Arts Center, MN

Mother Earth of Autumn

She covers her earth with a golden blanket
as she tucks her world to sleep.
She awakens to the feeling of autumn.

She cherishes her earth with the gift of life
as her warm homes hide behind the golden trees
just waiting… till the right day to come out.

The leaves fall from the trees and make the sound
as if you were walking the shoreline
hearing the water rustling.

It smells as if it were a fine fresh-aired sunrise
but no, I was just on my morning bus ride to school.

Essyonna Peschong, Grade 4
Breck School, MN

Fireworks

Fireworks
  are made out of all different things.
    Gunpowder, tubes, fuses
    all sorts of things.
They are illegal in some states.
They are colorful and cool from all different things.
Some make a popping noise, and different sounds.
Some make it explode.
Some are big and small.
Some fly up in the sky and some don't.
If they don't do much
    they are probably a dud.
Some are dangerous,
Some are not.
Some people are harmed from them.
They might have used them in a false way.
What makes them go up
    is gunpowder or something like that.
That is what makes them explode, too
I like fireworks…
You never know what you will see.

Cameron Dressen, Grade 4
Martin County West Trimont Elementary School, MN

I Remember…

I remember the day we decided to move.
I remember looking at a bunch of different houses.
I remember finding a new house.
I remember the day our old house was sold.
I remember crying myself to sleep.
I remember saying good-bye to my friends and teachers.
I remember when we got the Budget truck.
I remember the day loading up the Budget truck.
I remember unpacking.
I remember finally being home.

Samantha M. Kutsche, Grade 6
Campbellsport Elementary School, WI

Spaghetti!!!!!

You eat spaghetti.
You enjoy spaghetti.
With the sauce, noodles
and parmesan on top.
You smell it.
You spin your fork in it.
You dance.
You put it in your mouth you
think so tasty.
Then it's gone
you wipe your mouth
with your napkin.
So wonderful.
You cry. Boohoo.

Megan Grandstrand, Grade 6
St Francis Middle School, MN

Free Shot

I step up to the line
The crowd is cheering, I block them out.
It's just me and the basket.
Nervous butterflies flutter in my stomach.
The ball comes to me, I shoot.
A huge applause comes, and a grin comes on
to my face…I made it!
That's my first shot.
Now my second.
I shoot it up and it dances on the rim.
I close my eyes I could not watch.
It falls in.
We win the game!

McKenna Gieske, Grade 5
Blue Heron Elementary School, MN

Halloween Feels Like…

Halloween feels like…
wearing nice and scary costumes
and filling up my orange pumpkin basket
with lots of sweet candy
seeing all your friends walking around
Halloween is going to be scary and cold

Halloween is saying trick-or-treat
Going to lots of parties
and carving pumpkins into scary shapes
Halloween is playing with friends
Halloween is walking about 1 mile
Halloween is sleeping in the next day like a deer.

Tyler Buck, Grade 4
Kennedy Elementary School, MN

Ruby Red Roses

Red is a racing mustang,
A fire station, and when someone calls me "short."
Red is the taste of homemade apple pie,
And fresh picked raspberries.
Blooming roses smell red.
Talking in front of the class makes me feel red.
Red is the sound of me biting into an apple
and an apple falling from a tree.
Red is a barn and a red living room.
A screaming fire truck is also red.
A scary ghost movie is red, and pain is also red.
Red is a red hot pepper.

DeJay Bromund, Grade 6
Marinette Middle School, WI

Drip Drop

Drip drop one by one by one. It slowly drops.
And the chill in the air makes me hold in my breath.
And it makes me think of death.

Jeffrey Symens, Grade 6
St Francis Middle School, MN

If I Were a Horse

If I were a horse
I would taste alfalfa for breakfast.
I would be full of cockle burrs.
I would like to play with my friends.
I'd want to go for a trail ride at Yellow River State Park.

If I were a horse
I would run in open fields.
I would wish for friends my age.
I would love my mom and dad.
I would listen for mommy in case a predator came.
I would be a very good horse.

Morgan Chappell, Grade 4
Boscobel Elementary School, WI

My Name Is

My name is a quiet song.
My name is a fresh apple.
My name is a cup of fresh water.
My name is a new flower.
My name is a feather from a bird.
My name is a snowflake.
My name is an art piece.
My name is a white piece of paper.
My name is a growing tree.
My name is a fish in the lake.
My name is a word from a book.
My name is a piece of the end of a good book.

Ellie Ims, Grade 5
Sibley Elementary School, MN

A Birthday on Halloween

A birthday on Halloween
    is what I have.
My dad calls me a trick!
An exciting birthday.
I get presents and candy on the same day. Yay!
I know people
    that have the same birthday.
I bring treats to school.
It's the least I could do.
A birthday on Halloween…
    It's so interesting.
    It's what I have.

Jackie Frerichs, Grade 4
Martin County West Sherburn Elementary School, MN

Winter

W inter wonderland.
I nside with my family on Christmas Day.
N ever be sad on Christmas.
T ake time off and spend it with your family.
E njoy the holidays.
R ead if you have the time to.

Robert Harris, Grade 5
Stocker Elementary School, WI

My Empty Heart

Inside this empty cabinet
Lies secrets
Secrets of someone's death

Someone who was always there
There to catch me when I mess up
Yes they were there
For me and everyone they knew
They were always there

I didn't want to let them go
They went so fast
So fast it's not even real
In that dust on the empty cabinet
Lay their secrets
Just waiting to get out

I had to watch them both go
My great grandma
And my dog Shiloh
Loving sweet and kind

We all love and miss them
You never know what you'll find
In the empty cabinet of mine
Nicole Sternard, Grade 6
T J Walker Middle School, WI

It's Time for Fall

It's time for fall
It's getting cold
Leaves are changing from green
To apple red and sunny orange
Raking up leaves so we can have some fun.
I love to do body slams
Crunch! Crunch!

It's time for fall
That means treats
It's a month with scary ghosts
It's a month with rotting teeth
It's a month of Halloween spirit

It's time for fall
With its apple pie and apple cider
That means fun and games
Can you feel that crisp air?

It's time for fall
Let's get picking apples and pumpkins
And all sorts of things

It's time for fall
It surely can't be beat
Anthony Christofferson, Grade 4
Kennedy Elementary School, MN

Champion Basketball Trophy

Inside this basketball trophy
Is the sweat that dripped down our faces
The pain we felt
When we messed up
Like the loss of the game would be our fault

The screams of the people
When we made our last shot
This trophy sat waiting
For our warm hands to pick it up
To carry it
Proudly

When it walked out the gym door
As the lights clicked off
As a smile crept up my face
The door slammed
And it walked out
A champion
Rachel Miller, Grade 6
T J Walker Middle School, WI

What Lies Beneath My Pillow

Inside my pillow
on my bed
lie the dreams
of my childhood

it supports my head
when I feel sad
or when I fall
asleep

Inside my pillow
all my bad dreams
are stored away
with all the ones that
make me happy

I still have more
dreams to come that
are waiting to be told
Hannah Abrahamson, Grade 6
T J Walker Middle School, WI

Graceful Water

Graceful water
unlike brother fire
bright, blue, beautiful
so fragile
yet
so hard
can be furious
can be as gentle as a lamb
Jordan Warneka, Grade 6
St Francis Middle School, MN

Basketball

Orange and black balls
Shining lights
Lots of cheering
Bouncing balls
Focus
Pumped
SHOOT!
SHOOT!
SHOOT!
Swish!
BUZZZZZZ!!!
Greta Donnelly, Grade 5
Harriet Bishop Elementary School, MN

Goosebumps

A step on the carpet,
oh warm.
A step on tile…
frozen.
Chills rising up my back.
dot, dot, dots forming
ALL
over my body.
Goosebumps coming alive.
It never occurred to me now…
WHY DID I EVEN GET UP THIS MORNING?
Teresa Sukkert, Grade 6
Kosciuszko Elementary School, WI

Oh Apples

Oh apples! Oh apples!
How I love you so!
You make my taste buds sizzle with glee!

Oh apples! Oh apples!
How I love you so!
You make me happy with juicy fun!

Oh apples! Oh apples!
How I love you so!
You make me happy!
Courtney Babino, Grade 5
Riverdale Elementary School, WI

Maple

In the fall the leaves turn yellow
It's so peaceful, it's so mellow.
When the sun shines on the tall tree,
The air is filled with melody.

As the wind begins to blow,
The leaves fall down just like snow.
Now that they are on the ground,
They begin to make a great big mound.
Nicole Wydeven, Grade 4
Classical School, WI

Writer's Block

Writer's block is like Lebron James rejecting your shot while the crowd is saying "ohhhhhhhhh!" Pointing at you, you're embarrassed. It's like being rejected by a preppy girl, and all her friends giggle at you, and you blush. Being grounded and you have nothing to do about it, you're in trouble. You're locked in a cage, all by yourself like a zoo animal, who's scared while fat little kids point and cameras flash.

Pressure, you're losing your breath, as your older brother is drowning you while you try to ask for help, but the words don't come out. You want to drive on but there is a road block.

You want to write, and you use all your might, it's such a fight to scribble down one word. Writer's block is a hero's enemy, like Doc Ock and the joker. You lose your thoughts like a game of poker. When you lose it all and it seems like it's hopeless, and you think. Getting ideas, you make music, poetry, you tell stories, and there's a spark, like the Fourth of July, thousands of sparks popping, flashing, jumping off the sky. Pages of magic like a genie did all of it.

It was all you.

Corbin Smidzik, Grade 6
Linwood Monroe Arts Plus School, MN

Months

January is the month of my birthday, it just snows, snows, snows.
February is the month of romance, girls get cards and candy.
March is the month for luck of the Irish, St. Patrick's day is only days away.
April is the month of showers, it's cool and rainy because it also brings flowers.
May is the month of National Teacher's Day, all the teachers say hip, hip hooray!
June is the month when my dad turns 32 this year, on June 19th he'll say "Boohoo"
July is the month of Independence Day, fireworks soar across the sky all day!
August is the month of Friendship Day, friends will be nice to each other and come spend the day.
September is the month of Grandparent's Day, grandparents or grandchildren will come and visit.
October brings candy and costumes, all the kids say trick-or-treat!
November brings turkey to the table. Thanksgiving is celebrated on the 26th of November.
December is the month of Christmas, most children are very happy and full of cheer

Sydney Gustin, Grade 6
Gilmore Middle School, WI

I Remember

I remember playing and swimming in Mauthe Lake.
I remember waiting for my mom and sister to come to the lake.
I remember seeing my mom and my sister finally arriving, walking down a path.
I remember watching my sister come walking with a puppy behind her.
I remember my mom saying we were maybe going to keep the adorable dog.
I remember leaving the lake with the pup sitting on my lap in the car.
I remember the fun times we had playing and just having fun.
I remember naming him Eddie and him running away at night and then him coming back whenever he wanted to.
I remember coming home from school and having him wait for us at the front door.
I remember having to give him away.

Candace Westcott, Grade 6
Campbellsport Elementary School, WI

Softball

The ball was pitched as fast as a bullet.
The bat hit the ball as far as the distance to the moon and back.
The batter ran as fast as a deer.
She slid to third base leaving dust like a tornado.
She sprinted to home plate and dived head first past the catcher like a diver off a spring board.

Gretchen Bellefeuille, Grade 6
Harriet Bishop Elementary School, MN

My Little Bro

My brother is the only one I have.
He is a lot of fun, but also a lot of work.
You have to watch him like a hawk.
He can say lots of words for the age of one.
The one animal sound he can make is "me-ow" like a cat.
One of my favorite things about his is he gives hugs and kisses.
He's into balls. He knows lots of tricks with them.
He likes to crawl under our long chairs.
He has a REALLY good hiding place under his crib.
When I found out I BURST out laughing.
My brother is the most inspiring little brother ever.
He's funny, laughable, kind, loving, and playful.
He's the one who makes me smile before I go to school.
I say "I love you" and he blows me a kiss and gives me a hug.
He's like a little puppy that turns on my light switch.
I'm so happy he's my little guy!

Sierra Williamson, Grade 5
Martin County West Trimont Elementary School, MN

I Love Fall Because…

I love fall because…
Thanksgiving is like a big feast there are friends and
family stuffing themselves going crunch, crunch
with corn, ham, turkey, sweet potatoes, baked potatoes,
mashed potatoes, and other foods.
I love fall because…
Leaves fall like butterflies floating in the warm wind
on a hot fall day
I love fall because…
Bird's wings flapping in the wind going in v's like
figure 8 skaters dancing in the wind.
I love fall because…
As I eat my apple pie every bit I take
I can taste the summer sunshine.
I love fall because…
scratchy bark scratches me like a back scratcher.

Rachel Van Lear, Grade 4
Kennedy Elementary School, MN

The Big Adventure

The wind, sun, birds everything around me moving fast!
Jasmine sweaty and ready to win.
We are in the lead!
Open my eyes they are in front!
They win!
I laugh with my friend as our horses eat.
We head home.
As soon as we hit the canter stretch it happens!
The feathers and the squawk!
Jasmine jumps, my friend gasps then…
It's over.
We watch the turkey fly away to the woods.
Alone…
We trotted home stunned.

Brooke Imm, Grade 6
St Francis Middle School, MN

That Piece of Meat

Oh steak crackling
On a charcoal grill that smells
As if you were in heaven add the perfect spices
On the meaty juicy steak
Make the steak taste as if you were in a five star
Restaurant prepare the steak with the best of ingredients
Now when you take that first bite of perfection
Let the flavor dance acrossed your taste buds

Levi Ross, Grade 6
St Francis Middle School, MN

New York City

Central Park, Time Square,
When you reach those places
You know that you are there!
Meredith, Al, and Ann
Are all waiting to be seen right in Rockefeller
Plaza where the Today show is being done.
When you visit New York
You'll always know you're there!

Lauren Olmschenk, Grade 6
St Francis Middle School, MN

Bony Black

Black is a nightfall, a sky without stars, and sadness.
Black is the taste of juicy blackberries.
Too little air and charcoal smells black.
Black is the sound of silent death and booming in the morning.
Black is outer space, a basement and the dark side of the moon.
Mars is black.
A blackout in your room is also black.
Black is an owl in the trees at night or when your mind goes blank.

Tyler Dau, Grade 6
Marinette Middle School, WI

Family

Family!
My family is nice, fun, caring, lovable, and big.
My family or I have a big family.
My family care about each other and cares about other people too.
My family is fun to be with and play games.
My family is really nice to me my family and other people.
I have a big family with a lot of people.
That is my family! Family!

Isabel Jasch, Grade 6
St Francis Middle School, MN

Winter

W inter is here, it is time to cheer!
I nside it is warm and I drink hot cocoa.
N ow there is snow and time for a snowball fight.
T oday Santa Claus will come.
E verybody is cheering for Christmas.
R ight now everywhere has snow.

Adrian Sanchez, Grade 5
Stocker Elementary School, WI

Airplane

Blue airplane flying very high in the early morning
Sky getting louder then softer in the swirly clouds
Where is it going? When will it get there?

Blue airplane flying high in the 12:00 bright blue
Sky soft peaceful silence as it glides though the
Sky cushy seats in first class hamburgers to

Blue airplane flying very high we land

Richard Bailey, Grade 5
Harriet Bishop Elementary School, MN

Pretty Pink

Pink is inside of a sea shell, cooked shrimp, and soft silk.
Pink is the taste of cherry Kool-aid, roses, and
a newborn baby smells Pink.
Chicken Nuggets from Burger King make me feel pink.
Pink is the sound of a baby kitten, and soft music.
Pink is a fuzzy sweat shirt, claries in California is pink.
Bright ideas are pink, smart ideas are also pink.
Pink is warm like a dog.
Pink is painting my finger nails.

Crystal Johnson, Grade 6
Marinette Middle School, WI

Colors

Colors are everything
Red is the salamander crawling on the stone hard floor
Orange is the goldfish moving swiftly in the tank
Yellow is the lightning emerging from the sky
Green is the grass growing everywhere on Earth
Blue is the raindrops falling from the clouds
Purple is the flowers growing in the lush warm meadow
Black is a dark shifting thunderstorm cloud
Colors, colors, colors are everything

Samuel Carman, Grade 5
Harriet Bishop Elementary School, MN

Horicon Marsh

There is a place where the grass grows long
Where the animals frolic
Where the water's clear
Where people and muskrats play with cattails
Where people and nature are one
This place is the Horicon Marsh

Paul Derr, Grade 5
St Katharine Drexel School, WI

Soccer

Players passing, fans screaming
Fear, happiness, excitement, and determination
"Why didn't you shoot?"
Post dinging "Nice shot!"
Scoring, scoring, scoring

Emilia Widen, Grade 6
Harriet Bishop Elementary School, MN

Radiant Ruby Red

Red is fresh-picked roses,
Door County cherries,
and an oven at 450 degrees
Red is the taste of strawberry Kool-aid.
Cinnamon and cheesy pizza smell red.
Doing something ridiculous in front of all my friends
makes me feel red.
Red is the sound of wailing sirens and blasting fireworks.
Red is Pizza Hut, volcanoes,
and the planet Mars.
A glowing fire is red.
Yummy pepperoni is also red.
Red is a loving heart.

Jordan Jenquin, Grade 6
Marinette Middle School, WI

Glowing, Gorgeous, Green

Green is the shiny, wet grass and the beautiful
tall trees and the feeling of silky, velvety flower petals.
Green is the taste of frozen mint chocolate-chip ice-cream
melting on your tongue.
Grilled carrots and green beans
And a forest of vast evergreens smell
Green. Being independent makes me feel green.
Green is the color of baby blue birds and leaves of our
enormous apple tree rustling in the wind. Green is Ireland,
Greenland, and the Earth. Relaxing time with
My family is green. Hanging with my
Best friends is also green.
Green is my amazing color.

Brooke Pratte, Grade 6
Marinette Middle School, WI

Pinktatious Pretty Pink

Pink is a peach bloom, a flamingo, and the feeling
of a fuzzy, soft blanket.
Pink is the taste of strawberry milk.
Tulips in the spring
and a grilled steak
medium rare smell pink.
Being excited makes me feel pink.
Pink is the Easter bunny,
fresh, crisp bed sheets,
and a ribbon in a little girl's hair.
Bright ideas are pink.
Playing with friends is pink also.
Pink is a Starburst candy.

Renee Oesau, Grade 6
Marinette Middle School, WI

Hats and Gloves

The snow is out this morning I can't wait to go out and play!
Where are my gloves! Where is my hat?
Looks like I'm not going out in the snow today.

Ally Peterson, Grade 6
St Francis Middle School, MN

Stars and Stripes

Red, white, and blue; so cool,
Red, white, and blue; like 50 stars in the frosty blue sky,
Red, white, and blue; with 13 red and white stripes,
Red, white, and blue; for the U.S.A.,
Red, white, and blue; for you and me.

Savana Gee, Grade 5
Mazomanie Elementary School, WI

Winter

I feel the snowflakes as they fall upon my cheek.
I hear Christmas songs as I listen to the radio.
I see the snow falling to the ground as I stare out my window.
I smell Mom's cookies as they come out of the oven.
I taste the sweet vanilla in my coffee.

Kaelan Aker, Grade 5
Stocker Elementary School, WI

Football

Play it in warm or cold weather,
Crashing shoulders hard as possible,
Making a catch before it drops,
Rush in to the end zone for the score,
Dancing on the goal line for the fans in the stands.

Bradley Rindt, Grade 6
Campbellsport Elementary School, WI

Homer

Shredding objects out of boredom
Barking while on his leash wanting attention
Fetching tennis balls with never-ending energy
Begging for a treat while trying to act cute
Sleeping silently on his pillow

Jennifer Zimdahl, Grade 6
Campbellsport Elementary School, WI

My Name Is

My name is like fireworks in the night sky.
My name is like a firecracker in the night's darkness.
My name is like an explosion about to go off.
My name is like a calm sunset in the sky.
My name is like the American flag blowing in the breeze.

Dillion Vigesaa, Grade 5
Sibley Elementary School, MN

Thanksgiving

Thanksgiving
Turkey, pumpkin pie
Joy, excitement, care
Family, games, food, television
Talking, music, cars humming, TV, people cooking

Michael Gospodarek, Grade 4
Stocker Elementary School, WI

Halloween

Halloween is coming up for young and old,
the young getting costumes and the air is getting cold.
The young come knocking on the door trick-or-treat
and the old say sour or sweet they give the candy and
so they go home to eat.

Terrance Ward Jr., Grade 6
Messmer Preparatory Catholic School, WI

Winter

I feel as if Santa is going to come any second.
I hear bells jingling and carols all around that warm my heart.
I see millions of white crystals making a blanket.
I smell gingerbread with gumdrops and peppermint.
I taste warm, ooey, gooey chocolate cookies and hot chocolate.

Andrew Fairchild, Grade 5
Stocker Elementary School, WI

Cars

Cars taste like exhaust fumes going into my lungs.
Cars smell like a fresh coat of wax.
Cars look like fresh polished chrome.
Cars sound like the roar of the engine shifting gears.
Cars feel like smooth leather.

Samuel Dawson, Grade 6
Dr Dyer Intermediate School, WI

Halloween

Halloween
Candy, fog
Goo, nasty, candy
Ghouls, goblins, monsters, candy
Monsters, candy bag, running, laughing, yelling

Dante Gennaccaro-Archer, Grade 4
Stocker Elementary School, WI

Santa

Santa tastes like candy canes,
Santa smells like a gingerbread man,
Santa looks like a guy that should be working out more,
Santa sounds like a man with a cookie in his throat,
Santa feels like a mushy marshmallow.

Chandler Reinholtz, Grade 6
Dr Dyer Intermediate School, WI

Winter

I feel the Christmas joy inside me.
I hear the snow saying, "Finally I've come to Earth."
I see cold, fluffy cotton sitting in my use to be grass.
I smell Christmas Eve dinner and my Aunt Kim's perfume.
I taste the little snow that drops on my tongue.

Kylaira Harris, Grade 5
Stocker Elementary School, WI

Christmas

Christmas is not for fireworks booming in the air, beholding the sparkling sky, and parades going down the street.
Christmas is for the smell of hot cocoa being made.
Christmas is for celebrating Jesus in church.
Christmas is for time with your family.
Christmas sounds like the tearing of wrapping paper.
Christmas sounds like people singing Christmas carols.
Merry Christmas

Tim Weber, Grade 6
Campbellsport Elementary School, WI

Friendship

Friendship is as powerful as the sun beating down on the earth.
Having a friend can be as cold as ice, as hot as the sun, as big as life, and as small as a pebble.
Finding great friends like mine is like nailing jello to a tree…its impossible.
Friendship is like iron, it is extremely strong and very hard to break.
A good friend is like toothpaste, they are always there for you to squeeze.
Friendship is like a flashlight, shining through the darkest forest.
Best friends are as close to one another as peas are in a pod.

Ella Cavanor, Grade 6
Harriet Bishop Elementary School, MN

Softball

Bats, swinging as fast as airplanes
The ball is hit like a bullet
Hats are sitting on peoples heads
Chairs are waiting for the girls from the outfield to come running so they can sit and rest on them
The wind is whipping up the dirt like a tornado
The grass and the trees are just laying in the outfield
The shells from the seeds are piling up like a mountain next to the bench.

Audrey Pred, Grade 6
Harriet Bishop Elementary School, MN

Just Because

Just because my back is turned doesn't mean I can't hear you.
Just because you can't see me when you say it, doesn't mean that I won't find out.
Just Because I'm not in the room, doesn't give you permission to do it.
Just because you gossip, doesn't mean you're cool.
Just because everyone thinks you're popular, doesn't mean you have to be mean to all the "unpopular" people.
Just because…
Just because…

Aimee Lopez, Grade 6
Frank Lloyd Wright Intermediate School, WI

A Sunny Day

Finally a sunny day!
I open my door and a million dollars is at my door step!
  I also find a car in my driveway and a private jet, and was flown to the store.
I got free food because I was the millionth customer.
  I was flown to a Manchine and at the Manchine I moved in my belongings, ah what a sunny day!

John Green, Grade 6
St Francis Middle School, MN

Stars

Stars is a twinkle in my eye.
And they are so very high,
I feel like I can fly.
But when the sun comes out,
The stars go bye-bye.
They are so pretty,
I want to cry.
And when I wake up,
The sun is out.
I don't like it,
But I can scream and shout.
When night comes again,
I have to go in.
But I don't care.
I can stare out the window,
And then I will know,
That they like to glow
And that is what they will always show.

Jenna Fintelmann, Grade 5
Howards Grove Middle School, WI

The Simple Tree

Inside this
Small
Christmas tree
Lies glowing lights
Telling me to shine

Families just waiting
For Christmas Day
Inside this tree
Lies memories that
Have been given
To others

Inside the lights
On the tree
Lie happy or sad
Children
Waiting

Tina Guo, Grade 6
T J Walker Middle School, WI

What Is TV

What is TV?
TV is a world trapped in a box.
A mind with its own image.
From happy to tragic it will choose!

What is TV?
TV is life you just can't control
with rotating pictures throughout the show
and a sparkling screen for you and me.
That is TV!

Allison Lind, Grade 6
Valley Middle School, MN

Earth's Language

I speak the language of the earth
Birds chirping, rivers rushing
The sounds of nature

I speak the language of the earth
My voice changing all the time
In the spring, I tweet and sing
In the summer, I gargle as a river
In the fall, I sing the song of falling leaves
In winter, I am gone

I speak the language of the earth
The seasons come and go
I leave for winter
Because there isn't much noise
But at all other times
I speak the language of the earth

Erin Dollerschell, Grade 5
Wagner Elementary School, MN

My Cabin

The crisp sun setting with care
The sky instantly purple and pink
The lake as smooth as glass
The vibrant moon shines
Stars twinkling
Snap, crackle, pop, the bonfire is lit
I rest my head
Morning comes
Waves crash
Lightning bolts
Hail beating
Rain pelting
Trees rustling
Silence
Calming
Peaceful
Relaxing, relaxing, relaxing

Amy Prairie, Grade 6
Harriet Bishop Elementary School, MN

Kristen

What is a kind person?
  Someone who offers to help
  Someone that is friends with everyone
  Someone with manners
  Someone that cares about their friends
  Someone that gives kindness
  They give love to family
  Who helps the hurt
  Who cheers everyone up
  Who makes lonely people not lonely
  Kristen is kind
That is kind!

Marley Christophersen, Grade 6
Orfordville Elementary School, WI

My Black Feelings

Black looks like a spider
creeping down next to you.
Black sounds like evil singing
on top of you.
Black smells like a
marshmallow burning.
Black feels like cold air inside of me.
Black makes me
feel dark inside.
Black seems like I am Goth.
Black is a haunted house and a
haunted hay ride.
Black looks like a very very hairy gorilla.
Black is the night sky.
Black is a crow soaring in the night sky.
Black smells like
twilight standing in me.

Alicia Henry, Grade 6
Marinette Middle School, WI

Arrow

Green blue ribbons
Falling from the arrow

White bright stars
Deep blue sky

WOW!

Blue green ribbon
Blue green arrow

Why did the arrow
Come down that night?

Falling star
Falling star
Falling star

Taylor Fenhaus, Grade 5
Hewitt Texas Elementary School, WI

If I Were a Panda

If I were a panda
I would taste bamboo
I would be full of bananas too
I would like to run and play
I'd want to sleep all day

If I were a panda
I would play and play
I would wish to eat bamboo all the day
I would love to lay in bed every Tuesday
I would listen for enemies prowling the way
I would be proud of myself every Monday

Madalyn Wellumson, Grade 4
Boscobel Elementary School, WI

My Gracy

Hopping bunny,
Eating all the time!
Getting her vegetables,
Vegetables, Gracy, vegetables!
Going to sleep when I pet her,
Drinking her water,
Laying on the carpet.
She is so CUTE!!

Jacob Wehler, Grade 5
Mazomanie Elementary School, WI

Horicon Marsh

High in the sky the geese are honking
In the cattails, the muskrats are eating
The toads are hopping
The grasshoppers are jumping
The snakes are slithering
The milkweed is hatching
The wind is howling
It still seems so peaceful here today.

Christian Bahr, Grade 5
St Katharine Drexel School, WI

Lost

She walked out of her house,
With nowhere to go so she kept walking
The touch of wind on her face,
So cold, so soft.
The rustling of leaves beneath her feet
So loud, more than she wanted to hear.
She felt so safe, yet so scared.
Scared, she'd become lost.

Abby Ciesielski, Grade 6
Riverdale Elementary School, WI

The Cow

Moo, moo! Wake up!
Moo, moo! Time to eat!
Moo, moo! Milking time!
Moo, moo! Time to lay in the sand!
Moo, moo! Time to eat!
Moo, moo! Time to have some salt!
Moo, moo! Milking time!
Moo, moo! Good night!

Amber Putz, Grade 6
Riverdale Elementary School, WI

Chores

C leaning fast
H orrible
O range pop stains
R oving vacuum
E verlasting work
S uper boring

Amanda Smith, Grade 4
Chaska Elementary School, MN

NFL Teams

NFL
Football
Teams
Sad Dolphins,
Terrible Browns,
Disastrous, vile, unpleasant Cowboys,
Complicated, rough, obscure Steelers,
Those are a few.
Difficult Patriots,
Catastrophic Giants,
Running, catching, throwing Saints,
Smashing, juking, stiff-arming Broncos,
Calamitous Chiefs,
Robust Bengals
Rugged Buccaneers,
Gruesome Eagles,
Don't forget dreadful Lions,
Last of all — best of all —
I like exciting Vikings.

Nathaniel Graskey, Grade 5
Howards Grove Middle School, WI

Inside the Lonely Barn

There was a lonely cat
inside an empty barn
it never comes out
I try to get it out.

It's alone, I'm scared
it might die
I come back
it's gone, I loved that cat.

I was worried
Then I look around it's there
I thought it would never leave
I was so proud it was there.

I danced around the barn
I was so happy
I thought it would like a strand of grass
staying in one place.

Alexa Jennerjohn, Grade 6
T J Walker Middle School, WI

Sports, Sports, Sports

I like sports
The feel of the equipment
In my hands
Makes me feel excited
When I hear the crack of a bat
Or a swoosh of a basketball
Going through the net
I feel great

April Thornsen, Grade 6
Hillsboro Elementary School, WI

All About Madeline

M adeline is a nice girl
A pples are my favorite fruit
D ogs are my favorite animals
E ach year I am going to get older
L ike to bowl
I am in fourth grade
N ext year I am going to middle school
E xcellent girl I am

Madeline Bettinger, Grade 4
Tess Corners Elementary School, WI

Monkey

I have a monkey!
Do you have a monkey?
My monkey is brown.
She never has a frown.
She is a chunky monkey!
She likes to eat bananas.
Her name is Hannah!
I love my monkey so much!

Quinn Fitzgerald, Grade 5
Riverdale Elementary School, WI

Billy

My friend's name is Billy
Billy and I act really silly
Billy loves fruity flavored pop
He licks the rain when it drops
He likes to have snowball fights
His night light is like the sunlight
He likes to hunt for ducks
I like to hunt for bucks

Ethan Haffner, Grade 5
Riverdale Elementary School, WI

Horicon Marsh

The Horicon Marsh is peaceful
Listening to the geese as they call
Watching cattails wave in the wind
Seeing the beautiful colors on the trees
Caterpillars crawling on the road
Ripples in the water
Wonderful smell of the wildflowers
Watching birds fly north

Klahryssa Heinzen, Grade 5
St Katharine Drexel School, WI

Frogs

Jumping hopping through the day
Maybe even at the bay
Catching flies from the sky
Croaking as you pass by
Sleeping all through the night
Waking when they see a light

Gabby Calametti, Grade 6
St Francis Middle School, MN

Spiders

Spiders
Eight legs ugly
Scary black eyes
They scare people
Jump on webs
Lay eggs
Crawls on
People
Are very
Hairy
Kadija Sloans, Grade 5
Messmer Preparatory Catholic School, WI

Dogs

Playful, lovable
always having fun
It's just the right pet for me
You'll never be bored with this pet
A playmate for life and eternity
Man's best friend, he shall be
Best friends forever, you and me
Dogs and people
People and dogs
What would life be without you and me?
Mikayla Jakircevic, Grade 5
St Paul Evangelical Lutheran School, WI

Dreams*

Hold fast to dreams
For if dreams light,
Life is a great big bird
That is beautiful in flight.

Hold fast to dreams
For if dreams grow,
Life is a strong breeze
That gently blows.
Kristina Jeng, Grade 4
Classical School, WI
*Inspired by Langston Hughes' "Dreams"

Leaves

I feel the leaves rustling on the ground.
I hear the leaves crunching
When I step on each and every one.
I see the neighbor's leaf pile
As I walk by.
I spring into the air
And I land on my back in the now…
   Messed
Up   Leaf
     Pile.
Mollie McGrann, Grade 4
Breck School, MN

The Horicon Marsh

Hear the crickets chirping
See the marsh glistening
Reflections on the water
Beautiful berries with color
Water waves making sound
Ducks in the water splashing
Birds flying in the sky
The warmth of the sun on your face
Plants preparing for winter
Red, yellow, and purple leaves on trees
Walking on a path of leaves
People enjoying nature together
Ducks playing with each other
Mackenzie White, Grade 5
St Katharine Drexel School, WI

Colors

Pink is the color of uncooked meat,
White is the color of a white man's feet.

Gold is the color of my chain,
Brown is the color of a mud stain.

Black is the color of my shoelace,
Red is the color of my sun burned face.

Green is the prairie where flowers grow,
Yellow is the color of my swollen toe.

Now those are some good colors.
Tavares Adams, Grade 6
Gilmore Middle School, WI

Autumn Leaves

When leaves fall
Summer has come to an end.
Fall is one of the most
Beautiful sights on Earth.

I hear the soft wind
Rustling the leaves.
It almost sounds like screaming.
For winter is coming.

And it just keeps coming.
And it just keeps coming.
Max Sternberg, Grade 4
Breck School, MN

Friends

I meet my friends from day to day
We talk and hang
We have a gang
Don't just sit there let's play a game
Kyla Ingberg, Grade 6
St Francis Middle School, MN

Babies, Babies, Babies

Sweet babies
Fat babies
Ugly, mean, pukey babies
Hairy, skinny, sticky babies
Those are just a few
Silly babies
Messy babies
Nice, crying, loud babies
Quick, smart, snuggly babies
Pink babies
Sugar babies
Playful babies
And don't forget bad babies
Last of all
Best of all
I like cute babies!
Abbie Pickett, Grade 4
Boscobel Elementary School, WI

An Awesome Book

Inside a book
There are adventures to go on
In a book
Anything can happen

Others can get lost in a book
You can have feelings
Inside a book there are memories faded
In a book
In books you want to read more

Good books, just forgotten
Pages ripped
Feelings left behind a book
A mystery begins
Over and over again
Jasmine Severin, Grade 6
T J Walker Middle School, WI

Basketball

court
teams
lines
players
free throw
3 pointer
jump shot
lay ups
dunks
running
hoops
shooting
scoring
cheering
Zach Tucek, Grade 5
St Paul Evangelical Lutheran School, WI

Pillow

The sheep sits there
Under a little sheet
I feel wool and no hair
They just sit there with no heat

Those little sheep
They sit there and stare
They don't leap
I just don't think it's fair!

Kylie Cunningham, Grade 4
Classical School, WI

The Horseback Ride

Brown and white deer
Moving slow turtles
Green grass blowing in the wind
Sunny day, crystal clear, bright clouds
Some peaceful spooky feelings
Why do horses move a lot?
Restful
Restful
Restful

Katelyn Nardi, Grade 5
Hewitt Texas Elementary School, WI

Rain

Rain is fun
me and my brother can play in it
Rain can also be dreary
the sky is dark and gloomy
Rain is also helpful
the plants get a drink so they can grow
Rain can be nonhelpful
the rain could make a flood
But that is what rain is

Mckenzie Jirousek, Grade 6
Hillsboro Elementary School, WI

Winter

W ind whistles by my window
I nto the snow we go
N ewly fallen snow glistens in the sun
T aste the hot cocoa near the fire
E vergreens are covered with snow
R eading next to the fire

Brandon Saladis, Grade 5
Stocker Elementary School, WI

Horicon Marsh

M any birds to see
A mphibians hopping here and there
R eptiles slither through the grass
S liding snakes on the rocks
H ad so much fun

Zach Piechowski, Grade 5
St Katharine Drexel School, WI

Yellow

Yellow is the color of the sun on a bright sunny day, fireworks and a book that always works.
Yellow is the color of hay on a farm, lemons, and a pencil that works like a charm.
Yellow is the color of a cake that's really crazy, and a bee that's really lazy.
Yellow is the color of cheese on a plate, and a bus that's really late.
Yellow is the color of a car on black tar, and a rope that needs some soap.

Alyssa Davis, Grade 4
Boscobel Elementary School, WI

Memories

Memories are my favorite thing they remind me of everything the good ones the bad ones
Everyone works. My memories are my number 1 thing it helps with everything.
My memories take me back to fun times in my life but every memory isn't so bright.
The ones that help the most are the ones that deserve a toast.
My memories are great to see they're for you and me.

Nik Klessig, Grade 5
Howards Grove Middle School, WI

Winter

Winter time is for playing in the snow and drinking hot chocolate.
When I play in the snow I build snowmen and a fort and have fun-filled snowball fights.
Winter is not only about playing outside and drinking hot chocolate
but seeing the beautiful scenery and the snow falling.
Just sitting at the window and watch the most beautiful scenery in winter.

Taylor Berger, Grade 4
Tess Corners Elementary School, WI

Christmas and Winter

Winter is the sight of two kids playing in the snow and the smile on a snowman.
Christmas is the smell of hot chocolate and the smell of cookies.
Winter is the sound of blowing wind and some Christmas music.
Christmas is the feel of snow and the feel of ice.
Christmas is the taste of hot chocolate and the taste of marshmallows.

Pedro Diego, Grade 4
Boscobel Elementary School, WI

Green

Green is the color of snake scales, a green egg, and a stinky shirt.
Green is the color of a turtle's shell, a grasshopper's skin, and green broccoli.
Green is the color of crunching leaves, the green grass, and creepy spiders.
Green is the color of tasty cabbage, a healthy meal of lettuce, and green paper.
Green is the color of coloring crayons, a swimming fish, and crawling caterpillars.

Dallas Gunderson, Grade 4
Boscobel Elementary School, WI

Winter

Winter is the sight of snow in a bucket and sleds going down a hill.
Winter is the smell of cookies in the oven and popcorn getting popped.
Winter is the sound of an avalanche going down a hill and sleigh bells on a sleigh.
Winter is the taste of snow and candy canes being eaten.
Winter is the feel of a shovel scooping snow and cold ice on warm hands.

Eric Manders, Grade 4
Boscobel Elementary School, WI

A Day with the Monkeys

Apes, Monkeys, Chimpanzees,
You never know where they're going to be.

Running, climbing, and scampering around,
Making a mess and loads of sound.

Hungry for fruit, and tired from play,
Go to sleep to start a new day.

Apes, Monkeys, Chimpanzees,
My, that's the life I want to be!

Jacob Van Blarcom, Grade 6
Viroqua Middle School, WI

The Mighty Prowler

In the early sun.
I was hoping for a day of fun.
When the key was turned the track ready to be burned.
As the mighty Prowler moved so swift.
Over and through the snow drifts.
The snow blew.
As I flew.
When the engine roared my passengers screamed MORE!
Around and round
Till I slipped
And tipped and then I was finally whipped.

Cassie Kosloske, Grade 6
Dr Dyer Intermediate School, WI

Leaves

As I walk outside I wonder…
What would it be like to be a leaf falling
From the treetops?
I walk around feeling the leaves
With my fingertips.
I wonder, which one would be me?
Would I be soft and graceful?
Or would I be a leaf that simply lies waiting for winter?
And then I find it!
A simple leaf
Different, but me.

Julia Murphy, Grade 4
Breck School, MN

Snow

Sheep in the sky in groups of cotton,
They jump in a grassy hill.
Soon the hill is covered with sheep.
They think, "This is rotten."

Sheep, sheep start a new life.
Soon they get used to being cold in the spring.
All the sheep melt in the mountain,
Thinking, "This is getting old."

Joanna Carman, Grade 4
Classical School, WI

Brown

Brown, it feels like soft fur.
Brown, it feels like a leather baseball glove.
Brown, it feels like my soft, comfy couch.
Brown, it feels so nice.
Brown, it tastes like fresh turkey.
Brown, it tastes like meatballs.
Brown, it tastes like awesome chocolate.
Brown, it tastes so good.
Brown, it looks like small bunnies.
Brown, it looks like a gigantic moose.
Brown, it looks like a peaceful dear.
Brown, it looks so cool.
Brown, it sounds like a growling raccoon.
Brown, it sounds like a baseball hitting my glove.
Brown, it sounds like a cracking tree branch.
Brown, it sounds so violent.
Brown, it smells like wet doggies.
Brown, it smells like a forest of wood.
Brown, it smells like muddy pigs.
Brown, it smells so strange.

Emma Hakanson, Grade 5
Harriet Bishop Elementary School, MN

Halloween

Halloween might give you a fright,
Ghosts are marching on Halloween night.

It might be chilling,
And it is all very thrilling.

You will be scared soon,
Everything spooky will be out on a full moon.

Watch out! There might be snakes,
Be careful or you might trip over rakes.

You might see some mummies,
It will be so scary, it might even hurt your tummy.

Watch out for witches!
You might be so scared you'll need stitches.

People will moan.
You might even groan.

Gavin Greene, Grade 5
Seneca Middle School, WI

Winter

I see the snowflakes falling from above on the trees and
kids freezing from the snow that fell on their winter coats.
I hear the bells from Santa Claus on his reindeer sleigh.
I smell hot chocolate heating from the pot.
I taste the hot chocolate…ouch, it burnt my tongue.
I feel the very cold snow running down my back.

Hunter Proft, Grade 5
Stocker Elementary School, WI

A Walk in the Woods
Light
Pretty
ice

Sparkling snowflakes
Fall as the
Wind blows

Sparkling sunlight
Spills through
The trees
Cole Henkelman, Grade 5
Hewitt Texas Elementary School, WI

Our Nature Walk
Barking dogs, leaping frogs
This is our nature walk
Birds are twittering, chattering, chittering
While cotton seeds whiz through the air.
Buds are growing, waters flowing
Flowers are beautiful in the sunlight.
Winds are blowing as we are going
Through the curving path.
God has created these wonderful things
That we have seen today to reflect
His glory.

Hannah Hanson, Grade 5
Blue Heron Elementary School, MN

The Maple
Maple you are a beautiful tree
Your leaves like fire,

Fall off and blow free
Make music like a lyre.

In winter's chill
Your arms are bare,

They stay until
Snowflakes fill the air.
Lili Braatz, Grade 4
Classical School, WI

Halloween
Goblins, witches, bats, and ghosts
but candy is what I want the most.

Skeletons, pumpkins, spider webs and
haunted houses too.
Spooky ghosts floating by and
the scary owl says whoo
making all the kids laugh and scream
Happy Halloween.
Damaris Alexander, Grade 6
Messmer Preparatory Catholic School, WI

My Brother
Caleb

C ats are an animal he loves
A lways tries his hardest
L oves everyone in his family
E ven loves Sammie
B est brother I could ever have

Caleb
Quinn Bilitz, Grade 5
St Paul Evangelical Lutheran School, WI

Black
Black is your heart when it is sad,
Black is also the color of rage.
Black is the color of sadness,
Black is the color of hate.
Black is the color I want my hair,
Black is what I would wear every day.
Black is the color of tears
Black is everything faded away.
Black is depression.
Brittany Cieczka, Grade 6
Gilmore Middle School, WI

Trees Are Bears
In the woods
Trees are bears
They hide their hoods
They have branches in pairs

The bears growl
The wind makes trees howl
The trees move when no one can see
Of course, that's between the bears and me!
Maddie Waters, Grade 4
Classical School, WI

Halloween
I saw bats and black
cats on Halloween night.
I saw creepy crawlies,
and other creepy stuff,
but tonight was still the
BEST night ever!
Kiarra Reliford, Grade 5
Messmer Preparatory Catholic School, WI

Bunnies
Bunnies are soft and fluffy.
Bunnies are runny and cuddly.
Bunnies eat cute and travel in their cage.
Bunnies are nice to pet.
They nibble cute and nice like they smile.
Clayton Baker, Grade 6
St Francis Middle School, MN

Missing
Inside this puzzle I see the picture
But something's missing, a piece
As though a part of me has left
To never return…

I see it, I see it in the puzzle
Is it a tree? Is it a river?
Is it there? A piece, is it hiding?
No one can see it
Behind the picture in the puzzle

It is a missing puzzle piece
A missing part of me,
There's no way I can replace myself
My puzzle piece, will I find it?

It's a piece of me
And it's missing
Everyone's missing one piece of them
I will get it back

If I don't search I won't find it
Inside this puzzle I see the picture
But something's new…a piece
Allison Hensley, Grade 6
T J Walker Middle School, WI

Baseball
I thought that I would lose the game
I thought that I would lose my fame
My team was losing by three
Everyone stared at me

I stepped up to the plate
The pitch…I swung too late
I missed another ball
My team almost lost it all

It was our last chance
For our team to advance
The last ball was thrown
I started to groan

I swung hard at the ball
But I started to fall
The bases were loaded
Then the crowd exploded

I hit the ball out of the lawn
Going Going Gone
I won the game
And got my fame
Logan Wettstein, Grade 6
Orfordville Elementary School, WI

A Singer

I am a singer!
I wonder what song is next.
I see the crowd cheering.
I want to sing an encore.
I am a singer!

I pretend I'm always alone.
I feel the excitement in the room.
I touch the fan's hands.
I worry if I'll mess up.
I shout for joy at the end of the concert.
I am a singer!

I understand people make mistakes…
I say, "I can do this!"
I dream of playing guitar.
I try to satisfy the fans.
I hope I am a star forever.
I am a singer!

Courtney Serpe, Grade 6
Gilmore Middle School, WI

Superman

I am Superman
I wonder how I help people
I hear innocent people scream
I see bad guys
I want to save the innocent
I am Superman

I pretend I am a hero
I feel like a hero
I touch people's hearts
I worry about people
I cry when the innocent die
I am Superman

I understand everything
I say Superman
I dream of Super girl
I hope I live forever
I am Superman

Stefan Boyd, Grade 6
Gilmore Middle School, WI

Castles

Castles
Creepy, dark
Cold, massive
Towering, drafty, huge
Cold, defending, living
Hard, stony, powerful
Protective, helpful
Castles

Matthew Wilke, Grade 5
Classical School, WI

Chocolate

What is chocolate?
A warm sensation in your mouth
Creamy and tasty filled with nougat
So delicious it's hard to swallow
Blended with soft caramel
A sweet milky feeling
Inside a cookie
Looks so good you'll eat the plastic
Seems so small but tastes so big
That is chocolate!

Patrick Engen, Grade 6
Orfordville Elementary School, WI

Outside

I step outside into the cool crisp air.
I hear…
    Children yelling,
    Swings rusty chains squeaking,
    Balls bouncing on the rocky blacktop,
    Balls fling into goals.
I feel…
    The wind through my hair,
    Chills going through me.
That is what I hear and feel outside.

Melanie Roehrborn, Grade 5
Howards Grove Middle School, WI

Baseball

In your hands
Behind your back
Across the field to first
Upon first base
Between the first and second baseman
Upon second base
After the third baseman
Upon third base
Down the foul ball line to home
Upon home plate and SAFE!

Payton Bender, Grade 6
Orfordville Elementary School, WI

Dreams*

Hold fast to dreams
For if dreams come
Life is a musical
That makes all hum.

Hold fast to dreams
For if dreams smile,
Life is a rainbow
Stretching at least a mile.

Shannon Wilbourne, Grade 4
Classical School, WI
*Inspired by Langston Hughes' "Dreams"

We All Scream for Halloween

He screams
you scream
we all scream
for Halloween

Scary voices
in my head
monsters underneath
my bed
yanking my legs
from under the bed
as I try to get
out of the bed.

Zombies walking
zombies singing
Michael Jackson's video
is both scary and thrilling

As I run and scream
and as I dream
I finally realize
I don't like Halloween

Catera Stanfield, Grade 6
Messmer Preparatory Catholic School, WI

Snowman

Frosty and froze
Stand very bold
Shiny button eyes
An orange carrot nose
Buttons of coal
Fancy top hat
Two rough stick arms
And a broomstick in his hand
Snowman

Nicole Malecha, Grade 5
Sibley Elementary School, MN

I Am…

I am Shayane Andersen
I am 11 years old
I am in 5th grade
I am in a family of 5
I am a Christian
I am in love with animals
I am kind
I am a good drawer
I am good at skipping
I am a good dancer
I am a good singer
I am happy to be around friends
I am happy to be with my pets
I am Shayane Andersen

Shayane Zaina Dereeé Andersen, Grade 5
St Paul Evangelical Lutheran School, WI

Unwritten

Inside this empty notebook are pages unwritten
Imaginations have not yet told this lined paper the ideas
Ideas drowning the paper with no escape
They're whispering secrets, secrets that I have not yet discovered
They all hear my thoughts
Hoping I'll write
The undiscovered

The undiscovered
Blank pages
Lonely pages
They're screaming
Please write on me
All alone
The pages are bursting with excitement as I grip my pencil

Inside this empty notebook are pages unwritten
They speak to you
There's no escaping them
Blank pages
Unwritten

Hailey Benesh, Grade 6
T J Walker Middle School, WI

I Am

I am from playing video games
to riding my blue bike
I am from tripping to slipping
I am from chasing to being chased.
I am from running to walking
I am from jumping to falling
I am from the giant Science Museum
to sitting inside a car
I am from going to a great school
to going home
I am from sitting down to standing up
I am from calm St. Paul to light Minneapolis.
I am from crazy New York to calm Minnesota
I am from hot Mexico to cold Minnesota
I am from writing to reading
I am from eating a hot lunch to have recess
I am from playing with a football
to sitting by a wall
I am from talking to stopping
I am from being small to even more tall
From cleaning to playing on the computer.

Ray Lopez, Grade 5
Adams Spanish Immersion School, MN

Spaghetti and Meatballs

Mmm something smells good what is for dinner
We are having spaghetti and meat balls for dinner
Grab the forks so we can eat
Yum the spaghetti and meatballs taste really good.

Max Oberleitner, Grade 6
St Francis Middle School, MN

Wolves Howling

Wolves howling
The dark night sky stretches high above my head
I can smell the oak
I know I'm safe with Jack and Pa guarding the home
I listen to chirps of crickets
I look at the stars twinkling down at me
The wind is softly blowing the grass sideways
Making a soft whistle in the breeze
I fall asleep with no fears
And to myself I whisper
"Sweet dreams!"

Annika Dome, Grade 4
School of Technology & Arts I, WI

Beautiful, Bodacious, Blistering Blue

Blue is the clear summer sky, the peaceful ocean, and
overwhelming sadness.
Blue is the taste of warm blueberry pancakes.
Fresh juicy blueberries and freshly-baked blueberry
pies smell blue.
Death makes me feel blue.

Blue is the sound of crashing waves and bagpipes.
Blue is Noah's Ark, slow-moving rivers,
and funerals.
Gloomy rainy days are blue.

Nathan Peterson, Grade 6
Marinette Middle School, WI

Snow

So white and cold
whiter than a sheep's fur
colder than the wings of a penguin
snow
hiding like escaped prisoners from the suns rays
falling so gentle like a parachute
snow
when touched by heat it melts like tears
so many things you can make
snowmen, balls, and forts
SNOW

Reily Knutson, Grade 6
Ramsey International Fine Arts Center, MN

New Years Day

N ew Year
P **E** ople talking
Ne **W** York

People **Y** elling Happy New Year
E ating
A big celebration
Waiting fo **R** the big ball to drop at midnight
S houting and screaming

Morgan Wittman, Grade 5
Howards Grove Middle School, WI

Things You Should(n't) Say

You shouldn't say a few different things
  like "can't,"
    "Should I write this?"
      "I don't think I can do it."
There's really nothing to it.
Just be positive and say…
    "I can, I'm going to, YES!"
Even, if you're feeling down don't say
    the things you shouldn't say.
But say…
    "I can, I'm going to, YES!"
These three things
    always help me feel
      awesome!

Morgan Larson, Grade 6
Martin County West Trimont Elementary School, MN

Hope

Inside this single stitch in a quilt
Lies the strength of the person who stitched it
The strength that makes the single stitch hold the quilt together
And once held the person together

Inside this single stitch in a quilt
Lies the worry of the person who stitched it
The worry of how to go on
The worry of the future

Inside this single stitch in a quilt
Lies the hope of the person who stitched it
The hope of what's to come
The hope of everything and all things

Ruby Malek, Grade 6
T J Walker Middle School, WI

Dream Tree

Inside this maple tree
Are memories waiting to be
A playful kid's picnic or a starry night,
Under my branches, dreams take flight.

They sit under my branches for shade and for sorrow,
For the hope that things will be better tomorrow.
The birthday parties and winters I've seen,
Are the things I've been used for
But don't know what they mean.

So what am I good for but to be a maple tree and a spy?
Oh, to be there when people need me,
And to be part of many dreams until I die.

Abby Thiede, Grade 6
T J Walker Middle School, WI

A Soldier

A soldier is a fighter for freedom,
For family, for friends,
There aren't just soldiers on the
battlefield but also in our
communities. They bring us
together and make us all
feel safe.

Genoa Scott, Grade 6
Ramsey International Fine Arts Center, MN

Bedroom

Bed, soft and warm like a hug
Mirror, like the reflection in someone's eyes
Clock, like arms pointing
Bookshelf, like a brain full of books that you've read
Rug, soft and fuzzy like a dogs fur
Chair, like arms holding a baby
Pictures, like your heart full of good memories

Lizzie Hugo, Grade 6
Harriet Bishop Elementary School, MN

Winter

Winter is a time for sledding and hot chocolate
And time to put away summer clothes
And bring out winter jackets
When we have snow days there is no school
Winter is a time to get wet and cold
Then come in and have hot chocolate and marshmallows

Allyson Hunt, Grade 6
Orfordville Elementary School, WI

Winter

W isconsin is the best place to be if you like snow.
I n the winter the weather is unpredictable.
N o one can resist Wisconsin snow.
T ons and tons of pretty white snow.
E veryone in Wisconsin loves the snow.
R eady for December snow!

Brandon Willems, Grade 5
Stocker Elementary School, WI

Fall

I see a ginormous leaf pile
I feel the leaves tiny and large brush my skin
I hear a wonderful crunch!
I smell a spicy ginger pie.
I taste the crunched up leaves in my mouth.
Ewwwwwww!

Kendra Dobbins, Grade 5
Franklin Elementary School, WI

My Fish, Bubbles
Bubbles is the laziest fish
In the tank
He is two and
Likes to be cool
He thinks he rules the pool
He is orange, like Citrus
He swims around the
Bowl again and again
He lives on my dresser
Looking down at the messy ground
Around and around
Bubbles swims around
All day long
Carlin Wolleat, Grade 5
Blue Heron Elementary School, MN

Matt
Matt is a clone
Since when?
Forever,
The regrets piled thickly
Yet in the midst of his sorrow.
Matt found a glimmer of hope
He believed he could be something more.
"And I will be,"
Matt exclaimed.
But everything is not depressing.
It is his job,
To tame the hot desert air.
That is how it happened.
Angelica Kurth, Grade 6
Tomahawk Middle School, WI

Christmas Day
C heerful
H oliday
R eal good
I love the holiday
S erious day
T rees
M y presents
A Christmas day
S anta Claus

D ancing
A mazing
Y ears of dreaming
Jesse Schwoerer, Grade 5
Howards Grove Middle School, WI

Bees
Bees go to flowers
collecting nectar from them
passing by each one.
Justin Lein, Grade 6
Dr Dyer Intermediate School, WI

Asleep
Cool breezy grass
Under my back
Stars crack the darkness
Like a gunshot
From a distance
I hear wolves
Singing a sad
Sad song
Crickets rhythmic
Chirping serves
As a lullaby as
I gently fall
Asleep
Brad Vandenberg-Daves, Grade 4
School of Technology & Arts I, WI

Horicon Marsh
Leaves fall upon the trail
Plants losing their color, becoming brittle
Waters rippling in a calm way
Fuzzy caterpillars along the trail
The warmth of the sun on my face
Cattails as tall as I am
Colorful trees in the distance
Red and purple berries on their stems
Leaves lying on the trail
Sun sparkling on the water
Old barn off in the distance
Slimy snake on the trail
Leaves of many shapes and colors
Baysia Boschert, Grade 5
St Katharine Drexel School, WI

Horicon Marsh
H ad lots of fun
O utstanding field trip
R ushing wind everywhere
I was very tired after the trip
C ould see many geese in the sky
O ur first field trip in fifth grade
N ot many ducks were there

M y mom was there
A ir was cold
R eally warm in the building
S aw two snakes
H ad to write some papers
Rachel Fister, Grade 5
St Katharine Drexel School, WI

Fish
I caught a fish it was huge!
We took pictures.
And then we released it.
Bradley Johnson, Grade 6
St Francis Middle School, MN

Ghosts
Demon,
Phantom,
Haunted tombstone,
Cold ghosts,
Spooky, scary, creepy spirits,
Cold, white, luminous after life,
Those are a few.
Eerie cemeteries,
Mysterious specter,
Spooking, haunting, fighting ghouls,
Floating, coming, scaring ghosts.
Undead vampire too.
Spookiest cemetery,
Super natural phantoms,
Dark after lubes,
Don't forget apparition ghoul,
Last of all — best of all —
I like shady tombstones.
Emily Knier, Grade 5
Howards Grove Middle School, WI

Behind a Trumpet
Inside this trumpet
Are songs that haven't been played yet
Sad and joyful songs are waiting to sing

Inside this trumpet
Is a story with different sounds
Waiting to be let out

Inside this trumpet
The trumpet sings to
The veterans who have died
And to the happy couple at a wedding

Inside this trumpet
Is something special
Something not discovered
For that a new song it will sing
Samantha Mirkes, Grade 6
T J Walker Middle School, WI

Goblins
Fiction book
Fantasy world
Going to war
Ugly faces
Coming for me
I'm so scared
What about you?
Wonder what their going to do to me…
Watch out…
Watch out…
They're coming for you…!
Anthoni R. Kong, Grade 5
Harriet Bishop Elementary School, MN

Winter

I can see sparkling snow
I can hear the big snowplows go by
I can taste and smell the hot, hot chocolate
I can touch the very cold snow

Kyle Podskarbi, Grade 5
Stocker Elementary School, WI

My Fluffy Dog

Snuggled up by my pillow,
Crying to see me,
Quiet, relaxed, sleepy
A big teddy bear on my bed.

Neysha Rodriguez, Grade 6
Gilmore Middle School, WI

Football

Exhilarating, enlightening
Tackling, running, throwing
Exciting, anxious, anger, nervous
Gridiron

Anthony Silverman, Grade 6
Dr Dyer Intermediate School, WI

Leaves

In spring I am small
In the summer I am tall
In the fall, I fall

Mallory A. Topel, Grade 5
St Paul Evangelical Lutheran School, WI

Candy

Candy, candy, candy is fun
and it's good to eat
with a buddy

Kevin Marquez, Grade 6
Messmer Preparatory Catholic School, WI

Mountain Lion!

Rare mountain lions
Ate all the animals up there
No more animals.

Zachary Johnson, Grade 4
Stocker Elementary School, WI

Dog

A dog eating in peace
Suddenly a cat comes by
Dog chases the cat!

Indiria Clark, Grade 4
Stocker Elementary School, WI

Skiing Down a Hill

Skiing down a hill
Going 30 miles per hour
Wind rushing through your hair as you go
Flying down a hill
Soaring through the air
Bend your knees and brace yourself
CRASH!
You're on the ground; you can't get up
After a few minutes that feel more like a lifetime,
The pain begins to recede
You get up and try it again.

Skiing down a hill
Going 30 miles per hour
Wind rushing through your hair as you go
Flying down a hill
Soaring through the air
The sense of power rushing through your veins
The feeling that all time has stopped as you plummet down the slope
Bend your knees and brace yourself for the crash
But you're not lying on the ground this time.
You are still skiing down a hill.

Noah Agata, Grade 6
Lincoln Middle School, WI

Christmas

Kids getting cool gifts,
Christmas lights on the house,
Tasty treats on the table,
Christmas trees full of lights,
Santa Claus coming to town,
Kids screaming "Toys toys,"
Kids going outside to play snowball fights
People watching Christmas movies,
And everybody having fun with their family,
People going to their church to celebrate the day when Jesus was born.

Kameron Shembeda, Grade 5
Howards Grove Middle School, WI

Strike 3!!!

I'm ready for that wild pitch to punch me in the gut.
Instead I hit it back, HARD!
I'm rounding first, half way to second!
That little voice inside my head is yelling, GO! GO!
I started to speed like a burglar!!!
I wasn't quite done. I was going home!!
The ball was coming faster than ever.
I didn't know whether to dive or slide.
There was no turning back.
All of a sudden, there was a tornado of dust.
When it cleared off, the umpire screeched like a gorilla,
SAFE!!!
And that was that!
WE WON!!

Brenna Bentz, Grade 5
Harriet Bishop Elementary School, MN

Tigers

Tiger
Big, colorful
Purring, scratching, starring
Predator from the rain forest
Big cat

Aaron Hatlevig, Grade 6
Orfordville Elementary School, WI

Winter

I feel the fresh snow blankets.
I hear the spirit lifting Christmas music.
I see the wonderful tree.
I smell freshly baked cookies.
I taste great hot cocoa when I come inside.

Amber Mivshek, Grade 5
Stocker Elementary School, WI

Guitar

Guitar
Musical, graceful
Strumming, picking, vibrating
Musical note
Metal rock

Keegan Rhynas, Grade 5
Howards Grove Middle School, WI

In the World of Squirrels

Squirrels
El stupido nuisance
Chattering, fleeing, climbing
Hatred irritated awestruck amazed
Rat

Jarret Johnson, Grade 6
Dr Dyer Intermediate School, WI

Thanksgiving

Thanksgiving
Pie, turkey
Joyful, thankful, happy
Family, friends, colors, trees
Wind, talking, laughing, music, munching

Sarah Carlson, Grade 4
Stocker Elementary School, WI

Turkey

Turkey
Good, yummy
Furry, hard, smooth
Feathers, meat, grown, wilderness
Loud, gobble, silence, dying, eating

Brandon Erickson, Grade 4
Stocker Elementary School, WI

I Am

I am from one life, one you, some moments good, some piercing, some happy.
I am from traveling and movement
from speed and hiking.
I am from the thin dry air or the moist crisp air.
I am from biking, everything lost
except for the cool wind.
I am from freezing water, swimming in the icy Burntside,
to swimming in Lake Superior to swimming in the dirty Atlantic Ocean.
I am from soft musical instruments to enjoy or play.
I am from reading, and listening to a lovely book.
I am from visiting Zion, Redwood, Rocky Mountain, Yosemite, or the Big Tree.
Everywhere.
I am from architecture, from designing and creating to testing and using.
I am from waking up with the birds and listening to them: chirp-chirp-chirp.
I am from laughing so hard I cry.
I am from happy moments
I am from my life.

Aaron Kramer, Grade 5
Adams Spanish Immersion School, MN

I Am

I am from a spinning football into the air and catching it in the awesome end zone
I am from the coolest state in the world called Minnesota, I was born in St. Paul
I am from riding my bike to watching a movie at night
I am from doing my homework to playing shooting video games
I am from riding my gigantic bus to going to my good school
I am from praying for my food going to my holy church
I am from playing baseball to running to third base
I am from reading to doing math
I am from riding my awesome skateboard to playing with my good friends
I am from going to sleep to waking up and going to my good school
I am from listening to music to watching my cool TV
I am from swimming to playing with my kickball
I am from going to the zoo to riding my scooter
I am from eating pizza to watching TV
I am from going to the big Mall of America to going on the rides.

Kiko Carbajal, Grade 5
Adams Spanish Immersion School, MN

Sugar

Inside this piece of gum
there lies a piece of sugar
that's not been tasted.
Just that one piece of sugar not tasted.
But when you taste this piece you get that feeling of your taste buds rising.
By the time that taste passes you probably spit it out or keep chewing.
But if you spit it out you pull out another piece of gum.
Unwrap it, throw the wrapper away, then start chewing again.
But do you think of what you taste?
If you don't you're probably doing something else or thinking of something else.
And sometimes you can feel the sugar touching your tongue.
Then you lose track of what you're doing.
You think of what touched your tongue and that my friends is sugar.

Austin Jerome, Grade 6
T J Walker Middle School, WI

Christmas at My House

C aring for my family
H aving fun together
R eading Christmas stories
I nviting loved ones over
S haring great gifts
T hanking one another
M aking yummy cookies
A way in the manger
S inging Christmas carols
    late into the night.
Elizabeth Behling, Grade 5
Sheboygan Falls Middle School, WI

Tradewell

T alented
R ead
A wesome
D ude
E xciting
W ell
E xcelling
L oves food
L oving
Dillon Tradewell, Grade 6
St Francis Middle School, MN

In the Season of Winter

In the season of winter
Thousands and thousands of snowflakes
All from the sky.
In the season of winter
The snow is very white and puffy.
In the season of winter
Many children play in the snow.

In the season of winter
Cesar Castellon, Grade 5
Wagner Elementary School, MN

Friends

Friends are always here,
so never have that fear.
They will help you through it all,
and will never let you fall.
Friends love you,
almost as much as you love them.
Emily Drone, Grade 6
Riverdale Elementary School, WI

The Sunset

The Sun sets and rises
It looks like it is
Painting the sky
I love to see the sun set.
Eliza Carman, Grade 4
Classical School, WI

Open Mind

How was the world created?
And its constant changing in emotion?
How is it ever possible?

How does the world work,
the way it does?
How many wonderful worlds are there,
out in the universe?

So many glistening stars,
remind me every day,
that we may not be alone here!

Makes me wonder…
It just gives me an open mind…

What IS life?

How did it start?
When will it end?

The world may never know…
Emily Hayden, Grade 6
Lincoln Middle School, WI

Stalkers in the Forest

Hunters,
stalking through
the leaves, quietly
talking, occasionally
stopping, silently
blocking a squawking
bird among the
dappled trees, while
still walking.
Scout Savage, Grade 6
Riverdale Elementary School, WI

Let's Go Hunting Dad

Into the closet
In the door
Grab for the case
Snatch the bullets
Into the truck
Down to the field
Into the stand
Load your gun
Wait for the right deer
Gun to your cheek
Aim at the deer
Squeeze the trigger
Gut the deer
Show your friends
Eat the meat
Hunter Case, Grade 6
Orfordville Elementary School, WI

Band

Trombone,
Trumpet,
French horn,
Loud Saxophone,
Soft flute,
Squeak, vibrate, soothing oboe
Thunderous, noisy, dull drum
Those are a few.
Special bass
Boring drum
Hitting, sliding, tapping ensemble
Pushing, plucking, blowing orchestra
Famous piano too.
Shrill trumpet,
Energetic saxophone,
Nice French horn,
Don't forget tedious trombone
Last of all — best of all —
I like the magical clarinet.
Ryan Bell, Grade 5
Howards Grove Middle School, WI

Sports

Cross country,
Basketball,
Baseball,
Competitive football,
Energetic tennis,
Fun, rough, tiring track and field,
Skill, exciting, score water polo,
Those are a few.
Crashing football,
Professional basketball,
Throwing, running, catching baseball,
Shooting, passing, dunking basketball,
Hard tennis too.
Enemy football,
Block water polo,
Tough cross-country,
Don't forget active volleyball,
Last of all — best of all —
I like teamwork soccer.
Ashley Reinemann, Grade 5
Howards Grove Middle School, WI

Volleyball

What is volleyball?
Hard, rubber balls
Teammates yelling, "I got it!"
Knees pounding on the gym floor
The smack of a spike
My coach and teammates screaming,
"We won!"
That's volleyball!
Malayna McDaniel, Grade 5
Howards Grove Middle School, WI

I Am From…

I am from doing hard work
to playing and doing extremely fun things.
I am from the cold Minnesota
and I was born in the capital St. Paul.
I am from shooting at small targets at my grandma's big farm
to playing football in the big green field.
I am from skateboarding in the big park
to playing basketball in the small court.
I am from playing with my little dog
to being lazy and watching TV.
I am from eating extraordinary foods
to eating the same old thing every day.
I am from scaring my mom
to getting freaked out by my dad.
I am from doing crazy stunts
to being bored as can be.
I am from eating slowly
to having a fast wing-eating contest.
I am from a loud city
to a quiet, lazy country.

DeMarco Lindstrom, Grade 5
Adams Spanish Immersion School, MN

I Am From

I am from dancing with my sister
to reading to her at night

I am from loud wild parties
to soft sleepy music

I am from slumbering peacefully dreaming about my cat
to having a terrible fight about my hat

I am from my fuzzy black and white cat
to colorful bright lights

I am from reading large volumes
to encountering shiny rocks

I am from the city of St. Paul
to spending the weekend in the country

I am from big rocky mountains
to the salty tang of the sea

Anna Engelhardt, Grade 5
Adams Spanish Immersion School, MN

Senses

I was petting my puppy, I like the feel.
He was stinky and I could smell him from a mile away!
I saw dirt in his fur, that had to go!
I decided to give him a bath after I ate dinner.
I heard scratching in the bathtub
It was my puppy waiting for his bath!

Nina Doss, Grade 6
Gilmore Middle School, WI

Thanksgiving

T hanksgiving is here, I am so glad.
H unting will take over my mind.
A t school I won't be able to concentrate,
N ow that Thanksgiving is here.
K itchens are full of women preparing for dinner.
S o many orange coats dot the fields and trees.
G uys eat so much after hunting.
I n the living room, we're making too much noise.
V ery few people aren't excited for the food.
I know I am!
N ow Thanksgiving is over.
G ood thing I can give thanks again next year!

Kilian Boland, Grade 6
Seneca Middle School, WI

Beautiful Blistering Blue

Blue is the summer sky, waves crashing on the shore,
and losing your dog.
Blue is the taste of cotton candy.
Crystal clear water and winter's icy air smell blue.
When people die I feel blue.
Blue is tears running down my cheek and a quiet sea.
Blue is the Menominee River, my bedroom,
and a dark, cloudy day.
Getting good grades is blue.
A bruise from falling on my bike is also blue.
A blistering January wind is blue.
Blue is Hawaii.

Lynsee Bohan, Grade 6
Marinette Middle School, WI

24/7

Although I have hands I am different from you,
and I easily get ticked off.
I'm here to cause the time of your life,
whether your heart is hard or soft.

I spin around every day,
I'm changing all the time.
Remember to look at me,
'cause when you're having fun I fly!

What am I?
I'm a clock

Olivia Bien, Grade 5
Harriet Bishop Elementary School, MN

Basketball

Shoots, jumps, scores
Jumps under the hoop to catch the rebound.
It is a team sport.
Dribble, pass, box-out
Pass to the open person.
Runs down the court to make a lay-up

Annie Behrend, Grade 4
River Heights Elementary School, WI

My Grandparent's Land

Dirt roads, itchy grass,
Two trailers, four wheeler trails,
A long dock leading to a lake,
A hammock, brightness of yellows,
Greens, and red plants,
A bright sun beating down on me,
The dark and bright colors of the
Four wheelers,
Dogs barking, fish flopping,
Kids screaming that they have a
Fish, four wheeler's engine running,
Bait hitting the water,
How long are we staying here,
What type of fish are in the lake,
Happiness, sadness when leaving,
Excitement,
Happiness,
Happiness,
Happiness.

Parker Wiles, Grade 6
Harriet Bishop Elementary School, MN

Seasons

Flowers are blooming
Birds are singing
Children are splashing
Spring is coming

Schools are closing
Days are expanding
Kids are biking
Summer is coming

Leaves are tumbling
Trees are swaying
Schools are starting
Autumn is coming

Jackets are zipping
Snowflakes are falling
Parents are shoveling
Winter is coming

Abby Smith, Grade 6
Valley Middle School, MN

Snow

Snow snow snow
Anything with snow
I play in it
I build it
I lay on it
Minnesota is covered with snow
Snow snow snow
Just let it snow

Jonathan Nguyen, Grade 5
Harriet Bishop Elementary School, MN

The Balloon

Inside my 12th birthday balloon
slowly sinking
day by day
to the ground

The dark air inside this balloon
slowly finding places
to sneak out
into a very bright room

The dark air is like a person
that did something wrong
trying to find a place to get out
into a bright, bright free life

Ryan Jackson, Grade 6
T J Walker Middle School, WI

This Old Guitar

Inside this old guitar
Lies songs that are
Waiting to be heard
Just waiting to be heard

This old guitar is waiting
Wanting to be heard
Just wanting to be played
But isn't

But then there is a
Change of
Heart and it is
Finally played

Cody Clemons, Grade 6
T J Walker Middle School, WI

The Gears and Car

The gears
They make you go
Make you stop
When the engine roars you go

It makes you go
And you think
Go or
Stop

The engine
The gears go
The car and gears
Make you go

Hugo Reyes, Grade 6
T J Walker Middle School, WI

I Am

I am from tank tops to coats,
berries to cherries, apples to oranges,
dogs to cats, and wishing to fishing.
I am from teachers to coaches, no's to yes's,
boats to scooters, and blah to yum.

I am from pants to shorts, pencils to pens,
computers to printers, and dresses to skirts.
I am from short to tall, gross to pretty,
beach balls to snowballs,
and hip hop to classical.

I am from running to walking,
jogging to skipping, getting to giving,
and crying to laughing.
I am from heels to flats, bees to trees,
winter to summer, fall to spring,
and morning to night.

I am from peas to pods, sweet to sour,
and scary to silly.
I am from buttons to zippers, sun to moon,
hurting to healing, bows to ties,
and boxes to bags.

Grace C. Banks, Grade 5
Adams Spanish Immersion School, MN

I Am

I am from creative arts,
sparkly crafts,
activities, imagination,
and new things
to make every day.

I am from cooking new recipes,
new food to try out every day.
I am from making delicious cakes,
and baking sweet cookies
and eating my favorite cheesy pasta,
and Mexican rice with sour cream.

I am from colorful flowers and roses
I am from school math and art
I am from playing with my friends,
going to their fun parties.

But one important thing
Caring about them and loving my family.
I am from sweet watermelon
so fresh, so red
I am from drawing and playing
I am from dancing in my head.

Wendy Rios Renteria, Grade 5
Adams Spanish Immersion School, MN

Hunting

Hunting hunting worth being here
especially when you see a deer.
Always always grab your bow
don't forget before you go.
Kameron Moffatt, Grade 6
St Francis Middle School, MN

Snow

Snow is cold.
Snow is white.
Watch out you might
Get frostbite.
Maria Willner, Grade 6
St Francis Middle School, MN

Sun

Redness, far
Rotates, heats, flares,
Peaceful, relaxed, bright, friendly
' Star
Shiyue Xie, Grade 6
Dr Dyer Intermediate School, WI

The Zoo

The animals at the zoo.
Always make me feel blue.
Because they're in a cage.
With all that pent up rage.
Andrew Biesek, Grade 5
St Johns Lutheran School, WI

Carpet of Leaves

As I walk down the pathway,
The leaves fall and create
A red, yellow, and gold carpet
As if I am royalty.
Julian Frerichs, Grade 4
Breck School, MN

Blue Jeans

Blue jeans are all different colors:
Dark blue, light blue
Even in the middle blue
Torn up, raggedy, old blue jeans.
Sommer Storms, Grade 4
Jefferson Elementary School, WI

Maple

Every autumn day
You seem to fade away.
Your bright red colors
Always seem to beat the duller.
Caitlin Dempsey, Grade 4
Classical School, WI

I Am

I am from long brown hair and big brown eyes.
I am from my large dog Toby and riding on my dad's fast boat.
I am from small color crayons and loud violins.
I am from going outside and fun times.
I am from my ripped up blanket and going on planes.
I am from long cold Minnesota days and different kinds of chapstick.
I am from hot cooking and fun writing to mushy marshmallows and 5th grade.
I am from watching the big wide TV to swimming in the deep blue sea.
I am from playing hard soccer and reading scary books.
I am from eating gross coconuts in Mexico and my ok sisters.
I am from my dirty sweatshirts and my big family.
I am from colorful all star tennis shoes and being in fun kindergarten.
I am from fluffy warm pancakes and cold milk.
Jeniffer Ponce, Grade 5
Adams Spanish Immersion School, MN

Months

April is the month of my birthday YAY!
November is when New Moon comes out — go Team Edward!
August is when you scream I scream we all scream for ice cream AAAHH!
October is when we go to haunted houses and get chased by Jason!
December is when we unwrap our Christmas presents like wild animals!
July is when we see fireworks from the sky BOOM!
September is when school starts with new teachers — go Mrs. Paul!
February is when Edward and Jacob fight over Bella for LOVE!
June is when we get out of school and do whatever we want with NO TEACHERS
     all over us telling us what to do
May is when flowers jump out of the grass and LAUGH!
March is my brother's birthday and we go to Chuckie Cheese with Chuckie!
January is when snow falls and butterflies fly away!
Miguel Ramirez, Grade 6
Gilmore Middle School, WI

The Mummy

There once was a mummy
Who had an ache in his tummy.
He tried to call for help
But he couldn't even yelp.
The guards forgot to check
The daily checking for some reason they were playing cards.
Then they found that his stomach wasn't bound.
"Well no wonder why, pharaoh, your tummy hurts it's not bound." The guard said.
The mummy said that his hair is too long and needs to get out of his tomb
And get a groom.
The guards suggested that they have a feast
So, he can rest in peace.
Jacob Rasmussen, Grade 4
Ashby Elementary School, MN

Fall

The whistling wind blows through the fingers of the trees
The leaves dance to the beat of the music the wind makes
Flowers slowly close their petals and swiftly sway until winter's first breath
Coolness against my face makes a new song a new day, a new breath
Bronwyn Silk, Grade 5
School of Technology & Arts I, WI

Halloween Is Here!

Halloween is here
I see Halloween parties on every block
it sounds like a lion roaring in the zoo
Halloween is here…
I hear kids ringing doorbells everywhere
kids say trick-or-treat like
a parrot copying somebody
Halloween is here…
I touch candy and pumpkin guts
trying to make jack-o'-lanterns
the guts are like old munchy candy bars
Halloween is here…
I smell candy on every block
and sweet crisp autumn
the aroma smells like pumpkin pie fresh out of the oven
Halloween is here…
I taste soft caramels melting in my mouth
and crunchy candy it sounds like stepping on crunchy leaves

Jack Robinson, Grade 4
Kennedy Elementary School, MN

Pizza

Homemade pizza

Homemade pepperoni with warm dough
Toss into the cool air.

Bright red tomato sauce
Spread on top of the smooth dough.

Cheese sprinkles like rain falling from the sky,
Landing on red sauce.

The warm, delicious smell of pizza in the oven
Makes me feel like I am floating on a rainbow.

Pepperoni slices around like sleds
Sliding down a hill in the winter.

Pizza, HOT like the sun on a hot summer day!

Hunter Payne, Grade 5
Sibley Elementary School, MN

Dreams*

Hold fast to dreams
For if dreams fly,
Life is an amazing friend
That will never die.

Hold fast to dreams
For if dreams stay,
Life is a warm feeling
That will never go away.

Alexander Long, Grade 4
Classical School, WI
*Inspired by Langston Hughes' "Dreams Deferred"

Sheep

I have sheep.
They're sometimes a pest.
They're really loud.
But when we split
  the babies from their mom
  it is the worst thing ever.
My favorite part is
  when the babies are born.
  they are small and cute.
Sometimes we have to bottle feed them
  and it is really fun.
I feed the ewes with their babies.
I have to check
  if their mouths are cold.
If they are we have to
  put orange brown stuff
  in their mouths
  and then they feel better.
I hate when we send them to the market.
It is the worst thing ever.

Erin Tlam, Grade 4
Martin County West Trimont Elementary School, MN

The Guitar

Inside this guitar,
Are songs that have not been written
Just music notes with no sound
The strings, just no movement

Inside this guitar,
There is a song inside
For someone special to hear
No one else, just that special person

Inside this guitar,
There are symbols
That show its personality,
Its strength, and its cleverness

Inside this guitar,
Where the music is born,
Lays a heart of kindness,
Strings that won't be broken
And many songs that will never be forgotten.

Kyle Medlen, Grade 6
T J Walker Middle School, WI

Vamps

the paleness of their white skin makes them look lifeless.
you look into their eyes of black like you're hopeless.
their teeth sink into your skin the pain is deceiving
when you wake up you feel nothing.
and you thirst for the taste of blood.
you are now a vamp.

Ashley Stone, Grade 6
St Francis Middle School, MN

Fishing

Fishing is very fun.
I love when I get a bite!!
Sometimes fish make a big fight.
I catch walleye.
    Sometimes I hook it in the eye…Ouch!!!
I catch crappie, bluegill, and perch.
We search for hooks
    that we get
    in the weeds and reeds.
Northerns are big fish
    and hard to reel in.
Sometimes if we catch a lot
    we will string them
    through the gill
and out the mouth
    and tie them
    to the boat.
I love fishing!!!

Kooper Janssen, Grade 4
Martin County West Trimont Elementary School, MN

Black

Mmmm. Fresh picked blackberries in a big bowl,
Or the opposite, Nanny McFee's mole.
Black says, "No" and gives me commands,
And black prefers ACDC, the famous goth band.

What's that I smell? Smoke from a fire?
Black is rage, a feeling not admired.
A piano piece in the minor key,
Oh, it's kinda scaring me!

The midnight sky on a Halloween night,
With witches and goblins whose magic is not bright.
Black is dark and black is deep,
Wear black at a funeral and people will weep.

Black is not a friendly color,
Try to find one any duller.
BLACK, BLACK, BLACK!

Abby Herzog, Grade 5
Harriet Bishop Elementary School, MN

Rocking Ruby Red

Red is marching Marines, the United States flag, and the
Badger Games.
Red is the taste of tangy spaghetti sauce.
Roses on Valentine's Day and pepperoni pizzas smell red.
Getting bad grades makes me feel red.
Red is the sound of sirens and the dripping of blood.
Red is a volcano, a beating heart, and a burning building.
Car accidents are red.
Wailing of ambulances are also red.
Red is the love of my dog, Hershey.

Cali Nygren, Grade 6
Marinette Middle School, WI

My Crazy Cousins

The definition of CRAZY = loud, obnoxious, rude.
That's my cousins
and I would not
trade them for a
thing. Because
they're mine and
mine only. Rude
and I will always LOVE them.

Because that's
my big crazy
COUSINS!

Kardia Coulibaly, Grade 5
Eastern Heights Elementary School, MN

Colors of the World

My Red is a quart of lion's blood,
The Red is a blazing bonfire on a cool night,
This Red is a very bright laser,
This Blue is a sparkling lake,
My Blue is a shimmering Iris,
The Blue is an uprooted sky,
The Tan is Horatio Caine's hair,
My Tan is my ivory skin,
This Tan is the beaches coarse sand,
My Green is the algae on a shimmering lake,
This Green is billowing grass in a park,
The Green is the leaves of a tall maple tree.

Brody Bien, Grade 6
Harriet Bishop Elementary School, MN

Random Colors

The gold is a rich person's bath tub
The turquoise is the slippery soap in my bathroom
The orange is an orange
The red is the center of the earth
The blue is Neptune in space at 12 hundred
The yellow is a lemon
The gray is an old man's hair
The pink is a pink lemon
The brown is a chocolate bar melting on Tuesday
The white is the shiny snow on Christmas day
The black is a black hole in space
The purple is a grape

Luke Senta, Grade 5
Harriet Bishop Elementary School, MN

My Name Is Like…

My name is like a June day when everyone is relaxed.
My name is like a tornado getting furious.
My name is like a gift when a baby is born.
My name is like a flag touching the ground.
My name is like a math problem no one can figure out.
My name is like a fall day that has just arrived.

Kate Erickson, Grade 5
Sibley Elementary School, MN

The Fun Day

8:00 am
My alarm clock goes off
So I can go and set up the chairs for when my friends come over.
My mom goes to get the food
While my dad gets the candy and the movies.
Soon enough
My friends
Get here
And I'm still setting up the games
So my friends help me.
Then my mom gets home with
The food and my dad got
Home with the candy and movies.
Now we can watch
A movie while eating;
This is a fun fun day.

Hannah Courtney, Grade 6
St Francis Middle School, MN

Flame in the Fire Place

You're there, still there, still warm
And still bright
Not fading away behind a glass door
You can make a rhythm with your flame
And you can't stop

You are starting to burn out, but you come back
You can't go anywhere
Your flame is too strong to be broken
You can't go anywhere, you're too strong
To be gone

I think of you, a calm, nice flame
With your nice soft rhythm, you're unstoppable
Until air or water, I finally figured
Out you're my little flame.

Cameron Krishka, Grade 6
T J Walker Middle School, WI

Gorgeous Gooey Green

Green is a snapping turtle, a sparkling emerald,
and feeling envious.
Green is the taste of fresh dill pickles.
Spearmint
and stinky cheese smell green.
Jealousy
makes me feel green.
Green
is the sound of chirping crickets and
terrifying alligators.
Green is a wet rain forest, the Great Plains, and a
garden full of daisies.
Recycling paper is green.
A 4-H Club
is also green.
Green is slimy science goo.

Rebecca Dura, Grade 6
Marinette Middle School, WI

Glamorous Glossy Green

Green is grown grass, fresh zucchini, and the
swamp in our backyard.
Green is the taste of a
crispy, Granny Smith apple.
Haymaking and Christmas trees
smell green.
Zooming roller coasters
make me feel green.
Green is the sound of croaking
frogs and a spinning windmill.
Green is a rolling meadow, a
forest of evergreens, and Iceland.
Mowing the lawn is green.
Golfing in the summertime
is also green.
Green is a Shamrock on St. Patrick's Day.

Claire Carviou, Grade 6
Marinette Middle School, WI

Racing Ruby Red

Red is a delicious apple, an identical rose,
and a burning sunburn.
Red is the taste of spicy sauce.
Spectacular pizza and a bouncing rubber ball smell red.
A flaming fire makes me feel red.
Red is the sound of racing fire trucks
and screaming ambulances.
Red is a fire station,
Planet Mars,
and the humongous sun.
A sparkling marker is red.
A wonderful
Rainbow is also red. Red is
Being daring and brave.

Kaitlyn Berkebill, Grade 6
Marinette Middle School, WI

My Box of Crayons

The red is a hard dark brick
An orange is the edges of a blazing sun
The yellow is a planet looking down
My green is the beautiful leaves and grass
A blue is the dark night sky
The indigo is bright and dark all at the same time
My violet is my lilacs in my old yard
The black is my dog all curly and messy
My white is the glimmering snow all through the day
The gold is a shiny glowing jewel
Silver is what covers my snow
The pink is people's lips
A gray is the fog on a cold rainy day
My tie-dye is a group of stunning butterflies flying across the sky

Emma Gavnik, Grade 5
Harriet Bishop Elementary School, MN

Football

F eet running
O nly 32 teams
O ver 200 players
T oy footballs made
B alls flying
A thletes running
L eaping for a touchdown
NF **L**

Bryce Pedrin, Grade 5
Howards Grove Middle School, WI

Halloween

Just this morning I wanted to play
Butt when I woke up it wasn't day
I yelled for my mom she wasn't there
I looked around, the whole house was clear
I went outside I was so scared
But I think they left me that wasn't fair
There wasn't no sound
Nobody was around

Traveon Robinson, Grade 6
Messmer Preparatory Catholic School, WI

Come into the Presence of Dogs

Dogs are taught to do many tricks
They can be entered in dog shows
Golden Retrievers love to swim
Black labs love to hunt for ducks

Poodles are intelligent animals
The German shepherd works for police
People think the pug is actually a pig

Siada Loch, Grade 5
Wagner Elementary School, MN

My Old Cat

Straying in the basement
Away from the light
Unseen by people
Unknown by the world
People ask about her
I say she is a spirit
I wish I could be with her
In heaven.

Melissa Lui, Grade 6
Gilmore Middle School, WI

Autumn

Yeah it's starting to get cold,
Snow's coming!
We also get to jump in leaves.
Now where did I put my rake?
I love autumn.
It's so much fun!

Daniel Hanson, Grade 6
St Francis Middle School, MN

I Am

I am from lovely day dreaming
Inventing a whole new world like no other.
I am from a lot of reading
The amusingness of bold words converted into a
Wonderful picture in my mind.

I am from swimming
Going underneath what do you see?
Nothing just peaceful, relaxing, plain water.
I am from learning everything
Paying attention to everything my teacher tells me to do.

I am from falling all the time
Clumsy me falling all the time, do you want to see my almost deep scars?
I am from writing poems
Sometimes creative, sometimes sad.

I am from Mexico
I miss the cool hot place.
I am from me
I am creative, fun, laughable me
So this is me…bye.

Paola Casillas Ortiz, Grade 5
Adams Spanish Immersion School, MN

The Best Times in Fall Are…

Fall is, eating pumpkin pie fresh out
of the oven, with a melted cherry in the middle.
Fall is here…kids are screaming on Halloween,
being scared by spooky boys and girls in their
costumes, running to their parents.
Fall is here…touching the snow that falls to the ground,
and melts like an ice cube.
Fall is…going to friends' houses,
and ringing glowing doorbells and saying hi to friends.
Fall is…smelling waxy candles that glow,
kids making wishes while blowing on the candles.
Fall is, smelling the fall leaves with slimy bugs
crawling on them. Ew!
Fall is…tasting hot chocolate with whip cream on top,
It's like a wave of happiness inside my mouth.
Fall is…leaves falling and making pictures when
they fall onto the ground.
Fall is…hearing rain drops down into the pond,
it sounds like a music note. I hear frogs popping their heads out of the water.
Splash! The frogs stick out their tongues.

Allison Barber, Grade 4
Kennedy Elementary School, MN

Poster

The poster is as colorful as a beautiful rainbow flowing across the sky.
It's as square as a Wheat Thin ready to be eaten.
As thin as a little piece of lead rolling across the table.

Ajullu Jobi, Grade 6
Harriet Bishop Elementary School, MN

Monkeys
Ape,
Chimpanzee,
Mom sets,
Big gorillas,
Hairy chimps,
Brown, black, color gibbons
Ugly, gross, mean tarsiers
Those are a few.
Banana eater, tangerine
Fruit eater, tites
Came flashing, finding, hiding, night monkeys
Jumping, running, climbing simians
Funny squirrel monkeys,
Furry woolly monkeys,
Soft howler monkeys,
Small monkeys,
Don't forget —
Fool spectacled
Last of all, best of all,
I like fat spider monkeys.

Allyson Wasmer, Grade 5
Howards Grove Middle School, WI

The Reader
I am a reader.
I wonder why I love these things called books.
I hear nothing when I read.
I see the pages pass as I turn them.
I want to read forever.
I am a reader.

I pretend that what I read is real.
I feel different emotions as I read different stories.
I touch the covers as I hold them in my arms.
I worry I will not finish in time.
I cry when I read something sad.
I am a reader.

I understand that I can't read every written tale.
I say I'd rather go to the bookstore than the mall.
I dream to own every book I've loved
I try to get through them all.
I hope to read again tomorrow.
I am a reader.

Ayme Hernandez, Grade 6
Gilmore Middle School, WI

What's in a Name
My name is like a tornado
My name is like a snow storm
My name is like a golf swing
My name is like sharks in the ocean
My name is like a lightning storm in the night
My name is like the gym on soccer elimination day

Andrew Stoesz, Grade 5
Sibley Elementary School, MN

Crazy
Crazy is not something sad.
Crazy sounds like a very excited girl.
Crazy is a drunk person trying to dance.
Crazy sounds like a puppy whining.
Crazy sounds like someone laughing too hard.
Crazy sounds like a baby having to go.
Another word for crazy is hyper.
One thing about crazy is it's just fun.

Autumn Thoma, Grade 6
Campbellsport Elementary School, WI

Today's Broadcast
On the twelfth of October I woke up.
It was slightly rainy, slightly snowy,
slightly cold, slightly warm,
slightly happy, slightly sad.
I wish I didn't skip school today.
I will miss Stretch and having fun.
It is so much fun to spend time at Stretch
I wish I did go to school today.

Emma Tish, Grade 4
Martin County West Sherburn Elementary School, MN

The Walk
Snakes slither through the grass
Birds fly above singing a song
The wind is cold in the light blue sky
And the tree's leaves are falling off
But they leave a beautiful color on the ground
Hear the geese honking in the sky
But look at the sun set
And say good night

Elaina Bohlig, Grade 5
St Katharine Drexel School, WI

The Forest
A quiet place where fairies play
A place where you could think all day
Where the water trickles down the stream
Somewhere that animals work as a team
And the leaves ride on the breeze
You rarely ever hear a sneeze
A place where you can be who you want to be
Somewhere I can just be me.

Brett Burger, Grade 5
St Paul Evangelical Lutheran School, WI

In the Prairie
The dark sky is covered
wind whistling all around
the wolves singing to the moon
the horses' hooves stomping on the swaying grass
the creek rushing through the waves
in the prairie.

Anna McConahay, Grade 4
School of Technology & Arts I, WI

I'm in a Mirror

Inside this
mirror there is
a reflection waiting
to be seen copying
your every move

You look
at yourself
and get a memory
of when you were young
but you don't fully remember
so you reach in
the mirror
but nothing
comes out

You look in the mirror
and you think
and think and think
and think
it's coming to you
and it finally comes
out because of the mirror

Liam Hogan, Grade 6
T J Walker Middle School, WI

Strength

Inside this pencil
Is the
Key to
Ever even
Using
A pencil
It's lead

Lead that will
Never be
Broken
As long as
We as a community
Stay strong
And unite

Help
Help is what
We need, to stay strong
And save our Earth
So that we may have peace
So that we may all be happy
For as long as we live our lives

Sydney Tlachac, Grade 6
T J Walker Middle School, WI

Mmmm…Spaghetti!

S tringy and long
P erhaps I'll have one more bowl
A lways ideal
G o and try some yourself!
H eavenly taste
E veryone should have some
T ry some, you'll love it!
T oo good to pass up
I t tastes unbelievable!

Tanner Zocher, Grade 5
Campbellsport Elementary School, WI

The Big Maple Tree

Beautiful, colorful leaves,
Fall from a big maple tree,
Sap trickling down your chestnut bark,
Some of your branches have big marks.

Your trunk is so fat and fine,
I would not mistake it for a vine,
Your branches are tremendously high,
They almost touch the sky.

Alexis Killian, Grade 4
Classical School, WI

Bridgette with Her Eyes So Bright

Bridgette with her eyes so bright
Looks toward Heaven at midnight
On the longest night of the year
That's the one she holds most dear.

"Starry friends," she's often heard to say,
"How I wish that I could make you stay."
She knows, though they can't remain
Time will bring them round again.

Parker Summers, Grade 4
Classical School, WI

Winter

W hite snow falls in the night
I sit near the fireplace
N ever got used to the cold
T here goes the snow on top of the trees
E vergreen trees with white snow
R ed Christmas lights dance in the dark

Daniel Haugh, Grade 5
Stocker Elementary School, WI

Piggy Monkey

piggy monkey
was eating carrots
because he was hungry
at snack time
in the middle of the desert

Matt Sash, Grade 6
Harriet Bishop Elementary School, MN

True Sight

Inside this old pair of glasses,
I see a little child,
Eyes searching for one clear thing,
Wanting, needing sight.

Straining, struggling to
Find a sure path.
Yet the darkness doesn't fade.

And out of the darkness
Comes a gleaming beacon,
Forming a path of light.
Clear light.
Pure light.
And for once,
He saw the true
World in his own eyes.

James Champion, Grade 6
T J Walker Middle School, WI

Pretty Pink's Purpose

Pink is a strawberry, a barking poodle,
and the feeling of
love and happiness.

Pink is the taste of gummy worms.
A daffodil and bubble gum
smell pink.

Calm makes me feel pink.
Pink is the sound of
Children playing
and laughter.
Pink is Disney World,
a thorny rose patch, and magic.
Happy shih tzu puppies are pink.
A graceful ballerina is also pink.
Pink is a teacher smiling.

Hannah West, Grade 6
Marinette Middle School, WI

The Fall Journey

As I walk across the path,
I close my eyes.

I'm in a new world,
A new life that I, and only I
May enter.

I take my bow
And descend into a blanket of fall.
There's only one thing it may be…

The leaves.

Julia Gabriel, Grade 4
Breck School, MN

The Ways of Life

I used to be an amateur
But then I became good
Now I am an expert

I used to be immature
But then I became aware
Now I am mature

I used to be lonely
But then I got friends
Now I am popular
Kjersten Grinna, Grade 5
Howards Grove Middle School, WI

Little Deer All Alone

Little deer all alone
In a pile of leaves
It's a small deer
all alone

Little leaves
Around the deer
Beautiful colors…
Bronze, yellowish-green,
Orange-gold and most
Of all brown
Sofia Osuna, Grade 4
Breck School, MN

The Pebbles

The pebbles here
do not have long to wait,
'Til their view is gone
of the sky from the bottom of
the lake.
But one day
the stones will see a sight
that will make them glow.
Because once again
the sun has shown these age-old pebbles,
that it will melt the snow.
Andrew Salsbury, Grade 4
Breck School, MN

Fall Is Beautiful

red, orange, yellow ALL
come have a ball
build a pile of leaves
and jump in it
as many times as you please
cut the turkey
and have some fun
fall is cool
fall is FUN
Alexis Rogers, Grade 6
St Francis Middle School, MN

Rain!

What is Rain?
A piece of sky
A gift from above
A wet drop of peace
A tear drop from God
The wetness of life
The darkness and fear
A river of life
A helper of nature
A lovely little drop of fun
That's Rain!
Becka Groetken, Grade 6
Orfordville Elementary School, WI

This Is My Puppy

This is my puppy
His name is Otis
He is black and white
He's a cockapoo
This is my puppy
All cute and fluffy
He always wants a treat
He loves to eat
This is my puppy
I love him I do if I could
I would have another puppy!
Jenna Olson, Grade 5
Howards Grove Middle School, WI

Ice Cream

Ice cream
Chocolate chip cookie dough
Is the best
I like it on hot days
It's sweet
It's cold
Cones or dish
I like both
Chocolate chip cookie dough
Is the best
Ice cream
Jaycie Johnson, Grade 6
St Francis Middle School, MN

Pets

Pets are furry!
Pets are scary!
Pets are scaly!
Pets are cute (except for fish) !
Pets are fun to play with!
You will love pets if you have one!
Pets are so cute!
Pets are playful!
Pets are love!
David Klug, Grade 5
St Paul Evangelical Lutheran School, WI

I Am

I am from fun soccer
Running, kicking, blocking
And making an exciting goal!
I am from reading great
Thick books
Imagining being part of the amazing story
I am from spending time in Oaxaca, Mexico
Speaking lots of cool Spanish
Having great big fun
I am from juggling
Colorful beanbags
Throwing, catching, learning
I am from fluffy stuffed animals
Fuzzy cows,
Cute lions,
Soft monkeys
I am from Mexico to books
From stuffed animals to juggling
To soccer
I am me
Jeremy Skoler, Grade 5
Adams Spanish Immersion School, MN

I Got an F

I got an F.
I don't know why.
I don't understand.
I really did try.
I got an F
on my history report.
I guess it was
a little too short.
I got an F
I had a fit.
It's not fun,
but I'll live with it.
I got an F.
My mom got mad
and guess what she did?
She told my dad!
I got an F.
My report was hard
and guess where that F went?
On my report card!
Madison Davis, Grade 4
River Heights Elementary School, WI

Leaves

L ooks very colorful
E verything is changing
A ll the days are getting shorter
V ibrant bright colors
E ating Thanksgiving turkey soon
S o many different kinds of vegetables
Hunter Roberts, Grade 6
Seneca Middle School, WI

Seasons

Winter is so joyful and delightful
It's also a pleasant sight
to see snow and snow angels on
the ground and hearing Christmas songs
all around town.

Summer is hot and musty
people start to get crabby and rusty
Because it gets hot and they feel like
they are getting cooked in a pot.

Spring is flower's that are blossoming.
and people that are gossiping about how
the flowers look. That's all I should say
about a beautiful spring day.

Last but not least there's fall
The one I love best out of them all
Because that means a lot of crunchy
leaves that's why I love fall and it is
the best out of them all

Oriah Miller, Grade 6
Ramsey International Fine Arts Center, MN

The Crackling Leaves

Crunch…
the crackling golden leaves are slowly falling as I rake.
Woosh…the wind sweeps up the leaves.

The air is as cool as an ice cube
I can tell that winter is almost here.
Woosh…the wind sweeps up the leaves.

The wind is as foggy as a snowstorm
it whips the colorful leaves off the green grass and
brings it down like a thunderstorm of hail
Whoosh…the wind sweeps up the leaves.

You can hear the leaves pound on the cold ground,
as people jump in gigantic leaf piles
Then someone shouts "Thanksgiving!"
Woosh…the wind sweeps up the leaves

Before I knew it, it was Thanksgiving.
It was here at light speed. Now I'm surrounded by caring people.
Woosh…the wind sweeps up the leaves.

Dylan Olson, Grade 4
Kennedy Elementary School, MN

Two Wonderful Seasons

The leaves and long grass represent a fall day.
Snow and big puffy jackets represent a winter day.
How beautiful the fall day is!
How breathtaking a winter day is!

Brady Fox, Grade 6
Riverdale Elementary School, WI

Snowshoes

I am wearing boots.
My boots are wearing snowshoes.
A hat falls over my head,
A coat puffs me up.
Mittens turn my hands from five fingers
To two.

I trudge out to a wonderland.
Though the nighttime sky is pitch black,
The full winter moon is gleaming,
Shimmering the snow.

My snowshoes leave tracks
As I continue to trudge out into the woods.
I am blind now.
Not even the moon
Has sunken through a canopy of pines.

An owl hoots.
A mouse scatters.
But I am silent and still.

Not even my snowshoes are crunching through winter.

Tori Papke, Grade 5
Sibley Elementary School, MN

My Puppy Daisy

My dog Daisy is pretty lazy.
She is very naughty
    and looks really gaudy.
She never wants to play
    she just wants to lay.
She has a special spot
    and always wants to plot.
Never asks for any fun,
    she sits till the day is done.
My dog is the best.

Annalivia Grace Baker, Grade 4
Martin County West Trimont Elementary School, MN

What I Love About Fall

What I love about fall is…
looking at all the costumes you see
ghosts, ghouls, witches, and zombies
jack-o'-lanterns watching you from back to back

What I love about fall is…
roasting marshmallows over an open flame
and the smell of apple pie is as soft as wet sand at the beach

What I love about fall is…
touch of the delicate snow as it slowly drifts down

What I love about fall

Morgan Loch, Grade 4
Kennedy Elementary School, MN

Hidden Songs

Inside this guitar, lay unwritten songs of life, hope,
Faith, love, and many other things we don't know about
Inside this guitar lay peoples' dreams of becoming famous
And inside this guitar are many songs just waiting to be played

Inside this guitar lay dreams of making a difference
With songs and a chance to be
Who you are by expressing your feelings by music
And inside this guitar are hidden songs no one knows about

Inside this guitar songs are calling out to me,
Telling me to play them, I don't know what
Kinds of songs are in this guitar, they could be
Sad or happy but no one will ever find out unless

You hear the guitar's cry its cry to be
Played, to dream, express, listen, and believe,
Believe in yourself to make a choice and
Hear its cry to be played

Kyra Jahnke, Grade 6
T J Walker Middle School, WI

I Am...

I am a dancer
And a student
I am a sister
And an artist

I am a wonderer
And a questioner
I am a dreamer
And a believer

I am a thinker
And a hoper
I am a reader
And an Army daughter

I am what I am and if you don't like that
Then why are you still standing here because...
I am...
ME!

Grace Collier, Grade 5
Blue Heron Elementary School, MN

Bakugans

Bakugans are red, black, green, white, blue, and brown
They have different faces and abilities
Bakugans have traps that help you win battles
Some Bakugans are weak and some are strong
Their gate cards help them win brawls
Round and rolling Bakugans go to their cards
Pop! They open when they roll onto their cards
into different creatures

Eddie Pierce, Grade 5
Blue Heron Elementary School, MN

Fall

You can hear the wind whistling in your ear.
You can see critters making nests.
You can only imagine what fall will bring next year.
But my favorite part of fall is whistling winds, whirlwinds,
and the cold silence of what winter will bring.
The beautiful colors of fall are why fall is my favorite season.

What's yours?

Grace Nesheim, Grade 5
Mazomanie Elementary School, WI

one little sticky spider web

one little sticky spider web,
on a tiny tree,
lonely as can be,
the quiet wind sings a song to me,
somewhere,
somewhere,
somewhere,
there's a little sticky spider web on a tiny tree.

Lindsey Stagg, Grade 6
Harriet Bishop Elementary School, MN

Flags

A colorful piece of cloth
specially designed to represent or say something
for a country or state or business
big or small, rectangle, or triangle
as light as an ant on a diet
standing proud, tall, and powerful for what it represents
flapping in the wind, like a songbird's wings flying
Flags

Cole Utter, Grade 6
Harriet Bishop Elementary School, MN

A Singing Day

Yes, a singing day.
"Where are my lyrics"
Need those lyrics
My music my tune and my microphone too
My voice pitch is low I need some water
I found my lyrics my good oh lyrics
My music, my tune, and my microphone too
Ah, a singing day.

Eve Lee, Grade 6
St Francis Middle School, MN

Winter

W isconsin's great winter
I nside watching the snow fall
N ever eating candy canes whole
T o go down the largest hill with a snowboard
E KKK! No school snow day
R adio says it is going to be a white Christmas!

Zachary McGonegle, Grade 5
Stocker Elementary School, WI

The Best Time in Fall Is...

The best time in fall is jumping in the colorful leaves
with my friends here to there
I step on leaves crunch! Crunch!
The best time in fall is watching the gold leaves,
racing across the street making so much noise
they twirl and go round and round
The best time in fall is watching cold children
playing with their friends jumping into leaves
and then raking the leaves back up.
The best time in fall is the smell of fall
as good as a house with candles lit
friends playing here to there!
The best time in fall is grabbing first piece
of apple pie before anyone else gets it. I know it's fresh out
of the oven because it's hot!

Jenny Becker, Grade 4
Kennedy Elementary School, MN

The Black and Red Stripes

The black and red stripes, four to be exact
Along the board ready to be chopped up
The four stripes along the board soon to be cut
Black red black red just like an American flag

The black and red stripes soon to be cut
A friend soon to be thrown away
A special person down the drain
A person, a pet, a creature thrown away

The black and red stripes, four to be exact
The black red black red stripe pattern
Along the board ready to be shuttered
A lost friend black and red
The four stripes on the board

John Poh, Grade 6
T J Walker Middle School, WI

Boomer

Boomer is my dog
  he can run as fast as a car.
Sometimes he can be a dumbhead
  but in the end
  he is a good hunting dog.
Boomer is an extremely useful dog,
  he is super strong
    and young.
He is as hefty as a wolf.
  I like him very much.
He fetches like a pro
  and we can play hide and seek.
  He really likes to play tag.
He is a pure yellow lab
  and an awesome pet to have.

Karter Janssen, Grade 5
Martin County West Trimont Elementary School, MN

Fourth of July

I see the fireworks are blasting into the air.
Boom and bang all over the summer air.
People clapping and cheering for more and more.
Colors of fireworks red, purple, orange, and blue.
I like fireworks, how about you?
I hear the jets fly in the air.
I watch the fireworks bursting in a flair.
I love the Fourth of July!!

Zach Halom, Grade 5
Mazomanie Elementary School, WI

Bright Lights

Bright lights
The sun shining so bright
A flash of lightning in the middle of the night
The light from a flashlight staring you down
The beams of light coming from a town
And me
Running from it all

Sawyer Gilding, Grade 6
Dr Dyer Intermediate School, WI

My Best Friend

There was a girl named Star
She loves to give hugs a lot
She is eleven years old
She dislikes people who tell other people secrets

She lives in Wisconsin
She gives people a lot of respect

Brittany Riggs, Grade 5
Riverdale Elementary School, WI

War

War may be good but maybe even bad
you will not know until you are sad

When a war is nearby
you will know
there you will see
your friend or your foe.

Jose Escalona, Grade 6
Ramsey International Fine Arts Center, MN

October

O range pumpkins for carving faces
C reating silly costumes
T elling scary stories
O dd monsters lurching around your neighborhood
B egging for just one more piece of candy
E arning the first prize trophy for best costume
R acing up to people's houses for trick-or-treating

Abi Albright, Grade 5
Howards Grove Middle School, WI

Basketball

Basketball
Sweat, shoes
Shoes, wristband, points
Powerful, ready, cool, good
Fans, drums, music, clapping, squeaking
Marques Packard, Grade 4
Stocker Elementary School, WI

Cookie

Cookie
Hot, soft
Making, baking, cooling
Always made with love.
Treat
Tristan Schill, Grade 6
Campbellsport Elementary School, WI

Gracious Wind

The sound of the wind I can hear
It is blowing to stop my tears

You feel the cold wind as it blows
I hope it doesn't snow
Devin Peter Perez, Grade 6
Gilmore Middle School, WI

Guinea Pigs

Guinea pigs
Hilarious, adorable
Squeaking, dashing, biting
Funny, lovable, joyous, amazing
Miracles
Katelynn Schwarten, Grade 6
Dr Dyer Intermediate School, WI

Winter

I feel the cold white snow.
I hear the colorful birds sing.
I see the tall trees turning colors.
I smell delicious cocoa from my mom.
I taste huge apple pies.
Carlo Saldana, Grade 5
Stocker Elementary School, WI

Halloween

Candy, costumes,
pumpkins and a
whole lot of enjoyment
is what the Halloween
celebration is all about!
Demesha Rimmer, Grade 6
Messmer Preparatory Catholic School, WI

Months

January, the month that is cold, kids are having snowball fights.
February, the month of love and kindness, I'll send some valentines today
March, both of my sisters birthdays are today, we're celebrating that special day
April, the month of rain, grab your umbrella, the storm is on it's way
May, all the animals are born at the zoo, can't wait to see the baby monkeys
June, school is out, summer is here
July, Independence Day is coming, let's go see the fireworks.
August, time to go to the beach, bring your shovel and pail
September, my birthday is here, blow out birthday wishes
October, the spookiest time of year, everyone gets candy
November, let's go to the Thanksgiving feast, time to eat turkey and pie
December, my favorite month of the year, everyone gets presents.
Morgan Johnson, Grade 6
Gilmore Middle School, WI

Months

January is the month with a lot of snow that all the little kids play in.
February is the month of love because of Valentine's Day.
March is the month of green when everybody might sing.
April is the month of rain then all the kids play in the water.
May has a lot of bright beautiful flowers.
June is my sister's birthday.
July is the month with hot sunny days.
August is one of the months that has 31 days in it.
September is the month of my friend's birthday.
October is the month of Halloween
November is my birthday.
December is the month Jesus was born.
Gabby Ludwig, Grade 6
Gilmore Middle School, WI

Months

January is the month with New Year's Day and it will be a new year.
February is the month with Valentine's Day and people can send cards to their loved ones.
March 16th is the day of my birthday and next is St. Patrick's Day.
April is the month of April Fool's Day watch out and don't be fooled.
May is when the flowers burst and I will go outside to play.
June is when school is done and summer has just begun.
July is when the 4th of July will be and my brother will be 23
In August my mom will be 34 and she doesn't have to worry about 33 anymore.
In September summer is done and school has just begun.
October is Halloween and when you go trick or treating you will hear screams
In November there is Thanksgiving Day and you should be thankful.
In December there is Christmas and you get all sorts of things.
Jeremiah Megloun, Grade 6
Gilmore Middle School, WI

My Looks

My eyes are green like the grass getting shined on by the sun.
My hair is brown like a rabbit's furry hide.
My smile is bright and white like a polar bear's back.
My personality changes over time like the sky's shades from the clouds.
My heart is filled with peace and laughter that is filling like Thanksgiving dinner.
I live in my cell phone and eat my contacts.
Hannah LaVesser-Kendall, Grade 6
Dr Dyer Intermediate School, WI

Sunset

I am a sunset calming and peaceful.
I am a sunset who draws people to my attention
I am a sunset that blends well with fall colors
I am a sunset melting snow down to the grass
I am a sunset that people paint a lot
I am a sunset that is an alarm clock that tells me it's time for bed
I am a sunset that makes the blue sky turn to orange and yellow
I am a sunset that turns cattails purple
I am a sunset that brightens up people when they are sad
I am a sunset that colors the whole world
I am a sunset that brings people luck, joy, grace, and happiness
I am a sunset colorful, peaceful, wonderful, and amazing
I am a sunset

Erin Groskreutz, Grade 5
Wagner Elementary School, MN

Mom

I love having you home all the time so I can see you
I love snuggling with you and Lilly
Mom
I love baking chocolate chip cookies with you
I love going shopping with you at the mall
Mom
I love how you cheer me and Jake on in sports
I love having just a girls night going to the movies
Mom
I love sitting with you in the car on long car rides
I love going to hockey tournaments and going to hotels with you
Mom

Sarah Stowe, Grade 5
Sibley Elementary School, MN

An Autumn Kaleidoscope

Leaves twirling and dancing through the sky,
Scarlet, orange, brown, and gold.
The aroma of pumpkin and apple pies,
Float through the crisp, cool air.
Children's laughter and joyous shouts ring out.
Geese honk as they soar to their warm winter homes.
Leaves drift to the dry, golden grass,
Blanketing it with a thin layer of color,
Creating an autumn kaleidoscope.
Tree limbs have been stripped bare.
Sap slides through the strong trunk to the twisted knotted roots,
Where they will be stored for winter.

Kayleigh Kaminski, Grade 5
Jefferson Elementary School, WI

Chickens

The chickens are out in the yard.
They are scratching hay.
They are eating bugs and corn.
Their nests are in the barn and they are laying eggs.
Their feathers are all different colors.

Michael Odell, Grade 6
St Francis Middle School, MN

Gym Girl

Gymnastics is my favorite sport.
I really adore the floor with backhand
springs this way and that.
I think it's quite cool how hard I hit the mat
I really love bars I finally have my fly away
with a little bit of spot.
I have fun at tumble track 'cause when I hit the mat goes plop.
Back tucks are a riot when I do them everyone is quiet.
That is why I love gymnastics.

Rachel Owens, Grade 6
St Francis Middle School, MN

Lying Down by the Little House

Lying down by the little house
I spot and see a scuttling mouse
Gazing up at the starry light
I hear a snake slithering with all its might
It's hunting the mouse, the snake that is
Will he catch it? No doubt he is
A few minutes have passed just watching that snake
The grass is waving looking just like a lake
The prairie feels so peaceful and safe.

Ben Smith, Grade 4
School of Technology & Arts I, WI

Dreams

Dreams
A magical thing,
Happening while you sleep
As quiet as a tiptoe,
Creeping through the night
You get lost in your thoughts,
Until you wake up
Dreaming is like wondering, thinking and more
All in one package

Maggie Gillis, Grade 5
Harriet Bishop Elementary School, MN

Winter

W arm hot chocolate fills me inside
I gloos are being made with sparkly, white snow
N ever frown around Christmas time
T rees are covered with snowflakes galore
E ven though winter is cold it is still fun
R ivers freeze from the ice cold temperature

Jaime First, Grade 5
Stocker Elementary School, WI

Fall

The trees gracefully blowing in the wind
Branches waving their colorful leaves at me.
Frisky cold nights coming to be,
Kids raking both huge and tiny leaves.
Jumping for joy in the piles of leaves and branches.

Olivia Hackney, Grade 4
Classical School, WI

Winter

W hite beauty
I ncredible snow fall
N o two snowflakes are alike.
T is the season
E ntirely covered in snow
R apid snowfall

Gavin DeBoer, Grade 5
Stocker Elementary School, WI

Spring

It's here after winter
Playing outside
Running around
Igloos are gone
New flowers are ready to grow
Good times to have!

Elisabeth Rebrovich, Grade 5
Blue Heron Elementary School, MN

Halloween Sweets

Apple on a stick
Caramel and peanuts
Yummy and juicy
Good and sweet
Mighty yummy
It's a good treat!

Kayla Gaston, Grade 5
Messmer Preparatory Catholic School, WI

A Leaf's Life

I once was the lush color green.
With a stem ever so lean.
But now I am the dull color brown,
And on the dirty ground.
I am now lonely and scared.
For the time of winter has finally bared.

Louie Hardesty, Grade 6
Dr Dyer Intermediate School, WI

Thanksgiving

The smell of homemade pumpkin pie,
The taste of juicy turkey,
The look of delicate cranberries,
The laughter of everyone around you,
The wonderful day of Thanksgiving.

Keisha Verbeten, Grade 6
St Clare School, WI

My Sister

Amber
Cute, cuddly
Chattery, sassy, hungry
Very playful
Shimmering jewel

Ashley Schukow, Grade 5
Howards Grove Middle School, WI

I Am From...

Playing wii to drawing pretty me
I am from playing basketball to shopping at the awesome mall.
I am from eating yummy candy to watching the *Grim Adventures of Billy and Mandy.*
I am from whirling creepy tornadoes to hating gross tomatoes.
I am from wanting a cute dog to sitting on a rotten log.
I am from eating good mango to not being able to do the tango.
I am from having fun to not looking at the hot sun.
I am from having an annoying brother to being bad at my mother.
I am from smelling the beautiful flowers to reading for long hours.
I am from a wonderful place called Earth.
I am from dressing up to messing up.
I am from cool 5th grade.

Lalita Lira Greene, Grade 5
Adams Spanish Immersion School, MN

Colors

The White is the blanket of snow that covers our land every winter
The Blue is the ocean that perimeters our land
The Orange it the liquid in my cup I drink for breakfast
My Tan is the skin the covers my bones
The Pink is the perfect stick of bubble gum that I pull out of the wrapper
My Green is the Christmas tree that sits on my living room floor every year
The Red is the rose that grows in my garden
My Yellow is the sun that brightens up my day
This Purple is the car I get in every day
The Brown is the freshly baked brownies that break apart in my mouth
The Gold is the earrings that dazzle my appearance
The Black is the cat that screeches on Halloween Night.

Gina Maddaloni, Grade 6
Harriet Bishop Elementary School, MN

Grandpa

Grandpa
Demanding, caring, a tease and funny.
Grandpa of Justin, Cole, Luke, Tristan, Kaitlyn, Daley, Paige and Ashtyn.
Lover of America, freedom and people.
Who feels proud, daring, helpful.
Who needs food, ammo and health.
Who fears snakes, spiders and dying.
Who gave morphine, patches and weapons.
Who would like to see his family, friends and home.
Veteran

Justin Jungers, Grade 6
Campbellsport Elementary School, WI

My Brother

My brother is cool
My brother is smart
My brother laughs a lot and likes to play jokes on me
Sometimes my Dad and I laugh at my brother's laugh because it sounds funny
My brother is picky
My brother is good at hockey and soccer
But my brother always has a joke on hand no matter where he is
But I know I'll always love my brother

Natalie Neumann, Grade 5
Sibley Elementary School, MN

I Remember

I remember staying up late screaming "Happy New Year" while beeping a blow horn on January 1st at midnight waking up half the neighborhood.

I remember making a snowman with slushy snow, using potatoes instead of coal, and waking up seeing how it turned to ice.

I remember seeing the amazing fireworks show on the 4th of July.

I remember watching all the snow melt away and feeling the cabin fever for summer to kick in.

I remember feeling very ecstatic about summer vacation just when I got out of school

I remember the hot summer days when I went wake boarding and water-skiing.

I remember the end of summer, which meant school, snowboarding, and Christmas.

I remember doing this all over again.

Cody Kollmansberger, Grade 6
Campbellsport Elementary School, WI

Popularity Library

Inside this library books line the shelves but only the popular books are picked up and checked out. People pick the books that are big and bright and on display without thinking to search the shelves.

People only skim the crystal clear surface instead of diving into the dark depths to try to be different and find a book that may be old or may not because the books that haven't been read in years and years are the ones screaming to you saying, pay attention to me, love me, read me, and I may not be sparkly or new but I am just as good.

Inside this library there are books that have barely ever been opened and books that have been opened and closed hundreds of times. This is when I begin to wonder is a library just a fancy term for a book popularity contest or is it just a library.

Rachel Seizer, Grade 6
T J Walker Middle School, WI

On Rainy Days

On rainy days,
I wear my sweatshirt,
rain slicker,
or my coat,
but most likely my rain slicker.
On rainy days out in front of my house there are watery roads. Kids playing in the water.
On rainy days plants get water, soil gets wet and plants grow.
On rainy days some people think that they're sad but the sun is only around the corner on rainy days.

Carson Bettcher, Grade 6
St Francis Middle School, MN

Christmas

Christmas is not handing out valentines, kissing your parents, and getting hugged over and over again.
Christmas is drinking hot chocolate, going sledding, and counting down on a paper chain calendar to see my cousins.
Christmas is seeing my great family, making a cool Christmas play, and singing beautiful Christmas carols
Christmas is getting presents, having a big Christmas feast, and saying grace.
Christmas sounds like loud music going on downstairs, getting ready to do a play, and opening presents.
Christmas sounds like saying thank you to everybody, screaming when my family plays cards, and giving out hugs when you're leaving to go home.
Another word for Christmas is Christ.

Kimberly Firkus, Grade 6
Campbellsport Elementary School, WI

Dictionary

Full of information, I wait for someone to open me, in a small poof dust will fly out, my black words cover my dull white pages, my interesting words and their definitions will blow you away, I soar high on the shelves, I am the hawk of hardcover books, my cardboard cover protects me like the shell on a snail or the thorns on a rose bush, against the careless children, with me you will never be at a loss for words!

Rhianna Hajduch, Grade 6
Harriet Bishop Elementary School, MN

Sprinting

Jolting forward on the track
Feet throbbing as you go
Heart pounding
Lungs gasping for air
Eyes focused on the finish line

Leah Haebig, Grade 6
Campbellsport Elementary School, WI

Hunting

Wearing bright orange
Walking in the deep quiet woods
With a group of hunters
Hearing loud gun shots
Sitting in your stand waiting patiently

Brendon Ehlman, Grade 6
Campbellsport Elementary School, WI

Mike

There once was a little dog named Mike
Him and I were always alike
Even if he's aggressive
But his tricks are impressive
Oh how much I love my little tike

Samantha Hohs, Grade 6
Dr Dyer Intermediate School, WI

My Cat

Marshmallow
fluffy lazy
toasty gray
oh so cuddly
on a rainy day

Jacob Wegner, Grade 6
Riverdale Elementary School, WI

Skiing

As I fly down the hill
the wind stings my face
We get on the chair lift and sit and talk
We go again and say let's go in
In the lodge there's warm hot chocolate

Kelsey Paulus, Grade 5
School of Technology & Arts I, WI

White

Some people think of clouds
Some people think of angels
But they both have something in common
They are both floating in the air
Unless they go down.

Grace Jezuit, Grade 4
Tess Corners Elementary School, WI

Great-Grandma

Grandma as sweet as candy,
As lovely as the queen,
As helpful as beavers working together to make a home,

Everyone loved her, she was so sweet and kind,
She came to family holidays,
Gave wonderful hugs,
She donated quilts she made,
And helped everyone.

When she got sick, we were worried, but we knew it would be okay.
My cousins visited her in the big scary place, with lots of people in white dresses.
That day, Grandma told them she would be okay.

She died April 2009,
We had a memorial, everyone came,
Her quilts we donated,
She is remembered and loved.

We visited her and Grandpa's house later in the year,
We saw her favorite quilt she made,
With purple, green, blue and white stripes.

We love you Grandma,
Forever and Always, we'll love you.

Naomi Schmeck, Grade 5
Blue Heron Elementary School, MN

He Wasn't

He couldn't make himself believe that he was moving,
But here he was getting into the car leaving his friends and memories behind.
He couldn't leave without his friends,
Looking out the window, suddenly a tear came to his eye.

He swore he wasn't going to cry,
But he loved his friends so dearly he couldn't leave.
Fifteen miles past and he couldn't believe that his mother was making him do this,
He couldn't forget the picture of his friends standing in a group waving.

He didn't want to leave,
To leave his memoires, his friends, his school, and his house.
He couldn't think of himself without his loyal friends,
All the summers, all the fights, all the hot days with nothing to do.

He couldn't cry,
For if he'd cry he'd feel weak.
He wanted to stay strong,
For his mother, for his friends, for wherever he was moving to.

He couldn't picture himself living here in this place,
He's lonely and sad.
He couldn't think of his friends any longer,
For once in his life, he was without his friends.

Alissa Blais, Grade 6
Woodland Elementary School, MN

Memories Ticking Away

Inside this grandfather clock
Lies memories untold
Stories wanting to be heard
I can tell
I can tell by the faint smile on his face

He waves at me when I pass
His gloomy heart not yet satisfied
Who knows why

The memories may be good
The memories may be about me growing up
The memories may be about death
Or anything else

No one can ever know
No one can hear his voice
Just a faint tick or tock
From time to time

We can only wonder
Wonder what he wants to tell us
While inside this clock
Memories remain in the dark
Unknown, untold

Paige Frystak, Grade 6
T J Walker Middle School, WI

All About Samantha

Samantha Keller
Helpful,
Amazing,
Trustworthy,
Wishes to get a good education.
Dreams of being very successful in life.
Wants to help people that need it.
Who wonders what life will be like in 1,000 years.
Who fears roller coasters.
Who is afraid of getting in trouble by my mom.
Who likes to be with friends at all times.
Who believes in God.

Who loves my family.
Who loves my friends.
Who loves to play volleyball.
Who loves to play soccer.

Who plants to do really good in life
Who plants to get good grades.
Who plants to have a really fun life
Who plans to do what I want

Whose final destination is in heaven.

Samantha Keller, Grade 6
Gilmore Middle School, WI

I Am

I am from playing football with my friends.
I am from my loving dog Chola to my loving dog Georgie.
I am from brown eyes to black hair.
I am from riding my big bike.
I am from a great and loving family.
I am from a big house.
I am from delicious Mexican foods
from orange rice to soft tacos.
Even though we fight I guess my sisters are all right.
I am from playing complicated video games
to playing very easy video games.
I am from slipping to sliding to running to walking.
I am from going to the state fair to valley fair.
I am from happy to sad.
I am from playing outside to playing inside.

Titus McKnight, Grade 5
Adams Spanish Immersion School, MN

Bodascious Blossoming Blue

Blue is crystal clear water,
A cloudless sky and sadness way up high.
Blue is the taste of sweet cotton candy.
Vibrant violets
And delectable blueberries smell blue.
Collective calmness makes me
Feel blue.
Blue is the sound of tears pouring down your face
And waves on a sandy shore.
Blue is my beautiful bedroom,
An empty field,
And a cool quiet forest.
Listening to the ocean is blue.
Flowers blowing in the breeze are also blue.
Blue is being happy.

Katlyn Langer, Grade 6
Marinette Middle School, WI

What Fall Is to Me…

What fall is to me…
watching the colorful turkeys running around
and going gobble! Gobble as they run for their lives
What fall is to me…
smelling hot apple pie in the oven
it smells like a summer's day
What fall is to me…
mashed potatoes as fluffy as snow and the gravy
flows through your mouth like the Mississippi River
What fall is to me…
I hear big yellow school buses roaring through the air
like a jungle cat running at full speed.
What fall is to me…
I feel the leaves in my hand
going crunch! Crunch!

Alaina Kremer, Grade 4
Kennedy Elementary School, MN

Radio in the Doorway

Inside this radio in my doorway
just waiting to shout
eating my CDs and yelling the songs
out into my room's air

Inside my radio is a song
not quite sung
but what it sings is what to hear
dancing and singing to the rhyme

When they are quieted for the night
stuck in the speakers
waiting for me to turn it on
to pollute the air with its beautiful sound of music

Kesean Chapman, Grade 6
T J Walker Middle School, WI

The Flying Feather

Inside this feather that has fallen to the ground,
Are memories of when it was flying in the air,
Wishing, hoping
That one day it can have a purpose

Like it once had, swaying in the wind
Like it did before
Is what this lonely feather dreams about,
A tear comes even though it's dry,

Seeing the pain when it fell off a sparrow
Only making a wish,
And wondering if it will ever have
A meaning in reality again.

Mary Georges, Grade 6
T J Walker Middle School, WI

War

War is a game
A bloody and tearful game
You don't want to play the game
War is scary
Very very scary
Bombs and bullets fly around you
But, you stay out in the open not sure what to do
To help your fallen comrades
To take a bullet for a friend
There is so much emotion
And everything around is in motion
Something flies through the air
It looks like a flare
Realization hits, it's a bullet

Andrew Monk, Grade 6
Orfordville Elementary School, WI

Snow

Snow is as fluffy as a teddy bear.
Snow is like little balls of fur flying down.
Snow is as white as an albino deer.
Snow is like water on the ground everywhere.
Snow is like millions of little white pieces of paper flying.

Luke Schultz, Grade 5
Wagner Elementary School, MN

Hannah

Helps me out, always makes me giggle when I'm feeling down,
I know she's got my back whenever, wherever, and for whatever,
She means so much to me, she's practically my sister,
She is nice, loving, caring, funny, my buddy, my pal, and mostly,
My best friend forever, I couldn't live without her.

Cheyanne Renderman, Grade 6
Campbellsport Elementary School, WI

Two Best Friends

There once was a girl named Haley,
That hated a girl named Kaliy,
They used to be best friends,
Until it came to an end.
Because Kaliy stole Haley's boyfriend named Bailey.

Jena Krupp, Grade 6
Dr Dyer Intermediate School, WI

Winter

I feel the snow when I jump in it and pick it up.
I hear the wind whistling in my ears.
I see wonderful pure white snow.
I smell the fresh air of the outdoors.
I taste the cold snow dissolve in my mouth.

Bailey Santiago, Grade 5
Stocker Elementary School, WI

Fall

Fall
Pie, turkey
Leaves, plates, trees
Turkey, family, pumpkin, fruit
Munching, crunching, laughing, talking, chair moving

Trinati Cain-Kuykendall, Grade 4
Stocker Elementary School, WI

Winter

I feel the dazzling ornaments on my tree.
I hear nice Christmas music.
I see sparkly white snow in the winter time.
I smell cookies in the oven on Christmas Day!
I taste the breakfast I have with my family Christmas morning.

Grace Heide, Grade 5
Stocker Elementary School, WI

The Marsh

T he cattails waving
H eard birds tweeting
E verything looks pretty

M uskrat houses
A ir is blowing through my hair
R ed and yellow leaves falling
S nakes slithering
H onking geese
Hanna Kremsreiter, Grade 5
St Katharine Drexel School, WI

Football Is the Bomb

Football is the bomb
running
jumping
kicking
throwing
tackling
hitting
punting
Football is the bomb
Trentin Kirk Uttech, Grade 5
St Paul Evangelical Lutheran School, WI

The Maple

I know a maple
Who has red autumn leaves,
And in the winter
Snow it heaves.

In the spring
It will have new leaves that sway
And finally in the summer
That is where children like to play.
Elayne Rath, Grade 4
Classical School, WI

Colors

Red is the color of the sun
Blue is the color of fun
Green is the color of summer
Gray is always a bummer
White is daylight
Black is always midnight
Kevin Wszola, Grade 6
Gilmore Middle School, WI

Slam-dunk!!!

Yes, we're against the Eagles!
Where did I put my basketball?
I need my uniform, water bottle,
tennis shoes, and basketball, too!
Ah, I hope we win!
Samantha Henry, Grade 6
St Francis Middle School, MN

Zachary Sullivan

Z any as can be
A nd he loves to watch smackdown
C atches fish
H as a dog
A nd loves to play football
R aking the leaves in fall
Y acking on his cell phone

S illy
U sually playing video games
L ikes to go fishing
L ikes to go to his friend's house
I s eleven years old
V ery big bed
A nd loves to go bowling
N ever gives up
Zachary Sullivan, Grade 6
Gilmore Middle School, WI

The Big Bonfire

Crackling wood
Huge fire
Red, yellow, and orange

Colors of the fire
Shine in the night
The flying debris
Could land on the house
And then such a fright

I felt excited
As the fire rose
Into the night sky

Then I said
"Goodbye fire and goodnight"
Ethan Krohn, Grade 5
Hewitt Texas Elementary School, WI

My First Brewers Game

Jaw dropping
Warmth
Speechless
Bat cracking
Bernie heading down the slide
Wagging the flag
Back and forth
Excitement
Rumbling fans
Listening to the person
Saying drinks here
Amazing
Amazing
Amazing
Kyle Ninnemann, Grade 5
Hewitt Texas Elementary School, WI

Snow

It's so white and fluffy
I love to play in it
Every day it gets
me out of the house
that is very very stuffy
You can make snowmen,
forts, and snowballs
That's all I can
think about in
the school halls
Athan Karabetsos, Grade 5
Riverdale Elementary School, WI

What Is Football?

My favorite sport
A fun game
A physical game
A good time for everyone
My favorite time of the day
My favorite place to be
Fun and entertaining
A family time
A chill time
That is football.
Tanner Cowan, Grade 6
Orfordville Elementary School, WI

My Big Brother

My big brother is big and strong,
But he's really mushy and gushy.
He's smart, funny and weird, but cool.
He says he'll always protect me
If someone tries to hurt me.
He's no ordinary brother,
He's like Superman's son.
But he would not wear the uniform.
My big brother is the only brother I have,
So I think I'll keep him around.
Abbie Hald, Grade 5
Sibley Elementary School, MN

Basketball Rocks

B ouncing leather balls
A thletes compete
S creaming fans
Bas **K** ets are shot
E ntertaining
T eamwork helps
B uy or bring fan accessories
Everybody c **A** n play
L oud screaming fans
L ittle kids can play too
Rachel Richter, Grade 5
Howards Grove Middle School, WI

We Are Children of Puzzles

We are children of puzzles,
Each child is its very own puzzle,
It takes a while to figure out,
Soon enough parents start to put the pieces together,
And when they do,
They start to find out what their children like,
And when their children grow into adults,
The puzzle begins again.

We are children of puzzles

Kollan Rotzien, Grade 5
Wagner Elementary School, MN

Band

Band is so much fun
  when you get to play the instruments.
The sounds are so beautiful
  when you make them.
There are so many instruments
  like flute, trombone, and tuba.
You have to practice to get the notes right.
You can play at the football games.
If you practice really hard
  you will be good.

Brooke Anderson, Grade 5
Martin County West Trimont Elementary School, MN

Sea

Down below the murky water,
Down below the waves and the sunset,
Down there is a wonderful city of…
Coral and seaweed that sway through the water,
Painting the sea floor from the littlest grain of sand
To the biggest whale.
To the star fish that climb the sand like stairs.
To the flying fish that glide through the water.
And that's what it's like under the sea.
But at least that's what I see.

Ethan Ripp, Grade 5
Mazomanie Elementary School, WI

Green

Green is mellow
Green is calm
Green represents a calm calm song
Green is like an open field
Green is like the leaves off a tall tree
Green is what you might eat in your salad
Green is like a juicy apple
Green is like the snake when it wraps itself around its prey
Green is like a wonderful jungle
Green is a wonderful color in the rainbow

Giovanni El Rey Garcia-Jimenez, Grade 6
Gilmore Middle School, WI

Rain

Full of strength
But doesn't hurt you
Sounds soft
Like a blanket
During storms
It gets angry and full of its powerful strength
The after side is
Sidewalk puddles and dripping rooftops
Drip Drip Drip
Rain

Kayla Hepler, Grade 5
Sibley Elementary School, MN

Horicon Marsh

Horicon Marsh, a place where the cattails rustle
Where the muskrats play
Where the birds sing
Where the water ripples
Where the squirrels scamper
Where the ducks quack
Where the waves crash against the shore
Where the snakes slither
Where the colors glow
Where the air is pure

Ryan Christian, Grade 5
St Katharine Drexel School, WI

Pink

Pink is a nice tropical drink on a hot summer day.
Pink is the color of love and care.
Pink is the color of hearts and the February theme color.
Pink is the big eraser on your teacher's desk.
Pink is the color of blooming flowers in the garden in the spring.
Pink is strawberry cake with a fresh glass of milk on the side.
Pink is the teddy bear that's on my bed.
Pink is the color of your cheeks when you blush.
Pink is the color of flamingos standing on 1 leg.
Pink is my favorite color.

Brianna Horton, Grade 6
Gilmore Middle School, WI

I Can't Help Myself

Inside the string of Christmas lights
That I remember since forever…
I would catch myself staring
At the colorful twinkling lights…

Blues, reds, pinks, oranges, and yellows
I would sit there staring at the twinkling lights…
As if it wasn't real…
Like I was in a whole different world…
But that's just me…

Alyson Bailey, Grade 6
T J Walker Middle School, WI

Halloween Is...

Halloween is...
    Sweet, sugary candy
    from very friendly people
    scary haunted houses with
    skeletons, graves, strobe lights and much more

Halloween is...
    Hot apple cider freshly pressed
    from Honeycrisp apples
    sweet pumpkin pie as sweet as caramel

Halloween is...
    Jack-o'-lanterns with candles
    glowing like the sunlight in the day
    sweet, chocolatey candy melting
    through my body as I eat them

Halloween is...
    The best time in fall!

Sam Poncelet, Grade 4
Kennedy Elementary School, MN

Fall Is Here...

Fall is here...
I taste pumpkin pie as hot as a candle
with flaming sparks and cool down with
a white, icy whipped cream.
Fall is here...
I hear the hard, crunchy leaves
hit the ground with a crinkle, crackle and
squirrels collecting nuts for the cold,
icy, white and bright winter.
Fall is here...
I see pumpkins with faces with shiny lights like stars
that twinkle in the night.
Fall is here...
I smell warm apple cider as I take a cup
it warms my hands like a burning fire.
Fall is here...
I feel lumpy, bumpy
pumpkins in my cart
taking them home to carve for the season.

Dea Duesing, Grade 4
Kennedy Elementary School, MN

Today

Today's a new day; come on get out of bed.
You've got to clean up; come on brush your teeth.
Today's a new day; today's your day.
And you've got to remember, just that you matter.
Hopefully you'll remember, remember that it's time,
Time to share all the wonderful things,
That you were born with, 'cause it's time.
So get up and out of bed,
Because they're all waiting, waiting to see,
The gift that you were made with,
That you can share with me.
You don't need to practice; it's natural, of course.
Just remember that it's time,
Your time to share the beautiful smile,
That wonderful, true, and definitely yours, smile.
It is yours, not mine or theirs.
It's yours, so share it out loud
Without the faintest idea, of the good words,
That you will share, with just the touch of a single smile.

Kaytlyn Rowen, Grade 6
Hudson Middle School, WI

Friends

My friends are what complete me.
I am so glad I have them.
I have so many sometimes I forget them.
I have boy and girl friends.
    younger and older friends.
I have blonde haired friends,
    brown haired friends,
    black haired friends,
    even red haired friends.
I have lots of friends.
My friends mean so much to me.
If I lose one
    I am very sad.
But somehow...
    I always get them back.
It is hard getting through bad times.
Most of the time we get through it.
I feel grateful to get through fights.
I really like having friends.

Ashley Lyon, Grade 4
Martin County West Trimont Elementary School, MN

The World

The world is a wonder, what a great sight.
God is a power with all of His might.
School is made for kids to learn,
But it keeps them from the fun they yearn.
What is the world? A thought not so tight.
And when is the day everyone says goodnight?
The world is a wonder with joys everywhere.
What is the world? That's the question we share.

Hunter Presny, Grade 5
Mazomanie Elementary School, WI

My Name

My name is reading in my invisible hammock,
My name is writing outside on my bench,
My name is my dogs playing in the snow,
My name is *The Black Book of Secrets*,
My name is a bird singing,
A dog barking,
A fish swimming,
And everything else good in the world.

Timothy Gasior, Grade 5
Sibley Elementary School, MN

Parents

Mom
Friendly, clever
Understanding, affectionate, caring
Always there for me
Worrying, wondering, watching
Prepared, strong
Dad
Courtney Dorzok, Grade 6
Campbellsport Elementary School, WI

Science

S uper scientific
C ool discoveries
I nventions
E nergy
N ew ideas
C oming close to success
E ntering inventions
Haley Wolf, Grade 4
Chaska Elementary School, MN

Horses

Cantering, galloping, walking
Horses are fun
Bouncing, trotting
What would we do without them
Riding horses, having fun
All day in the sun
Horses
Caroline Kloster, Grade 6
Hudson Middle School, WI

Football

Football is a tough sport.
You need guts to join.
There is a lot of running and tackling.
You need about eight different pads,
thigh pads, knee pads, side pads,
tail bone pads, shoulder pads,
helmet, and mouth guard.
Austin Bloom, Grade 6
St Francis Middle School, MN

Soccer

Gather up all your friends,
Don't forget the soccer ball,
Now all you need is teamwork!
Once you have that,
Then you can make some goals.
The game is over,
So it is time for some high fives!
Jorden Atkins, Grade 6
St Francis Middle School, MN

It's Time for Fall...

It's time for fall...
the sweet pumpkin pie as warm as a summer day long gone.
I sip my hot apple cider a waterfall of warmth.

It's time for fall...
on this lonely day I can hear the cold fall air
The leaves try hard to hold on Whoosh! They let go.

It's time for fall...
the summer green leaves turn into red, orange, and yellow fall leaves.
Crows on scarecrows peck away at it's golden straw insides
all this golden makes me think about jack-o'-lanterns glowing
in the mist of the twilight.

It's time for fall...
my nose catches the smell of cookies I follow the smell inside
I see cookies each on with a pumpkin and a ghost
I take one then open the door and smell cool, Smokey fall air.

It's time for fall...
Wham! My cold body hits the cold, wet grass. I decide to carve my pumpkin
I snatch it up and feel the bumpy, rough surface.
I carved a big smile on it for this day has been a great day!
Josephine Pechous, Grade 4
Kennedy Elementary School, MN

Today and Tomorrow

It was early in the morning,
I dressed up and finished eating,
Things were all prepared last evening,
I walked out readily before school bus coming.
Today gave it a shot, tomorrow will rock!

I greeted my teacher and everyone, so,
The English class started with a spelling show,
The teacher asked for five words ending with "o,"
"Potato, piano, hero, solo, and go" — I happened to know.
Today gave it a shot, tomorrow will rock!

After P.E. was a music class,
We appreciated a Mozart masterpiece,
We learned new tricks with keyboard plus,
And music notes, dynamics, flats and sharps...
Today gave it a shot, tomorrow will rock!

It's just another day,
Full of cool activities and fun plays,
If it continues to accumulate,
The world is a more beautiful place.
Today gave it a shot, tomorrow will rock — as my mom and dad say!
Stone Wang, Grade 5
Lincoln Elementary School, WI

Willow Tree

Why do you weep so?
Is it because the creek no longer flows?
Is it because the birds no longer sing?
Do you miss the touch of their delicate wing?
Do you wish you could play with the children again?
Or is it because no one will stop to listen to the song
Your branches weave in the moonlight's soft winds?
Are you lonely atop that mighty mountain you sit?
Oh willow, why do you weep so?

Zoë Wurzel, Grade 6
Hudson Middle School, WI

Who Am I?

We are tough and we eat a lot of stuff,
Some people think that we stink,
We don't like the Vikings,
We have a coach and his last name is Macarthy,
We are from Wisconsin,
One of are team members got traded to a bad team,
We have a lot of fans from our state,
One of our team members has a restaurant named after him,
And we have a big stadium.

Emily Durham, Grade 5
Harriet Bishop Elementary School, MN

The Sun Hits the Beach

When the sun hits the beach it
feels good, when it hits the water it
feels refreshing, when it hits my face I
feel warmth, when it hits my hair it
feels strong, when it hits the sand it
feels hot, when it hits me it feels
good, refreshing, warm, strong, and hot
but, mostly I don't worry about that
because all I do is enjoy it.

Skylar Mundy, Grade 6
Ramsey International Fine Arts Center, MN

Mother Maple

Mother Maple's body is a mystery,
For when it is warm she wears a thick green coat,
And she takes everything off when it gets chilly.
Before she takes it off she turns red and hot,
And when summer returns in the coming year,
She lays her coat back on her arms neatly,
Then does a dance when the wind blows freely.

Kalen Klitzke, Grade 4
Classical School, WI

Babies

Babies, lying in their cribs.
Crying when they need their diaper changed.
Lying there smiling at you.
So little, so cute.

Maddie Weinman, Grade 6
St Francis Middle School, MN

Red

Red is the smell of a red rose,
Red is the taste of ripe strawberries,
Red is the color of a baby Robin,
Red is the sound of a racecar zooming around the track,
Red is the soft sweater that my mom and dad bought me,
Red is the flying ladybug buzzing around my ear,
Red is the hot molten lava rushing down a mountain,
Red is the spicy Habanero salsa my mom made,
Red is the color of leaves in autumn.

Veronica Velazquez, Grade 6
Gilmore Middle School, WI

Come into the Presence of Animals

As the eagle soars across the sky
Its feathers spread to make shadows above
Wolves cry at the glittering black sky
Caribou and reindeer walk at sunset

The golden wings of a butterfly glisten in the day
The sparkly eyes of a tiger watch you at night
Where the owls hoot in the darkness
And the horses stare up at the glistening night sky

Makenna Larson, Grade 5
Wagner Elementary School, MN

The Horicon Marsh

The rhythm of the water sounded so peaceful
Heard many different sounds
Everything was so calm

My favorite part were the leaves changing
A bird hummed peacefully
Roaring wind through the cattails
Splashes on water echoes the cry of the geese
Here the animals live

Morgan Moreau, Grade 5
St Katharine Drexel School, WI

Heartbeat Storm

The storm is blasting!
The rain is blowing against my window from the strong wind,
sounding like crashing thunder.
The dog is howling so loud that my eardrums are pounding.
As soon as the storm gets really bad, it ends.
Now there is a pretty rainbow
and everyone is happy and calm.

Caitlyn Sweesy, Grade 6
St Francis Middle School, MN

Hunting

Hunting from dawn to dusk
Sitting in the stand waiting
Looking for the big whitetail
Hoping that today will be the day that I get the big one.

Ty Bender, Grade 5
Howards Grove Middle School, WI

The Opposite
House
Cozy, warm
Cleaning, working, playing outside
Downstairs, room, football, dogs
Talking, laughing, talking on the phone
Cool people, trash
Street
Haley Kilfian, Grade 4
River Heights Elementary School, WI

The Winter Bird!
I look out my window,
The moon is coming up,
An owl swoops by,
White as if it's born from the snow,
So graceful to watch,
At the right moment,
It looks like it has the moon on its wings!
Sophia Elworthy, Grade 5
Mazomanie Elementary School, WI

Somewhere Cold and Somewhere Hot
North pole
Cold, windy
Snowing, blowing, freezing
Ice, Santa, kangaroo, desert
Fishing, swimming, snorkeling
Hot, sunny
Australia
Reid Path, Grade 4
River Heights Elementary School, WI

Halloween
Some people have fun on Halloween
Some people don't
Some people are funny on Halloween
Some people are scary on Halloween

Some people like candy on Halloween
But I don't like Halloween.
Xavier McElwee Lloyd, Grade 6
Messmer Preparatory Catholic School, WI

A Sunrise
It bleeds into the night
Bringing sunshine
Bringing light
With a rainbow across the sky
It makes the new day;
Bearing light into the world,
The sun rises for today.
Madrigal von Muchow, Grade 6
Lincoln Middle School, WI

Winter
Winter is the sight of Santa Claus at the mall and children building snowmen.
Winter is the smell of fruit cake on the table and eggnog in a cup.
Winter is the sound of the wind on a cold winter night and carolers singing.
Winter is the feel of the mistletoe above you and snow on the ground.
Winter is the taste of fudge bars on a plate and marshmallows in your hot cocoa.
Lily Scallon, Grade 4
Boscobel Elementary School, WI

Winter
Winter is the sight of Santa Claus on the roof and sleds in the snow.
Winter is the smell of hot chocolate in the microwave and cookies in the oven.
Winter is the sound of the wind in a stormy blizzard and sleigh bells on Santa's sleigh.
Winter is the feel of snow that falls from the sky and wrapping paper to wrap presents.
Winter is the taste of fudge in a pan and candy canes from the tree.
Rachel Yahn, Grade 4
Boscobel Elementary School, WI

Green
Green is the color of sweet grass in the summer, and money in my pocket.
Green is the color of a juicy green apple, and a cucumber in my grandma's garden.
Green is the color of a green pepper on my pizza and a sour lime.
Green is the color of a newborn caterpillar and a soft warm blanket on a cold night.
Green is the color of a noisy frog and the leaves in the wind on a fall night.
Emily Johnson, Grade 4
Boscobel Elementary School, WI

Phones
Don't phones ever get tired of being used?
Do they wish they could just shut down even if they worked perfectly fine?
Don't they ever get tired of people pushing their buttons?
Do they ever wish they were never bought?
Desiree Thomas, Grade 6
Gilmore Middle School, WI

Boats
Boats skidding by. Wave crashing into things, kids laughing dogs swimming.
The suns bright and warm shining in the water.
My dog walking around in the boat. I wonder the time but I can't stop having fun.
Water splashing in my face. Air drying me in a jiffy all I say is fun fun fun.
Carter Rush, Grade 6
Harriet Bishop Elementary School, MN

Christmas
Some people may love Christmas and some people may hate.
For me it's the best time of the year.
I am one of the people who loves Christmas in every way.
For the people who hate it's a big long day of hatred. But the thing that counts is family.
Matthew Faust, Grade 4
Tess Corners Elementary School, WI

Silver
Some say silver is like a shiny moon
shining on me. It's a pitch black night
and all you can see is the silver moon.
Almaya Loosemore, Grade 4
Tess Corners Elementary School, WI

Winter
Winter has arrived
Snowflakes falling toward the ground
Making world all white
Erin Penzel, Grade 6
Dr Dyer Intermediate School, WI

Sunset
Burning
Beautiful
Dazzling
That's the relaxing scene
Of the beautiful sunset

And the animals go quiet
Which is a peaceful sound

The eerie glow of
The red and orange
Circle

Coming down between
The trees

Glowing
Glowing
Glowing

Good night sun.
Gabriel Schwister, Grade 5
Hewitt Texas Elementary School, WI

I Am
I am from skiing at Afton
to horrible water rafting
I am from playing violin
to making big grins
I am from eating yummy ice cream
to having big dreams
I am from the play Cinderella
to the bright color yellow
I am from playing games with friends
to great ideas that never end
I am from reading big books
to exploring small nooks
I am from being pretty tiny
to the smell of lemon limey
I am from my little brother Sam
to being vegetarian, no ham!
I am from being happy and outgoing
to loving when it's snowing
I am from jumping, and playing,
and cool drawings too,
But that is just me, and I am not you!
Liza Strom, Grade 5
Adams Spanish Immersion School, MN

Lacrosse
Crowds of people, bright and sunny,
people cheering when a goal is made
the whistle going off at the end of the game,
tweet tweet tweet, players tired.
Joshua Cuellar, Grade 6
Harriet Bishop Elementary School, MN

Notebook
Waiting to be written in,
Cover in so many colors,
College rule paper,
Smooth pages lined neatly,
Perfect for doodling,
Magnificent for stories and poems,
Easy to tear-out pages,

Perfection.
Alyssa Ford, Grade 5
Harriet Bishop Elementary School, MN

Once I Got a Dog
Once I got a dog
I named him Dakota
His nickname is Coda
I give him a bone
It's hard as a stone
And he eats it
Like its gum!
But that's my dog
And I love him so much
Samantha McCray, Grade 6
Dr Dyer Intermediate School, WI

The Long Journey
Out the wooded door
Around my pine tree
In the green garage
Throughout the triangular window
Across the brownish lawn
By the blue pond
Down the hill
Towards the gas station
Into the birthday party
Katelyn Harnack, Grade 6
Orfordville Elementary School, WI

Hungry
A clap of thunder in the night
the roar of a lion gives me fright
water crashing from a fall
a volcano erupting blowing rocks and all
and me
with my stomach growling
Moses Retana, Grade 6
Dr Dyer Intermediate School, WI

My Bumpy Little Tractor
Motorized vehicle
Lime green, fast
Flying, speeding, turning
Get in, buckle up and ride
Go-cart
Kyle Prochnow, Grade 5
Campbellsport Elementary School, WI

My Amazing Dog
This is my dog

He is fifteen years old.
He is still energetic even though he's so old.

This is my dog

All fury and frantic,
When I look at him
He reminds me of a puppy.

This is my dog

He attacks the garbage can,
He tears it all up,
I don't like it at all
And neither would you!
Jacob Rautmann, Grade 5
Howards Grove Middle School, WI

Deer Hunting
Fun relaxing,
You get to hang
out with your
cousin.

You get to
see what a
deer looks
like up close.

You get to carry a gun,
and learn safety
they kick like a northern
pike biting you.

The best thing is looking
The wildlife you see.
Ryan Trettel, Grade 5
Blue Heron Elementary School, MN

Mickey Mouse
M y favorite mouse
I loved it when he was black and white
C olorful now
K icking comedy
E verybody loves him
Y ear after year he brings joy

M any kinds of episodes
O ther people think he's awesome
U gotta love him
S ee him at Disneyland
E mily's favorite cartoon!
Emily Bornick, Grade 4
Jefferson Elementary School, WI

Horicon Marsh

It is so peaceful I must say
all the cattails gently sway.
The ducks, the birds, the babies play
mothers look for food all day.
As people watch for winter to come
birds fly south because winter isn't fun!

Patrick Caine, Grade 5
St Katharine Drexel School, WI

Winter

W histling leaves
I smell the sweet taste of apple pie.
N ever-ending season
T asting a lot of sweet choices on this day.
E verybody loves Christmas!
R eady for a great year!

Erika Maceira, Grade 5
Stocker Elementary School, WI

Leaves in Fall

Orange leaves, yellow and red
They're all so colorful,
I never wanna go to bed.
Leaves are fun to rake,
I wouldn't want to make a mistake.
Brown leaves, yellow and red.

Brynn Tyczkowski, Grade 4
Classical School, WI

Life

What's life
Magical and mysterious
A miracle after miracle
Taken for granted
A wonderful thing
That's life

Joyell Glocke, Grade 5
Howards Grove Middle School, WI

Dance Dance Dance!!

Need to go to dance!!
Forget to practice!
Where are my shoes?
So much to do!
Ballet is so graceful !
Tap makes so much noise!

Danielle Nordling, Grade 6
St Francis Middle School, MN

Tigers

Tigers
Fast, brave
Prowling through the night
Fierce

Kathryn Crump, Grade 4
Tess Corners Elementary School, WI

The Empty Alarm Clock

Inside my broken alarm clock there are so many technological things
I've always wondered what's inside
Every morning when it called to me get up
And at night when the numbers started to blink and then it was blank

I tried to make it work but it was broken
So when I was about to throw it away it somehow said to me
Even though I'm broken I still have a heart of stone
So up until this day

I have that same alarm clock
All alone on my cold empty shelf
And every night when I go to climb in bed it speaks to me and it says
James thank you for not throwing me away

I am a living breathing thing just like you
And thank you for saving me and my heart
Because even though things don't have use
They might still be very useful for the rest of your life good bye.

James Konarzewski, Grade 6
T J Walker Middle School, WI

Halloween Howl

Midnight strikes on Halloween night
Witches and wizards, are riding their brooms around the town square
And the ghouls and ghosts,
Swarming around families and giving them a scare
Houses and homes are guarded by gnomes
Against trespassers like giants and trolls,
Hunting for treats and sweets
And forget about all the monsters,
They're at the dance, with their friends
And gents having a good time
Drinking there coffee,
Till the morning light
And though there time is over
They live inside us…
In fear.

Arooooooooooooooo!!
HA,HA,HA,HA,HA!!!!!!!

Justin Hunt, Grade 5
Harriet Bishop Elementary School, MN

The Naughty Little Boy

My dog Freddy was like a naughty little boy
He always got into trouble, but he gave me great joy
He ate Grandma's banana bread, while she scolded him he let out a big burp
Boy, I miss that little twerp!

Always in trouble and never would listen, like naughty boys do
But he could always make me smile when I was blue
As a lay in bed thinking of crazy things, I close my eyes to sleep
The thought of that lovable naughty little boy always makes me weep.

Sami Berth, Grade 4
Classical School, WI

Angels of Love

A ngels of love, hope, and justice.
N ever ending dreams.
G ivers of faith
E aters of darkness
L eaders of friendship

O nly sparkling in the dark
F ountaining flowers in the light

L oving little angels
O ffering to play with you
V ery nice when sheltering you
E ach made of sparkles

Jackie Rodewald-Jones, Grade 6
Ramsey International Fine Arts Center, MN

I Love You

I wake up on a cool summers day. Then
I went outside hoping the sun will smile
upon me. The rays of the sun felt good on the
cool day. I laid on the wet green grass
letting it tickle my bare feet. The wind picked
up and blew the grass giving me a soft breeze.
The clouds covered the sun and my smile went
away. It started to rain but I did not move.
The sweet smell of rain reminded me of my
grandmother. I looked up as the sun reappeared.
Now I know my grandmother is near, smiling
down on me. "I love you" I whispered into
the cool breeze letting the wind carry my words to her.

Rayven Janae Collins, Grade 6
Ramsey International Fine Arts Center, MN

Christmas

Christmas is the time of year.
Time for toys and time for cheer.
My Uncle Thad's birthday is today.
And I am very excited!
I think I'll give him his favorite movie.
That he's been wishing to have.
That will make him very happy.
He will give me a hug and thanks.
School is out for a break.
All the children get to play in the snow.
Oh…I almost forgot!
Do you know why this is a special holiday?
Because our Savior, Jesus Christ was born today.

Skylar Tumbleson, Grade 4
Martin County West Trimont Elementary School, MN

I Play Hockey

I play hockey. It is fun! You play with a puck.
If you don't skate hard, the coach makes you do skating drills.
You play at an ice arena. The ice is a cool temperature.

Max Greene, Grade 6
St Francis Middle School, MN

I'll Always Remember the Rain!

When it rains, I'll always remember
hearing the rain drops going tick tock like a clock.
When it rains, I'll always remember
going outside and smelling nature.
When it rains, I'll always remember
the rain drops shining like diamonds all around.
When it rains, I'll always remember
going outside without my umbrella
waiting till those shiny raindrops wet me.
When it rains, I'll always remember
seeing the shiny grass sparkling around.
When it rains, I'll always remember
seeing the clouds gray not blue.
When it rains, I'll always remember
worms coming out of their homes.
When it rains, I'll always remember
flowers closed instead of opened.
The most thing I'll remember about the rain
is all those wonderful things it has.
I'll always remember the rain!

Sarahi Ruiz Velasco, Grade 6
Ramsey International Fine Arts Center, MN

Bible

I'm the Bible
   Moses was asking the king of Egypt
   to let the slaves go.
The king would not.

Moses said again and again.
Finally the Lord sent plaques
   and poison frogs, but the king
   still would not let them go.
So the Lord sent the ghost of
the Holy Spirit and
   killed the king's oldest son
   and other Egypt people's oldest son
   if they did not put lamb blood
   on the top of their doors.

Then the king
   let the people go.
The teachings of the Bible
   tell the truth and rule.

Cole Owens, Grade 4
Martin County West Trimont Elementary School, MN

Enjoying It All

The screaming and yelling at a concert
the sound of a electric guitar with a big bass
the drums banging as loud as they can
the singer singing at the top of his lungs
and me
enjoying it all

Cole Miller, Grade 6
Dr Dyer Intermediate School, WI

One Wish

I won't forget
That one day
My mom took down
The canopy

When she turned the corner
The wind picked up
The wind carried her
A short distance but she landed
Hard on her head

She was knocked unconscious
I had never felt so terrified
In my life

My sister and I got her inside and called 911
The police and ambulance came
And they took her

She was in the hospital
For four days because she
Fractured her head in two parts

She's better now but
Can't smell or taste

Nikki Sauter, Grade 5
Blue Heron Elementary School, MN

The Best Times in Fall Are…

The best times in fall are
leaves falling from trees
as if they were falling from a cliff
then I turn and see kids trick-or-treating
wearing their creative costumes
and see smiles on their faces that show their glee!

The best times in fall are
all of the raindrops that fall from the sky
it feels like a waterfall pouring on my head, it soaks me.

The best times in fall are
pumpkin seeds baking in the oven
as popcorn is popping in the microwave
you can smell the butter melting.

The best times in fall are
the terrific tasty apple crisp fresh from the oven
with a cinnamon taste in the middle and a thick crust
that warms me like sitting next to a fire.

The best times in fall are
the leaves crunching and crackling below my feet
every time I put my foot down
Whoosh! Whoosh! I hear the wind breezing by.

Kiera McBeath, Grade 4
Kennedy Elementary School, MN

The Hill Failure

Once I went upon a hill
To sing my song of thrill.
But on that hill I slipped and fell
So now this is my story to tell.
Now after I had slipped and fell
I looked like an egg that had broken it's shell.
So, since I have just broken my shell
I will pick up my cell and tell
All that has happened when I fell.

Julia Turner, Grade 5
Ashby Elementary School, MN

Realistic Autumn Dream

I'm having the most wonderful day of autumn,
with the most beautiful field of leaves crunching under my feet.
But instead of the leaves yelling at me,
they fill me with love and joy.
They encourage me to crunch them
more and more,
until I wake wondering how it felt…
So,
So real.

Alex McFarland, Grade 4
Breck School, MN

Butterfly

Pretty,   f   o   i   g
        l   w   n
                   s
                 e
              i
           l
Stopping, sits,   f
Butterflies are very pretty
Moth

Madison Melms, Grade 6
Orfordville Elementary School, WI

Winter

W inter means fun.
I n the snow.
N estle hot chocolate running down my throat.
T he taste of victory in a snowball fight.
E vergreens decorated with lights.
R unning down the stairs to find your gifts.

Jarrad Hoffman, Grade 5
Stocker Elementary School, WI

Winter

I feel frosty and ice snow against my warm skin.
I hear people singing Christmas carols.
I see frosty snow glistening in the sun.
I smell the warm fire burning.
I taste warm, delicious hot chocolate with marshmallows in it.

Gracie Schiesl, Grade 5
Stocker Elementary School, WI

The Guitar

The broken guitar
There lies a soul
A soul
That I can remember

I remember playing it
All day
All night
Songs
After songs

I will never forget it
Loving
Winning or
Playing
Brenden Gutchak, Grade 6
T J Walker Middle School, WI

Fall's Emotions

Fall can be mad.
Very mad.
But fall can be happy.
Very happy.
Fall can be sad.
Very sad.
But when fall is mad,
It might grab you
With its scratchy trees.
But when fall is happy,
It's golden meadows
Will put you to sleep.
But when fall is sad,
It will drench you with rain.
Fall has many emotions.
Brendan Conroy, Grade 4
Breck School, MN

My Dog

This is my dog
So fat and brown.
He is a chocolate lab.
He is so cool.
And not a fool.

This is my dog
So happy and energetic.
When I go he's always next to me.
And loves to lick me.

This is my dog
So smart and funny.
Sometimes tackles me.
And is so kind and loves me.
Malik Griessmeyer, Grade 5
Howards Grove Middle School, WI

Autumn Leaves

Autumn leaves drop off trees in fall.
But they come back in spring.
When they return,
It reminds me of a flower dying,
Hibernating for next year's spring,
Like millions of monarch butterflies
Overlapping for warmth.
Josie Flanders, Grade 4
Breck School, MN

The Maple

All gaze upon the maple
In its autumn beauty.
All hail this autumn god
When it's in its glory.
Even when it's pouring,
It's never ever boring
For it's the god of autumn beauty.
Keegan Chesney, Grade 4
Classical School, WI

Wonderful Oranges

O ranges are great
R eally good treat
A n orange is juicy
N othing can beat the orange
G reat oranges are from Florida
E verybody can eat an orange
S o delightful to eat
Paige Rastello-Weber, Grade 5
Howards Grove Middle School, WI

The Mushroom

The mushroom,
Sitting so vulnerable there.
Makes me want to help it,
But I stare.
What happens?
Sitting with fright.
Looking into the frosty night.
Darian Dominski, Grade 4
Breck School, MN

Winter's Coming

As the big white ghost comes
The skeleton trees grab for you.
If they get you with their frosty hands
They'll give you the chills
But if you sit by the fire
You'll be cured
In no time.
John Steinbergs, Grade 4
Breck School, MN

The Bright Christmas Lights

String Christmas lights
Hanging from a hook
Don't know when it is going to fall
Don't fall
Stay up there

Inside it's glowing
It's happy but oh no
It's gone out
It's sad
You need to help it.

Go up, be a good person
Change the light bulb
Then it will be happy
Not sad
Have a heart
Don't break theirs.
Brandon Krause, Grade 6
T J Walker Middle School, WI

Inside This

Inside this Kleenex box are tears that I once
Shed over my grandpa's dead body.
My grandma kept hugging him when he
Was in the coffin, I patted him on
The shoulder, just as my dad did.

I don't know why I'm writing
About this sad memory but just so
You know, my grandpa meant a lot
To me, and he always will even
Though he is dead.

In case you are wondering, he died
Of a heart attack and he worked
At Gibraltar as a janitor and died
In the auditorium and he was the
Announcer of the Athletics (A's) of
Baileys Harbor.
Siera Renee Becker, Grade 6
T J Walker Middle School, WI

High Heels

High heels
Clickity clack
Leather covers
Stilettos
Pumps
Rare colors
Pop goes the heels
They're useless now
But I'll keep them anyhow
High heels rule
Saffya Harris, Grade 5
Harriet Bishop Elementary School, MN

Colors of the World

My green is the broccoli on my plate. The red is a ruby on a necklace. My yellow is a bright sun on a beautiful day. My orange is a carrot in my mouth. The blue is a shimmering sea. My purple is a violet in the warmth of summer. The brown is a thick woods just waiting there. My black is a misunderstood bat. My gray is the so very depressed sky. My pink is the skin of a noble swine. My hot pink is a rose for the love of my life. The lime green is a caterpillar munching on a leaf. The colors of the world are very unique and elegant and we should recognize them more.

Jacob Norling, Grade 6
Harriet Bishop Elementary School, MN

Fishy

I remember when I caught my first blue gill fish; it was 2 inches long and was very slimy and gooey
I remember all the seaweed I caught, all green and mushy
I remember digging out the worms from wet shredded paper in an old sour cream container.
I remember putting on the damp, orange life jacket.
I remember putting my hand into the warm spring water to wash off the worm slime.

Victoria Konstanski, Grade 6
Campbellsport Elementary School, WI

Blue

Blue is a flower swaying in the breeze, a shirt you are wearing, a piece of paper, a balloon given to you.
Blue is a sticker, a marker you can write with, a globe you can look at.
Blue is a blueberry you can eat, and some juice you drink, a piece of candy you shouldn't eat.
Blue is a flag you can feel, a pencil you write with, a toy you play with, a piece of soap you wash with
Blue is a blue jay singing, a nice blue ocean, a folder flapping.

Gideon Dalton, Grade 4
Boscobel Elementary School, WI

Hawaii

Hawaii is a beautiful place to be with dolphins and sharks along with their babies.
They jump out of the water and watch the colorful butterflies fluttering high above.
High palm trees with coconuts and birds so pretty it makes surfers want to surf even more and visitors cheerful.
Hawaii.

Katie Goodman, Grade 4
Chaska Elementary School, MN

The Rain

I hear a pattering as I sit in the silence as I wonder what it is. As the pattering continues so steadily I hear a rumble following. I now realize that the pattering is rain. As the rain comes down harder there is a bigger rumble and strikes of lightning Right now in the middle of the storm I realize that you should look on the bright side and I realize how relaxing and environmentally it can sometimes be.

Natalie Wasche, Grade 6
St Francis Middle School, MN

The Inside of This Smart Board

Inside this Smart Board there are wires and chips and circuits and all sorts of things. How does a Smart Board know? You can type in anything and a Smart Board will show it. How does it know, it blows my mind. The Smart Board is magical! Inside this Smart Board there are wires and chips and circuits. This is what's in a Smart Board. What's in you?

Christian Mallien, Grade 6
T J Walker Middle School, WI

My Puppy Taytor

I love my puppy Taytor! He is so beautiful because he is mostly white and light brown. Around his eyes, nose, and mouth, it is black. He has little black freckles on the top of his nose. The reason he is so many colors is because he is a Saint Bernard. His name is Taytor but I call him Taytor-Bug!

Tayllor Raymond, Grade 6
Riverdale Elementary School, WI

This Is My Fish
Pets
Orange, tropical
Watching, feeding, cleaning
Swimmers of the tank
Fish
Hailey Ebert, Grade 6
Campbellsport Elementary School, WI

Christmas
I feel the wrapping paper.
I touch the ornaments.
I taste the good eggs my dad makes.
I see all the presents under the tree.
I smell the candy cane.
Jeremy Socher, Grade 4
Tess Corners Elementary School, WI

My Brother Josh
Josh
Jumps, eats messy, never listens
He does it to annoy me
But I still love my brother
Josh
Jarin Boettcher, Grade 4
River Heights Elementary School, WI

Friskey
Friskey, you adorable little cat
You sleep all day, just like that you stare
Out the window at my other cats.
You look at the TV like what is that?
Friskey, Friskey, why do you act like that?
Heather Johnson, Grade 5
Sibley Elementary School, MN

The Teacher
The teacher,
On her computer,
Hour after hour,
In a silent classroom,
Finishing the day's work.
Sharlacia Shaw, Grade 6
Gilmore Middle School, WI

Frog
There was a little green speckled frog,
Sitting all alone on a log,
It was in the water,
It could see an otter,
While it's floating in a cranberry bog.
Aylah Wright, Grade 6
Dr Dyer Intermediate School, WI

15 Beautiful Things
The sound of crickets
Walking in the snow after dark
Working with the flowers at the farmers market with my grandparents
Soft jazz music
Painting in art class
Hearing taps at camp
Walking my dog
A hug from my mom
Friends
Getting homework done
Relaxing after school
Fallen leaves
Vacation
Seeing birds in summer when school is out
And playing with my friends at the pool
Jake Thomas, Grade 5
Sibley Elementary School, MN

The Beach
The sand and the blue ripple
Told the shells to shout
Over the valley hills
Passing through the rippling waves

The rippling waves
Passed along the shoreline as the waves crashed on the sandy beach

Sitting on the sandy beach a sailboat can be seen in the distance
The sail boat cruised along,
The sailboat moving across the water was like a really good orchestra

The sail boat then had to go home
And the sea shells had to go to the floor of the great blue water
And the blue ripple will become very calm as the sun sets on the horizon
Lauren Miller, Grade 5
Blue Heron Elementary School, MN

I Am From
I am from playing with my fun dog to feeding the shy sheep in England.
I am from super sour candy to puffy brown hair.
I am from sweet and salty mashed potatoes to dreaming of exotic new animals.
I am from climbing up the MASSIVE Eiffel Tower
to going into the super deep catacombs.
I am from swimming in exotic xl-ha to colorful smelly markers.
I am from playing awesome soccer to reading tons.
I am from super delicious spaghetti to going to a very fun family reunion.
I am from Wisconsin Dells to stepping on a different continent.
I am from going to new exotic restaurants each year
to doing confusing secret Santa with my cousins each year.
I am from running very long miles to watching very good TV.
But that's just me!
Simon Cloutier, Grade 5
Adams Spanish Immersion School, MN

You Can

You can swim in the pool
You can jump on a trampoline
You can ride on a ride
You can drive a car
You can hunt a deer
You can get hurt on a bike
You can hear the waves at the ocean
You can fly a plane
You can dream in your bed
You can run a marathon
You can try bungy jumping
You can do anything if you set your mind to it
You can hop like a frog
You can climb like a monkey
You can do it!

Nicholas Bartels, Grade 5
St Paul Evangelical Lutheran School, WI

Radiant Remarkable Red

Red is crisp roses, the morning sky
and a soft bear.
Red is the taste of ripened cherries.
Tasty cherry juice and delectable strawberry jam smell red.
The morning sun on my face makes me feel red.
Red is the sound of florescent bouncy balls
and tapping heels on the floor.
Red is a squealing ambulance, a honking
fire engine and, a colorful candy shop.
A burning sun burn is red.
Picking sweet raspberries is also red.
Red is the night sky.
Red is a blazing fire.
Red is the smell of autumn leaves.

Kimmie Kienitz, Grade 6
Marinette Middle School, WI

Christmas

Christmas time is the best time of the year
People are full of happiness and cheer.

You know Christmas is near
When you hear the clatter of Santa's reindeer.

My family and I decorate a Christmas tree
For everyone to enjoy and see.

Each year we bake holiday cookies
My favorite kind are the cut-out cookies.

This is a time for sharing and giving
It always comes after Thanksgiving!

Sarah Gardner, Grade 5
Howards Grove Middle School, WI

Winter

I see people shopping for gifts for their little ones.
I hear bells jingling from above. (If I didn't know any better
I'd say Santa and his reindeer are coming early).
I smell everything from apple pie to hot chocolate coming
from every house on the street.
I taste the snowflakes as they fall and popcorn from the string.
I feel the frostbite on my hand from making snowmen all day.

There is no better gift than being with your family on
Christmas Day!

Gabrielle Young, Grade 5
Stocker Elementary School, WI

Flowers

Flowers are so pretty,
They're so beautiful when they bloom.
They're colorful and bright,
They make your eyes go boom.
I love flowers in the summer,
They are everywhere.
I like to watch them brighten up,
Because once they bloom, their smell fills the air.
They smell so good and look so pretty,
I love flowers everywhere.

Lindsey Baumann, Grade 5
St Katharine Drexel School, WI

I Could

I could be playing outside
on the playground down the slide
in a forest in a cave
but to routine I have to slave
My schedule's full my calendar's booked
I don't even have time to read a book
In and out
Out and in
and this is how my life has been.

Samuel Jerome Lee, Grade 6
Ramsey International Fine Arts Center, MN

Christmas

Christmas is a time for fun, to laugh and play with your family.
Christmas is a time for celebrating that our Savior was born.
Christmas is a time in the snow, and having snowball fights.
Christmas is a time to feast and eat great meals.
Christmas is a time to decorate your tree with so many colors.
Christmas is a time to give, and not get.
Christmas is a time to be happy, not sad.
I like Christmas. How about you?
I'll have the Christmas spirit. How about you?

Noah King, Grade 5
Mazomanie Elementary School, WI

Youthful Yelling Yellow
Yellow is a flickering firefly, buzzing bees,
and lightning
striking the paved ground.
Yellow is the taste of
gooey honey on warm toast.
Sweet, silent spring
and blooming daffodils smell yellow.
Yellow is
the sound of jumping tennis balls
and kids slurping lemonade.
Yellow is vibrant highlighter,
Inside a sunflower,
and the sun bouncing off the dew-filled grass.
Day dreams are yellow
A man's smiley-face tie
Is also *yellow*.
Yellow is the color of happiness.

Elizabeth Poisson, Grade 6
Marinette Middle School, WI

John's Life
John is a man who has a good life
Who has a good job with good pay and no strife
The job he has might seem plain
But he always said that it was far from lame.
John has a well-behaved family
And they would be friends with you and me
When his kids wake up in the morning
John tells them to play and that nothing is boring.
John is very educated in lots of stuff
He is eager to learn and will never be rough
He is also very nice to boot
His friends like him from head to foot.
John knows that he is not perfect
But a good man will always have a good effect
John knows that not everything will go his way
But he always has a very good day.

Tommy Gennaula, Grade 6
Ramsey International Fine Arts Center, MN

My Mother
My mother can get sad at times,
   so can everyone else.
My mother can get mad at times,
   so can everyone else.
What nobody else has but her
   is her loving, caring, and comforting abilities.
She cares for me when I'm ill,
   she gives the right medicine.
She comforts me when I'm sad,
   when I lose a basketball game.
And the most important thing of all…
   she loves me with all her heart
   and I KNOW she would never let that love go.

Logan Weber, Grade 6
Martin County West Trimont Elementary School, MN

Fishing at the Pond
Fishing at the pond,
is more thrilling than you know,
the worms squiggle as you put them on the hook,
casting the line into the open water,
sit and wait for the line to yank,
Bobbers bobbing, the fish pulls
Snag and reel it in.
The fish flips and flops
ending on my grill.

Matthew Schumacher, Grade 5
St Paul Evangelical Lutheran School, WI

Hoses
Hoses are long and so are snakes.
Both are slimy and neither like rakes.
My dad waters the lawn and it may sound silly,
But he sings as he does it all willy-nilly.

He swings the hose like all cowboys should.
And lassoes the snakes, as if he could.
Snakes never venture into our yard
'Cause Cowboy Dad makes it too hard.

Katie Hulce, Grade 4
Classical School, WI

Best Friends
Best friends are fun to hang out with
   at the mall, a party, and your house, too.
Best friends are there for you
   when you're down in the blues.
When you have best friends
   you know you're gonna have friends
     that like you.
They'll be with you even when you move away.
   I guess they're the best!

Jenna Steele, Grade 5
Martin County West Trimont Elementary School, MN

The Maple
The hard Maple,
A great strong tree in Canada,
Its branches sway in the wind.
When at night it looks creepy and cruel,
It bleeds red leaves which puddle on the ground.
The Maple stands tall and proud,
In Canada.

Logan Strasburg, Grade 4
Classical School, WI

Hard Work
Leaves, wind
Crumbled, grass, rake
Trees, bags of leaves, people, sticks
Wind, leaves, whistle in the wind, cars passing, birds

Austin Pankratz, Grade 4
Stocker Elementary School, WI

My Room

My room is never messy, just filled with clothes.
It is hot pink and orange, that's what I like about it.
My bedspread is hot pink with flowers on it.
If you turn it over it has colorful stripes, really cool.
My closet is fairly big, I have clothes all over.
In my room I have an awesome chair, it is pink and fuzzy.
My dresser and my desk are wooden.
My bed is queen sized.
My fan is white and my TV is silver.
My rug is white with a nail polish stain (because of me).
When I look outside there is a very messy lawn (p.s. it is my lawn).
There is a big tree with a frisbee on a branch.
On my dresser is a polka-dotted jewelry box
That holds all my jewelry (of course).
My shelves over my bed hold all my collections.
Beanie Babies, collective Barbies, and my glass items.
So that is my room.

Cara Behrends, Grade 5
Martin County West Trimont Elementary School, MN

A Notebook That Never Got Used

Inside this yellow notebook
Lies things that have never been said
And things that need to be spoken

I once had a poem written inside of me
But now I'm alone
For my writer has forgotten about me
These words have a wrong and right

Now I'm just a small little notebook with no ideas to share
Even if it's up in a classroom I don't care, I want to be shared
Now I'm sitting on a tree house and it's downpouring hard
And I'm afraid now all my pages are gone

No one can use me, no one now,
But once again here is how it sounds
The last is that it cries and shatters

Kyrie Snow, Grade 6
T J Walker Middle School, WI

Months

January is a New Year, time for joy, time for cheer.
February, the month of love, look at cupid flying above.
March is my sister's birthday. Want to come over and play?
April, ha-ha month of jokes! I laugh at all the little folks.
May, May, May, the month of Mother's day.
June is when we get out of school, watch out! Into the pool!
July, the month of sun, eating hot dogs and hamburger buns.
August, I laugh, I play, I hope you have a good day!
September is my friend's birthday I wish I can go over and play.
October, BOO! Trick-or-treating, I like to do.
November is my birthday, I will be 13 next year. It's coming my way!
December, HO-HO-HO! Santa is coming with lots of snow!

Kimberly Langenfeld, Grade 6
Gilmore Middle School, WI

Blue

Blue is the color of Kool-Aid, a flower, and a blue jay.
Blue is the color of books, a box, and fishing hooks.
Blue is the color of crayons, a shirt, and a rubber band.
Blue is the color of the sky, a tie, and a ladder ten feet high.
Blue is the color of birds, a clock, and words.
Blue is the color of a bag, a magazine, and a rag.
Blue is the color of posters, an eraser, and a roller coaster.
Blue is the color of eyes, a chair, and a car speeding right by.
Blue is the color of a baseball bat, a crayon box, and a fishing hat.

Alexxis Riley, Grade 4
Boscobel Elementary School, WI

B.G.

My hair is brown like a caramel chocolate candy
My eyes are golden brown like a fall leaf on a tree
My lips are soft like silky rose petals
My smile is bright like a solar eclipse
My heart holds energy
This is neon colored as a bouncy ball trapped in a box
I live on a basketball court
And eat lots of squeaky shoes

Breanna Grenier, Grade 6
Dr Dyer Intermediate School, WI

Autumn

As I walk outside to play with my leaves,
To make a pile to jump in,
All of a sudden I notice people
Taking their dogs for walks.
People playing.
Then I see leaves and hear their crunch.
And I finally realize autumn is very wonderful,
Every day.

Paige Olowu, Grade 4
Breck School, MN

Friendship

Friendship is trust
Everywhere I go there is friendship
You have to trust care and have fun
It's like a world of roses
Laughter is in the air when I am with friends
There are laughs, cries, and hard times
But we get through it with friendship
I have so much friendship

Sierra Coleman, Grade 6
Orfordville Elementary School, WI

Winter

I see the white snowflakes falling from the sky.
I hear the dogs howling to get in.
I smell the warm chocolatey cocoa my mom is making.
I taste the warm pie that my grandma made.
I feel the cold breeze coming from the windows.

Karlie Barnes, Grade 5
Stocker Elementary School, WI

The Memorable Game Controller

Inside this game controller
Are so many memories, remembered or lost
So many experiences to be made
Being thrown into the air when we won
Being thrown to the ground every "game over"
And many more to come

This controller has heard many scoldings
Like "Get off that stupid machine!"
And
"You play that thing too much!"
Or
"Go do something!"
But they aren't yelling at you controller
They are yelling at me
So don't get down because
We have a lot more experiences to share
A lot more throwing
And many more bonds

Josh Augustson, Grade 6
T J Walker Middle School, WI

The Bleeding Heart

T he bleeding heart
H and in hand with magic
E ngaging in danger

B reathing it in deeply
L oving the feeling of magical power
E ating at the thought of why
E njoyable magic
D eciding what choice to make
I nnocently choosing to try
N ever thinking what could happen
G etting it to work could mean good-bye

H oping, wishing, and waiting
E xcruciating madness
A waiting for it to happen
R eady set BOOM!
T he bleeding heart

Lilly McLaughlin, Grade 6
Ramsey International Fine Arts Center, MN

Ready for Christmas

C aroling to many houses filling people with joy
H eaps of snow piling up
R udolf shining his big, bright, red nose
I ce freezing on your doors
S anta laughing HO HO HO!!!
T he Christmas presents AWESOME THINGS!!!
M antles being lit
A unts and uncles come to town
S ledding down the bumpy hills

Alexandria Durn, Grade 5
Campbellsport Elementary School, WI

Fluffy Kittens

Fluffy kittens soft ones, raggedy ones, stray ones,
Fluffy ones, cute ones. Kittens are so cute they're
all of these things. Playing with kittens is almost
a joy to everyone. Some people hate cats some
people love cats. Most of the time when people
are sad they play with their cats (or if they don't
have cats they play with their dogs) most of them
make them happy most of them are just mad.

Chethra Chhan, Grade 6
St Francis Middle School, MN

Halloween

It was Halloween on one late night.
The sky was dark, but the moon was bright.
There were witches in the air that made a Halloween scare,
as the ghosts and the goblins came out of their lair.
The pumpkins were scaring the children by three,
I hope that they don't scare you or me.
As you finish this poem you will feel something soft,
the ghosts will scream your name and then vanish right off.

Sophie Dominguez, Grade 5
MacArthur Elementary School, WI

Darkening Home of the Prey

D eep black abyss of the day
A nother word for the night
R ustle, rustle
K ale gets flattened under the raccoon's soft paw
N umerous nocturnal creatures creep about
E ver shifting time of life
S ay good-bye to your garden
S ecure does not describe one's precious foods from the hungry

Kirsten Lloyd, Grade 6
Campbellsport Elementary School, WI

Snowflakes

Swishing, swirling,
On a winter's day.
Tossing, tumbling,
Time to go out to play.
Floating, flittering,
Let's take a ride on the sleigh.
Whirling, twirling,
All night and day.

Erica Heinig, Grade 6
Elkhart Lake Elementary-Middle School, WI

Winter

W ind is blowing beautifully on my face.
I nside the house, no one is out.
N ever-ending falling snow.
T rees are dancing because Christmas is here!
E verybody opens presents on this Christmas Eve!
R iding cars get stuck on snow and can't get out.

Galilea Arizmendi, Grade 5
Stocker Elementary School, WI

Fireworks

Lights flashing
Warmth of
The fire

Boom
Boom
Boom

Crackle
Red, white,
And
Blue
And more

Fireworks
Are awesome.

Nicholas Juers, Grade 5
Hewitt Texas Elementary School, WI

Colors

Orange is a color in the sky.
White is a seagull ready to fly.

Gray is the color of a rim.
Blue water makes you want to swim.

Yellow is the sun's rays
Red fires of a campfires blaze.

Green is the color of grass.
Gold coins are a blast.

Silver is the color of the Eiffel tower.
Pink is the color of a pretty flower.

What are colors to you?

Jacob Zimmerman, Grade 6
Gilmore Middle School, WI

Turkey Hunting

T is for turkeys praying not to get shot.
U is for under treetops looking for game.
R is for ready to fire at any time.
K is for knowing turkeys will come.
E is for every minute in the woods.
Y is for yummy food we eat.

H is for hunting with pride.
U is for under pressure at gunfire.
N is for no noise in the woods.
T is for tender meat cooking.
I is for in the woods at all times.
N is for never hunt at night.
G is for guns firing all day.

Ian Joy, Grade 6
Seneca Middle School, WI

Basketball

Ball,
Hoop,
Net,
Tough tiger,
Rough court,
Energetic, exciting, thrilling players,
Orange, round, big basketball,
Those are a few.
Winning teamwork,
Losing teamwork,
Yelling, throwing, shouting teamwork,
Dribbling, running, passing teamwork,
Fun shoes too.
Skilled players,
Hard coaches,
Loud fans,
Don't forget center line shots too.
Last of all best of all…
I like tough basketball.

Samantha Yancy, Grade 5
Howards Grove Middle School, WI

Wolf

Wolf,
Dog,
Animal,
Strong fangs,
Ugly monster,
Fat, fast, brave creature,
Strong, healthy, hungry wolf,
Those are a few.
Boney legs,
Sharp fangs,
Killing, playing, barking dog,
Howling, eating, running pups,
Dangerous pack, too.
Ugly monster,
Pretty fur,
Healthy leader,
Don't forget scary animal,
Last of all — best of all —
I like dangerous wolves.

Brandon Meyer, Grade 5
Howards Grove Middle School, WI

December

D ancer is a reindeer
E lves create presents
C laus gets ready
E lderly fart through the night
M oments remembered
B ig plans are made
E ven God celebrates Christmas
R eindeer don't fly

Dimitri Luna, Grade 5
Luna Home School, MN

Fireworks

Splashing colors
Over my head
If you were standing by me
You would be in awe
Listen to the crackles, booms
And explosions
Come with me next time!

Lydia Hoffman, Grade 5
Hewitt Texas Elementary School, WI

Mystery Books

Books are so fun.
They are so big and so long.
They are entertaining and fun.
They are so educational.
You learn who did it.
How they did.
You are done.

Quinn Gard, Grade 6
St Francis Middle School, MN

My Summer Joy

Racing
Rough, dirty
Smashing, jolting, vaulting
Two wheels, gas motor
Finishing, winding, falling
Adrenaline, sweaty
Motocross

John Meyer, Grade 6
Campbellsport Elementary School, WI

Fly Me Away

Night, light
I fly so high
To catch the stars that are so bright
Fly me away, fly me away
So I can get my way
I always try
To fly

Elena Xiong, Grade 5
Monroe Elementary School, WI

Ultra Enjoyable Stories

Reading
Delightful, fresh
Motivating, captivating, engaging
Whisking me off to a new place
Intriguing, inspiring, amazing
Enjoyable, innovative
Books

Ariana Strupp, Grade 5
Campbellsport Elementary School, WI

Into the Night

Moonlight cast shining light through bare trees,
creating onyx shadows on the snow.
I'm perfectly still, my silhouette perched on the branch
of an icy tree.
I am a work of art, the sparkling snow my canvas.
I lift myself off the branch, and my heart soars
just as my body does.
My outstretched wings appear on the glistening snow,
flying gently through gently swirling flurries.
I glide and dip, a treasure in the chilly air
that's gentle on my face.
I fly gracefully into the night sky, free.
   I am beautiful.
   I am king of the night.
   I am an owl.

Rachel Carboni, Grade 6
Lincoln Middle School, WI

The Flag

I was tattered and torn
   and all with holes.
I still stood there with stars and stripes.
I looked below.
   I saw people with fright.
Some dropped dead
   with blood all over their clothes.
I thought why not run?
Then I knew why they were still fighting.
They were standing up for their country.
Then I heard no more bombs.
I looked and saw
   the ships were leaving.
I heard cheers.
Then I realized that we won!

Joshua Bjerken, Grade 5
Martin County West Trimont Elementary School, MN

Angel

Cute,
Loving,
Loyal,
Wishes she could have a bone every 4 minutes
Dreams of chasing squirrels
Wants to check out every dog that goes by
Who wonders where everyone is
Who fears shots
Who is afraid of a new person
Who likes bones
Who believes every dog needs a home
Who loves naps on my bed
Who loves everyone
Who plans a nap in the sun
Who's faithful to her stomach, to her nose, and to her family.

Jonathon Blaisdell, Grade 5
St Paul Evangelical Lutheran School, WI

The Mischievous Noise

As I walk along the hall
I hear a strange call.
The noise hits me like
waves fragmentizing the shore,
fireworks exploding in the sky,
an eagle thwacking its stupendous wings.
As I emerge from the corner
the lights flash, then go out,
the noise is coming from everywhere.
As I start floundering around I bump a shelf
the lights come on
in the chair is my worst nightmare,
it was…it was
I let out a shrill gasp
it was Grandpa snoring!

Kaitlyn Reece Cook, Grade 5
Martin County West Trimont Elementary School, MN

Leaves

Leaves fall from their treetop perch
giving the dark, blue sky
new spirit
the wind is crisp and cold that blows
russet leaves to the sky will they reach the moon
nobody knows
the sound is nature's symphony cricket plays his violin
and the wind sings her song
to the willows who are whispering among themselves about
the coming of snow
the night sky is now russet with the leaves
like butterflies spreading their beautiful wings
when soaring in the night sky
which is now a pinkish mist sunrise on the
horizon

Avery Laffey, Grade 4
School of Technology & Arts I, WI

My Best Friend

Buck
cute,
yellow,
sensitive
Wishes he could run through the house,
Dreams of sitting on laps,
Wants to play all day long,
Who wonders why he can't run through the house,
Who fears thunder,
Who is afraid of strangers,
Who likes milk bones
Who believes he weighs 20 pounds,
Who loves me,
Who plans to hunt,
Who loves food, people, and Dad.

Yancey Daniel Beard, Grade 5
St Paul Evangelical Lutheran School, WI

Africa!

The lion roars loudly
As he hunts on the grassy plain
He is a carnivore.

Javantae Dampier, Grade 4
Stocker Elementary School, WI

Octopus!

An octopus scared
An enemy approaching slowly
SQUIRT! — gets scared off!

Ruben Garcia-DeLeon, Grade 4
Stocker Elementary School, WI

School

Bell rings
Teacher enters
Time to work.

Dazsanae Sherrod, Grade 6
Gilmore Middle School, WI

Toad!

Rains all day
Hopping on a lily pad
Hopping all day.

Bria Hollingsworth, Grade 4
Stocker Elementary School, WI

Horsefly!

As a pesky horsefly
Swarms around in your house
You try to kill it.

Andrew Herrera, Grade 4
Stocker Elementary School, WI

Racing

Big wheels, gleaming chrome
revving engines, shifting gears
racing down my road

Jacob Bergdorf, Grade 6
Campbellsport Elementary School, WI

April!

Children play outside
In April birds begin to sing
Softly in the trees.

Olivia Lehrke, Grade 4
Stocker Elementary School, WI

Dog

Big, brown, and shaggy
Swimming in the cold, blue lake
My dog is happy.

Travis King, Grade 4
Stocker Elementary School, WI

Changing from Fall to Winter

When I walk down the street I see the leaves flying off the trees and onto the sidewalk.
I hear the leaves crunching as I walk on them,
I smell pumpkin pie on a table ready to be eaten,
As I see the tree in our backyard I can visualize the storing sugars,
And the leaves producing the sugars that will be stored for winter,
But I begin to wonder why the leaves change color?
I know that the leaves fall off the trees because they lack sunlight to keep photosynthesis.
As fall slowly drifted away the trees became bare.
Then the flowers will be gone as the little flakes of white gently float through the
air until they softly touch the ground.
The streets will be all white with snow, same with the trees.
I hear kids having a snowball fight and building a snowman.

Bailey Dietzen, Grade 5
Jefferson Elementary School, WI

Spirally Locked Bindings

Inside the spiral binding, there is a story, a story that hasn't been written.
This story is aching to come out, to be explained.
But the spiral binding is holding it in.

This story is an interesting one, and the spiral binding knows that.
But the binding is afraid, afraid to tell, afraid to let it out.

Eventually the binding gets weaker,
The binding starts to uncoil. And finally, the story gets told.
Inside this binding, there is a story, a story that is told.
A story that will no longer linger in the shadows of the spiral binding.
The binding will no longer hold any stories.

Alec Fischer, Grade 6
T J Walker Middle School, WI

The 12 Months of Fun

January is the first month of a New Year, so everyone parties and says, "Here here!"
February is the month of my sister's birthday. Also the birthday of Washington.
March is the beginning of my favorite day. It is when spring begins.
April is my birthday month. It's on April Fool's Day, too.
May is one of my favorite months. It's my mother's birthday.
June is always fun because we're not in school and can always play.
July is a month that we never forget. It's the Fourth of July, a holiday!
August means money for some. It is both my brother and father's birthday in this month.
September is leafy. All of the leaves from the trees begin to fall off.
October is scary. Even more on Halloween!
November is peaceful because it's Thanksgiving
December is the worst. It is always freezing cold.

Joanna Jaimes, Grade 6
Gilmore Middle School, WI

Tom

My eyes are brown like a melted Nestle bar
My hair is tiny like little blades of grass
My teeth are white like a smooth white pearl
My feet are huge and heavy like big rocks
My heart holds happiness that is orange and blue like the Chicago Bears
I live in an awesome blue house and eat everything that doesn't eat me first

Thomas Petrick, Grade 6
Dr Dyer Intermediate School, WI

The Lock Guarding the Door

The lock guarding the door
Is guarding me
From what is behind it
The secrets and mysteries
Behind it, behind me

The gears and wheels of the lock
Keep me out
I try the lock every day
Still to find it
Locked away

The lock makes me think
Of what's within it?
Within me?

I look at the lock
Staring me down
And I think I should open it
Secretly

If only I had the key
Ariel Laxo, Grade 6
T J Walker Middle School, WI

You Shouldn't Drink

If you drink a lot,
don't drive home.
If you drive home,
don't crash into a tree.
If you crash into a tree,
be mad at yourself.
If you're mad at yourself,
it's your fault
because you shouldn't drink.
Julia Forseth, Grade 5
Mazomanie Elementary School, WI

The Mall

Crawling with people
Colorful stores
Numerous lights everywhere
Not a dark spot in sight
Noisy
Not very peaceful
Why, Why, Why so many shoppers
Excited
Overjoyed to go on really cool rides
Ecstatic to shop in so many stores
Numerous
Numerous
Numerous
Shoppers
HOORAY!
Lindsey Allen, Grade 5
Harriet Bishop Elementary School, MN

I Love Volleyball

I love the *thump* of the serve
As it flies over the net
I love the *thud* of the sturdy pass
With perfect angle to the setter
I love the quiet pleasure of the set
An arc towards middle
I love the *thwack* of the hit
As it hits ground
hard

I love the scampering of feet
Scrambling to get under the ball
I love the yelling of the team
Communicating with teammates
I love the mounting voices of the fans
Cheering on their home teams
I love the unique feeling I get
When I play volleyball
Olivia Grace Jensen, Grade 5
Blue Heron Elementary School, MN

A Watch with a Beep

This watch when it beeps
It tells me to do something
It talks to me

When it talks to me
I feel like talking to it

But when I turn the beep off
It stops talking to me
And I stop too
And I feel sad inside

The watch reminds me
Of a friend I lost and I miss

I miss my friend
But this watch has a beep
I don't forget.
Brandon Braun, Grade 6
T J Walker Middle School, WI

Basketball

Basketball
A coach with assistant coaches
A basketball to play with
8 players that play basketball
2 teams of at least 10
A basketball court
A referee with a whistle
1 of the teams home
A bottle of water
BASKETBALL ROCKS
Casey Etter, Grade 5
Harriet Bishop Elementary School, MN

Football

Up and down the field
Left and right
In the air, on the ground
In and out of the hands
"Fumble" they yell
Picked it up
It's ran back for a touchdown
Jude Rosauer, Grade 5
Riverdale Elementary School, WI

New Year's Eve

New Year's Eve
Fireworks and the countdown ball dropping
Scented candles burning
Horns and noise makers
A bowl of ice cream
Icy ground
New Year's Eve
Matthew Clune, Grade 6
Campbellsport Elementary School, WI

Great-Grandpa

I never got to see him
I never got to love him
I never got to run and jump into his arms
He never got to hold me
He never got to love me
He never got to see me
He died before he could
Haley Paulson, Grade 4
Tess Corners Elementary School, WI

New Year's Eve

New Year's Eve
People gathering for a party
All different types of foods
Everyone shouting 3, 2, 1
Yummy treats
Comfy bed after midnight
New Year's Eve
Hannah Mrochinski, Grade 6
Campbellsport Elementary School, WI

It's Night

It's night
I hear the crickets chirping softly
in the tall grass
I hear wolves howling loudly
to the moon
I see stars twinkling in the sky
I hear prairie owls hooting
Desirae Schaefer, Grade 4
School of Technology & Arts I, WI

Airplane

Driving to the airport at five a.m.
Security, wow what a long line!
Wait, what's this? We get to go ahead.
Now all that's left is to get on the plane.
Section one, two, three, four, that's us!
Come on let's get window seats.
Ding goes the light. Time to buckle up.

Left and right, now right again.
Taxiing to get to the runway.
Whoosh goes the engine. That tells us it's time to go.
Speeding, see the earth outside
and now we're up. Quick, look down!
There are so many colors, and most are natural.
See the water sparkle in the sun.
Now we're going through the clouds.
Within an hour and a half
we have reached our destination.

Zooming in the sky, making sure the runway's open.
Down we go. Clink, we've hit the ground.
Time to get off. See you next time, airplane.
Isabella Mandli, Grade 5
Mazomanie Elementary School, WI

The Music Note

Inside this music note
lies secrets yet to be told
waiting, just waiting
to be told

No one knows when
no one knows how
but someday this note,
will come alive.

The longer it waits to come out
the more secrets come to life.

Some day this note will have so many secrets
that it will explode and make songs
that make you happy, sad,
that make you feel good, and independent.

When that day comes that note will expand
and yet have more secrets to be found,
and more secrets to be found.
Ryan Mueller, Grade 6
T J Walker Middle School, WI

Blue

Some say blue is like the midnight sky.
The midnight sky that is calm and quiet, and
full of twinkling stars.
Zoie Weiss, Grade 4
Tess Corners Elementary School, WI

Inside This Poem

Inside this old poem I
have so many ideas, that can't wait to
go and just let it all out. When I wrote it down I just
couldn't get it right.

Deep inside this oh so deep inside there is this big, big idea it is
as big as the blue sky in the middle of July and I'm about
to tell you what it is. You see it's the biggest poem
about to be reborn. It's about a young little baby
in Caligsburg County that just has his first
Christmas.

He just opened his
newest young present that he
has ever gotten. As he drools on it as
most babies do he looks up at the ceiling he
awakens the newborn baby deep, deep inside of him.
Robert Hohlfelder, Grade 6
T J Walker Middle School, WI

My Name

My name is a gorilla scaling a tree in the rain
forests of Brazil.

My name is like an evil demon dueling a foe.

My name is a storm that is pouring rain while lightning is
flashing and thunder is sounding, calling to others to challenge me.

My name is like a koala, often daydreaming, often tired.

My name is a postcard
traveling all over

My name is like a strand of hair,
always wanting to stop but still continues.

My name is Zeke.
Zeke Vanderwood, Grade 5
Sibley Elementary School, MN

Months

January the month where everything is new but very few like it new.
February the month of love where you probably see a dove.
March the month of my mom's birthday and she gets cake.
April the month of laughness and trickeries
May the month where kids play
June school is out soon and you play all afternoon
July the days of independence where there is remembrance.
August you go to a barn and play in the hay.
I have my birthday in September I never forget I always remember.
October the month of terror and scream.
November on the table the turkey of every day.
December the month everybody remembers.
Adonis Merino, Grade 6
Gilmore Middle School, WI

Stage Acting

When you see the stage,
see the lights,
makes you feel like you're on top of heights.
You feel so special,
you feel so amazed,
but you can also feel nervous,
and maybe sort of dazed.
But the people you meet,
the friends you make,
whatever is thrown at you,
you'll know you can take.
And when the lights and eyes are on you,
just be yourself,
don't be so blue,
just smile and think of
how great
you
will
do.
Sarah Fogelman, Grade 6
St Francis Middle School, MN

Mice

Mouse,
Rodent,
Meises,
Crafty mousy,
Albino mousies,
Black, brown, white mice,
Tan, long, thin tail,
Those are a few.
Sweet fruit,
Crunchy nuts,
Running, scampering, walking wheel,
Chewing, eating, squeaking chew block,
Orange carrots too.
Sharp teeth,
Mini paws,
Bright eyes,
don't forget tiny tracks,
Last of all — best of all —
I like spotted mice.
Zoe England, Grade 5
Howards Grove Middle School, WI

Rain

Yes, rain!
Now I have an
Excuse to stay inside
And read!
Where is my book?
I need a snack!
Chair, music, book,
Snack, check.
Carter Weigel, Grade 6
St Francis Middle School, MN

I Wake Up

I wake up
Looking out my bedroom window
The trees are branching off
Like sparkling water

The sky
Blue
Is like violets on the river
The trees seem like
They're dancing in the cool wind

Something outside is glittering
Bright as the sun
I feel like going to the thing
But something tells me not to
Michael Felix, Grade 5
School of Technology & Arts I, WI

Angels Singing

Why does the grass grow?
Why does the wind blow?
Why do the bells ring?
Why do the angels sing?

The grass grows.
The wind blows.
The bells ring.
Because the angels sing.

The angels sing because…
The grass grows.
The wind blows.
The bells ring.
And that's why the angels sing.
Star Gates, Grade 5
Riverdale Elementary School, WI

Mr. Nobody

Mr. Nobody is invisible
Like a living ghost
Mr. Nobody sits on the bench
Alone
Mr. Nobody is alone
In a big world
Full of people
Mr. Nobody wants a friend
But somebodies
Won't be his friend
Mr. Nobody is fun
But somebodies
Won't ever find out
That Mr. Nobody
Is somebody
Katie Bartelt, Grade 5
Howards Grove Middle School, WI

The Bear

Scary
Shocking
Thrilling

Seeing a big black
Blob running
On a crisp evening

Hearing the shouts of shock
And amazement

Thinking if it could
Hurt us

Feeling shocked, scared, and thrilled

That's what I remember when
I saw the bear
Brennen Pozorski, Grade 5
Hewitt Texas Elementary School, WI

I Am a Soccer Player

I am a soccer player.
I wonder if I can achieve.
I hear that I play well.
I see that I want to win.
I am a soccer player.

I pretend that I'm going pro.
I feel I will be able to win.
I touch the soccer ball with my feet.
I worry that I'm not good enough.
I cry if I break my ankle.
I am a soccer player.

I understand that if I try I will get better.
I say that I will be a pro.
I dream that I can be good enough.
I try to play very aggressively.
I am a soccer player.
Emilio Toscano, Grade 6
Gilmore Middle School, WI

An Ode to Pigs

Ode to pigs who give
us pork chops.
Pigs eat and eat
they never stop.
Oh, pigs you are
so fat and pink.
You roll in mud and
always stink.
Oh, pigs you are so cool
maybe I'll bring you to school.
Jason Lange, Grade 5
St Katharine Drexel School, WI

I Can

I can
I can run
I can draw
I can color
I can name animals
I can name cars
Alexander Roy Brocker, Grade 5
St Paul Evangelical Lutheran School, WI

Soccer

S ports
O ffense
C heering
C ompete
E nd of the game!
R un
McKenzie Couey, Grade 5
Riverdale Elementary School, WI

Spring

S unlight shining on me in the morning,
P rancing in the day light,
R ivers running free and wild,
I ce cream after a long day,
N othing but jumping in puddles,
G reen grass coming to life.
Olivia Stauss, Grade 5
Howards Grove Middle School, WI

School

S chool at SFMS
C ool
H olidays off
O utside for gym
O ut of school suspension
L earning something every minute
Cameron Pettis, Grade 6
St Francis Middle School, MN

My Love

I just want to let you know
In these words my love will show
Yes you are the true, true one
Whose beauty is just like the sun
I hope that you will keep on knowing
That my love for you is always growing
Madelyn Brost, Grade 5
Medford Middle School, WI

The Waves

I hear the waves rush up to the sand
little turtles follow their mother
and leave little footprints on the sand
the waves washed them away
Alyssa Bjorge, Grade 5
School of Technology & Arts I, WI

Big Bass

Big Bass Lake is a calm beautiful place that is full of things to do.
The lakes smells the pancakes that Mom flips on the griddle and the bacon searing away.
In the morning the lake breathes last night's fire.
Big Bass Lake gets bounced off of and ripped apart
As kids jump in the water and the boats split the lake in half.
In the afternoon the lake's population sinks just like a stock market on a bad day.
At night Big Bass Lake smells marshmallows roasted on the fire. He eats a s'more.
At night Big Bass Lake is dead silent.
As silent as when someone is standing outside in the cold and is shivering.
James Miller, Grade 5
Sibley Elementary School, MN

Blue

Blue is the color of the wavy strong sea
Blue is my favorite color
Blue is the color that the earth is most filled with
Blue is the color of the big amazing sky
Blue is the color of the ribbon when you win the first prize at the fair.
Blue is the color of the ice at the north and south poles
Blue is the color of the tears that come out of your eyes.
Blue is the color of the rain that comes down from the big sky
Blue is the color of yummy blueberries.
Txhais Yang, Grade 6
Gilmore Middle School, WI

The Basketball Stadium

Inside the stadium is a madhouse. So intense in some moments that you can hear a pin drop. The guy next to me is a hyena screaming and laughing with his high pitched voice with the ref's every call and blow of the whistle. Then there are players, who like lions pounce on every moment they get to become a legend and become remembered forever. Then there is the coach who is like the wise owl, calling all the shots trying to make sure that their team will win, and trying to give his team the edge against the villains of the other team. For me I am not either, I'm the guy who captures all the moments you want to see again and again in my camera.
Jack Shaw, Grade 6
Holy Family Parish School, WI

Thanksgiving

Thanksgiving
Turkey, pumpkin pie
Warm, hot, good
Leaves falling, people raking, turkey on table, pumpkin
Rain falling, people talking, knocking at door, people eating, people laughing
Jori Alvarez, Grade 4
Stocker Elementary School, WI

Finding a Friend Like You

Looking for a friend like you is like looking for a four leaf clover in a clover patch,
I have to scan every single clover to make sure I don't miss that four leaf clover,
I have found that four leaf clover,
I searched every clover patch,
It was hard but worth it.

Brianna Eittreim-Davis, Grade 5
Northwinds Elementary School, MN

Friends

A friend is like
a kid with a bike,
a dog with a bone,
a place to call home.
Then your friend turns their back on you
and you feel like
a kid with no bike,
a dog with no bone,
no place to call home.
The world stops turning.
There's nowhere left to run.
It seems like nothing is fun.
But don't feel bad
acting like you never had
a real friend in this world.
If you never fight
you just might
not have a real friend.
Because as strange as it seems,
Fights just might
make your friendship stronger.

Jakan Young, Grade 5
Riverdale Elementary School, WI

Things About Gymnastics

Flips, grips, rips
Flips on the floor
Flips, grips, rips
Grips on the bars
Flips, grips, rips
Rips on your hands
Flips, grips, rips
Balance on the beam
Flips, grips, rips
Run on vault
Flips, grips, rips
Jump on the trampoline
Flips, grips, rips
Being flexible helps
Flips, grips, rips
You exercise a lot
Flips, grips, rips
A very fun sport
Flips, grips, rips
A sport for all year long
Gymnastics

Grace Braatz, Grade 4
River Heights Elementary School, WI

Books

Books are long
Books are short
Books are fun
Books are boring

Trevor Maloney, Grade 6
Riverdale Elementary School, WI

Inside This Notebook

Inside this notebook
Unwritten words
Inside this notebook
Homework not given

On these papers
Are unwritten words
Or maybe
Words of description

Inside these words
Mean different things to different people
Or might mean the same things
Or they could mean nothing at all

Inside this notebook
Are words unwritten
Inside this notebook
Is meaning to life

Tommy Safranski, Grade 6
T J Walker Middle School, WI

Dogs

Dogs,
Dogs,
Dogs,
Tall Great Dane,
Happy Golden doodle,
Swift, quick, active pup,
Skinny, loyal, obedient dog.
Those are a few.
Pretty Shi tzu,
Fat Bulldog
Jumping, running, sleeping puppy,
Biting, eating, fetching canine,
Ugly Rotweilers too
Bald K-9
Nice Golden retrievers,
Bouncing Black labs,
Don't forget mangy Yorkies.
Last of all — best of all —
I like cute yellow labs.

Miranda Zerger, Grade 5
Howards Grove Middle School, WI

Snow

The snow is so white.
The snow is so sensitive to a single touch.
It's so cold and unforgiving.
It's so cold.
It's so beautiful.
It seems to go on forever.
It's so cold and unforgiving.
It's so cold.

Austin Belford, Grade 6
St Francis Middle School, MN

I Am

I am cute
I wonder if cats can fly
I hear noises when I'm alone
I see my friends every day
I want $999, 999, 000.00
I am a student at Gilmore

I pretend to be dorky
I feel AMAZING
I touch pencils every day
I worry about my dog
I cry when I'm sad
I am hilarious

I understand my work
I say funny things
I dream I can fly
I do my best at sports
I hope it's time to go
I am cool

Courtney Collins, Grade 6
Gilmore Middle School, WI

Christmas

In this season of bells,
You hear me jingle,
Give me a ring.

In this season of tinsel,
Hang me high,
Or hang me low.

In this season of reindeer,
Soaring high through the night,
Pulling a sleigh, and being polite.

In this season of joy,
Hear the Christmas carolers,
And see the presents under the tree.

In this season of white,
White as snow and
Santa's beard.
Christmas is a time of white.

Mackenzie Knorr, Grade 5
Wagner Elementary School, MN

Winter

W inning the sled race
I ce on my driveway making my family fall
N ever let the holidays bring you down
T here's no place like home
E vergreens are topped off with fresh snow
R eindeer showing the way

Bridget Stella, Grade 5
Stocker Elementary School, WI

Colors

What is green?
A marker that you draw with.
What is red?
The apples in the tree.
What is blue?
Blue is the sea.
What is orange?
A marble on the floor.
What is white?
Snow on the ground.
What is brown?
Chocolates in a box.
What is purple?
A plum in a tree.
What is pink?
A pig on a farm.

Dylan Friedland, Grade 5
Riverdale Elementary School, WI

Happiness

Bring me happiness,
In the brightest of day,
In the darkest of night.

Bring me happiness,
When the tunnel has no end,
When no hope can be found.

Bring me happiness,
When winter never ends,
And spring never starts.

Bring me happiness,
After a river of tears ends,
When I read this poem,
Bring me Happiness.

Lu'Cinda Peña, Grade 6
Valley Middle School, MN

The Hike

We went for a hike,
Me and my dad.
We almost fell into a river,
Man was I glad!

We saw mosquitoes
We saw some bees.
We saw animal tracks,
We saw some streams.

I love to hike,
I love to climb.
In the wild frontier,
Hiking is sublime!

Daniel Zahn, Grade 6
Gilmore Middle School, WI

The Colors

The color blue is the color of the sky.
Yellow is great because it shines.

Purple is the color of grapes.
Sometimes gray can be the color of a cape.

Pink is a nice color for a rose.
Red is cool because it glows.

Brown is the color of my hair.
Green is the color of the chair.

Ronderia Perry, Grade 6
Gilmore Middle School, WI

Autumn

A beautiful fall day, finally!
Finally!
The leaves are so colorful,
Bright on the trees.
But in about two weeks
They will all fall off,
The trees will be bare.
I'll get to rake the leaves
And jump into the piles.
This will be so much fun!

Rachel Vouk, Grade 6
St Francis Middle School, MN

BMX

BMX is fun.
On a sunny day, you
Take out your bike and ride it
On the track for a race.
There are different places to race
When you're in the main
You will get tickets for your trophies
But some won't get them
There are different levels like
Novice, Inner, Expert, and so on.

Mikayla Hendrickson, Grade 6
St Francis Middle School, MN

Summer

Summer morning always light,
Make our days oh so bright.
Summer afternoons as hot as can be,
Being outside is the best to me.
Summer evening sunny still so,
We make a few water balloons to throw.
Summer night is such a delight,
Lightning bugs to keep it light.
Now it's dark and time for bed,
And rest our heads for the great day ahead!

Syanne Melchert, Grade 5
MacArthur Elementary School, WI

A Pumpkin's Life

I used to be a pumpkin
But then I became carved
Now I am a jack-o'-lantern

I used to be a jack-o'-lantern
But then my candle blew out
Now I am moldy

I used to be moldy
But then I got thrown away
Now I am alone

Erika Pfeifer, Grade 5
Howards Grove Middle School, WI

What Is a Tiger?

What is a tiger?
A mammal
A colorful creature
A striped animal
A hunter
A carnivore
An aggressive and fierce animal
An endangered species
A thought to be man-eater
A fast runner
That is a tiger!

Collin Hatlevig, Grade 6
Orfordville Elementary School, WI

What Is Pepsi…

a drinkable beverage
awesome in liquid form
brown in color
fizzy goodness
better than Coke
red, white, and blue
cans and bottles
makes me hyper
full of toxins
dentist approved
That is Pepsi.

Peter Bouc, Grade 6
Orfordville Elementary School, WI

Maple Leaf

Standing boldly by my house,
Like a skyscraper to a mouse,
Beautiful autumn leaves fill up my soul,
Maple syrup fills up my bowl.

Its arms all reaching to the sky,
Length of maple grows so very high,
Drops lots of leaves for me to play,
I hope this wonderful tree will stay.

Maia Diedrich, Grade 4
Classical School, WI

The Little Gymnast

She walks along so steadily
Upon that sturdy beam.
She tenses up quite suddenly
As she glances at the other team.

She completes a perfect glide swing
Upon those uneven bars.
She quickly dreams of the day
When she's performing with the stars.

She dives into a front hand spring
Upon that dusty floor.
She cannot help but smile
As she finished off one more.

That day was truly a great one
She comes home with the gold.
She says "I'll see you next year."
But, that's a whole other story to be told.

Claire Turner, Grade 4
Ashby Elementary School, MN

Inside This Bone

Inside this bone lies a secret
A secret of something lost, just gone
A family missing this
Bone of a fish, a washed up fish

People lose things
In a matter of seconds
A friend, a ring, a toy, a life
The grief of losing something dear

Even though a fish
You lose something dear
This family from that fish
Is grieving over their loss

This family of fish could
Have forgotten about him
But I have not
He lies in my hands

Jessamy Tremper, Grade 6
T J Walker Middle School, WI

Clouds

Clouds
white and puffy
stretched across the sky
pictures in the swirly mist
light as air
floating over the treetops
big and fluffy
dreamy

Elizabeth Schwarz, Grade 5
Harriet Bishop Elementary School, MN

Big Green Tractor

Breath taking
Riding up the hill
Sun coming through the cab

Happy
Awesome
Bouncing

And not feeling a thing
In the air ride seat
Proud
Proud
Proud

Nicholas Walters, Grade 5
Hewitt Texas Elementary School, WI

White

White is the color
of paper waiting
to be written on
the color of walls
with no color of paint
the color of shirts
that have no color
clouds that are big
and puffy and
waiting to rain
pages of a book
that have no end
white

Kennedy DeVries, Grade 5
St Paul Evangelical Lutheran School, WI

Halloween

The night is cold
The moon is bright
Kids in costumes
Giving frights.

A night of fear
A night of scares
Parents giving out candy to share.

Halloween parties
Halloween fun
But when the day is over
It's all done.

Javon Duncan, Grade 6
Messmer Preparatory Catholic School, WI

Winter

White flurries going
snow melting, feeling your skin
winter has arrived

Chantel Weyrauch, Grade 6
Dr Dyer Intermediate School, WI

Shark!

The menacing shark
Swims in the dangerous waters
In the dark, dark sea.

Connor McIntosh, Grade 4
Stocker Elementary School, WI

Owl!

The owl soaring
High over the waterfall
During the night.

Kallie Snowtala, Grade 4
Stocker Elementary School, WI

Bull Frog!

A sleeping bull frog
Under a green lily pad
So quietly he sleeps.

Kolin Meyer, Grade 4
Stocker Elementary School, WI

Water

Crashing against rocks
Making deep puddles on streets
Falling from dark clouds

Tanner Ramthun, Grade 6
Campbellsport Elementary School, WI

Winter Blanket

Snowflakes falling fast
From the clouds they're coming down
Sprinkling the ground

Suzanne Mason, Grade 4
River Heights Elementary School, WI

Birds!

Birds flying over
A tree singing and chirping
Sitting on the tree!

Jaskirat Sidhu, Grade 4
Stocker Elementary School, WI

Sea Shells!

Laying on the sand
Getting washed by the waves
Shining in the sun!

Zachary Morris, Grade 4
Stocker Elementary School, WI

Haunted Manor
Through the door
Into the manor
Over the booby-trapped rug
To the left
Past the scary monsters
Down the stairs
To the right
Through the zigzagging room
Past the moving armor
Up the rickety lift
Through the maze of mirrors
Down some more stairs
Past the talking portraits
Out a door
Into a tree
Out another door
Into freedom
Zach Klick, Grade 6
Orfordville Elementary School, WI

Fun in the Sun
Swimming at the beach.
Tanning in the sun.
Eating some ice cream.
It's all so fun.

Playing some baseball.
Mowing the yard.
Earning some money.
Stay on guard.

As you can see,
this is all so fun.
Next time there's summer,
it'll be number one.
Robbie Whitney, Grade 6
St Francis Middle School, MN

Wind
How lovely is the wind!
The gentle breeze is soothing,
easing away your pain.
Carrying away the worries and
the lies we have told.
However, if the wind gets mad
it throws a tantrum,
wrecking everything in sight.
Sometimes even picking up water,
thrashing it everywhere.
The wind is so violent and painful,
yet so calming and soothing.
Faith Tisdale, Grade 5
Riverdale Elementary School, WI

Hermit Crabs
Hermit crabs
Sitting in the ocean
Eating dead fish
Hiding from starfish
Blue ocean
Bright lights
Snip!
Clank!
How big can they get?
Surprised
Awesome
Hermit crabs!
Hermit crabs!!
Hermit crabs!!!
Noah Gilbertson, Grade 5
Harriet Bishop Elementary School, MN

That's Not Any Ordinary Light
Inside this light
is no ordinary light
it's a Christmas light
surrounded by memories

this string of white lights
holds stories
they see you every year
opening their eyes to the world

every light holds another
day until Christmas
when one shuts its light down
their story comes alive
Nicole Tlachac, Grade 6
T J Walker Middle School, WI

fisheys
fish
big fish small fish
mini fish
dead fish
cool fish
hooked fish
any kind of fish
Aaron Lorenzen, Grade 6
St Francis Middle School, MN

Wausau East Lumberjacks Log Game
Cold
Fans roaring
Pads smacking
Mascot
Chopping down evergreens
Hot chocolate
Burning me
Cheering mouth
Wausau East vs Wausau West
East,
East,
East.
Hunter Behnke, Grade 5
Hewitt Texas Elementary School, WI

Fall
Happily starting school
Raking lots of crisp leaves
Jumping in crunchy leaves
Carving gooey pumpkins
Trick or Treating on Halloween
Kids dressing up in scary costumes
Eating delicious pumpkin pie
Picking juicy apples
Eating tender turkey
Harvesting lots and lots of crops
Sun setting earlier and earlier every day
Family gathers and has fun
Jared Shearer, Grade 5
Harriet Bishop Elementary School, MN

Starry Night
As I stood outside
I stare at the sky
And make out many constellations
They light up my face
And make my smile grow
And take away my exhaustion
Orion's belt
The little dipper
Those are just a few
If you look at the sky
And stare into the night
You might see them too
Jazmine Spitzer, Grade 6
St Francis Middle School, MN

Index

Author Autograph Page

Author Autograph Page

Author Autograph Page

Author Autograph Page

Author Autograph Page

Author Autograph Page

Author Autograph Page

Author Autograph Page

Author Autograph Page

Author Autograph Page